Correctional Counseling and Treatment

Correctional Counseling and Treatment

Evidence-Based Perspectives

ALBERT R. ROBERTS

Rutgers University

Upper Saddle River, New Jersey 07458

Library of Congress Cataloging-in-Publication Data

Correctional counseling and treatment : evidence-based perspectives / Albert R. Roberts.
    p. cm.
  ISBN-13: 978-0-13-613287-5
  ISBN-10: 0-13-613287-1
  1. Criminals—Rehabilitation. 2. Prisoners—Counseling of. 3. Prisoners—Mental
health services. 4. Juvenile delinquents—Counseling of. 5. Juvenile delinquents—
Mental health services. 6. Correctional psychology. I. Title: Correctional counseling
and treatment. II. Roberts, Albert R.
  HV9275.C633 2007
  365'.66—dc22

                                                          2007014611

Senior Acquisitions Editor: Tim Peyton
Editorial Assistant: Alicia Kelly
Marketing Manager: Adam Kloza
Production Editor: Vikas Kanchan, Stratford / TexTech
Project Manager: Barbara Marttine Cappuccio
Managing Editor: Mary Carnis
Manufacturing Manager: Ilene Sanford
Manufacturing Buyer: Cathleen Petersen
Senior Design Coordinator: Mary Siener
Cover Design: Eva Ruutopold
Cover Image: Bettmann/CORBIS
Composition: TexTech

Pearson Education Ltd.
Pearson Education Australia PTY, Limited
Pearson Education Singapore, Pte. Ltd
Pearson Education North Asia Ltd
Pearson Education Canada, Ltd.

Pearson Educación de Mexico, S.A. de C.V.
Pearson Education—Japan
Pearson Education Malaysia, Pte. Ltd
Pearson Education Inc., Upper Saddle River, New Jersey

ISBN 13: 978-0-13-613287-5
ISBN 10:   0-13-613287-1

Contents

---------------- ❖ ----------------

Prologue

Reaffirming Rehabilitation in the 21st Century

Francis T. Cullen

I have had the good fortune of being in the field of criminology for three decades—words I cannot imagine I am writing! I am not certain that longevity and wisdom are linearly related or, for that fact, related positively. But there is perhaps one sage insight that I have arrived at, whether through age or dumb luck: Liberals deny the pathology of offenders, whereas conservatives deny the humanity of offenders.

These two denials are, I believe, inordinately consequential. They are at the heart of two approaches to corrections that are colossal failures: nonintervention and mean intervention. In the 21st century, we must move beyond these largely ideological, nonscientific, and ineffectual paradigms. It is time to build a science of correctional treatment that will improve the lives of offenders and serve to protect the public. It is time to reaffirm rehabilitation.

THE DENIAL OF PATHOLOGY AND NONINTERVENTION

Despite mounting evidence from life-course criminology, liberals wish to deny that offenders are, to varying degrees, different from noncriminals. When taken together, these individual differences, such as antisocial cognitions and low self-control, make offenders "pathological." By pathological, I do not mean that offenders are completely different from the "rest of us." But I do mean that they have a propensity that allows them to steal, vandalize, and assault at levels that "normal" people, who might sporadically do such things, would never contemplate. Some offenders also feel perfectly comfortable carrying, brandishing, and even using weapons, at times for utilitarian purposes (to get something) and at times senselessly (for being "disrespected").

Why do liberals—and I include progressive criminologists at the core of this category—deny the pathology of offenders? They have two good reasons. First, they are inalterably opposed to prisons. At times, they suggest that they are against prisons because they are costly and deplete the public treasury, but this complaint is a bit disingenuous. After all, liberals do not worry about spending money on virtually any other government service. The real reason is that when liberals look inside correctional institutions, they do not like what they see. They view these facilities as needlessly painful, riddled by violence, coercive if not brutal, and stifling of the human spirit. What kind of society creates and puts its members in such places?

They will admit that the "dangerous few" might have to be incarcerated, but even this is confessed grudgingly. One gets the sense that they really mean that "just a few" should be in prison (i.e., a small number of offenders) and not a sizeable minority of those now incarcerated. This policy proposal—that the vast majority of current inmates "do not need to be behind bars"—inevitably leads to the related idea that most offenders are not such bad folks. They are not part of the dangerous few and thus can be placed "safely" in the community. Certainly, they do not merit the stigmatizing label of "pathological."

The second reason liberals deny pathology is that they do not wish to "blame the victim." For liberals, the unavoidable reality of prisons is that they disproportionately contain minority and poor men. It is not a coincidence that social inequality is reproduced within the correctional system. Indeed, many of these men (and the women who join them in prison) faced dismal life chances as youngsters. If we could take a time machine back to when they were 8 or 10 years old, we would have called them victims of heartbreaking personal and social experiences that no child should ever have to confront. We would have predicted a wayward future for these high-risk youths and wondered why nobody was doing anything to knife off this inevitability. Back to the future, it now seems unjust to liberals to impose yet another debilitating life experience—years in prison—upon them. And it seems a matter of utter bad faith to call these offenders "pathological."

I happen to share many of these sentiments. But the reality is that "savage inequalities," as Jonathan Kozol so eloquently called them, do have consequences for individuals. They distort how people understand and react to their world. They create individual differences that cause once innocent children to grow into predatory adults. The larger structures of inequality merit our attention, but this does not mean that we can ignore the pathology in individuals that these conditions ineluctably foster.

This denial of pathology is not simply an academic matter; it has had dire policy consequences. The main problem is that it has rendered liberals, including criminologists, bereft of any plausible answers as to how to confront crime in the United States. The roster of liberal proposals for crime control—keep offenders out of prison and in the community, perhaps try some restorative justice, or give offenders more legal rights and protections—is oriented to minimizing harm to criminals by limiting the criminal justice system's intervention in their lives. But this approach does not strike the average American as very responsible. It seems to show no compassion for the discomfort—ranging from mere inconvenience to fully ruined lives—that crime victims experience. And it seems to be cavalier in its willingness to risk the victimization of innocent citizens because liberals do not want predators to suffer in prison. This noninterventionist approach appears to be a case of misplaced empathy and values. Is it any wonder that "get tough" crime control proposals seem to make more sense?

The collateral policy mistake is that liberals are led to reject correctional rehabilitation. There is an initial doubt that anything done by "state officials"—especially those working in prisons—could ever be effective. But added to this suspicion is the underlying notion that offenders are not pathological and thus do not require any real intervention. If there are no true individual differences, then there is nothing to "target for change." In the end, liberals suggest that if we just put offenders into the community and got them good jobs, all would be well. If only it were that simple!

DENIAL OF HUMANITY AND MEAN CORRECTIONS

Conservative crime policies are even more troubling. Let me hasten to say that I think we could hold an honest debate over the true size of the group of high-risk offenders who should be incarcerated (I truly do not know) and over how much crime we save through sheer incapacitation (meaningful—perhaps 30 percent—but expensive and not the only option). But over the past three decades, I have recoiled at the harsh rhetoric and gratuitously mean-spirited policies put forward by right-wing politicians. Lock everyone up; impose three-strikes laws; build tent cities for jails, bring back the chain gang; take away the opportunity for college education, make prisons harsher by eliminating "country club amenities" like television, temperature control, and recreation.

What accounts for this mean season in corrections? I think that it mainly occurred because voicing "get tough" slogans got people elected, which itself is rooted in two considerations—one noble and one not so noble.

First, in the 1960s and 1970s, liberals committed the sin of overidentifying with the plight of offenders. I know that most liberals would follow their stinging critique of prisons and their call to place "unjustly brutalized" inmates in the community with this caveat: "Of course, we care about victims too." But to be honest, this afterthought rang hollow. By contrast, conservatives truly empathized with victims—at their loss, which at times was inordinate and tragic. They gave voice to victims and to the anger that we justifiably direct at those who wantonly damage property and damage people. And they offered to do what liberals would not do: lock up these wayward, if not wicked, offenders so they could not harm so soon again.

So, there was a core of nobility inherent in this defense of current and potentially future victims. But less noble was the second reason why conservative punitive policies flourished: many Americans—really, white Americans—came to define offenders as "not like us." Offenders were increasingly black or brown, and they were poor. Race and class thus matter, erecting a barrier—much like the wall surrounding a gated community—between "us" and "them." As James Unnever has taught me, as we distance ourselves from these offenders, we lose our empathy—our ability to imagine that these unfortunate souls in prison could have been a family member or, with a few bad breaks, even ourselves. It becomes easy to objectify offenders as completely different and as completely pathological. We thus start to embrace, if not actively help to construct, a social reality in which offenders are described, to use John Dilulio's popular label, as "super-predators." They belong to a dangerous class populated by those without conscience and without any hope of being saved.

When this occurs, offenders lose their humanity. They become "the other"—not of and created by our society, but some sort of subspecies or aberration that we should safely place in a cage. Offenders are no longer people who have lost their lives to crime and damaged others in the process. There is no sense of crime as a human tragedy, for all concerned.

The denial of humanity places virtually no limits on how mean we are willing to be. It is why many of us are not so sure we really oppose torturing "the terrorist out to destroy us." In corrections, it opens the floodgates to the vilification and ill-treatment of offenders. Of course, it also makes it easy to claim that "nothing works" to change offenders. In this context, rehabilitation almost seems absurd. Superpredators—those young men from the ghetto who glare at us defiantly through prison bars—are not of our world. We take comfort in their incarceration and vote for those who promise to keep us safe by locking them all up. In so doing, we forfeit the vision that, like us, they can be saved and come to lead lives of value.

REAFFIRMING REHABILITATION

It is time for us to relinquish our ideology and move to a more reasoned position on crime policy. The denial of pathology ignores that offenders will likely keep offending if we do not do something to change them. Nonintervention is a recipe for failure; it is a do-nothing approach that allows mean-spirited policies to monopolize the conversation on how best to prevent our victimization. The denial of humanity ignores that offenders are people who have the potential to change. After we heap our nastiest punishments upon them, they will return to society from prison—almost certainly no better off and, as research increasingly shows, often more inclined to victimize. The reality is that offenders are people whose criminality cannot be ignored but whom we belittle and demean at our own risk.

What should be done? There is no perfect alternative because corrections is an arena marked by much failure. It is unrealistic to expect that the correctional system will be uniformly effective in fixing society's mistakes—in transforming persistent waywardness, developed and deepened over a lifetime, into law-abidingness. But interventions can be more or less efficacious. In this context, I propose that our "best bet" is to reaffirm rehabilitation as the guiding correctional paradigm.

The rehabilitative ideal inspires because it offers both to improve offenders and to protect the public. At its core, the rehabilitative ideal accepts the pathology of offenders—they have differences that need to be changed. It also accepts the humanity of offenders—we have played a role in producing them and we can play a role in saving them. One payoff from rehabilitation is that the lives of offenders, heretofore lost to crime, are possibly rescued. The other payoff is that criminal careers are cut short, and thus countless victimizations never occur. Public safety is enhanced.

It seems that the opportunity is widening to reaffirm rehabilitation. The failures of punishment-oriented programs (e.g., intensive supervision, scared straight, boot camps) are too consistent to ignore. By contrast, there is a growing body of scientific evidence—as represented in the current volume's chapters—showing that treatment interventions do, in fact, "work" to reduce recidivism. Further, public opinion polls conducted over the past quarter century clearly demonstrate widespread support for rehabilitation as a goal of corrections. To be sure, Americans are not without their punitive side. They want serious crime punished seriously, and they oppose allowing dangerous offenders to roam their communities while receiving only perfunctory supervision. But justice and safety are only two elements of the trinity of values that inform citizens' views on offender control. Americans also are firm in their belief that an integral purpose of corrections should be, in the end, to correct offenders.

The special challenge for reaffirming rehabilitation in the 21st century is devising a credible intervention strategy. We must avoid the hubris of early reformers who overpredicted their ability to change offenders and were thus guilty of promising too much. This inability to "come through" exposed rehabilitation to legitimate criticism. After all, if "nothing works"—or works well and consistently—why should anyone support correctional treatment?

For rehabilitation to be a viable correctional paradigm over the long haul—if we are to avoid the "nothing works" criticism—three obstacles must be surmounted. First, corrections must be a profession that is based on scientific evidence and whose members develop expertise in delivering interventions. Medicine is a worthy model, though criminal justice is unique in that elected officials have the discretion (judges) and the power (politicians) to shape what happens to offenders. Still, even within a politicized system where foolhardy interventions are proposed, correctional officials and practitioners must stand firm in saying, based on the evidence, what will and will not work.

Second, we must develop more efficient conduits for technology transfer. As researchers develop increasingly sophisticated modalities for intervention, we need ways of communicating this evolving knowledge to agency personnel. Part of the obligation for receiving this evidence rests with those in the field; a hallmark of a profession is its openness, not its resistance, to new scientific information. But the obligation to transfer treatment technology also lies with the producers of the evidence. It is likely, of course, that the Internet will be a useful tool in disseminating knowledge.

Third, there is an inordinate amount of work to be done in discovering how to ensure that programs are implemented correctly. It is too much to expect that those in agencies will know how to implement new treatment knowledge effectively, and it is too much to expect that researchers who produce such knowledge will travel agency to agency to ensure that programs are "done right." There is a need to develop training systems—whether at centralized locations or through distance learning—that can enable practitioners to achieve a high level of program integrity.

Despite these challenges, I remain optimistic. Throughout much of the 1980s and 1990s, corrections was in a truly dreary state. "Get tough" ideology and policy seemed virtually hegemonic. But the limits of what this mean season in corrections has achieved and the devotion during this difficult period of those committed to discovering evidence-based treatments—a group that includes many authors of the chapters in this volume—have combined to create opportunities for change. I sense that we are on the verge of a new progressive era in corrections. This will be a time in which evidence will matter and in which programs that demonstrate reductions in recidivism will be embraced. The labor to produce effective, evidence-based programs—as *Correctional Counseling and Treatment* so richly illuminates—is well under way. Let this important work continue and let us thus get on with the task of showing why rehabilitation deserves to be reaffirmed.

Preface

❖

The planning and development of correctional treatment and counseling has grown too complex for any one person to believe that he or she is an expert in all of its facets. This book was compiled and edited to help fill the current information gap in correctional literature, by presenting an in-depth analysis of major treatment components in corrections. Each chapter was designed especially for this book and discusses appropriate methods of treatment based on the author's extensive knowledge and experience. Twenty-one prominent correctional authorities, with multidisciplinary background, present their guidelines for specific types of therapeutic activities for juvenile and adult offenders.

Students, professors, and practitioners of corrections have been searching for a textbook that provides appropriate guidelines and methods for planning and implementing correctional treatment programs. This book is designed to meet that need. It offers challenging reference materials for those students and practitioners who are concerned with effecting vital changes in correctional programs. It will also be useful as a primary text for undergraduate and graduate courses and for in-service workshops on correctional treatment.

Correctional Counseling and Treatment is a "how to" book, which is pragmatic and reality oriented. The chapter topics were selected after much deliberation and review because they reflect what appear to be the most promising programs for the future. Keeping in mind the objective of a cohesive book, without duplication of treatment components, specific topics were assigned to recognized experts who have extensive experience and publications in their designated area.

The treatment approaches described throughout the book would be most effective in community-based, rather than institutional, settings. This philosophy is echoed by several contributors. However, it is unlikely that all institutions will be closed and replaced by community correctional centers in the near future because of the financial limitations and political priorities of our correctional systems. Therefore, it is recognized by those of us who are reality oriented that—until such time as community-based treatment prevails—correctional programs will, of necessity, continue to be undertaken in institutional surroundings.

There is no panacea for upgrading the overall quality of correctional treatment in America's prisons. To achieve real change in correctional treatment, a total effort is required; legislators, administrators, and staff must cooperate to develop new facilities, program resources, evidence-based treatment protocols, equipment, and training modules. Other critical components are building a therapeutic alliance and motivating the offender to change. Without counseling staff who are committed to building on inmates' inner strengths and potential for positive change, the status quo will remain.

In the past, although positive efforts were attempted, the results were often disappointing because only fragments of the total treatment process were improved. Preservice and in-service training for correctional treatment specialists is one of the important vehicles for achieving meaningful change. Total commitment from administrators, custodial officers, counselors, teachers, social workers, and psychologists is needed. Correctional administrators and staff should work hand in hand with inmate groups, college and university faculty, students, and community leaders in planning the total milieu.

Correctional Counseling and Treatment provides a thorough analysis of program options that should be developed in the setting of a therapeutic milieu. These treatment approaches are presented as systematic alternatives for combating the destructive elements of traditional maximum-security prisons. With support from citizen groups, legislative bodies, and concerned practitioners, policy makers will be able to activate the development of viable treatment options—including community-based treatment and reentry programs—as recommended in this book.

Albert R. Roberts, Ph.D.
Piscataway, New Jersey

Acknowledgments

❖

First and foremost, I thank my prominent author team of experienced correctional practitioners and academic scholars for contributing important chapters to this book. Special recognition also goes to Kathy Glidden, Senior Project Manager at TexTech Inc., who was conscientious and responsive in coordinating all of the book's production activities.

I am grateful to Frank Mortimer, former Senior Editor in Criminal Justice, for agreeing with me about the critical needs for this text. Special thanks to Tim Peyton, the current Senior Editor in Criminal Justice at Prentice-Hall, for his enthusiastic endorsement and sponsorship of this volume. A highly supportive editor is the key to the success of any new textbook in criminal justice.

The helpful insightful suggestions and discussions with mentors and colleagues over the past forty or so years have been invaluable. The following professors and administrators have influenced my thinking on correctional treatment and rehabilitation over the years: Peter P. Lejins, J.D., Ph.D.; Commissioner Joseph Cannon, M.S.W.; Ann Wolbert Burgess, D.N.Sc.; Glenn Kendall, Ed.D.; Stanley L. Brodsky, Ph.D.; John Irwin, Ph.D.; Harris Chaiklin, Ph.D.; Vernon Fox, Ph.D.; and Nathaniel Pallone, Ph.D. Recent writings by Michael Jacobson, Ph.D.; David P. Farrington, Ph.D.; Lennox S. Hinds, J.D.; Francis T. Cullen, Ph.D.; James M. Byrne, Ph.D.; Michael Welch, Ph.D.; and Todd Clear, Ph.D. have influenced my perspectives on correctional counseling and treatment.

I thank my parents, Harry and Evelyn Roberts, who instilled within me a dedication to caring for vulnerable groups and persevering to complete all projects and activities no matter how time-consuming—like this my thirty-sixth book. Finally, I thank Beverly Schenkman Roberts, my wife of thirty-five years, for her sage counsel and being my most important sounding board in all that matters.

List of Contributors

❖

Jemel P. Aguilar, Ph.D.
School of Social Work
University of Texas, Austin

Donald A. Andrews, Ph.D.
Department of Psychology
Carleton University
Ottawa, Ontario, Canada

Kimberly Bender, M.S.W.
School of Social Work
University of Texas, Austin

Pia Biswas, B.A.
Department of Criminal Justice
Faculty of Arts and Sciences
Rutgers—The State University of New Jersey
Livingston College Campus, Piscataway

William M. Burdon, Ph.D.
UCLA Integrated Substance Abuse Programs
University of California, Los Angeles

James M. Byrne, Ph.D.
*Department of Criminology and Criminal
  Justice*
University of Massachusetts, Lowell

Harris Chaiklin, Ph.D.
School of Social Work
University of Maryland, Baltimore

Francis T. Cullen, Ph.D.
*Department of Criminology and Criminal
  Justice*
University of Cincinnati
Cincinnati, Ohio

Craig Dowden, Ph.D.
Department of Psychology
Carleton University
Ottawa, Ontario, Canada

Diane L. Green, Ph.D.
Department of Social Work
Florida Atlantic University, Boca Raton

Sabrina R. Haugebrook, M.P.A.
Department of Planning and Research
New Jersey Department of Corrections

April Pattavina, Ph.D.
*Department of Criminology and Criminal
  Justice*
University of Massachusetts, Lowell

Michael L. Prendergast, Ph.D.
UCLA Integrated Substance Abuse Programs
University of California, Los Angeles

Albert R. Roberts, Ph.D.
Department of Criminal Justice
Faculty of Arts and Sciences
Rutgers—The State University of New Jersey
Livingston College Campus, Piscataway

Shahid M. Shahidullah, Ph.D.
Department of Sociology,
*   Criminal Justice, and Social Work*
Virginia State University

David W. Springer, Ph.D.
School of Social Work
University of Texas, Austin

Mark H. Stone, Ph.D.
Adler School of Professional Psychology
Chicago, Illinois

Faye S. Taxman, Ph.D.
Criminal Justice Program
Department of Government
*   and Social Sciences*
Virginia Commonwealth University, Richmond

Kathi R. Trawver, M.S.W.
Department of Social Work
University of Alaska

Stephen J. Tripodi, Ph.D.
School of Social Work
Florida State University, Tallahassee

Harry K. Wexler, Ph.D.
National Development and Research
*   Institutes (NDRI)*
New York, New York

Kristen M. Zgoba, Ph.D.
Department of Planning and Research
New Jersey Department of Corrections

PART I

Introduction and Overview

❖

1

Introduction and Overview of Correctional Counseling and Treatment

Albert R. Roberts and Pia Biswas

Correctional counseling and rehabilitation, in the broadest sense, seeks to transform a convicted felon into a responsible and productive member of society. The focus in correctional counseling should be on changing behavior and helping offenders to enhance mental health and cognitive functioning as well as academic, vocational, and social skills. This chapter includes the summary findings of a nationwide survey on the state of the art of correctional counseling and treatment, staffing patterns, medical and mental health needs of offenders, and academic and vocational education programs. Twenty different state departments of corrections (DOCs) will be highlighted in terms of specific evidence-based assessment counseling and treatment programs.

This chapter is not designed to give definitive solutions to all problems and issues in the correctional counseling of offenders; rather the goal is to formalize ideas, raise issues, and document best practices from which effective programs can be replicated. A foundation will be delineated so that program planners and administrators may better be able to meet the individual and special needs of the inmate population.

There is wide variation in corrections from state to state and differences within some states on whether offender counseling and treatment programs are offered on a very limited scale or on a daily and intensive level. Correctional administrators have a tremendous amount of discretionary power in terms of the extent to which offenders are provided with opportunities for individual and group counseling, substance abuse treatment, and academic education or vocational training. The underlying basis of whether correctional administrators are punitive versus rehabilitation-oriented grows out of their political beliefs and views of both inmates in general and specific types of offenders. We believe that through intensive counseling and treatment most offenders have the ability to change their antisocial and law-breaking patterns of behavior as long as they are motivated to change. We also firmly believe that if you treat inmates like wild animals and continually punish them, in all likelihood, they will become more hardened and violent upon release. Therefore, the objective of this chapter and the text is to put "corrections" back into policies and practices with offenders. This can be done when a full range of opportunities for individual and group treatment is provided to all inmates regardless of the offense they have been committed for.

TREATMENT STRATEGY

The availability of program and service choices should be maximized to the extent that each offender can participate in rehabilitation programs. The philosophy underlying this therapeutic approach is that each person possesses unique needs, abilities and dispositions, and requires a flexible program. Instead of depersonalizing offenders through rigid regimentation of their time, attempts should be made to bolster self-confidence, individuality, and socialized identity. Most men and women have the potential to rationally and selectively plan their own destiny, and come to grips with the problems of free choice in our complex industrialized society. Offenders have failed in society; in order to motivate them for success after release, facilities should resemble free society in some areas, such as providing several program options.

An offender's chances for success the second time around are diminished if conditions in the prison are totally unlike those outside. "Success" in a traditional prison is dependent on the abnegation of responsibility for one's actions and passive acceptance of living conditions, food, medical services, and so on. Success in the outside world, however, is not measured by those criteria but by independently meeting one's own needs, working for a living, earning a good wage, having self-confidence, and attaining prestige in the eyes of the community members. To attain success after release, offenders must be able to handle free choice wisely and make decisions which are accepted as law-abiding. They can benefit from intensive individual and group counseling or staff role models, but, most importantly, they must be aware that to go straight and "make it" in free society depends on a willingness to work toward goals, make sacrifices, and be responsible for themselves and their family. The rigid paternalistic correctional philosophy of "I know what is best for you" has failed time and time again. In a truly therapeutic correctional environment, each individual has the continuous opportunity to make a number of program choices. By choosing to pursue a particular vocational area, for example, it is hoped that inmates will learn to make rational decisions, and transfer this ability to the community when they are released.

The organizational milieu in most correctional institutions is conflict-prone. The emphasis on security and punitive control measures exerted by custodial personnel all too often conflict with the therapeutic objectives of professionally trained treatment specialists. A treatment specialist provides supportive counseling and promotes initiative and positive self-direction among prison inmates.

Conflict arises because most correctional officers have little training in human relations and are threatened by the nonpunitive approach of treatment specialists. For example, a counselor may recommend that inmates become involved with vocational training in the sheet metal shop; he or she may also order 20 pounds of clay for inmate hobby time.

Although professional counselors recognize that clay modeling provides a healthy, non-violent outlet for a prisoners' aggressive energies, and vocational training in a marketable skill contributes to rehabilitation goals, many guards are disdainful of such efforts, regarding them as permissive and a means of coddling inmates. From the guard's frame of reference, the clay will only be modeled into a replica of a 38-revolver or made to resemble a man's head, to be placed on a cot so as not to arouse suspicion while the inmate attempts to escape. The sheet metal shop is thought of as the place where all the shivs and shanks are made.

The diametrically opposed attitudes of the untrained guard and the treatment specialist undermine and inhibit the rehabilitation effort of the treatment team. The custodial orientation leads to the growth of an inmate code that requires loyalty to other inmates, opposition to the entire prison staff, and at most lip service to so-called treatment programs.

There are several different conceptions of the ideal characteristics of therapeutic milieu, but the most significant aspect is that, if the inmate is to achieve any self-respect, he or she must be treated as an individual worthy of the respect of others. When both professional and nonprofessional staff work together to provide a therapeutic atmosphere and when inmates have the opportunity to make decisions and choose programs options, the necessary climate for a therapeutic milieu emerges. Early rehabilitation efforts overlooked the relationship between fostering positive attitudes and values and building the offender's initiative, self-direction, and responsibility.

If rehabilitation is to be a reality, the development of a therapeutic community is of paramount importance. In accordance with the psychotherapeutic ideals of Maxwell Jones, a therapeutic community allows the inmate to "act out" within acceptable limits and to become motivated to participate in available rehabilitation programs. The major objective is to reverse the regimented authoritarian structure of traditional prisons by encouraging communication among all levels of staff, and between staff and inmates.

Several therapeutic communities can be set up at each correctional facility so that inmates can begin to act responsibly for the welfare of their community. Although it is more difficult to initiate therapeutic communities in the highly regimented structure of most maximum-security institutions, they can be developed and operated effectively. In maximum-security prisons, each tier or cell block can be a therapeutic community; in minimum-security settings, the location of the community can be a dormitory. Within these physical confines, the inmates and staff make collective decisions based on democratic principles. Examples of some of the decisions that can be made are permitting of inmates with minimum-security ratings to attend a funeral of a close family member in another state without a guard, allowing the better educated inmates to tutor educationally disadvantaged adults in an inner-city basic education program, initiating a program to train inmates and guards to work as crisis counselors on a prison suicide prevention team, and suspending a correctional officer who harasses the inmates by turning off the television 15 minutes before the suspenseful climax of the Wednesday night movie.

The primary goal of comprehensive therapeutic services is to help offenders build self-esteem, adjust to the correctional facility, learn to communicate more effectively with family and community members, and be able to confront and act on alternatives available to them as they consider their future. In some cases, these goals can be accomplished through informal, everyday contact with staff and through the group counseling sessions. In many other cases, individual methods of treatment will be more beneficial.

INTERNAL VERSUS EXTERNAL CONTROL

Individual and group counseling is recommended for all committed offenders. Several techniques of counseling should be employed by the staff in fostering offender's increased self-awareness of self-destructive patterns and appropriate alternative behaviors. Some of the available treatment approaches are behavioral diagnosis, cognitive-behavioral treatment, counseling with focus on internal-external locus of control, milieu therapy, family counseling, psychodrama, and guided group interaction.

Counselors, and other correctional treatment specialists, are concerned with determining why some inmates seem motivated to try to reach socially acceptable goals, while other inmates do not seem to expend any task- or goal-oriented effort. Characteristics of inmates who do not manifest goal-oriented behavior are feelings of helplessness, alienation, and powerlessness. Offenders who are motivated to invest the necessary efforts to attain specific goals appear to be more capable of coping with the situations that affect their daily lives.

The degree to which inmates feel they have control over their environment has a significant influence on their behavior. The control expectancy notion allows treatment specialists to observe offenders with regard to the degree to which they feel able to give direction to, or have control over, their own lives. The "internal-external locus of control" is derived from J. B. Rotter's social learning theory. Internal control refers to the feeling of individuals that they have some measure of control over their destiny. They feel that the outcomes of positive and/or negative events are consequences of their own actions. On the other hand, those individuals who perceive that control is outside themselves and that their destiny is in the hands of fate, chance, luck, or powerful others have an external locus of control.

The implications of studying the internal-external control orientation relate to the desire for identifying and changing inmates' feelings of lack of control over their environment. If inmates believe that their actions can positively affect their future, there is a greater chance of their actively participating in a successful rehabilitation plan. In changing the low expectancies of inmates with an external orientation, the goals are to increase their literacy rate and improve goal-oriented behavior.

Marvin Seeman's research findings indicated that inmates with an internal locus of control were more willing to correct their deficiencies through participation in rehabilitative programs. He presented three kinds of information to 85 inmates at Chillicothe Federal Prison to measure their expectations of controlling their own destiny. The three types of information related to the individual's awareness of and ability to learn about the following: successful achievement of parole, the immediate reformatory situation, and their long-range prospects for a criminal career. Seeman's study indicated that "internals" retained a significantly greater number of parole-related items than did "externals," but no significant difference was found in their ability to learn the other two kinds of information.

Achieving parole status is one of the most important goals of an inmate. Obtaining parole puts the offender in a better position to control his environment. Therefore, an internal inmate would be more likely to invest the effort necessary to learn the information relevant to obtaining a parole than would an external inmate. The internal is motivated to learn information related to achieving parole because he or she views this information as essential to achieving this goal. In contrast, the external, perceiving that obtaining parole is unrelated to his or her efforts, would see little purpose in learning such information.

Research by Peters in a medium-security institution for adult felons in North Carolina provides further evidence of inmates' differing motivations for participating in occupational education programs. His results indicated that internals were more likely to participate in courses such as baking, small engine repair, typing, and high school refresher courses than were externals.

Treatment specialists should receive training that will enable them to foster an increased sense of control in external inmates. Implementation of the prison option system developed in this chapter can increase inmates' cooperation and participation in treatment programs by allowing the inmates to have a feeling of control over some of the events and programs that most directly affect them.

The authors have emphasized the need to reduce the external's low expectancy of control, thereby encouraging self-direction and goal-oriented behavior. In contrast, the inmate with extremely high internal control can be just as maladjusted as the extremely external individual. Highly internal offenders have been referred to as sociopaths, who feel compelled to dominate their environment. Two counseling approaches may be recommended for the "sociopath": helping them accept and adjust the aspects of their environment which they cannot or should not control and helping them to channel their aggressive energies into constructive and socially acceptable pursuits.

Methods for helping externals to become more internally controlled are to reinforce internal statements, to replace external control statements with internal questions, and to assist inmates to recognize the consequences of their behavior. This may be accomplished by helping them search for alternate behaviors that could have changed the outcome of events in the past and that can influence current and future events. The relationship between individual expectancies of control and inmate behavior has been shown. Treatment efforts geared toward reducing extreme expectancies of internal or external control may well result in inmates' improved self-concept, participation in rehabilitation programs, and successful readjustment to community life.

GROUP THERAPY

Group treatment programs in which small groups of offenders meet with a leader are becoming increasingly popular in correctional settings. Pressure to adopt group methods of treatment may be an outgrowth of the fact that: it is less costly to hire a group therapist who works with many inmates at one time than it is to employ a counselor who sees inmates only on an individual basis. Also, some prison administrators subscribe to the widely accepted sociological theories of crime causation which imply that criminal behavior is learned through association with deviant peer groups. By this reasoning, an anticriminal peer group would be a viable means for unlearning or renouncing criminal behaviors.

For group treatment to be effective, the group leader should be aware of the need to overcome initial resistance and conning on the part of group members. There are two distinct classes of group treatment with offenders—group psychotherapy and group counseling. The role of the group leader/therapist varies accordingly. The primary methodological distinction between the two is that group psychotherapy focuses on a psychotherapeutic approach toward the individual group members, while group counseling focuses on changing behaviors and interaction of the members through group process.

There are various advantages of group therapy for offender rehabilitation. Often times, individualized therapy is not as effective as group therapy because inmates endure an enormous amount of peer pressure to conform to certain types of behavior. Criminal behavior tends to thrive in a criminal subculture, where many people share certain views that promote and justify deviant behavior. It can be said that a vast majority of inmates were exposed to that subculture, which led to their deviant acts. Prisons naturally are a haven for these views since most criminals retain their beliefs from the criminal subculture during the time of their incarceration. Therefore, creating a change in the views and attitudes through therapy of the group, as opposed to the individual, allows for a greater likelihood that new views and attitudes will be adopted and sustained because they will now be part of the subculture. If a few or many of the inmates begin to embrace what they learn during the counseling sessions, the attitude of the subculture as a whole will begin to change as well. Additionally, group therapy allows for the group specialist to simultaneously reach out to more individuals, whereas it may be more difficult to set up individual sessions for each inmate. Also, if sessions are set up for individuals, they probably will not be held as frequently as group sessions are held.

The primary goal of group therapy is to prepare inmates for life in the outside world by teaching them to become law-abiding citizens. A crucial part of attaining this goal is to ensure that the subculture within the prison shifts toward more socially acceptable behavior. Though there has not been any definitive reason to believe that group therapy, in and of itself, reduces the recidivism rate of offenders, it appears that it does at least improve the interaction between offenders in prison. Staff members also reported that their communication with inmates undergoing group therapy had improved and that those individuals seemed to get into less trouble on average than other inmates.

Individuals who seem to have benefited the most from the group therapy sessions were those who were more extroverted and open to new ideas. Additionally, those who committed multiple offenses in the company of others were influenced the most by group therapy sessions. In sharp contrast, the introverts, or loners, tended to be less receptive to the therapy treatment and were more likely to recidivate upon release. Therefore, those who are most likely to be influenced by peers are more likely to adapt to the group therapy methods. Voluntary participation in group therapy will lead these extroverted individuals to emerge and self-select themselves for treatment. Staff members can also assist in the process to ensure that those who are susceptible to treatment are the ones being selected for the group therapy.

The type of leaders selected for group therapy sessions does not seem to make much of a difference in terms of the effectiveness of the treatment as long as the leaders are able to conduct discussions and convey warmth and encouragement to the offenders. Other factors, such as the specific type of training or background of the leader, do not seem to have as much of an impact on the level of effectiveness.

Group therapy should mainly focus on creating discussions, which are the most conducive way to promote active participation from all of the group members. Once group members are engaged in the discussion, they are more receptive to the ideas that are being conveyed to them. Since group therapy essentially tries to persuade offenders to adopt new and more socially acceptable behavior, the best way to go about this is by reinforcing positive behavior and discouraging any antisocial behavior.

Offenders should be seated in a circle to promote a roundtable-type discussion. There should be at least more than a handful of individuals in the group to prevent anyone from feeling uncomfortable or defensive; however, there should not be too many members, which may cause some to feel intimidated by the large crowd. The topics to be discussed in therapy sessions will vary from one group to another. Inmates may wish to discuss problems or issues that they are presently dealing with or topics in which they all share interest. Incorporating psychodrama (to be discussed next) allows for self-expression and discussion. Regardless, one topic that should be discussed is the inmates' life in the outside community upon release.

If possible, group members should be selected in accordance with the peer groups that naturally form in the institution. Since those who are most susceptible to treatment are the extroverted individuals who are influenced by their peers, creating a group in which these individuals are among their peer, will allow for more persuasion into socially acceptable behavior. By experiencing treatment as a group, the individuals may feel as though they are beginning to conform to the new norms (post-therapy) of the group. Thereafter, the whole group's views may begin to shift away from deviant behavior and may transition toward more law-abiding behavior. This, in turn, will help to prepare them for interaction and acceptance in the outside community.

Psychodrama

Psychodrama is a group therapeutic technique involving the dramatic enactment of events and issues that are important to the individual. The technique has been used mainly with people suffering from alcohol, marital, psychotic, and neurotic problems. Psychodrama is, however, a valuable technique for prison inmates, though it has been used by only a few innovative correctional psychodramatists.

When psychodrama is used with offenders, the scenes that are acted out may be part of their past, present, or future lifestyle. Psychodrama offers offenders an opportunity to act out antisocial and illegal behaviors in a controlled setting. In addition to depicting an important issue, it provides for open discussion and candid feedback by other group members.

The word *drama* comes from a Greek word meaning "action" or "a thing done." J. L. Moreno, the renowned founder of this approach, defines psychodrama as "the science which explores the truth by dramatic methods." Ideally, a particular area should be designated for psychodrama. The groups should know that they can step up on the platform whenever their emotions require dramatic expression.

Psychodrama can provide inmates with an outlet for characterizing experiences that are of such intensity that words alone are insufficient. The unique population of the prison makes the reaction to psychodrama different from what it is on the outside. Inmates who hear through the grapevine about a new group therapy approach may well be cynical and skeptical that it will turn out to be a psychologist's leading another group meeting. But psychodrama is different; it allows inmates to vent their pent-up hostility and frustration at the system and authority figures, at the fear of losing a girlfriend or spouse, and even over the anxiety of reintegration into an unknown society. Guided by a skilled therapist trained in psychological and dramatic techniques, psychodrama is a new and unique method of treatment for inmates.

This process is especially valuable in "future projections" in which the inmate, role-playing a future situation, can get the feel of actions, attitudes, and responses commensurate with a law-abiding person. Future situations that may pose a particular problem for offenders are applying for and maintaining a job, being reunited with family, participating in community life, and relating to parole and other correctional personnel.

In psychodrama, the pressure of the other group members makes distortion or conning difficult and causes inmates to more carefully assess their words and actions. Through psychodrama, offenders are able to reenact past behavior, project future actions, and reflect upon effective methods for coping with life's difficulties—without resorting to unlawful activities.

CHEMICAL DEPENDENCY AND ADDICTION TREATMENT

Convicted felons tend to be abusers of both alcohol and illegal drugs. In fact, a large percentage of state inmate populations are substance abusers. The percentage of the total state inmate population with drug addiction problems ranges from a low of 25 percent in North Carolina to a high of 80–85 percent in Kentucky, Maryland, Montana, and New Hampshire. States also differ in the types of chemical dependency programs they provide, vanaina from 6- to 12-month therapeatice communities to 12-step programs that meet 7 days a week. Some states like South Carolina have Addiction Treatment Units (ATU) where a therapeutic community model is maintained 24 hours a day, with three to four intensive groups per day. Other states like Wisconsin have residential treatment programs specializing in substance abuse treatment, aftercare and transitional programs, and treatment for dually diagnosed inmates. Other states like Maryland have modified therapeutic communities with an emphasis on cognitive-behavior counseling.

The three different types of programs for chemical dependency are Residential, Intensive Outpatient, and Outpatient. The Residential Program provides an entire unit of housing for inmates participating in substance abuse treatment. In the duration of this program, various methods are used, including acupuncture, mental health, therapeutic communities, and cognitive behavioral approaches. The program is for 6 months and offers two group sessions per week as well as one individual session every two weeks. The Intensive Outpatient Program is offered to inmates who do not reside in a special unit but receive rigorous treatment. The program runs for approximately 6 months and targets cognitive behavioral rehabilitation. Finally, the Outpatient Program is offered as an aftercare program, which consists of weekly group meetings after the completion of the two previous programs. This type of treatment is provided to the inmate indefinitely or until the time of release.

PSYCHOLOGICAL SERVICES

This type of treatment provides inmates with the opportunity to discuss any issues of concern in the protected group environment. Individuals receive feedback from the psychologist as well as other members of the group. The objective is to enhance offenders' problem-solving skills. There is no prerequisite in receiving psychological services; however, preference is given to those inmates who are monitored clinically. Additionally, there is finite time frame for the sessions; inmates may receive them as needed on an indefinite basis.

ANGER MANAGEMENT

Anger Management Group therapy is provided for inmates to help them determine what causes anger and discover methods by which the anger can be controlled. Elements include relapse prevention, stress reduction, conflict resolution, and training in assertive and rational behavior. By teaching offenders about anger as well as other negative emotions, negative and aggressive behavior can be prevented. Learning how to control their anger allows inmates to improve self-expression and their relationships with others. The average duration for the therapy course ranges from 8 to 20 weeks, with an average of 12 weeks. Classes are held once a week for approximately 90 minutes on average.

COGNITIVE INTERVENTIONS

The Cognitive Interventions Program is presented in a group format and strives to help participants better understand themselves and train them to better control their lives. The underlying notion of the program is that how individuals think determines how they will act; so if we can modify their thought process, the corresponding actions will be sure to follow. By showing offenders how to control their thoughts, they are able to control more aspects of their lives. The duration of this program ranges from 12 to 36 weeks, with an average of 15 weeks. The average groups meets approximately twice per week for 2 hours; however, this varies slightly from one location to the next.

NATIONAL SURVEY FINDINGS

In reviewing the national survey findings, we were struck by the low priority given to employing treatment staff—social workers, psychologists, or counselors—by many of the state correctional systems. In sharp contrast, many states have a low ratio of guards per inmate possibly due to an administrative priority of custody and punishment or to the strong unions, which advocate for custodial officers. More specifically, two southern states stand out as deficient when it comes to employing full-time clinical staff. Mississippi's DOC has 23 counselors and 1 psychologist treating 23,996 inmates, with a ratio of 1 clinician per 1,000 inmates. There's a dramatic difference when examining the ratio of inmates per guard 1:13 with a total of 1,843 guards.

On a more positive note, several states stand out for their demonstrated commitment to offender counseling and rehabilitation. New Hampshire and Wisconsin seem to be innovative and progressive with a ratio of 1 clinician for every 35.5 inmates incarcerated in the state of New Hampshire and 1 clinician for every 64 inmates incarcerated in the state of Wisconsin. At the same time, these two rehabilitation-oriented states are still concerned for public safety and holding inmates accountable for their behavior, with a ratio of 1 guard for every 4 inmates in New Hampshire and 1 guard for every 6.1 inmates in Wisconsin. The state of Washington has an even more impressive record with a ratio of 1 clinician for every 34.4 inmates and 1 guard for every 5.4 inmates—the best ratio of the states which were examined.

EXEMPLARS OF SEX OFFENDER TREATMENT PROGRAMS

Examining the Wisconsin DOC sex offender treatment program in more detail conveys the high level of commitment that the state has toward the rehabilitation of offenders. Wisconsin offers a selection of different offender programs, which include educational-based programs, psychotherapeutic interventions, and customized therapy groups that cater to the needs and risk level of the offenders. Participants of the programs undergo an evaluation and are provided with the treatment, that best suits offender's individual needs. All three programs manage the offender's risk of recidivism through supervision and polygraph exams. Involvement in at least one of the programs is mandatory under the offender's supervision rules. Failure of offenders to comply can lead to increased sanctions.

A plethora of factors are considered before placing an offender into a program, including the length of the offender's sentence, parole eligibility, mandatory release dates, the offender's willingness to participate in treatment, the accessibility of programs that best cater to the offender's needs, the amount of security risk that the offender poses, and other program needs of the offender. Once these factors are considered, the offender is then placed into one of the treatment programs: the Education Awareness Sex Offender Program, Pretreatment/Deniers, Sex Offender Treatment, Sex Offender Treatment Program, or Beacon Residential Program, as well as programs for juvenile offenders.

The Education Awareness Sex Offender Treatment Program is an entry-level program designed to prepare offenders for a more comprehensive treatment program. In this program, offenders receive approximately 25 hours of programming in 1.2 to 2.5-hour increments for groups ranging from 12 to 25 offenders. The staff generally consists of two people who are either psychologists or licensed social workers. The waiting list for the program varies from 12 to 24 months.

The Deniers program is a mandatory program for all sex offenders. The offenders in this group represent a wide range of resistance to programming, from vehement denial to reducing the significance of the offense. The program's goal is to encourage offenders to participate in treatment in a nonthreatening manner by informing the offenders that they will ultimately require treatment to reduce the risk of recidivism. This program is offered for 3 to 4 months and meets once a week for 2 hours. Groups of 10 to 12 offenders are supervised by one or two staff members, a psychologist or a social worker. Average waiting lists for these programs are relatively short, ranging from 3 to 4 months.

The Sex Offender Treatment (SOT) provides therapeutic interventions and is voluntarily attended by the offender. A majority of the treatment groups consist of a heterogeneous mix of offenders who show a less compulsive and repetitive pattern of sexual deviancy. Offenders who require special attention are placed in targeted offender groups such as SOT Female Offenders, SOT Spanish-speaking, SOT Lighthouse for the lower functioning, SOT Special Management Unit for the cognitively challenged and/or emotionally disturbed, SOT Child Victim, and SOT Adult Victim. The general group program runs from 6 to 12 months and meets once or twice a week for 1.5 to 2 hours for groups of 6 to 12 offenders. The staff consists of either two psychologists or one psychologist facilitator in conjunction with one treatment specialist, crisis intervention worker, or social worker.

The Sex Offender Treatment Program varies a bit from the program mentioned above in that it is a long-term residential program for offenders who display predictable patterns of compulsive and repetitive acts of sexual deviancy. The course of the program is 152 weeks and is provided to groups of 12 offenders. The staff consists of one Psychologist supervisor, one unit manager, one psychological services associate, two psychologists, two social workers, and one treatment sergeant. The average waiting list varies for this program, depending on the offender.

The Beacon Residential Program is a new three-phase residential program, which is an alternative to the traditional sex offender program. The program attempts to change impulsive behavior by gaining an understanding of the offender's past to create a relapse-prevention plan and to change any dynamic risk factors. The length of the program is approximately 104 weeks with groups of 8 to 10 offenders. The staff includes approximately five people, including at least one psychologist and four social workers. The average wait for this program is approximately 96 months but is less for those who have a Sex Offender Treatment Program need.

Special programs also exist for juvenile offenders, which are part of comprehensive four-phase treatment plan. The four-phase program addresses offense description, sex history, social history, and relapse prevention. Youths must satisfactorily complete one phase of treatment to move up to the next phase. The length of the program ranges from 1 to 1.5 years and is offered to groups of 8 to 10 offenders. The staff consists of psychologists, social workers, and youth counselors. The average waiting lists ranges from no wait to 6 weeks, depending on the location.

COMMUNITY AFTERCARE

Although various types of drug abuse treatment in prison are extremely beneficial for offenders, community aftercare is an essential step in reducing relapse and recidivism. Community aftercare essentially provides individuals with treatment after release into the community to assist in the rehabilitation of the individual. In order for aftercare to be most effective, it should mimic the type of treatment offered during incarceration. Whether offered during supervision or after supervision has ended, it helps to maintain discipline among offenders.

Intensive drug treatment programs focus on cognitive and behavioral treatment, group therapy, health and wellness, and role-playing, as well as techniques to boost self-esteem. Many programs hire ex-addicts to serve as examples for the groups, some even train the group. Treatment programs during incarceration can last anywhere from 6 to 12 months, however, aftercare does not have a definitive time frame. Some programs screen inmates to see which individuals would be best suited for particular programs, while others take all.

Each drug treatment program varies in its approach. For example, the Key-Crest Program (Martin, 1995) is an intervention program which has three phases. The first phase is therapeutic community for inmates in prison. The second phase entails releasing inmates into a community work release center; here, they have jobs but still reside in a facility and continue to receive treatment from phase one. The last phase releases individuals into the community under some form of supervision. The results of the program show that residential treatment in conjunction with the aftercare significantly reduced recidivism rates.

Oftentimes, intervention after release is more effective than treatment during incarceration. According to the New Vision residential treatment program, individuals who participated in aftercare, in addition to treatment during incarceration, had a recidivism rate of 7 percent for new convictions, whereas individuals who did not participate in aftercare had a recidivism rate of 16 percent. The study examined individuals within six months of release. Additionally, a study conducted by Wexler also confirms that those who had received community aftercare were considered lower-risk offenders than those who did not receive the aftercare. Therefore, the effectiveness of treatment during incarceration can be increased with community aftercare post-release.

In this text, we will examine various facets of the corrections systems and make recommendations as to the effective treatment and rehabilitation approaches.

PRISONER RE-ENTRY PROGRAMS

Approximately 650,000 prisoners are released from federal and state prisons into communities throughout the nation each year. According to the 2006 National Governors Association (NGA) Center for Best Practices report, about 67 percent (435,500) are rearrested and 50 percent (325,000) are re-incarcerated within 3 years of release. In past decades many of these ex-offenders have not been prepared to obtain realistic and marketable job skills, steady employment, substance abuse and mental health services, and/or subsidized and transitional housing upon release. Because of the dearth of prison vocational training and counseling programs, and prisoner re-entry programs available during the 1980s and 1990s, many released offenders commit new offenses and/or violate parole policies within 3 years of release.

A promising major federal initiative began in 2001. The Serious and Violent Offender Re-entry Initiative was developed by the Federal Office of Justice Programs of the U.S. Department of Justice and the National Institute of Corrections. Cosponsors of this large project also include the U.S. Department of Labor and the U.S. Department of Housing and Urban Development (HUD). This major national project provides funding to develop federal, state, and local community-based transition and re-entry programs for juvenile and adult ex-offenders. The overridding goal of prisoner re-entry programs is to help ex-offenders seek, find, and maintain employment as well as the full range of housing and social services.

In recent years, this federally funded program has received increased funding. In 2002, $100 million was given to 68 programs in 49 states to support prisoner re-entry programs. In 2005, President Bush proposed and then supported a $300 million 4-year expansion of the federal prisoner re-entry program.

There are many examples of comprehensive prisoner re-entry programs. For example, the National Governors Association's Center for Best Practices is currently operating seven prisoner re-entry academies in six states–Georgia, Idaho, Massachusetts, Michigan, Rhode Island, and Virginia. On the local level, Exodus Transitional Community Program in East Harlem, New York, seems to be highly effective in preventing recidivism. It served 213 ex-offenders in 2002 , and just 6 were returned to prison. Exodus served 290 ex-offenders in 2003, and only 3 of the men were returned to prison. The City of Memphis, Tennessee developed the Second Chance re-entry program over three years ago and has served over 1500 ex-offenders–only 4 ex-offenders were returned to prison.

During the 1960s, new prisoner re-entry programs were referred to as Federal Prerelease Guidance Centers, reintegrative programs (e.g. work-release and study-release centers), in-prison social education programs, and job information and placement labs at the federal and state level. Unfortunately, many of these programs lost funding and staff during the punitive era of the 1980s and 1990s. However, the re-emergence of comprehensive prisoner re-entry programs in recent years is extremely promising if the goal is to sharply reduce recidivism while rehabilitating and resocializing offenders.

2

The Emerging Role of Clinical and Actuarial Risk Assessment in an Evidence-Based Community Corrections System

Issues to Consider

James M. Byrne and April Pattavina

Revised and Expanded Version of an Article by Byrne and Pattavina in *Federal Probation* 70 (2): 64–67 (Sept, 2006).

❖

INTRODUCTION AND OVERVIEW

The risk assessment process is undergoing major change in federal, state, and local community corrections agencies across the country. New assessment instruments are being introduced, outdated case management systems are being redesigned, and the roles and responsibilities of line staff and management in community corrections agencies are being reassessed and redefined, in large part due to the application of new, "soft" computer technology in community corrections agencies (Pattavina and Taxman, 2007). As Gottfredson and Tonry (1987) predicted in the late 1980s, "both the literature and practical application of science-based prediction and classification will continue to expand as institutions evolve to become more rational, more efficient, and more just" (vii). While rationality, efficiency, and justice are laudable goals for any criminal justice organization, we suspect that ultimately, it is the effectiveness of the community corrections system—both in terms of short-term offender control and long-term offender change—that really matters to the public, and by extension, to policy makers and practitioners. In the following chapter, we examine three key issues related to assessing the effectiveness of risk assessment procedures that need to be addressed: (1) how can evidence-based practice be used to establish a link between risk assessment and risk reduction; (2) the implications of both actuarial and clinical assessment for line staff and management; and (3) the need to combine individual risk assessment and community risk assessment in the next generation of risk-driven community corrections strategies. We conclude by offering three simple recommendations designed to improve the effectiveness of the risk assessment process in federal, state, and local community corrections agencies: (1) Emphasize on risk reduction as the primary purpose of risk assessment; (2) design simple, yet powerful, assessment tools; (3) incorporate community-level risk factor into the assessment process in recognition of the importance of the person environment motivations.

ISSUE 1: EVIDENCE-BASED PRACTICE AND THE (MISSING) LINK BETWEEN RISK ASSESSMENT AND RISK REDUCTION

When the term *best practices* is used, it typically refers to the results of an evidence-based review of the research on a topic of interest (e.g., scared straight programs, prison and community-based treatment programs, etc.). Essentially, there are three different types of evidence-based reviews: (1) the "gold standard" evidence-based review focuses only on randomized, controlled experiments; (2) the "bronze standard" evidence-based review includes both experimental and well-designed quasi-experimental research, while using nonexperimental research studies to confirm findings from higher quality research; and (3) the unscientific (or nonsense) review, which does not identify specific study review criteria, relying instead on a selected subset of all studies available for review on the topic of interest. Not surprisingly, the last category of unscientific reviews is usually written by advocates of a particular program or strategy. In their most extreme form, the authors of the review simply allude to an evidence-based review or to "best practices," with no supporting documentation. Unfortunately, much of what is currently available in the corrections field—both institutional and community corrections—falls into this last category.

Applying the "gold standard" for evidence-based reviews to the "risk assessment" process in community corrections mandates that at least two randomized field experiments must have been conducted in this area (i.e., the link between classification level, community corrections intervention, and risk reduction) before we can offer an assessment of "what works" (see, e.g., the reviews conducted for the Campbell/Cochrane collaboration at www.campbellcollaboration.org). Unfortunately, no experimental research has been conducted on this specific topic in community corrections, leading us to conclude that we "don't know" whether there is a link between risk *assessment* (i.e., classification of an offender into high-risk, medium-risk and low-risk classification categories) and risk *reduction* (i.e., a lower rate of recidivism for offenders than anticipated, given their risk level) due to the types of supervision and services we make available to offenders at each level of risk. Given the ongoing debate between advocates of a control-oriented community corrections system (e.g., Farabee, 2005) and advocates of a treatment-oriented community corrections system (e.g., Latessa, 2004), the completion of experimental research testing both models would certainly answer an important question about whether what probation and parole officers do—in the areas of surveillance and/or treatment services—matters in terms of risk reduction.

Much of what we currently do in community corrections is based on assumptions about the risk-reduction effects of placing offenders into different supervision levels that have not been tested empirically, using randomized field experiments. What would happen, for example, if we placed high-risk offenders under "medium" or "low" supervision? Alternatively, what impact would placing a low- or medium-risk offender under "maximum" supervision have on these offenders? Until we have the results of quality, experimental research to review, we will continue to make assumptions about "what works" and "best practices" in terms of both risk assessment and risk reduction that are simply not supported by a careful, "gold-standard" evidence-based review.

ISSUE 2: THE IMPLICATIONS OF ACTUARIAL AND CLINICAL ASSESSMENT FOR LINE STAFF AND MANAGEMENT

One argument that can be made concerning the use of clinical versus actuarial risk assessment is that the line staff currently hired in community corrections do not have the background and qualifications necessary to conduct "clinical" assessments of offender risk, particularly for special category (e.g., mental health, substance abuse, sex offender) and multiple problem offenders. Assuming for the sake of argument that you want to introduce clinical assessments in your federal, state, and local community corrections agency, you have two choices: (1) recruit/hire line staff with the necessary qualifications to conduct clinical risk assessments (perhaps with minimal additional training); or (2) privatize the assessment process, using the network of current mental health treatment providers as your "target" potential provider. Indeed, it could be argued that by moving away from clinical and toward actuarially based risk assessments, we are attempting to simplify classification/decision making in an effort to reduce the need for higher-skilled line staff (i.e., the "dummying down" of community corrections). In this scenario, it is possible to envision a probation or parole agency where line staff are responsible for case planning and supervision, but other functions (assessments, treatment, and services) are subcontracted to agencies in the private sector.

While improving staff quality and/or privatization are options to consider *even if* you are not using clinical assessments, the evidence available from major reviews of the available research certainly suggest that you will not *improve* the risk assessment system using clinical assessments, because actuarial risk assessments consistently "outperform" clinical risk assessment procedures (see Harris 2006; and Gottfredson and Moriarty 2006). However, we should point out that the new generation of "actuarial" risk assessment instruments currently being used in community corrections agencies—including the popular LSI-R instrument . . . actually requires both objective and subjective (or clinical) assessments by line staff. In fact, the distinction between actuarial and clinical assessment is becoming blurred, with consequences for line community corrections personnel (and management) that are important to consider. It is our contention that if we continue further in this direction, then changes in either staff quality or the privatization of the assessment function may be needed.

According to a recent review by Brumbaugh and Steffey (2005), three of every four probation and parole agencies in this country employ "objective" risk/needs instruments to classify offenders, using either the shorter Wisconsin risk/needs assessment instrument or the longer, 54-item LSI-R mentioned earlier. Both instruments require line staff to make both *objective* assessments (e.g., prior convictions, current employment) and *subjective* assessments (e.g., extent of drug problems, attitude, mental health). Not surprisingly, the results of a number of inter-rater reliability studies reveal that line community corrections staff are much more consistent in their scoring of objective than subjective items (see, e.g., Austin, 2006; Byrne and Robinson, 1991; and Harris, 2006).

The use of a large number of items in a risk instrument is likely to exacerbate the inter-rater reliability problem. Austin (2006) for example, pointed out that (in an inter-rater reliability study he conducted) of the 54 items included in the LSI-R (37 yes/no items and 17 Likert scale items), only 16 items had an agreement rate of 80 percent or higher, with 38 other items scoring in the 60–70 percent range. Overall, Austin found that these scoring differences on individual risk items resulted in disagreement on the scoring of the offender's risk level in 29 percent of the 120 cases reviewed by the two staff members included in the inter-rater reliability test.

We can only speculate about how such differences in the scoring of individual risk items would affect risk assessment (and the classification of offenders into high-, medium-, and low-risk categories) across an entire department. However, Austin's research certainly suggests that new strategies need to be developed to improve the level of inter-rater reliability *before* the agency embarks on the time-consuming risk assessment construction/validation process. Our recommendation is to collect data on fewer items, focusing primarily on objective items that are relatively easy to code. Austin (2006) found that he could improve both the reliability and validity of the LSI-R by focusing on a subset of only eight of the 54 original LSI-R items. According to Austin, "not only do these items have better predictive ability, but also they reduce the 'high risk' category" (2006). Since most observers (see, e.g., Lowencamp and Latessa, 2005) recommend providing the highest level of supervision and services to high-risk offenders, the cost-effectiveness of a more precisely defined—and smaller—high-risk classification category should be obvious.

In addition to Austin's research, the findings from other inter-rater reliability studies indicate that line staff characteristics (e.g., age, gender, race, location, experience) will likely affect the scoring of risk assessment instrument items in ways that are important to consider. For example, Byrne and Robinson (1990) identified gender bias as a potential problem affecting inter-rater reliability. In their study of inter-rater reliability among 130 probation officers, they distributed two different versions of a "case study": in version A, the juvenile (Sandy) was described as female; in version B, the juvenile was described as male. There were no other differences between the two case studies. Significant differences in overall risk scoring were identified, with the female version of the case receiving *higher* scores than the male version of the same case, resulting in a greater proportion of the female cases being classified as high risk (40.4 percent) than their male counterparts (33.1 percent).

We suspect that in addition to variations in scoring and consistency due to *offender* characteristics (such as gender, race, class), there will be variation in scoring and consistency due to the characteristics of the line probation/parole officers completing the assessment (see, e.g., Byrne and Robinson, 1990).The findings from both the Austin study and Byrne and Robinson study underscore the importance of conducting an inter-rater reliability study, not only to support initial risk instrument development but also to examine the very real possibility that bias (related to both the characteristics of offenders and the characteristics of line staff) is having a detrimental effect on the risk assessment process.

One other area where clinical (subjective) judgment enters into the classification process is in the agency's risk scoring "override" policy. While there will undoubtedly be circumstances where an offender will be either overclassified or underclassified by line staff members, and/or by management decisions to ignore risk altogether (e.g., offense exclusions for sex offenders), it is critical that the level, type, and circumstances of override usage be monitored on an ongoing basis. A simple rule of thumb for this type of review is to apply a 10 percent rule: if more than 10 percent of the agency's risk scoring decisions are being changed, then the agency has a problem in this area that needs to be resolved.

Finally, our discussion of the utilization of clinical and actuarial risk instruments in community corrections would be incomplete without mention of the "validation" problem. According to a recent study by Hubbard, Travis, and Latessa (2001), "only 30% of the agencies that use an assessment instrument reported that the instrument was validated for their local population" (as summarized by Brumbaugh and Steffey, 2005:59). Without the completion of the necessary validation research, there is no way of knowing whether the risk instrument being used by a particular agency results in an accurate classification of offenders into the low-, medium-, and high-risk categories used to allocate scarce probation and parole resources, both in terms of supervision and in terms of services.

While there certainly has been much discussion of the need to apply the "risk principle" (risk, needs, responsivity) to offenders supervised in the community corrections system (see, e.g., Andrews, et.al., 1990, Lowencamp and Latessa, 2005), it appears that the determination of "risk level" may be inaccurate for a significant number of these offenders. Recent attempts to *improve* the risk assessment process using actuarial instruments may have made matters worse, because of the inter-rater reliability problems associated with the more complex risk assessment instruments currently being used, such as the 54-item LSI-R. The implications of our brief review of the use of actuarial versus clinical assessment are straightforward: in order to improve both reliability and validity, risk assessment instruments need to be designed using a small number of objective risk items and tested (for reliability and validity) on an ongoing basis.

We anticipate that the continued development of LSI-R type assessment instruments, along with the use of offender-specific assessment devices (e.g., sex offender, mentally ill offender, substance abusing offender, multiple-problem offender) will require more qualified line staff and/or the use of private sector assessment centers. However, current line staffs in community corrections agencies are certainly qualified to classify the risk level of offenders using the simplified versions of the actuarial risk instruments advocated by Austin (2006). The challenge for community corrections is to allocate resources to offenders placed in various risk classification levels in a manner that maximizes the system's overall effectiveness. Getting the assessment "right" is the critical initial step, but it must be followed by improvements in treatment classification, and subsequent case planning strategies (see, e.g., Taxman, 2006).

ISSUE 3: THE NEED TO COMBINE INDIVIDUAL AND COMMUNITY RISK ASSESSMENT

A number of recent evidence-based reviews of the research in community corrections have identified statistically significant, but modest (10 percent) recidivism reduction effects associated with a variety of community treatment strategies (see Welsh and Farrington, 2006). We suspect that the recidivism reduction effects identified in these studies would be even more pronounced if *individual*-level assessments of risk were combined with *community*-level risk assessments (Byrne, 2006; Pattavina, Byrne, and Garcia, 2006), based on the premise that community-level risk assessment is a necessary "second step" in the offender assessment process.

We offer this assessment based on two related factors: first, there is a large body of research supporting the notion that an individual's risk of re-offending is affected—both positively and negatively—by the community in which he/she resides while under community supervision (Sampson and Bean, 2006; Kubrin and Stewart, 2006; Sampson and Raudenbush, 2004; Pattavina, Byrne and Garcia, 2006). As Gottfredson and Taylor concluded twenty years ago: "Bad risk offenders fail more seriously when released to bad environments and do better if released to good environments" (1986:148). The explanation for this person-environment interaction, according to a recent study by Pattavina, Byrne, and Garcia (2006) is that there is a differential surveillance and control model operating at the neighborhood level: "It does appear that both residents (via informal surveillance/control activities) and the police (via formal surveillance/control activities) respond differently to (high vs. low risk) offenders in different (high vs. low risk) neighborhoods."

A second factor related to the need for assessing the risk level of a particular neighborhood is that the treatment resources available to offenders (and community residents attitudes toward treatment) will also likely vary by the "risk level" of the neighborhood, with higher-risk neighborhoods offering fewer (and lower-quality) treatment options to offenders living in these areas, while also affording offenders more opportunities for relapse. According to a recent study by Jacobson (2006:1) focusing on drug treatment service location in high-risk neighborhoods, ". . . conditions around the treatment site may also influence treatment outcomes, particularly social and economic stressors such as disadvantage and violence, visible drug activity, and drug availability." The challenge for community corrections will be to develop strategies that move beyond the simple admonition that an offender "move out" of these high-risk neighborhoods. Unfortunately, individual offender relocation strategies have not worked particularly well because, inevitably, offenders—when they do move—move from one socially and economically disadvantaged "poverty pocket" area to another (Pattavina, Byrne, and Garcia, 2006; Kling, Ludwig, and Katz, 2004).

Accuracy of the individually based *risk* classification system will likely improve with the inclusion of overall community risk level (high vs. low/medium risk, for example, based on offender density and/or the area's crime rate), along with selected community "risk" characteristics (e.g., unemployment rate, proportion residents living in poverty, size/characteristics of first generation immigrant population). Similarly, the accuracy of the individually based *treatment* classification system (linking offenders at different risk levels to appropriate treatment) would also be improved by an assessment of community risk level, because this classification decision could be based on an assessment of the likely impact of community culture (e.g., attitudes toward substance use, criminal thinking, etc.) on the attitudes and behavior of offenders residing in "high-risk" and low/medium-risk neighborhoods (Sampson and Bean, 2005).

Our current system of federal, state, and local community corrections agencies essentially relies on about 100,000 probation and parole officers to manage—or control—the behavior of almost 5 million offenders. Until recently, inadequate attention has been given to the fact that the majority of these offenders reside in a relatively small number of structurally disadvantaged neighborhoods; and in these neighborhoods, a unique combination of formal and informal social control mechanisms affect offender behavior (Gottfredson and Taylor,1986; Pattavina, Byrne, and Garcia, 2006; Byrne and Taxman, 2006). When viewed in this context, it is apparent that we cannot reasonably expect probation and parole officers to "change" offenders until we change the communities in which they reside.

For many readers, this assessment will be problematic, because they do not view community change as the "job" of community corrections. However, it is our contention that a better understanding of community context will improve not only the *accuracy* of individual offender risk assessment but also the *content* and *quality* of the subsequent community supervision/service plans. As a result, at least some improvement in the overall risk reduction effects of community corrections is likely, even without major changes in the two factors most often cited as explanations for the relationship between concentrated disadvantage and crime: (1) structural social disadvantage and (2) cultural social isolation. As Sampson and Bean (2005:16) recently concluded: ". . . in structurally disorganized slum communities a system of values emerges in which crime, disorder, and drug use is less than fervently condemned and hence expected as part of everyday life. These ecologically structured tolerances in turn appear to influence the probability of criminal outcomes. . . . The social isolation fostered by the ecological concentration of urban poverty deprives residents not only of resources and conventional role models but also of cultural learning from mainstream social networks that facilitate social and economic advancement in modern industrial society." In the next generation of risk assessment, such person-environment interactions must be assessed and integrated into existing offender-based classification schemes; and new intervention strategies need to be developed based on the results of the assessment of both offender and community risk level.

CONCLUSION

While there have been significant improvements in the individual offender assessment procedures used by community corrections agencies over the past two decades, our brief review suggests the following: (1) we need to conduct high-quality experimental research on the effectiveness of both risk and treatment classification systems, using *risk reduction* as our primary outcome measure; (2) we need to consider simpler alternatives to both the general (e.g., LSI-R) and offender-specific (e.g., mentally ill, substance abuser, sex offender) risk assessment devices; and (3) we need to incorporate community-level risk factors into our current assessment system. In the next generation of risk assessment instruments, the links between individual and community risk level and individual/community risk reduction strategies will be much more clearly defined, in large part as a result of a new emphasis on evidence-based community correction strategies.

REFERENCES

Andrews, Don, James Bonita and Robert Hoge. (1990). "Classification for Effective Rehabilitation: Rediscovering Psychology." *Criminal Justice and Behavior* 17:19–52.

Austin, James. (2006). "How Much Risk Can We Take? The Misuse of Risk Assessment in Corrections." *Federal Probation* 70(2):58–63.

Brumbaugh, Susan and Danielle Steffey. (2005). "The Importance of Constructing and Validating Risk Assessment Instruments in Community Corrections Settings," *Justice Research and Policy* 7(2):57–86.

Byrne, James M. (2006) "Introduction: Why Assessment 'Matters' in an Evidence-Based Community Corrections System." *Federal Probation* 70(2):i–ii.

Byrne, James and Faye Taxman. (2005). "Crime (Control) Is a Choice: Divergent Perspectives on the Role of Treatment in the Adult Corrections System," *Criminology and Public Policy* 4(2):291–310.

Byrne, James and Robin Robinson. (1990). *Juvenile Risk Classification in Illinois: An Examination of Inter-Rater Reliability* (Springfield, Illinois: Administrative Office of the Illinois Courts).

Byrne, James, Robin Robinson and Anthony Braga. (1992). "An Examination of Gender Bias in the Classification and Treatment of Juvenile Offenders," unpublished manuscript.

Farabee, David. (2005). *Rethinking Rehabilitation: Why Can't We Reform Our Criminals?* (Washington, DC:AEI Press, American Enterprise Institute).

Gottfredson, Don and Michael Tonry. (1987). *Prediction and Classification: Criminal Justice Decision-Making* (Chicago, University of Chicago Press).

Gottfredson, Stephen and Moriarty, Laura. (2006). "Clinical versus Actuarial Judgements in Criminal Justice Decisions: Should One Replace the Other?" *Federal Probation* 70(2):15–18.

Gottfredson, Steven and Robert Taylor. (1986). "Person-Environment Interactions in the Prediction of Recidivism," pp. 133–155 in James Byrne and Robert Sampson, editors, *The Social Ecology of Crime* (New York: Springer-Verlag).

Harris, Patricia. (2006). "What Community Supervision Officers Need to Know about Actuarial Risk Assessment and Clinical Judgement." *Federal Probation* 70(2):8–14.

Kling, Jeffrey, Ludwig, Jens, Katz and Lawrence. (2004). Youth Criminal Behavior in the Moving to Opportunity Experiment. Working Paper 482. Industrial Relations Section. Princeton University, available at http://www.irs.princeton.edu/pubs/workingpapers.html.

Kubrin, Charis E. and Eric A. Stewart. (2006) "Predicting Who Reoffends: The Neglected Role of Neighborhood Context in Recidivism Studies." *Criminology* 44(1):165–197.

Latessa, Edward J. (2004). "The Challenge of Change: Correctional Programs and Evidence-based Practices." *Criminology and Public Policy* (4):547–560.

Lowencamp, Christopher T. and Latessa, Edward. (2003). *Does Correctional Program Quality Really Matter? The Impact of Adhereing to the Principles of Effective Interventions.* Unpublished manuscript available from Edward.latessa@uc.edu.

Pattavina, April and Faye Taxman. (2007). "Community Corrections and Soft Technology" pp. 327–344 in James Byrne and Don Rebovich, editors, *The New Technology of Crime, Law, and Social Control* (New York: Criminal Justice Press).

Pattavina, April, James Byrne and Luis Garcia. (2006). "An Examination of Citizen Involvement in Crime Prevention in High Risk Versus Low to Moderate Risk Neighborhoods." *Crime and Delinquency* 52(2):203–231.

Sampson, Robert and Lydia Bean. (2005). "Cultural Mechanisms and Killing Fields: A Revised Theory of Community-Level Racial Inequality" in Peterson, Krivo, and Hagan, editors, The Many Colors of Crime: *Inequalities of Race, Ethnicity and Crime in America* (New York: New York University Press). Retrieved from Robert Sampson's webpage.

Sampson, Robert J. and Stephen W. Raudenbush. (2004). "Seeing Disorder: Neighborhood Stigma and the Social Construction of 'Broken Windows.'" *Social Psychology Quarterly* 67(4):319–342.

Sampson, Robert J., Jeffrey Morenoff and Stephen Raudenbush. (2005) "Social Anatomy of Racial and Ethnic Disparities in Violence." *American Journal of Public Health* 95(2):224–232.

Sampson, Robert J. and Stephen W. Raudenbush. (2001). "Disorder in Urban Neighborhoods—Does It Lead to Crime?" *Research in Brief* (February):1–5.

Taxman, Faye. (2006). "Assessment With a Flair: Offender Accountability in Supervision Plans." *Federal Probation* 70(2):2–7.

Welsh, Brandon and David Farrington. (2006). "Evidence-Based Crime Prevention," pp. 1–20 in Welsh and Farrington, editors, *Preventing Crime: What Works for Offenders, Victims, and Places* (New York: Springer).

P A R T I I

Assessment and Treatment of Juvenile Offenders

❖

3

Assessment, Classification, and Treatment with Juvenile Delinquents

Jemel P. Aguilar and David W. Springer

Between 1991 and 2003, the number of juveniles in residential corrections programs increased by 27 percent. In practical terms this means that over 96,000 juveniles are in residential correctional programs (Snyder & Sickmund, 2006). In addition to the large number of juveniles in residential programming, a recent research study (Teplin et al., 2002) showed that over 60 percent of young male offenders and 73 percent of young female offenders had a mental health diagnosis, such as major depression, generalized anxiety disorder, attention-deficit/hyperactivity disorder, conduct disorder, or obsessive-compulsive disorder. Hence, the juvenile justice system faces the task of serving a number of youth who have committed delinquent offenses and possibly contending with one or more mental health disorders.

Following a number of critical reviews of evaluations, in particular Lipton, Martinson, and Wilks (1975), the accepted wisdom in the field related to juveniles became one of "nothing works." Today, researchers are conducting complex statistical tests of the effectiveness of interventions with juvenile offenders. Lipsey and Wilson (1998), for example, conducted a meta-analysis of experimental or quasi-experimental studies of interventions with serious and violent juvenile delinquents. They reviewed 200 programs, 83 of which involved institutionalized juveniles and 117 involved noninstitutionalized juveniles. McBride et al. (1999, p. 58) summarize the findings of Lipsey and Wilson's meta-analysis. Now researchers are confident that some interventions are effective in stemming juvenile delinquency (cf. Lipsey, Wilson, & Cothern, 2000).

Among the programs in *noninstitutional* settings, those that demonstrate good evidence of effectiveness include behavioral therapies (family and contingency contracting), intensive case management (including system collaboration and continuing care), multisystemic therapy (MST), restitution programs (parole- and probation-based), and skills training. Program options that require more research to document their effectiveness include 12-step programs (AA, NA), adult mentoring (with behaviorally contingent reinforcement), after-school recreation programs, conflict resolution/violence prevention, intensive probation services (IPS), juvenile versions of Treatment Accountability for Safer Communities (TASC), peer mediation, and traditional inpatient/outpatient programs. Program options that do not show evidence of effectiveness include deterrence programs, vocational training or career counseling, and wilderness challenge programs.

In *institutional* settings, evidence of effectiveness has been demonstrated for behavioral programs (cognitive mediation and stress inoculation training), longer-term community residential programs (therapeutic communities that employ cognitive-behavioral approaches), multiple services within residential communities (case management approach), and skills training (aggression replacement training and cognitive restructuring). More research is needed to determine the effectiveness of day treatment centers, as there were too few studies to review. Those programs that have been shown ineffective are juvenile boot camps, short-term residential facilities, and state training schools.

MacKenzie, Gover, Armstrong, and Mitchell's (2001) national evaluation of boot camps, for example, demonstrated that boot camps do not include the therapeutic elements that are effective in producing long-term behavioral changes in offending youth. MacKenzie, Gover, Armstrong and Mitchell (2001) compared 27 boot camp programs to 22 traditional corrections facilities to evaluate the impact of particular institutional environments on the outcomes of these facilities. They found that youth and staff reported many positive aspects of boot camps, such as providing a safe and structured environment, maintaining a high level of activity, and helping youth to be more prepared for their release back into the community. MacKenzie et al.'s research documents that many positive aspects of boot camps are apparent to both juvenile offenders and staff members. However, compared to traditional facilities, boot camp programs are not effective in reducing recidivism. Thus, practitioners unaware of boot camps' ineffectiveness may recommend this type of intervention, assuming that it will result in long-term changes, when in fact boot camps will not.

Accurate assessment and classification is a significant aspect of effective treatment of juvenile offenders (Shepard, Green, & Omobien, 2005). Thus, we argue that practitioners must accurately assess juvenile offenders' biopsychosocial development, classify offenders according to their level of risk for future acts of delinquency, and employ empirically-based and effective intervention methods that target the multisystemic influences on juvenile offenders' behavior.

Practitioners new to the juvenile justice field and those already familiar with it need guidance regarding the best tools to assess, classify, and treat juvenile offenders. In this chapter we aim to (1) provide new and experienced practitioners with an overview of the biopsychosocial model of assessment; (2) discuss two classification tools—the Youth Level of Service Inventory and the Child and Adolescent Functional Assessment Scale—frequently used with juvenile offenders; and (3) discuss evidence-based treatment models that focus on youth, family, and/or the social environment.

Beginning with a biopsychosocial model of assessment, we then discuss the two classification tools and how these provide a standardized categorization of the offender based on an understanding of his or her strengths and weaknesses. We also review several treatment options that have considerable empirical support. In all, we offer this chapter as a systematic guide for practitioners working with juvenile offenders and a means to update one's knowledge of the leading practices within the field of juvenile justice.

ASSESSMENT

The biopsychosocial model of assessment examines the biological, psychological, and social processes that influence development and behavior. In this model, practitioners conduct systematic observations of a young offender's medical history, personality, cognitive abilities, emotional development, family environment, and neighborhood (Austrian, 2002; Jordan & Franklin, 2003; Springer, 2002). The strength of a multisystemic assessment is that delinquency research and theories of human development agree that behavior is the result of complex interactional processes across intrapsychic, family, and community interactions (Aguilar, 2006). For example, youth offenders referred to treatment for delinquent behaviors are more apt to present as "involuntary clients" considering they are attending to fulfill a programmatic or court-related requirement (Rooney, 1992, 2002). Practitioners who engage with these youth may attribute difficult or resistant behaviors to the youth's developmental stage or temperament, thus ignoring the involuntary nature of the practitioner-client relationship. However, we assert that addressing the involuntary nature of the relationship during the assessment phase can assist the practitioner in differentiating the behavior as developing from temperament or the context of the relationship (Corcoran & Springer, 2005; Rooney, 1992, 2002).

Several sources of information can further assist the practitioner in constructing a comprehensive analysis of the youth's circumstances and development over time. These are extensive interviews with a client and his or her family, interpretation of standardized instruments, reviews of documents related to juvenile justice or mental health system involvement, and knowledge of human behavior in the social environment (Jordan & Franklin, 2003). Most programs conduct an intake, which is an initial interview of the youth to determine the reasons for referral, psychosocial and family history, current medications, legal status, and areas of strength and vulnerability. Including measures of experiences or situations that place youth at risk for further delinquency can assist in defining problems and identifying areas of intervention. These measures can also aid in determining which factors are more amenable to change, compared to those more stable and longer-lasting factors (Bloom, Fisher, & Orme, 2006; Jordan & Franklin, 2003). For example, malleable risk factors include the number of delinquent peers, limited free-time activities, or the absence of pro-social mentors.

In the classification section, we describe two standardized instruments used to measure a juvenile offender's level of functioning and/or risk factors for future delinquency. Using these instruments along with the other assessment data, practitioners can also construct baseline measures of the multiple influences on a juvenile's behavior. Bloom, Fischer, and Orme (2006) assert that establishing baselines prior to intervention is crucial to understanding the frequency, stability, and intensity of the presenting problems, as well as for practice evaluation. Jordan and Franklin (2003) also write that in an assessment process practitioners should construct a baseline understanding of the presenting problem to facilitate evaluation.

Many scholars argue that practice evaluation is a significant underpinning of effective and ethical social work practice (Bloom, Fisher, & Orme, 2006; Jordan & Franklin, 2003). Evaluation is the process of determining the effectiveness of a given intervention by establishing a baseline, implementing an intervention, and then measuring changes in relevant variables or constructs (Barker, 1999; Bloom, Fischer, & Orme, 2006). In addition to determining the effectiveness of a given intervention, evaluation is a part of ethical and responsible practice (Bloom, Fisher, & Orme, 2006; Jordan & Franklin, 1995).

CLASSIFICATION

Using the findings or results of an assessment can inform classification of a juvenile offender. Classification, defined by Austin, Johnson, and Weitzer (2005), is "the process of determining at what level of custody an offender should be assigned" (p. 5). Other definitions of classification include references to diagnosis or the process by which a practitioner categorizes a person as exhibiting traits associated with a group (Bisman, 1999). To aid in the process of classification, researchers suggest the use of standardized instruments (Austin et al., 2005; Jordan & Franklin, 2003; Springer, 2002). We will discuss two such instruments, the Youth Level of Service Inventory and the Child and Adolescent Functional Assessment Scale.

Youth Level of Service Inventory

Hoge and Andrews (1994) developed the Youth Level of Service Inventory (YLSI) to assist professionals in the process of determining a young offender's area of risk and needs. For this instrument, risks are defined as those situations or experiences that increase the likelihood of a negative outcome, such as delinquency or violence. Risks offer the practitioner insight into possible areas of intervention and services that the practitioner can provide to reduce some risks, while acknowledging that other, more stable risks may require long-term programming to facilitate change.

The YLSI is based on a social-psychological approach to criminal behavior and as such suggests that youth identified with higher areas of risk and needs require more supervision and services than youth identified with lesser risks and needs (Hoge & Andrews, 1994). The YLSI measures eight areas of risk: prior and current offenses or dispositions, family circumstances and parenting, education and employment, peer relations, substance abuse, leisure and recreation, personality and behavior, and attitudes and orientation. Areas of strength are also recorded, however, strengths are not considered when calculating the level of risk. A total scale score of 8 indicates a low level of risk for recidivism, while 9–22 is medium risk, 23–34 is high, and 35–42 is very high (Hoge & Andrews, 1994). According to the developers (1994), juveniles with higher levels of risk are in need of more intensive supervision and services compared with those youth whose scores show lower levels of risk. The eight risk area scores and the total level of risk score can then guide practitioners in the formulation of measurable treatment objectives and goals.

Child and Adolescent Functional Assessment Scale

The Child and Adolescent Functional Assessment Scale (CAFAS; Hodges, 2000) is a standardized multidimensional assessment tool that is used to measure the extent to which the mental health/substance use disorders impair functioning of youths ages 7 to 17. It is completed by the clinician, and requires specialized training. A major benefit of the CAFAS in helping practitioners determine a youth's overall level of functioning is that it covers eight areas: school/work, home, community, behavior toward others, moods/emotions, self-harmful behavior, substance use, and thinking. The adolescent's level of functioning in each of these eight domains is scored as severe (score of 30), moderate (20), mild (10), or minimal (0). Additionally, an overall score can be computed. These scores can be graphically depicted on a one-page scoring sheet that provides a profile of the youth's functioning. An appealing feature of recent versions is that the CAFAS now includes strength-based items. While these items are not used in the scoring, they are useful in treatment planning (Springer, McNeece, & Arnold, 2003). The psychometric properties of the CAFAS have been demonstrated in numerous studies (cf. Hodges & Cheong-Seok, 2000; Hodges & Wong, 1996). One study on the predictive validity of the CAFAS supported the notion that this scale is able to predict recidivism in juvenile delinquents (Hodges & Cheong-Seok, 2000). Higher scores on the CAFAS have been found to associate with previous psychiatric hospitalizations, serious psychiatric diagnoses, restrictive living arrangements, below-average school performance and attendance, and contact with law enforcement (Hodges, Doucette-Gates, & Oinghong, 1999).

CASE #1: JUAN

Patricia is a social worker for a metropolitan child guidance clinic. Patricia's position requires her to conduct a biopsychosocial assessment on youth brought to the agency, to identify treatment goals, and to make recommendations to the treatment team regarding the services that should be provided. Patricia met with Juan, a 16-year-old Latino male who was brought to a child guidance clinic because he is chronically truant from school and is charged with violating the citywide curfew. Since moving to this new community, Juan has frequently been truant and/or skipped individual classes. Juan's parents report that they suspect that he is getting involved with the "wrong crowd" and they are very concerned because they found marijuana in his room. Juan lives with his mother, father, two siblings, and maternal grandmother. Juan's aunt, uncle, and cousins live in the house next door and they are frequently involved in supervising Juan when his parents are at work.

All of Juan's family members describe him as a "good kid," quiet, who keeps to himself most of the time. Juan's parents have noticed lately that Juan seems angry most of the time and, because of his temper, he has gotten into what his father describes as "minor scrapes" with neighborhood boys. Juan's dad says that Juan is just getting used to living in this new neighborhood and is probably having trouble making friends but says, "Juan will grow out of it." Juan's grandmother says she is worried because they moved to this house a year ago and he is still having trouble. Upon interviewing Juan, Patricia discovers that he has very few friends in the neighborhood and in school. Patricia notices that Juan does not make overtures that indicate that things will change for him in the near future. Also during the interview Patricia finds that Juan has trouble sleeping at night and so he skips school because he is so tired in the mornings. Juan also admits his friends "hooked him up with some weed" and that smoking weed makes him feel relaxed. Juan says that he is thinking about dropping out of school because he thinks he "isn't smart enough anyway," but has not said anything to his parents because they would be disappointed.

Initial Assessment

Patricia's initial impression of Juan is that he is a "good kid" but he is struggling with changes that occurred in his life. Patricia's initial interview with Juan indicates that he is attempting to develop his own identity outside his home environment, understand the implications and value of his Mexican American identity, and acclimate to his new neighborhood and school. Patricia also notes some symptoms of a depressive disorder, but these symptoms may be indicative of Juan's coping with his current situation. Juan's family is very supportive of him and provides extensive supervision. Patricia is somewhat concerned that his family may not understand the extent of the problems that Juan is facing. Alternatively, Patricia recognizes that Juan's family may not feel comfortable with providing their insights to a stranger whom they are *required* to meet with for a number of sessions. Juan scored in the low-risk range on the Youth Level of Service Inventory and the subscales did not strongly indicate particular risks that needed individual attention. Patricia enters the following diagnosis on the intake assessment:

Axis I: 309.0 Adjustment disorder with depressed mood, chronic; 300.4 Dysthymic Disorder, early onset (Provisional)

Axis II: v71.09 No diagnosis

Axis III: None

Axis IV: Fighting with peers, school truancy, marijuana use.

Axis V: GAF = 60

Several recent meta-analyses suggest that the most effective approaches for treating juvenile offenders, such as Juan, are those with a cognitive-behavioral component combined with close supervision and advocacy. There is also evidence that more positive treatment effects are realized in community settings than in institutional settings (Deschenes & Greenwood, 1994). We now turn our attention to such treatment approaches.

TREATMENT

Juveniles in the corrections system can undergo a variety of treatment programs that differ in how they go about bringing long-term changes in the youthful offender's behavior. Practitioners, such as Patricia, can become overwhelmed by the array of options available to treat youth offenders, but research can guide her decision-making process by outlining models that garnered favorable empirical support. In this section, we identify those empirically supported interventions used in juvenile corrections. To that end, we first describe the intervention, its goals, the populations the interventions are tested with, and its strengths and weaknesses.

Multisystemic Therapy

Multisystemic therapy (MST; Henggeler & Borduin, 1990; Henggeler, Schoenwald, Borduin, Rowland, & Cunningham, 1998) is a family- and community-based treatment approach that is theoretically grounded in a social-ecological framework (Bronfenbrenner, 1979) and family systems (Haley, 1976; Minuchin, 1974), and as such, is a form of treatment that addresses the multiple influences for youth's problematic behavior (Borduin et al., 1995; Henggeler et al., 1986). Essentially, MST intervenes in the "transactions" between adolescents and their "pertinent systems" such as family, school, or peer groups to alter how these interactions bring about antisocial or negative behaviors (Henggeler et al., 1986). Intervention modalities must address the various ways intrapsychic, family, and community systems operate on the developing youth because, as the developers of this treatment strategy assert, these interactions can produce delinquent and antisocial behaviors in a young person (Borduin et al., 1995). Individual factors such as a child's cognitive strengths and weaknesses, physical appearance, coordination, attitudes, beliefs, and presence of disabilities should be considered in interventions; as well as presence of delinquent peers, family interaction patterns, sibling interactions, quality and resources of the youth's neighborhood, and parental involvement in educational systems.

MST can accommodate multiple theories of behavior change and/or intervention because it does not subscribe to any specific theoretical framework. Thus, MST clinicians can include cognitive skills, behavioral modification techniques, or psychoeducational treatment into an MST program. What is more, other professionals and teachers can reinforce treatment plans in their context by working with practitioners on learning to reinforce the skills and methods included in the intervention plan. MST, however, requires that practitioners have a reduced caseload and be available to clients 24 hours per day. This, along with the extensive training required to effectively implement this model, may be a barrier to successful implementation.

Extensive evaluations of MST reveal that this intervention model produces significant changes in youths' intrapsychic functioning, their interactions with parents, and educational outcomes (Henggeler et al., 1986). In one such evaluation, Henggeler et al. (1986) found that as parents increasingly became involved in their son's or daughter's education, the youth would perform better in school and demonstrate increased motivation for academic achievement. In that same study, the behavior problems decreased and overall interactions between the youth and his or her family improved. The authors remarked that youth were included in family decisions, intraparental communication improved, and parents reported that the child demonstrated fewer behavior and emotional problems (Henggeler et al., 1986). Based on the extensive research supporting MST as an intervention for juvenile offenders, the study authors argue that MST is a promising and effective treatment for juvenile offenders, benefiting the juvenile and also family interactions (Borduin et al., 1995; Henggeler et al., 1986).

Through the Campbell and Cochrane Collaborations, Dr. Julia Littell, a social work professor at Bryn Mawr College in Pennsylvania, has conducted her own systematic review on the effectiveness of MST (Littell, 2005; Littell, Popa, & Forsythe, 2005). In her review, Dr. Littell includes both published and unpublished studies, as is standard practice for reviews conducted through the Campbell and Cochrane Collaborations. In total, Dr. Littell and her colleagues identified 35 unique studies and included 8 in their review. For example, Dr. Littell discovered an unpublished study that had been led by Dr. Alan Leschied, who conducted a trial of MST with 409 youth in Canada. Dr. Littell presented her findings at a recent meeting of the Campbell and Cochrane Collaborations, suggesting that MST may not be as effective as has been previously thought. The most recent development in this line of inquiry has appeared in the form of letters to the editor of *Children and Youth Social*

Services, both from Dr. Scott Henggeler, the developer of MST, and his colleagues (Henggeler, Schoenwald, Borduin, & Swenson, 2006), and from Dr. Littell (2006).

Cognitive-Behavioral Therapies

The broad category of cognitive behavior therapies includes those therapeutic interventions designed to alter both a youth's cognitions and behaviors related to their poor conduct or offending. Cognitive behavioral therapy is an umbrella category for contingency management, cognitive behavioral treatment, guided-group interaction/positive peer culture, and milieu therapy (Pearson, Lipton, Cleland, & Yee, 2002); however, two subcategories are evident. First, behavioral modification is the administration of positive reinforcement when an appropriate behavior is exhibited by a person. For example, when a youth offender completes a classroom exercise without engaging in disruptive behaviors, such as talking out of turn, then the instructor will provide the youth with a reward, such as a favored activity. Essentially, reinforcement is meant to draw youths toward appropriate behaviors by rewarding them (Pearson et al., 2002). The second subcategory is cognitive-behavioral treatments. Cognitive-behavior treatments are those interventions that target behavioral processes and lead to changes in one's ways of thinking (Pearson, Lipton, Cleland, & Yee, 2002). Social skills training, problem-solving education, role modeling, cognitive behavior and rational emotive therapies are all forms of cognitive behavioral treatments.

In an evaluation of the effects of cognitive skills programming on recidivism, Pearson and his colleagues (2002) found that social skills development and cognitive skills training can decrease the probability of recidivism. Pearson's et al.'s evaluation confirms Izzo and Ross's (1990) early studies of cognitive-behavioral interventions, thus lending even more support for this line of therapeutic intervention.

Cognitive-behavioral interventions have significant strengths that facilitate applying this type of intervention to juvenile offenders (Pearson et al., 2002). For example, clinicians can encourage family and peer group members, mentors, school personnel, or a client's coworkers to reinforce the youth's behavioral changes. As a youth moves from a supportive treatment environment back into his or her social context, the assistance of community members in reinforcing behavioral changes can increase the likelihood of sustained change over time. Similar to MST, cognitive-behavioral treatments can be coupled with other forms of treatment to enhance the range of interventions offered to juvenile offenders. For example, practitioners can include cognitive-behavioral treatments with family therapies to bring about changes in a youth's and family's functioning or include psychoeducational components to aid the family in better understanding a youth's behavioral problems while the youth undergoes treatment.

Conversely, implementation can be a considerable weakness in creating a cognitive-behavioral program. Practitioners may have different understandings or professional training in cognitive-behavioral treatments. Consequently, when treatment facilities implement a cognitive-behavior treatment focused on building social skills and practitioners unwittingly design more behavior modification interventions in their work with clients, programmatic outcomes will be affected. Hence, staff members' level of training in the methodology, a clear explication of the treatment method and sample exercises, and ongoing supervision of practitioners are all needed to create an effective and cogent cognitive behavioral program.

Victim-Offender Mediation

Victim-offender mediation is an intervention model that brings together victims and their offenders to discuss the impact of a crime, determine appropriate forms of restitution, and allow victims to be advocates in the justice process (Flash, 2003; Umbreit, 1993). Victim-offender mediation, as stated in the definition, includes all relevant parties directly involved in the crime and a trained mediator who facilitates the process.

Victim-offender mediation begins when victims approach a mediator and request to meet with their offender. Offenders are then asked if they are willing to participate and if they agree, then individual sessions are set. These sessions provide the mediator with an opportunity to introduce the process of victim-offender mediation and help both parties reflect on what they would like to discuss in the mediation. After several individual sessions, the mediator establishes a meeting between the two parties and addresses any concerns that either party may have. At the meeting, the mediator restates the ground rules for the mediation and then "sits back" as the two parties have an opportunity to discuss the offense, ask and answer questions, and determine the restitution for the offense. At the end of this session, the mediator writes a contract that outlines the restitution and any stipulations that the parties mutually agree on, and then both parties sign it.

Victim-offender mediation has significant strengths that make it a useful form of intervention with juvenile offenders. First, victims are directly involved in achieving a just outcome to the crime they have experienced (Flash, 2003; Umbreit, 1993). Adjudicatory processes typically involve many players, such as lawyers and judges, who take control of the process, leaving victims feeling revictimized by the justice system (Flash, 2003; Umbreit, 1993). Umbreit (1993) found that directly involving victims and offenders in the process creates a sense of ownership by both parties, focuses the criminal event as affecting human beings, and is empowering to victims and offenders.

Next, victim-offender mediation is a low-cost alternative to adjudication (Flash, 2003). The structure of victim-offender mediation requires direct involvement by victims and offenders, instead of attorneys representing all parties and judges presiding over the judicial process. Mediation uses experienced and well-trained mediators who can be community volunteers or professionals to work with both parties throughout the process. Umbreit suggests that a small paid staff can manage a cadre of well-trained volunteers, thus reducing the need for an extensive staff member base.

This simple process reduces the costs in time for district and defense attorneys, probation offenders, and other personnel typically associated with a juvenile adjudication process. Next, several victim-offender mediation researchers state that the focus is on "humanizing of the justice system." In focusing "on problem-solving rather than vindictiveness, and an offender as seen as being against a person, not against the state, this view allows the victim to play a part in the proceedings, ask questions of the offender, and be empowered, rather than disempowered, by the justice process" (Flash, 2003, p. 512). Mediation practitioners are moving into using this intervention process with more severe and violent offenders with impressive results (Umbreit, Coates, & Vos, 2003). However, practitioners must gain a number of skills to effectively mediate between parties and understand the types of crimes (i.e., domestic violence) for which mediation is inappropriate. Victim-offender mediation is becoming increasingly popular as form of intervention for offenders and crime victims and, as research demonstrates, has a significant effect on both parties, aside from the provision of restitution.

Wraparound Programming

The eco-systemic natural wraparound model is similar to MST in that it focuses on the multiple systems influencing behavior. The wraparound model, however, uses the existing strengths and resources within a youth's environment to bring about positive changes for the youth. The creators of this model comment that unlike other models, youth and their families are not required to change their beliefs or values to participate in wraparound programming. Instead, practitioners encourage families to maintain their beliefs and gather together many community supports that interact with the youth to determine the best ways to support a youth to adopt pro-social behaviors (Flash, 2003; Northey, Primer, & Christensen, 1997). Hence, families are thought to already have the resources they need to facilitate change in their social environment and value system (Flash, 2003; Northey et al., 1997).

The theoretical foundation of this intervention model rests on systems theory and constructivism (Northey et al., 1997), sometimes referred to by proponents of this approach as a systems-of-care perspective. Systems theory is explained in the section on assessment, therefore we will not repeat those points in this section. Scholars of constructivism assert that the appearance of an objective reality is false and instead argue that reality is actually "constructed by people" (Blumer, 1968; Flash, 2003; Northey et al., 1997). In interactions with others or one's context, people develop an understanding or definition of a situation or object. For example, through interactions with family members a child learns that "daddy is daddy." A child also learns to define these objects through further interactions. Thus, daddy is defined in a way that is specific to the child and his or her family context, such as daddy is the man whom I live with and love (Blumer, 1968; Flash, 2003; Northey et al., 1997).

The authors of this model use systems theory and constructivism to form a basis or premises for wraparound programming. According to the model, (1) youth's behavior is derived from meanings, attachments, and potentialities; (2) successful wraparound programming reduces recidivism; (3) a youth's self-perception or concept is an important element of wrap-around programming in that intrapsychic factors can inhibit wraparound programming; and (4) wrap-around programs must not only consider the interactions within systems but also interactions between different systems (Flash, 2003; Northey et al., 1997). The foundational elements guide the practitioner as he/she reviews assessment and classification reports and/or establishes treatment goals along with the client and his/her family.

Natural eco-systemic wraparound models use social supports already present in a youth's environment to provide a range of services. For example, supportive people and resources may advocate alongside a youth for services, assist family members with home-care difficulties, provide tutoring for a youth with academic difficulties, or be an additional supportive adult in the youth's life. Using such natural resources reinforces the notion that family members can solve their problems using the resources already available to them. Moreover, family members can clearly attribute their successes to their own interventions (Flash, 2003; Northey et al., 1997).

Eco-systemic natural wraparound programming has considerable benefits. First, the model encourages a strength-based perspective for the families of juvenile offenders instead of assuming that a juvenile offends because of inadequate parenting (Northey et al., 1997). Using social supports already present in one's social environment also provides a family with support after the service is discontinued, which can help sustain changes created by the intervention. Moreover, the active involvement of family members in the treatment and evaluation process gives families ownership in their own treatment, while also permitting cultural factors to be included in treatment planning. For example, families are encouraged to develop plans for situations in which the family typically enters "crisis mode." For some families, crises are the means to demonstrate one's resilience or are what bring families closer together. In collaboration with therapists, however, family members plan for crises and work to avoid them in the future.

Finally, eco-systemic natural wraparound models help family members recognize the considerable resources and strengths already that exist in their social environment. This model also respects a family's values and norms while addressing unhelpful or problematic situations that lead to a young person engaging in delinquency.

Multidimensional Treatment Foster Care

Multidimensional treatment foster care (MTFC) is an effective model for treating juvenile offenders (Fisher & Chamberlain, 2000). Fisher and Chamberlain (2000) state, "MTFC capitalizes on more than 40 years of research and treatment activities that have supported the notion that families, and particularly parents who are skilled and supported, can have a powerful socializing role and positive influence on troubled youth" (p. 156). Chamberlain and other researchers argue that MTFC is effective with troubled youth because this model takes initiative in stemming behavior problems before they occur and maintaining a consistent environment that supports lasting changes (Fischer & Chamberlain, 2000). MTFC is based on the philosophy that for many youth who exhibit antisocial behavior, the most effective treatment is likely to take place in a community setting, in a family environment in which systematic control is exercised over the contingencies governing youth's behavior. MTFC parents are the primary treatment agents for program children and adolescents; additionally, youths' own biological/step/adoptive/relative families help shape their youngsters' treatment plan and participate in family therapy and home visits throughout placement to prepare for reunification with their children/adolescents at the program's end. To provide youth who have serious and chronic problems with delinquency with close supervision, fair and consistent limits, predictable consequences for rule breaking, a supportive relationship with at least one mentoring adult, and limited exposure and access to delinquent peers.

Program staff members pay close attention to the individual youth's progress/problems in the foster home and at school. Case managers typically carry a smaller caseload, MTFC parents are carefully recruited and a high level of preservice training as well as ongoing support and supervision are provided to them. MTFC parents are the eyes and ears of the program, maintain close communication with the case manager, and help identify target behaviors and formulate treatment plans. MTFC parents are strongly and repeatedly encouraged to call the case manager at any hour of the day or night if they are concerned or have a question about the child placed with them. Parents also participate with program staff in daily data collection on child problems/progress and program implementation via the parent daily report (PDR) calls and engage in weekly supervision/support meetings with their case manager and other MTFC parents.

RECOMMENDATIONS FOR JUAN

Based on the assessment and understanding of what treatment programs work best for young people, Patricia recommends that Juan and his family engage in the wraparound program

Treatment Methods Table

Treatment Type	Focus of Treatment	Benefits of Treatment Model	Limitations of Treatment Model
Multisystemic Therapy	Individual, family, and community influences on behavior	Produces changes in intrapsychic functioning and interactions with parents	Requires reduced caseload and extensive training for practitioners
Cognitive Behavioral Therapy	Youth's cognitions and behavior	Ease of implementation Focuses on youth's cognitions and behaviors	Implementation can be impeded by different understandings of cognitive behavioral therapy
Eco-systemic Natural wrap-around Models	Individual, family, and community influences on behavior	Targets the multiple influences on youth's behaviors Uses family strengths and community volunteers	Youth and family must have community supports willing to engage in the program
Victim-Offender Mediation	Impact of crime on victim and offender	Reduces court costs Humanizes justice system	Both parties must agree to participate Not appropriate for all types of crime
Multidimensional Treatment Foster Care	Youth's problem behavior	Forty years of empirical support Includes close contact between foster parents and social work staff	Extensive training and supervision of foster parents Foster parents must have a clear understanding of the purpose of multidimensional treatment foster care

in her. From her research, eco-systemic wraparound programs will use Juan's family strengths and resources within their environment to support lasting behavior changes for Juan. Eco-systemic wraparound programs will also allow Juan's family members to help direct his treatment in ways that are in line with his family's values and norms. Eco-systemic wraparound programs will provide Juan's family with the latitude to include additional members outside of the immediate family that interact with Juan in school or that could connect him with other youth in neighborhood programs. Finally, engaging Juan in wraparound programming will enable his allies to discuss and monitor the depressive symptoms identified through his interview. If a depressive disorder is developing and the wraparound community decides treatment is needed, then the wraparound community can refer Juan for services and Juan's wraparound team can educate each other on depression and its treatment.

Patricia decided against using other types of interventions because Juan's situation did not warrant placement outside the home given that his family was willing to be involved in Juan's treatment. Thus, Patricia was immediately able to rule out treatment modalities such as multidimensional foster care. Patricia also thought that cognitive-behavioral treatment would be beneficial for Juan. However, based on her assessment data, Patricia decided to leave this treatment decision up to the wraparound team because she thought his symptoms of depression were related to the family's move to a new community. Patricia did not think that victim-offender mediation was necessary at this time because Juan was not at risk for adjudication for his fight with the neighborhood boys. As Patricia examined the assessment data she gathered and considered the empirically-based treatment options available in her area, she decided that a wraparound model best suited Juan and his family.

CONCLUSION

When working with youth who have committed crimes, social workers should be sensitive to the risk factors that have the greatest impact on recidivism. In a study recently conducted by Rivaux, Springer, Bohman, Wagner and Gil (2006), substance abuse predicted recidivism individually as did older age and being male. These findings highlight the need for a focus on prevention and early intervention services with delinquent behaviors, particularly for substance-abusing youth and for males. This study also found that greater levels of family problems predicted recidivism for Latino youth, while increased levels of psychological problems predicted recidivism for African American youth. Knowledge of these predictors could help social workers in assessments of risk and in targeting interventions in a culturally useful way. For example, such a finding might suggest a greater emphasis on family dynamics when working with Latino youth. The intersection of these various predictors of recidivism also highlights the need for prevention and intervention programs that are responsive to issues of both ethnicity and gender.

McNeece, Bullington, Arnold, and Springer (2005) assert that treatment should be linked with a *harm reduction approach*. The harm reduction strategy promotes public health rather than the criminal justice perspective when determining what to do about drug users. Thus, all drug use, whether of "licit" or illicit substances, is seen as potentially problematic. Proponents of this approach assert that the distinctions made between legal and illegal substances are totally artificial and have led to a myopic focus solely on illicit chemicals (McNeece et al., 2005). We should make the receipt of federal funding contingent on the repeal of a number of state laws, including those that prohibit the free distribution of needles and syringes to intravenous drug users.

Traditionally, therapeutic interventions with substance-abusing youth and violent juveniles have been driven more by practice wisdom than by scientifically based outcome studies (evidence-based practice). While we should not abandon our accumulated practice wisdom, to the extent that it is available, practitioners are encouraged to also use evidenced-based practice to guide their treatment planning. In short, it is critical that practitioners remain up-to-date on the best practices available, which will be critical in maximizing our effectiveness in treating juvenile delinquents. Given the limited resources that are currently directed to troubled youths, an interdisciplinary commitment to help these youths is warranted if we are to reduce their substance abuse, delinquency, and associated problems.

REFERENCES

Aguilar, J. P. (2006). *Invisible offenders, violence crimes: Young women's identity, social environment, and violent behavior.* Unpublished dissertation, University of Minnesota School of Social Work.

Andrews, D. A., Zinger, I., Hoge, R. D., Bonta, J., Gendreau, P., & Cullen, F. T. (1990). Does correctional treatment work? A clinically relevant and psychologically informed meta-analysis. *Criminology, 28,* 369–404.

Austin, J., Johnson, K. D., & Weitzer, R. (2005). *Alternatives to the secure detention and confinement of juvenile offenders.* Juvenile Justice Bulletin: U.S. Department of Justice, Office of Justice Programs, Office of Juvenile Justice and Delinquency Prevention.

Austrian, S. G. (2002). *Developmental theories through the life cycle.* New York: Columbia University Press.

Baer, R. A., & Nietzel, M. T. (1991). Cognitive and behavioral treatment of impulsivity in children: A meta-analytic review of the outcome literature. *Journal of Clinical Child Psychology, 20,* 400–412.

Bisman, C. D. (1999). Social work assessment: Case theory construction. *Families in Society, 80,* 240–246.

Bloom, M., Fischer, J., & Orme, J. G. (2006). *Evaluating practice: Guidelines for the accountable professional* (5th ed.). Boston: Allyn & Bacon.

Blumer, H. (1968). *Symbolic interactionism: Perspective and method.* Berkeley: University of California Press.

Borduin, C. M., Mann, B. J., Cone, L. T., Henggeler, S. W., Fucci, B. R., Blaske, D., & M., Williams, R. A. (1995). Multisystemic treatment of serious juvenile offenders: Long-term prevention of criminality and violence. *Journal of Consulting and Clinical Psychology, 63,* 569–578.

Bronfenbrenner, U. (1979). *The ecology of human development: Experiences by nature and design.* Cambridge, MA: Harvard University Press.

Corcoran, J., & Springer, D. W. (2005). Treatment of adolescents with disruptive behavior disorders. In J. Corcoran, *Strengths and skills building: A collaborative approach to working with clients* (pp. 131–162). New York: Oxford University Press.

Deschenes, E. P., & Greenwood, P. W. (1994). Treating the juvenile drug offender. In D. L. MacKenzie & C. D. Uchida (Eds.), *Drugs and crime: Evaluating public policy initiatives* (pp. 253–280). Thousand Oaks, CA: Sage.

Fisher, P. A. & Chamberlain, P. (2000). Multidimensional treatment foster care: A program for intensive Parenting, family support, and skill building. *Journal of Emotional & Behavioral Disorders, 8,* 155–165.

Flash, K. (2003). Treatment strategies for juvenile delinquency: Alternative solutions. *Child and Adolescent Social Work Journal, 20,* 509–527.

Goldstein, E. G. (2001). *Object relations theory and self psychology in social work practice.* New York: Free Press.

Haley, J. (1976). *Problem solving therapy.* San Francisco: Jossey-Bass.

Henggeler, S. W., Schoenwald, S. K., Borduin, C. M., & Swenson, C. C. (2006). Letter to the editor. Methodological critique and meta-analysis as Trojan horse. *Children and Youth Services, 28,* 447–457.

Henggeler, S. W., & Borduin, C. M. (1990). *Family therapy and beyond: A multisystemic approach to treating the behavior problems of children and adolescents.* Pacific Grove, CA: Brooks/Cole.

Henggeler, S. W., Rodick, J. D., Borduin, C. M., Hanson, C. L., Watson, S. M., & Urey, J. R. (1986). Multisystemic treatment of juvenile offenders: Effects on adolescent behavior and family interaction. *Developmental Psychology, 22,* 132–141.

Henggeler, S. W., Schoenwald, S. K., Borduin, C. M., Rowland, M. D., & Cunningham, P. B. (1998). *Multisystemic treatment of antisocial behavior in children and adolescents.* New York: Guilford Press.

Hoge, R. D. & Andrews, D. A.(1994). *YLS/CMI: Youth level of service/Case management inventory user's manual.* Tonawanda, NY: MHS.

Hodges, K. (2000). *The child and adolescent functional assessment scale self-training manual.* Ypsilanti: Eastern Michigan University, Department of Psychology.

Hodges, K., & Cheong-Seok, K. (2000). Psychometric study of the Child and Adolescent Functional Assessment Scale: Prediction of contact with the law and poor school attendance. *Journal of Abnormal Child Psychology, 28,* 287–297.

Hodges, K., Doucette-Gates, A., & Oinghong, L. (1999). The relationship between the Child and Adolescent Functional Assessment Scale (CAFAS) and indicators of functioning. *Journal of Child and Family Studies, 8,* 109–122.

Hodges, K., & Wong, M. M. (1996). Psychometric characteristics of a multi-dimensional measure to assess impairment: The Child and Adolescent Functional Assessment Scale. *Journal of Child and Family Studies, 5,* 445–467.

Izzo, R. L. (1990). Meta-analysis of rehabilitation programs of juvenile delinquents. *Criminal Justice and Behavior, 17,* 134–142.

Jordan, C., & Franklin, C. (2003). *Clinical assessment for social workers: Quantitative and qualitative methods* (2nd ed.). Chicago: Lyceum Books.

Kurtz, A. (2002). What works for delinquency? The effectiveness of interventions for teenage offending behaviour? *The Journal of Forensic Psychiatry, 13,* 671–692.

Lipsey, M. W., Wilson, D. B., & Cothern, L. (2000). *Effective intervention for serious juvenile offenders.* Juvenile Justice Bulletin: U.S. Department of Justice, Office of Justice Programs, Office of Juvenile Justice and Delinquency Prevention.

Lipsey, M. W., & Wilson, D. B. (1998). Effective intervention for serious juvenile offenders: A synthesis of research. In R. Loever & D. Farrington (Eds.), *Serious and violent juvenile offenders: Risk factors and successful interventions* (pp. 313–344). London: Sage.

Lipton, D. S., Martinson, R., & Wilks, J. (1975). *The effectiveness of correctional treatment: A survey of treatment evaluation studies.* New York: Praeger.

Littell, J. H. (2006). Letter to the editor. The case for Multisystemic Therapy: Evidence or orthodoxy? *Children and Youth Services, 28,* 458–472.

Littell, J. H. (2005). Lessons learned from a systematic review of multisystemic therapy. *Children and Youth Services, 27,* 445–463.

Littell, J. H., Popa, M., & Forsythe, B. (2005). Multisystemic therapy for social, emotional, and behavioral problems in youth aged 10–17. *The Cochrane Database of Systematic Reviews, 4.* Article No: CD004797.pub4. DOI:10.1002/14651858.CD004797.pub4.

MacKenzie, D. L., Gover, A. R., Armstrong, G. S., & Mitchell, O. (2001). A national study comparing the environments of boot camps with traditional facilities for juvenile offenders [Online]. *National*

Institute of Juvenile: Research in Brief. Retrieved June 26, 2006 from *www.ncjrs.gov/pdffiles1/ nij/187680.pdf*

McBride, D. C., VanderWaal, C. J., Terry, Y. M., & VanBuren, H. (1999). *Breaking the cycle of drug use among juvenile offenders* [Online]. Retrieved October 24, 2002, from www.ncjrs.org/pdffiles1/ 179273/pdf

McNeece, C. A., Bullington, B., Arnold, E. M., & Springer, D. W. (2005). The war on drugs: Treatment, research, and substance abuse intervention in the twenty-first century. In R. Muraskin & A. R. Roberts (Eds.), *Visions for change: Crime and justice in the twenty-first century* (4th ed., pp. 88–120) Upper Saddle River, NJ: Prentice Hall.

Minuchin, S. (1974). *Families and family therapy*. Cambridge, MA: Harvard University Press.

Northey, W. F., Primer, V., & Christensen, L. (1997). Promoting justice in the delivery of services to juvenile delinquents: The ecosystemic natural wraparound model. *Child and Adolescent Social Work Journal, 14*, 5–22.

Parent, D. G. (2003). *Correctional boot camps: Lessons from a decade of research*. National Institute of Justice, U.S. Department of Justice, Office of Community Oriented Policing Services. Retrieved May 17, 2006, from www.ncjrs.org

Pearson, F. S., Lipton, D. S., Cleland, C. M., & Yee, D. S. (2002). The effects of behavioral/cognitive-behavioral programs on recidivism. *Crime & Delinquency, 48*, 476–496.

Rivaux, S. L., Springer, D. W., Bohman, T., Wagner, E. F., & Gil, A. G. (2006). Differences among substance abusing Latino, Anglo, and African-American juvenile offenders in predictors of recidivism and treatment outcome. *Journal of Social Work Practice in the Addictions 6*(4), 5–29.

Shepard, J. B., Green, K. R., & Omobien, E. O. (2005). Level of functioning and recidivism risk among adolescent offenders. *Adolescence, 40*. 23–32.

Snyder, H. N., & Sickmund, M. (2006). *Juvenile offenders and victims: 2006 National report*. Rockville, MD: U.S. Department of Justice, Office of Juvenile Justice and Delinquency Prevention.

Springer, D. W., McNeece, C. A., & Arnold, E. M. (2003). *Substance abuse treatment for criminal offenders: An evidence-based guide for practitioners*. Washington, DC: American Psychological Association.

Springer, D. W. (2002). Assessment protocols and rapid assessment instruments with troubled adolescents. In A. R. Roberts & G. J. Greene (Eds.), *Social Workers' Desk Reference* (pp. 217–221). New York: Oxford University Press.

Teplin, L. A., Abram, K. M., McClelland, G. M., Dulcan, M. K., & Mericle, A. A. (2002). Psychiatric disorders in youth in juvenile detention. *Archives in General Psychiatry, 59*, 1133–1143.

Umbreit, M. S., Coates, R. B., & Vos, B. (2003). *Community peace-making project: Responding to hate crimes, hate incidents, intolerance, and violence through restorative justice dialogue*. Center for Restorative Justice & Peacemaking, University of Minnesota School of Social Work. Retrieved May 29, 2006 from www.rjp.umn.edu

Umbreit, M. S. (1993). Crime victims and offenders in mediation: An emerging area of social work practice. *Social Work, 38*. 69–73.

4

Overcoming Sisyphus

Assessment of Mental Health Disorders and Risk of Reoffending among Juvenile Offenders

Albert R. Roberts and Kimberly Bender

❖

INTRODUCTION

This chapter examines risk and mental health assessment tools that are commonly used with delinquents. There are two central goals of youth assessment in juvenile justice: (1) predicting the community's safety; and (2) predicting the outcomes of clinical treatment. In order to address the goals of reduced recidivism and rehabilitation, assessments must be comprehensive and cover several domains. Comprehensive assessments include offense history, family/ environmental factors, education/employment history, peer relationships, and psychosocial functioning. Since the overwhelming majority of juvenile offenders have co-occurring mental health and substance abuse disorders, ongoing assessments of psychosocial functioning are particularly critical while they are under the jurisdiction of juvenile justice authorities. Furthermore, these psychosocial factors, including personality characteristics, behaviors, affects, attitudes, beliefs and interpersonal constructs, are predictive of youths' infractions while incarcerated as well as their behavior patterns once released into the community.

In this age of accountability and performance-based measures, criminal justice professionals are being increasingly required by state and federal agencies to demonstrate the reliability and validity of their assessment instruments including brief symptom inventories, diagnostic tools, and violence risk assessment measures. Risk assessment tools assist institutional classification boards as well as parole boards to: (1) determine an initial security rating and placement into a particular facility and program(s); (2) develop a rehabilitation treatment plan; (3) assess eligibility for early release; and (4) determine the type of supervision needed while on parole. This article first describes how the juvenile justice system assesses youths' risks and needs through juvenile assessment centers, then explores common components of assessment in the juvenile justice system, and concludes with an examination of the most commonly used risk and mental health assessment tools and the evidence that supports their use.

All experienced probation officers, juvenile counselors, and forensic clinicians should have skills in risk assessment. Clinical assessment knowledge and skills provide the foundation for clinical judgments, applied research, and evidence-based practice. Within the juvenile justice system, prediction can be operationally defined as an assessment of future lawbreaking for the juvenile offenders who are officially processed through the system.

There are two primary types of prediction: clinical and actuarial. Clinical predictions are made by trained juvenile justice and forensic specialists after they have examined an individual's criminal and psychosocial history, and the results from psychosocial scales and inventories. Actuarial prediction methods are based on known properties, parameters, and statistical formulas applied to identical sets of data (e.g., demographic data, criminal history). Because of the two authors' backgrounds in forensic mental health and social work, we focus on clinical judgments and the most commonly used assessment scales for measuring mental health status, psychosocial functioning, and future criminality.

There is no single scale or assessment tool that can predict future mental health status or criminality with 100 percent certainty. Behavior, abilities, peer influences, family factors, and deviant behavior patterns are not static. They often change with age and different experiences. Empirical evidence from classic longitudinal studies indicates that violent juveniles are strongly influenced by male siblings of similar ages and delinquent gangs, as well as small groups of delinquent friends (Farrington & Loeber, 2000; Farrington & West, 1990). Therefore, it is critically important to use multiple assessment tools with clients at different points in the juvenile justice process.

Clinical prediction is based on perceptions and judgments in which the juvenile justice professional and/or mental health clinician uses different data sources, such as clinical diagnosis, ratings and scores on psychosocial risk assessment scales, interviews, psychotherapy records, and criminal history data to make judgments about the offender's placement in institutional or community-based treatment programs, progress and discharge from probation.

The early roots of prediction in juvenile justice can be traced to the establishment of the first juvenile court mental health clinic in Chicago in 1909 (Roberts, 2004), and the rapid growth and development of over 600 child guidance clinics by the late 1950s connected to juvenile courts throughout the United States (Roberts, 2004). In these clinics forensic psychiatrists and social workers collaborated on behalf of troubled juveniles.

By the late 1990s, most state juvenile correctional agencies included formal and informal dangerousness and risk of further violence and reoffending in their intake classification and assessment centers. The goal of risk assessments is twofold: (1) to predict the probability that a juvenile offender will reoffend; and (2) to predict which youths are at high risk of exhibiting violence in the institution or residential treatment facility, or upon release to parole supervision in the community. In general, classification decisions are made based on forecasts regarding which treatment/rehabilitation program is likely to be effective in changing the behavior patterns of specific types of juveniles, generally viewed as either property-related offenders or violent offenders adjudicated for offenses against persons.

One of the most overlooked components of the juvenile justice system is the assessment and treatment of juvenile offenders with mental health disorders, especially comorbid psychiatric disorders. Research indicates that at least two-thirds of juvenile detainees have one or more mental health disorders in addition to their juvenile offenses. Incarcerated juveniles suffering from impulsiveness, hopelessness, and depression are at an increased risk of suicide ideation, suicide attempts, and death (Rapp-Palicchi & Roberts, 2004). The death rate from suicide is 4.6 times higher in juvenile detention centers than in the general population (Sheras, 2000). Therefore, it is imperative that experienced mental health professionals be hired by juvenile justice agencies so that they can conduct extensive assessments at the preadjudicatory, incarceration, and community release stages (Rapp-Palicchi & Roberts, 2004). At the present time, most large juvenile probation departments do have a few probation officers with expertise in forensic mental health assessment and treatment. However, the time is now ripe for the National Juvenile Detention Association (NJDA), as well as the American Correctional Association (ACA), and state and county correctional administrators to follow the lead of the American Probation and Parole Association (APPA) in giving priority to setting standards, and encouraging their members to hire and train staff in all aspects of juvenile assessment and treatment.

JUVENILE ASSESSMENT CENTERS

A promising advancement of juvenile assessment is the innovative development of centralized, single-point-of-entry, intake juvenile assessment centers. These assessment centers are based on a general model for bringing together a variety of community agencies to one centralized location in which all justice system–involved youth can receive thorough assessment. Juvenile justice, law enforcement, school truancy, diversion programs, and other human service agencies are centrally located allowing for efficient and comprehensive assessment of youths' risks and service needs (Dembo, Schmeidler, & Walters, 2004).

Key elements of juvenile assessment centers (JACs) include (1) a single, 24-hour, centralized point of contact for all youth in contact or at risk of contact with the juvenile justice system, (2) screenings and comprehensive assessments of youths' circumstances and service needs, (3) management information systems that centralize information to avoid repetition and ensure appropriate treatment, and (4) case management services that integrate information in order to recommend appropriate referrals and follow up on youth after they are referred (Dembo et al., 2004).

Juvenile assessment centers got their start in the early 1990s in Florida and quickly gained the attention of the Florida legislature that was struggling with prison overcrowding. With a growing budget due to special appropriations, JACs quickly spread to several counties across Florida and were eventually established in other states, including Colorado and Kansas. Investing further in assessment centers with an initiative in 1996, the Office of Juvenile Justice and Delinquency Prevention (OJJDP) allocated funds to two assessment centers, in Denver, Colorado, and Lee County, Florida, designated as planning sites to develop more assessment centers. Additional funds supported improving services at two designated enhancement sites in Jefferson County, Colorado, and Orlando, Florida (Dembo, et al., 2004).

JACs vary considerably by location due in large part to access to resources and the unique needs of the communities they serve. For example, many Florida JACs work closely with nearby juvenile addiction receiving facilities to provide detoxification, assessment, and stabilization for youth with substance abuse problems. JACs differ in the range of services they provide from those with only juvenile justice agencies to those such as the Hillsborough County, Florida, JAC that provides an array of services, including booking, supervision, detention center screening, diversion, and truancy programming at one site. JACS located in urban settings tend to have longer hours, process many youth, and thus conduct more thorough off-site assessments (Dembo et al., 2004).

Despite these differences, JACs share common benefits to the juvenile justice system. They provide a centralized site for legally required mandates to be carried out more efficiently, saving time locating youth, completing multiple screenings, and providing information to courts for decision making. Integrating information into one information system allows for better-informed decisions regarding need for services and necessary level of supervision. Accessing all system-involved youth, JACs create a prime opportunity for prevention and early intervention. Finally, on a macro level, information from JACs informs the community of broader juvenile justice trends and needs for new services (Dembo et al., 2004).

Dembo et al. (2004) note an ongoing struggle for funding experienced by many JACs. Consistent funding at the federal and state levels is needed in order to provide decent salaries to well-trained staff, thereby reducing staff turnover and improving quality of service. Additional funds would also allow JACs to maintain their original goals of comprehensively responding to youths' multifaceted needs, and preventing JACs from skimming services and becoming mere processing centers.

With necessary funding and support, the future utility of JACs is broad and influential. JACs have the potential to play a major role in developing empirical knowledge in the future. With large sample sizes, JACs' information systems could easily gather data on youths' characteristics, service needs, and outcomes in different treatment programs, providing juvenile justice research with difficult-to-obtain information. This information can then be used to inform program development and service provisions for juvenile offenders.

JACs can also provide much-needed solutions to assessment, referral, and service delivery in the future. By integrating information among many agencies, JACs can help to identify youth who slip through the system by failing to follow through on treatment recommendations. Furthermore, providing objective measures of substance use through urinalysis screening is an invaluable service offered through JACs and has implications for validating youths' self reports of substance use and subsequent appropriate treatment placements. Finally, JACs ensure investment in prevention efforts, keeping youth from further developing delinquency careers; these prevention efforts inversely relate to the number of youth requiring long-term incarceration that is expensive and fairly ineffective (Dembo et al., 2004).

COMPONENTS OF RISK AND NEED ASSESSMENT

The central goals of youth assessment in juvenile justice are (1) the safety of the community by preventing reoffending, and (2) youth rehabilitation and clinical treatment. In other words, mental health assessments seek to identify both *risk and treatment needs.* Assessments must be comprehensive and cover several domains. Comprehensiveness includes assessing a youth's offense history, family/environmental factors, education/employment history, peer relationships, and psychosocial functioning.

Assessing psychosocial functioning is particularly important as the juvenile offender population has elevated rates of mental health and substance use disorders (Teplin, Abram, McClelland, Duclan, & Mericle, 2003). Furthermore, these psychosocial factors (i.e., personality characteristics, behaviors, affect, attitudes, beliefs, and interpersonal constructs) predict youths' infractions while incarcerated and their behaviors once they are released into the community (Cauffman, 2004; Hathaway & Moncachesi, 2003).

Mental health status is often underassessed and consequently undertreated in the juvenile justice system. This is because of a lack of resources and trained staff, as well as a punishment mentality. Teplin, Abram, McClelland, Washburn, and Pikus (2005) report that only 15.4 percent of detained adolescents who needed mental health treatment received treatment in detention centers; it is estimated that as many as 13,000 detained youth with major mental health disorders go untreated (Teplin et al., 2005). Effective mental health assessment and treatment are critical for achieving effective juvenile justice.

In 2002 the Consensus Conference brought together nationally recognized experts in the areas of mental health, juvenile justice, and child welfare service systems. More than 20 researchers with expertise in mental health assessment and juvenile justice convened, with the aim of developing recommendations for mental health assessment in the juvenile justice system. The conference was guided by data from a national survey of current mental health assessment practices conducted by the Center for the Promotion of Mental Health Assessment in Juvenile Justice. Directed by Gail Wasserman at Columbia University's Department of Child Psychiatry, the center's national survey provided information on the current practices and needs of juvenile justice systems across the nation. From these findings, the Consensus Conference was then able to create recommendations for standardizing mental health assessment practices on a national level. The Consensus Conference recommended that four levels of assessments should be conducted:

1. Emergent risk needs should be assessed immediately upon arrival at a secure facility.
2. A comprehensive mental health assessment should be conducted on all youths juvenile facilities to identify those who need more thorough mental health assessments.
3. Prior to community reentry all youth should be assessed for the purposes of facilitating transition and referral to community mental health services.
4. Continued reassessments should take place after the youths have returned to the community to prevent reoffenses.

In the past two decades, several measures have been developed to assess juvenile offenders' mental health and associated risks (Grisso, 2005). These measurement instruments aim to be accurate, reliable, and thorough, while being fairly quick and inexpensive to administer.

TOOLS FOR MENTAL HEALTH AND ASSOCIATED RISK ASSESSMENT

There are currently several well-validated assessment measures used to predict the likelihood of reoffending upon release, mental health treatment needs, and danger toward self (suicide ideation and suicide attempts) and others, based on the presence or absence of substance abuse, suicide ideation, personality traits, thought disturbance, and depression-anxiety. Below we describe several of the most common assessment tools used in juvenile justice research and practice. Several scales are actuarial in nature, whereas others integrate actuarial assessment with supplemental clinical judgment. Instruments are categorized according to their utility as brief screening tools, comprehensive assessment instruments, or risk assessments predicting recidivism or dangerousness in the future. Descriptions are intended to give a brief overview and should not be considered full reviews. For more detailed information on each of these instruments, readers are directed to Grisso, Vincent, and Seagrave's (2005) *Mental Health Screening and Assessment in Juvenile Justice* or to literature by each scale's developer.

Brief Screening Tools

Brief screening tools are instruments that can be administered quickly (usually in 30 minutes or less) and help staff to identify youth who may be of immediate risk to self or others. Furthermore, the screenings should help staff identify youth in need of more comprehensive mental health assessment. These instruments should be easily administered by frontline staff with little specialized training, allowing for quick and inexpensive use. Brief screening tools should not be used to inform treatment plans; instead their utility is in identifying those youth in need of emergency mental health services or those who need more comprehensive assessment that can then inform treatment needs. Table 1 describes the strengths and limitations of three commonly used brief screening tools.

MAYSI-2.   The Massachusetts Youth Screening Instrument—Version 2 (MAYSI-2) was developed by Grisso and Barnum (2003) as a self-report measure to identify youth entering the juvenile justice system with thoughts, feels, or behaviors indicative of mental health problems. The MAYSI-2 is available by pencil-paper or by CD-ROM and consists of 52 yes-no questions asking whether each item is true for the youth. Seven subscales are assessed, including alcohol/drug use, angry-irritable, depressed-anxious, somatic complaints, suicide ideation, thought disturbance, and traumatic experiences. This objective measure includes cutoff scores from a normative juvenile justice sample that can be used as indicators of clinical significance (Grisso & Quinlan, 2005). Research evaluating the reliability of the MAYSI-2 reports internal consistency ranging from .61 to .86 (Grisso, Barnum, Fletcher, Cauffman, & Peuschold, 2001) and support for test-retest reliability on most subscales (Cauffman, 2004). Similar positive findings were found in studies of validity comparing the MAYSI-2 to other standardized scales (Espelage et al., 2003) and to the DSM-IV (Wasserman et al., 2004). Of interest, were several studies that found the MAYSI-2 to predict future behaviors such as institutional maladjustment, sentence length, and necessary intervention for suicide risk and assaultive behavior (Cauffman, 2004; Stewart & Trupin, 2003). Cauffman

TABLE 1   Strengths and Limitations of Commonly Used Brief
Assessment Screens

Instrument (developer)	Strengths	Limitations

MAYSI-2
Grisso and Barnum (2003)
	Low cost
	Brief administration time
	Ease of administration
		Potential social desirability
		Need thought disturbance
		    for girls
		Test applicability to ethnic
		    minority youth

POSIT
Rahdert (1991)
	Identifies youth in need
	    of further assessment
	Public domain instrument
		Administer to one youth at
		    a time
		Test applicability to ethnic
		    minority youth

CAFAS
Hodges (2000)
	Easy training for
	    administration
	Helps prioritize interventions
	Objective measures
	    of functioning
		Requires time investment
		    in observing behaviors
		    and collecting collateral
		    information

and MacIntosh (2006) recently found different properties on some subscales, in particular the alcohol/drug use, anger-irritability and suicide ideation subscales, across ethnic and gender groups. Further research should continue to examine the extent to which these subscales are valid measures for female and ethnic minority youth.

POSIT.   The Problem-Oriented Screening Instrument for Teenagers (POSIT) was developed by Rahdert (1991) as a self-report brief screening to identify troubled youths' problems in psychosocial functioning requiring further assessment. The POSIT, available by pencil-paper or by CD-ROM, consists of a self-administered questionnaire with 139 yes-no questions and assesses 10 functional areas including substance use/abuse, physical health, mental health, family relations, peer relations, educational status, vocational status, social skills, leisure/recreation, and aggressive behavior/delinquency (Dembo & Anderson, 2005). Youths' total scores in each problem area can be compared to empirically based cutoff scores, allowing for a classification as low, medium, or high risk for that problem area. While objectively scored, collateral information is recommended to validate youths' responses. Research evaluating the reliability of the POSIT indicates internal consistency was above .70 and test-rest reliability significantly better than chance (Knight, Goodman, Pulerwitz, & DuRant, 2001). Hall, Richardson, Spears, and Rembert (1998) found high construct validity for the POSIT. Preliminary research indicates the POSIT is useful in classifying youth by predicting return to the juvenile justice system (Dembo et al., 1996).

CAFAS.   The Child and Adolescent Functional Assessment Scale (CAFAS) was developed by Hodges (2000) to assess youths' everyday psychosocial functioning across school, home, community, and work settings. Different ratings (parents, teachers, youth) of youth's behaviors are obtained across 10 subscales (school/work, home, community, behavior toward others, moods/emotions, self-harmful behavior, substance use, thinking, material needs, and family/social). Questions are asked for each subscale that identify severe, moderate, mild, or no impairment and also included are questions that indicate strengths or protective behaviors exhibited by the youth. Raters score the CAFAS after collecting information based on both their own observations and a family of instruments that assess the youths' and their caregivers' perspective on everyday functioning. Studies report positive results for test-rest reliability, validity, and ability to predict level of service needs (Hodges & Wong, 1997).

Comprehensive Assessment Instruments

Before forensic mental health specialists, correctional counselors, and probation officers can recommend a treatment plan, comprehensive risk assessment data must be collected. In comparison to brief assessment tools, comprehensive assessment instruments more thoroughly assess several domains of youths' mental health, personality, and psychosocial characteristics. These assessments often involve longer, more intensive interviews, and several also collect collateral information from other settings in the youths' life (i.e., teachers, parents, or chart information). Comprehensive assessment instruments help to clarify mental health needs, can inform treatment planning, and are most often conducted by professionals or require more involved training. Table 2 describes the strengths and limitations of three commonly used comprehensive assessment instruments.

TABLE 2   Strengths and Limitations of Commonly Used Comprehensive Assessment Tools

Instrument (developer)	Strengths	Limitations
DISC Shafer, Fisher, Lucas, Dulcan, & Scwab-Stone (2000)	Results in diagnosis allowing for more thorough planning No professional training required in administration Computer administration may ease disclosure of suicidal ideation	Computer skills necessary Does not address other social or environmental domains Potential social desirability
MMPI-A Archer (1997)	Widely used Useful in assessing change over time Ease of administration	Requires trained professional to administer Ability to predict violent recidivism has not been evaluated
MACI Millon (1993)	Minimum training for administrators Built-in measure of validity and reliability Consistent with DSM-IV	Relies on client retrospective reports rather than file data More research needed to assess predictive ability in juvenile justice setting

DISC. The Diagnostic Interview Schedule for Children: Present State Voice Version (Voice DISC) was developed by Shafer, Fisher, Lucas, Dulcan, and Scwab-Stone (2000) to assess mental health problems and provide a diagnosis by evaluating how youth meet DSM-IV criteria. Now self-administered on the computer, a unique pattern of questions is based on respondent's answers to previous questions, assessing the degree to which they meet criteria for more than 30 diagnoses (Wasserman, McReynolds, Fisher, & Lucas, 2005). Subscales include anxiety, mood, disruptive behavior, substance use, and miscellaneous (eating disorders, tic disorders, etc.). After the assessment tool determines a youth meets diagnostic criteria, further questions inquire about the severity and frequency of these problems in an attempt to understand impairment. However, youth may be limited in their ability to recognize the consequences of their own behaviors, and it is suggested that clinicians use collateral information to determine impairment. DISC reports include a list of those diagnoses for which the youth met criteria, impairment and symptom scores, and a list of "clinically significant symptoms." Acceptable reliability for most diagnoses and good test-retest reliability have been reported (Shaffer et al., 2000). Moderate to poor correlation with clinician diagnosis has been found (Aronen, Noam, & Weinstein, 1993).

MMPI-A. The Minnesota Multiphasic Personality Inventory—Adolescent (MMPI) was developed by Archer (1997) and adapted for adolescents by Butcher et al. (1992), and is the most widely used personality assessment (Archer & Baker; 2005). The MMPI consists of 478 items with validity scales (e.g., defensiveness, tendency to exaggerate, response consistency), clinical scales (e.g., psychopathology such as depression, anxiety, schizophrenia, antisocial behaviors), content scales (e.g., externalizing behaviors, anger, low self-esteem), and supplementary scales (immaturity, repression). Raw scores are converted to t scores and are compared to normative scores, resulting in classification of youth who clinically elevated, marginally elevated, or typically adolescent. Early research found scale 4 (psychopathic deviate) especially helpful in predicting delinquency (Hathaway & Monachesi, 1963). This is confirmed in later studies that found scale 4 (psychopathic deviate), scale 8 (schizophrenia), and scale 9 (hypomania) predictive of higher rates of delinquency (Archer, Bolinskey, Morton, & Farris, 2003). Over 100 studies have examined aspects of the MMPI-A, and a good resource is a review by Forbey (2003).

MACI. The Millon Adolescent Clinical Inventory (MACI) developed by Millon (1993) is a short assessment that provides clinical information on a variety of psychological problems, including psychopathology, peer difficulties, family problems, and confusion about self (Salekin, Leistico, Schrum, & Mullins, 2005). It also assesses a balance of externalizing/ delinquency risk factors as well as suicidal tendency and risk toward self. Based on the DSM-IV, the MACI includes 3 validity scales (disclosure, desirability, debasement); a reliability scale; 7 clinical syndrome scales (eating dysfunction, substance abuse, delinquent predisposition, impulsive propensity, anxious feelings, depressive affect, suicidal tendency); 12 personality scales (introversive, inhibited, doleful, submissive, dramatizing, egotistic, unruly, forceful, conforming, oppositional, self-demeaning, borderline tendencies); and 8 expressed concern scales (identity confusion, self-devaluation, body disapproval, sexual discomfort, peer insecurity, social intensively, family discord, child abuse). Base-rate scores are calculated and are interpreted by mental health professionals who first examine validity and reliability before identifying problem scales with elevated base-rate scores. The MACI is shown to have good internal and test-retest reliability and concurrent and predictive validity (Millon, 1993). A recent study by Taylor, Skubic-Kemper, Loney, and Kistner (2006) extends support for using the MACI as a tool for classifying subtypes of serious juvenile offenders. Furthermore, the MACI has been shown useful in assessing clinical change from intake to discharge in inpatient settings (Piersma, Pantle, Smith, Boes, & Kubiak, 1993) and is predictive of recidivism (Salekin, Ziegler, Larrea, Anthon, & Bennet, 2003).

Risk for Recidivism and Dangerousness Assessment Tools

Research has identified several factors that put youth at risk for future violence or recidivism. While no definitive list of factors has been developed, research has shown that there are common pathways to recidivism that can be predicted with some accuracy. These factors have been used to compose assessment tools that measure youths' risk of reoffending once released into the community. These instruments help juvenile justice centers make decisions to protect the community and identify need for further services such as case management. Risk for recidivism assessments often involves collection of collateral information from parents or chart materials in addition to interviews with the youth, and is a time-intensive process. Thus, these assessments require specialized training or a professional degree to administer and score. Assessments of future risk behavior include varying degrees of clinical judgment to interpret the results and make decisions. Table 3 describes the strengths and limitations of three commonly used assessments of future risk.

YLS/CMI.   The Youth Level of Service/Case Management Inventory (YLS/CMI; Hoge, Andrews, & Leschied, 2002) is designed to predict juvenile offender recidivism as well

TABLE 3   Strengths and Limitations of Commonly Used Assessments of Future Risk

Instrument (developer)	Strengths	Limitations
YLS/CMI Hoge, Andrews, & Leschied (2002)	Can be administered by "front-line" staff Assesses risks and needs	Requires time to review collateral materials Low reliability on one subscale
SAVRY Bartel, Borum, & Forth (2000)	Does not provide a decision or cut off point requiring knowledge of how identified factors relate to behaviors	No training formalized training Predicts case specific violence not general violence likelihood
PCL:YV Forth, Kosson, & Hare (2003)	Identifies risk factors for potentially very serious offenders	Complex training and advanced graduate degree recommended for administering assessment Controversy over stigmatizing youth with psychopathy label

as case management needs, making it especially useful in planning for transitions out of the juvenile justice system. The YLS/CMI assesses the offender as high- or low-risk, assesses need by targeting services due to risk factors, and assesses responsivity or reaction to interventions. The YLS/CMI is composed of six sections: (1) assessment of risk and needs (42-item checklist assessing prior/current offenses, family circumstances, education/employment, peer associations, substance abuse, leisure, personality/behavior, and attitude); (2) summary of risk/need factors (comparing scales to normative ranges); (3) other needs/special circumstances (situational information such as parental drug use or behavioral records that add information specific to youth); (4) professional override feature (asks clinician to use clinical judgment considering all relevant information to rate youth's risk level); (5) contact level (intensive services should be recommended for high-risk youth); and (6) case management plan (specific goals and objectives for reaching goals). Due to the complexity and knowledge required, the YLS/CMI is completed by a trained professional and purposely incorporates a degree of clinical judgment to supplement the objective portions of the assessment. Adequate internal consistency (Rowe, 2002) and interrater reliability have been found in empirical studies (Schmid, Hoge, & Robertson, 2002) except for the leisure/recreation subscale which as a wide range of interrater reliability (.05–.92). Several subscales of the YLS/CMI have been correlated with other externalizing measures (Rowe, 2002). Ability to predict new charges, new convictions and serious offense charges have been consistently demonstrated with males and more inconsistently for girls (Rowe, 2002; Schmidt et al., 2002).

SAVRY.   The Structured Assessment of Violence Risk in Youth (SAVRY; Bartel, Borum, & Forth, 2000) involves professional judgment based on systematic appraisal of the degree to which youth demonstrate risk factors for future violence. The appraisal involves assessment of six protective factors (e.g., prosocial involvement, strong social support, strong attachments and bonds, positive attitude toward intervention and authority, strong commitment to school, resilient personality traits). The instrument also assesses 24 risk factors in three domains: historical (history of violence, of nonviolent offending, early initiation of violence, history of self-harm, childhood exposure to maltreatment, parental criminality, early caregiver disruption, poor school achievement); individual (negative attitudes, risk taking/impulsivity, substance use difficulties, anger management problems, low empathy/remorse, ADHD difficulties, poor compliance, low interest/commitment to school); and social/environmental (peer delinquency, peer rejection, stress/poor coping, poor parental management, lack of personal/social support, community disorganization). Information should be gathered by the examiner through interviews with the youth, review of records, and observation (Borum, Bartel, & Forth, 2005). Numerical ratings are not the goal of this assessment; identifying empirically validated risk factors specific to each youth is the goal. Thus, clinicians are faced with reviewing the identified risk factors and making a clinical judgment about a youth's overall risk. Interrater reliability is moderate to high (.81) (Catchpole & Gretton, 2003) and studies show support for concurrent validity as compared to the YLS/CMI and PCL:YV (Catchpole & Gretton, 2003). Moderate yet significant correlations were found between the SAVRY and measures of violence and aggression (Gretton & Abramowitz, 2002; McEachran, 2001). Additionally, those youth characterized as low-risk had violent recidivism rates (6%), much lower than those characterized as moderate- (14%) or high-risk (40%) (Catchpole & Gretton, 2003).

PCL:YV. The Hare Psychopathy Checklist: Youth Version (PCL:YV; Forth, Kosson, & Hare, 1990) uses multiple sources of information across interpersonal, affective, and behavior domains to identify symptoms predictive of serious psychopathy in adolescents. The examiner uses information from an intensive interview with the youth, collateral sources, and review of the chart to rate the youth on 20 items according 20-item checklist, including impression management, grandiose sense of worth, stimulation seeking, pathological lying, manipulation of personal gain, lack of remorse, shallow affect, lack of empathy, parasitic orientation, poor anger control, impersonal sexual behavior, early behavior problems, lacks goals, impulsivity, irresponsibility, failure to accept responsibility, unstable interpersonal relationships, serious criminal behavior, serious violence of conditional release, and criminal versatility. Total scores provide the number of psychopathic features observed for each youth but do not result in cutoff or classification. However, raters can compare youth's scores to percentiles scores based on institutional, probation, and community samples. After the extensive training required to administer the PCL:YV, interrater reliability scores are generally high (.90–.96) and internal consistency is adequate (.85–.94) (Forth et al., 2003). Moderate correlations with reports of delinquency, externalizing symptoms, and aggression are reported, though the PCL:YV (as intended) does not correlate with measures of internalizing disorders (Cambell, Porter, & Santor, 2004). Recent studies report the PCL:YV significantly predicted both violent and nonviolent recidivism (Corrado, Vincent, Hart, & Cohen, 2004), as well as clean urine screens and participation in treatment (O'Neill, Lidz, & Heilbrun, 2003). Eden, Buffington, Colwell, Johnson, and Johnson (2002) further support the ability of the PCL:YV to predict disciplinary infractions in their sample juvenile sex offenders. However, Spain, Douglas, Poythress, and Epstein (2004) found negative results, with no relationship evident between the PCL:YV and treatment progress.

CONCLUSION AND SUGGESTIONS FOR FURTHER RESEARCH

Several brief assessment screens have been developed, and research supports their ability to identify youth with emergent risk and in screening for youth who should receive more comprehensive mental health assessments. A study by Wasserman et al. (2004) confirms that such brief tools as the MAYSI-2 are useful for identifying youth who have a possible mental health problem so that they can be further evaluated by such tools as the DISC to identify a more specific diagnosis. These brief assessment tools should be utilized for these purposes and they are most effective when administered promptly upon the youths' arrival at a secure setting.

Several of the took described in Table 2 address the aim of tapping different domains of functioning in the assessment. Some tools utilize multiple sources of data such as files and collateral sources of information in addition to self-reports, whereas others do not. This reflects the constant struggle to provide thorough assessment with limited time/expense resources. Considering the importance of accurately assessing and treating offender mental health problems, we conclude that assessments that tap into a range of information sources are worth the time and effort.

It is unclear from the current empirical evidence how effective the assessment tools reviewed here are in reassessing risk once the youth has been reintegrated into the community. Further research is needed to clarify whether current assessment tools are useful for postincarceration reassessment or whether other assessments, which take into consideration the importance of environmental transition, should be developed for that purpose.

It is important to mention that, while great progress has been made in beginning to understand and assess juvenile offender mental health risk, there is much work to be done in testing the ability of these assessment tools to generalize beyond the population for which they were developed. Recent research by Wasserman, McReynolds, Ko, Katz, and Schwank (2005), examining the prevalence of psychiatric disorders among youths at probation intake, reported that violent female offenders were up to five times more likely to report anxiety disorders than their male counterparts. Furthermore, of youth with conduct disorder, girls seemed to be more likely than boys to have complex diagnoses due to elevated rates of co-occurring internalizing disorders. Research also shows that ethnic minority youth are overrepresented in the juvenile justice system, yet few mental health risk assessment tools have been tested across gender or ethnic groups (Devine, Coolbaugh, & Jenkins, 1998). Considering the elevated mental health needs of females and the ethnic representation of those being served in the juvenile justice system, assessment tools should not be tested predominantly on white male samples. Further research is needed to evaluate assessment instruments with female offenders and ethnic minority offenders as research suggests adaptations may need to be made to accurately assess the needs of these vulnerable groups (Cauffman et al., 2006).

One additional facet of risk assessment appears particularly lacking in the field of juvenile justice. Risk assessments of juvenile offenders need to identify those youths who are likely to reoffend into adulthood, and who are likely to be the chronic career criminals. Several classic studies have documented the pattern of desistance of delinquent behavior in young, adulthood (Elliott et. al., 1983; Gottfredson and Hirshi's 1990; Farrington & West, 1977; Gottredson & Hirschi, 1990). Key finding was that most juveniles discontinue their delinquent acts into early adulthood. Farrington and West's classic study (1977) indicated that only 22.6 percent of their research subjects had subsequent convictions as adults. Elliott and associates (1983) found that only 2 to 3 out of every 10 adjudicated violent juveniles were arrested for violent crimes in adulthood. Also noteworthy is the fact that while the majority of delinquent youth do not seem to present a long-term risk of reoffending in adulthood, there is a small group of 5 to 6 percent of different cohorts who chronically persist in crime into adulthood and are responsible for a high volume of multiple offenses. In the Wolfgang, Figlio and Sellin (1972) birth cohort study, the authors reported that approximately 6 percent of their subjects were responsible for over 50 percent of the official crimes by the cohort. These chronic offenders were likely to have poor school grades and achievement, low IQ test scores, be of nonwhite racial background, low socioeconomic status, and school dropouts. Farrington (1985) found similar results of chronic offending by a small percentage of offenders—6 percent committing 49 percent of the criminal offenses.

Risk assessment instruments to date have not been well tested as to their ability to differentiate those youth who will chronically offend into adulthood from those who are temporary adolescent offenders. Perhaps Hare's Psychopathy Checklist comes closest to beginning to identify this type of particularly serious long-term offender. However, it is clear that while short-term outcomes are important to assess, much work is needed so that current assessment tools are consistently used in all jurisdictions to identify both short-term and potentially long-term chronic offenders.

These instruments do not take long to administer, are understood by the youth, and are easy to score. The biggest problem is that they are not consistently used in all juvenile detention intake units, juvenile reception centers, and institutions so that a large database can be built and modifications made to increase their reliability and validity. What is critically needed is full implementation and not one more instrument.

REFERENCES

Archer, R. P. (1997). *MMPI-A: Assessing adolescent psychopathology* (2nd ed.). Mahwah, NJ: Erlbaum.

Archer, R. P., & Baker, E. M. (2005). Minnesota Multiphasic Personality Inventory—Adolescent. In T. Grisso, G. Vincent, & D. Seagrave (Eds.), *Mental health screening and assessment in juvenile justice* (pp. 240–252). New York: Guilford Press.

Archer, R. P., Bolinskey, P. K., Morton, T. L., & Farris, K. L. (2003). MMPI-A characteristics of male adolescents in juvenile justice and clinical treatment settings. *Assessment, 10,* 400–410.

Aronen, E. T., Noam, G. G., & Weinstein, S. R. (1993). Structured diagnostic interviews and clinicians' discharge diagnoses in hospitalized adolescents. *Journal of the American Academy of Child and Adolescent Psychiatry, 32,* 674–681.

Bartel, P., Borum, R., & Forth, A. (2000). *Structured Assessment for Violence Risk in Youth (SAVRY): Consultation edition.* Tampa: Louis de la Parte Florida Mental Health Institute, University of South Florida.

Borum, R., Bartel, P., Forth, A. (2005). Structural Assessment of Violence Risk in Youth. In T. Grisso, G. Vincent, & D. Seagrave (Eds.), *Mental health screening and assessment in juvenile justice* (pp. 311–323). New York: Guilford Press.

Butcher, J. N., Williams, C. L., Graham, J. R., Archer, R. P., Tellegen, A., Ben-Porath, Y. S., et al. (1992). *Minnesota Multiphasic Personality Inventory—Adolescent (MMPI-A): Manual for administration, scoring and interpretation.* Minneapolis: University of Minnesota Press.

Cambell, M. A., Porter, S., & Santor, D. (2004). Psychopathic traits in adolescent offenders: An evaluation of criminal history, clinical, and psychosocial correlates. *Behavioral Sciences and the Law, 22,* 23–47.

Catchpole, R., & Gretton, H. (2003). The predictive validity of risk assessment with violent young offenders: A 1-year examination of criminal outcome. *Criminal Justice and Behavior, 30,* 688–708.

Cauffman, E. (2004). A statewide screening of mental health symptoms among juvenile offenders in detention. *Journal of the American Academy of Child and Adolescent Psychiatry, 43*(4), 430–439.

Cauffman, E., & MacIntosh, R. (2006). A Rasch differential item functioning analysis of the Massachusetts Screening Instrument. *Educational and Psychological Measurement, 66*(3), 502–521.

Corrado, R. R., Vincent, G. M., Hart, S. D., & Cohen, I. M. (2004). Predictive validity of the Psychopathy Checklist: Youth version for general and violent recidivism. *Behavioral Sciences and the Law, 22,* 5–22.

Dembo, R., & Anderson, A. (2005). Problem-Oriented Screening Instrument for Teenagers. In T. Grisso, G. Vincent, & D. Seagrave (Eds.), *Mental health screening and assessment in juvenile justice* (pp. 112–121). New York: Guilford Press.

Dembo, R., Schmeidler, J., & Walters, W. (2004). Juvenile assessment centers: An innovative approach to identify and respond to youths with substance abuse and related problems entering the justice system. In A. R. Roberts (Ed.), *Juvenile justice sourcebook: Past, present and future* (pp. 512–536). New York: Oxford University Press.

Dembo, R., Turner, G., Schmeidler, J., Sue, C. C., Borden, P., & Manning, D. (1996). Development and evaluation of a classification of high-risk youths entering a juvenile assessment center. *International Journal of Addictions, 31,* 303–322.

Devine, P., Coolbaugh, K., & Jenkins, S. (1998). Disproportionate minority confinement: Lessons learned from five states. *OJJDP Juvenile Justice Bulletin, December* 1–11.

Eden, J., Buffington, J., Colwell, K., Johnson, D., & Johnson, J. (2002). Psychopathy and institutional misbehavior among incarcerated sex offenders: A comparison of the Psychopathy Checklist-Revised and the Personality Assessment Inventory. *International Journal of Forensic Mental Health*, *1*(1), 49–58.

Espelage, D. L., Cauffman, E., Broidy, L., Piquero, A. R., Mazerolle, P., & Steiner, H. (2003). A cluster-analytic investigation of MMPI profiles of serious male and female juvenile offenders. *Journal of the American Academy of Child and Adolescent Psychiatry, 42*(7), 770–777.

Farrington, D. P. (1985). Predicting self-reported and official delinquency. In D. P. Farrington & R. Tarling (Eds.), *Prediction in Criminology* (pp. 150–173). Albany: SUNY Press.

Farrington, D. P., & Loeber, R. (2000). Epidemiology of juvenile violence. *Child and Adolescent Psychiatric Clinics of North America, 9*, 733–748.

Farrington, D. P., & West, D. (1990). The Cambridge study in delinquent development: A long-term follow-up of 411 London males. In H. J. Kerner & G. Kaiser (Eds.), *Criminality: Personality, Behavior, and Life History*. Berlin: Springer-Verlag.

Farrington, D. P., & D. J. West (1977). *The Cambridge Study of Delinquent Development*. Cambridge, England: Institute of Criminology, University of Cambridge.

Forbey, J. D. (2003, June). *A review of the MMPI-A research literature*. Paper presented at the 38th Annual Symposium on Recent Developments in the Use of the MMPI-2 and MMPI-A, Minneapolis, MN.

Forth, A. E., Kosson, D. S., & Hare, R. D. (2003). *The Hare Psychopathy Checklist: Youth Version*. Toronto: Multi-Health Systems.

Gretton, H., & Abramowitz, C. (2002, March). *SAVRY: Contribution of items and scales to clinical risk judgments and criminal outcomes*. Paper presented at the biennial conference of the American Psychological-Law Society, Austin, TX.

Grisso, T. (2005). Evaluating the properties of instruments for screening and assessment. In T. Grisso, G. Vincent, & D. Seagrave (Eds.), *Mental health screening and assessment in juvenile justice* (pp. 71–96). New York: Guilford Press.

Grisso, T., & Quinlan, J. C. (2005). *Massachusetts Youth Screening Instrument—Version 2*. In T. Grisso, G. Vincent, & D. Seagrave (Eds.), *Mental Health Screening and Assessment in Juvenile Justice* (pp. 71–96). New York: Guilford Press.

Grisso, T., & Barnum, R. (2003). *Massachusetts Youth Screening Instrument—Version 2: User's manual and technical report*. Sarasota, FL: Professional Resource Press.

Grisso, T., Barnum, R., Fletcher, K. E., Cauffman, E., & Peuschold, D. (2001). Massachusetts Youth Screening Instrument for mental health needs of juvenile justice youths. *Journal of the American Academy of Child and Adolescent Psychiatry, 40*(5), 541–548.

Grisso, T., Vincent, G., & Seagrave, D. (Eds.). (2005). *Mental health screening and assessment in juvenile justice*. New York: Guilford Press.

Hall, J. A., Richardson, B., Spears, J., & Rembert, J. K. (1998). Validation of the POSIT: Comparing drug using and abstaining youth. *Journal of Child and Adolescent Substance Abuse, 8*, 29–61.

Hathaway, S. R., & Monachesi, E. D. (1963). *Adolescent personality and behavior: MMPI patterns of normal, delinquent, dropout, and other outcomes*. Minneapolis: University of Minnesota Press.

Hodges, K. (2000). *Child and Adolescent Functional Assessment Scale* (3rd ed.). Ypsilanti: Eastern Michigan University.

Hodges, K., & Wong, M. M. (1997). Psychometric characteristics of a multidimensional measure to assess impairment: The Child and Adolescent Functional Assessment Scale (CAFAS). *Journal of Child and Family Studies, 5*, 445–467.

Hoge, R. D., Andrews, D. A., & Leschied, A. W. (2002). *Youth Level of Service/Case Management Inventory: User's manual*. North Tonawanda, NY: Multi-Health Systems.

Knight, J. R., Goodman, E., Pulerwitz, T., & DuRant, R. H. (2001). Reliability of the POSIT in adolescent medial practice. *Journal of Adolescent Health, 29*, 125–130.

McEachran, A. (2001). *The predictive validity of the PCL-YV and the SAVRY in a population of adolescent offenders.* Unpublished master's thesis, Simon Fraser University, Burnaby, BC, Canada.

Millon, T. (1993). *Millon Adolescent Clinical Inventory.* Minneapolis, MN: National Computer systems.

O'Neill, M. L., Lidz, V., & Heilbrun, K. (2003). Adolescents with psychopathic characteristics in a substance abusing cohort: Treatment process and outcomes. *Law and Human Behavior, 27,* 299–313.

Piersma, H. L., Pantle, M. L., Smith, A., Boes, J., & Kubiak, J. (1993). The MAPI as a treatment outcome measure for adolescent inpatients. *Journal of Clinical Psychology, 49,* 709–714.

Rahdert, E. R. (1991). *The Adolescent Assessment/Referral System.* Rockville, MD: National Institute on Drug Abuse.

Rapp-Palicchi, L., & Roberts, A. R. (2004). Mental illness and juvenile offending. In A. R. Roberts (Ed.), *Juvenile justice sourcebook: Past, present and future* (pp. 289–308.) New York: Oxford University Press.

Roberts, A. R. (2004). The emergence of the juvenile court and probation services. In A. R. Roberts (Ed.), *Juvenile justice Sourcebook: Past, present and future* (pp. 163–181).

Rowe, R. (2002). *Predictors of criminal offending: Evaluating measures of risk/needs, psychopathy, and destructive behavior disorders.* Unpublished doctoral dissertation, Carleton University, Ottawa, ON, Canada.

Salekin, R. T., Leistico, A. R., Schrum, C. L., & Mullins, J. (2005). Millon Adolescent Clinical Inventory. In T. Grisso, G. Vincent, & D. Seagrave (Eds.), *Mental health screening and assessment in juvenile justice* (pp. 253–264). New York: Guilford Press.

Salekin, R. T., Ziegler, T. A., Larrea, M. A., Anthony, V. L., & Bennet, A. D. (2003). Predicting dangerousness with two Millon Adolescent Clinical Inventory Psychopathy Scales: The importance of egocentric and callous traits. *Journal of Personality Assessment, 80,* 154–163.

Schmid, F., Hoge, R. D., & Robertson, L. (2002, May). *Assessing risk and need in youthful offenders.* Paper presented at the annual conference of the Canadian Psychological Association, Vancouver, BC, Canada.

Shaffer, D. M., Fisher, P. W., Lucas, C., Dulcan, M. K., & Scwab-Stone, M. E. (2000). NIMH Diagnostic Interview Schedule for Children Version IV (NIMH DISC-IV): Description, differences from previous versions, and reliability of some common diagnoses. *Journal of the American Academy Child and Adolescent Psychiatry, 39,* 28–38.

Sheras, P. (2000). Depression and suicide in juvenile offenders. In *Juvenile Justice Fact Sheet.* Charlottesville: Institute of Law, Psychiatry, and Public Policy, University of Virginia.

Spain, S. E., Douglas, K. S., Poythress, N. G., & Epstein, M. (2004). The relationship between psychopathic features, violence, and treatment outcome: The comparison of three youth measures of psychopathic features. *Behavioral Sciences and the Law, 22,* 85–102.

Stewart, D., & Trupin, E. (2003). Clinical utility and policy implications of a statewide mental health screening process for juvenile offenders. *Psychiatric Services, 54*(3), 377–382.

Taylor, J., Skubic-Kemper, T., Loney, B. R., & Kistner, J. A. (2006). Classification of severe male juvenile offenders using the MACI Clinical and Personality Scales. *Journal of Clinical and Adolescent Psychology, 35*(1), 90–102.

Teplin, L. A., Abram, K. M., McClelland, G. M., Washburn, J. J., & Pikus, A. K. (2005). Detecting mental disorder in juvenile detainees: Who receives services. *American Journal of Public Health, 95*(10), 1773–1780.

Teplin, L. A., Abram, K. M., McClelland, G. M., Duclan, M., & Mericle, A. A. (2003). Psychiatric disorders in youth in juvenile detention. *Archive of General Psychiatry, 59,* 1133–1143.

Wasserman, G. A., McReynolds, L. S., Fisher, P., & Lucas, C. P. (2005). Diagnostic Interview Schedule for Children: Present State Voice version. In T. Grisso, G. Vincent, & D. Seagrave (Eds.), *Mental health screening and assessment in juvenile justice* (pp. 224–239). New York: Guilford Press.

Wasserman, G. A., McReynolds, L. S., Ko, S. J., Katz, L. M., Cauffman, E., Haxton, W., et al., (2004). Screening for emergent risk and service needs among incarcerated youth: Comparing MAYSI-2 and Voice DISC-IV. *Journal of the American Academy of Child and Adolescent Psychiatry, 43*, 752–761.

Wasserman G. A., McReynolds L. S., Ko, S. J., Katz L. M., & Schwank, J. (2005). Gender differences in psychiatric disorder for youths in juvenile probations. *American Journal of Public Health, 95*(1), 131–137.

Wasserman, G. A., Jensen, P. S., Ko, S. J., Cocozza, J., Trupin, E., Angold, A., Cauffman, E., & Grisso, T. (2003). Mental health assessments in juvenile justice: Report on the Consensus Conference. *Journal of American Academy of Child and Adolescent Psychiatry, 42*(7), 752–761.

Wolfgang, M. E., Figlio, R. M., & Sellin, T. (1972). *Delinquency in a birth cohort.* Chicago: University of Chicago Press.

5

Effective Family Interventions for Youthful Offenders

Some Important Considerations

Craig Dowden and D. A. Andrews

ACKNOWLEDGMENTS

The authors would like to thank Drs. Charles Borduin, Scott Henggeler, and colleagues for additional analyses on gender and racial groups.

ABSTRACT

Family-based programs are one of the most widely utilized and frequently evaluated types of correctional intervention for youthful offenders. However, despite recent advances in terms of our knowledge base concerning "what works" within these programs (e.g., appropriate adherence to the principles of risk, need, and responsivity), still relatively little is known about the impact of other potentially important issues on program effectiveness. This chapter begins to provide an answer to this question by recognizing that although the principles of risk, need, and responsivity are of paramount importance for maximizing program success, other variables that have been virtually ignored previously (e.g., staff characteristics/practices, program integrity) have meaningful roles to play in providing a complete answer to the question of what works. The chapter concludes with a series of recommendations for program deliverers and developers to consider in their work with youthful offenders and their families.

INTRODUCTION

In the field of criminal justice, considerable research has focused on the effectiveness of rehabilitation for offenders. This is evident when you examine the number of meta-analyses that have been conducted on the correctional treatment literature. Meta-analyses, which statistically aggregate the findings of a particular research area, have emerged since the mid-1980s with the seminal work of Garrett (1985), and their popularity has increased since that time. The selection of meta-analysis as the review method of choice for determining the therapeutic potential of correctional programming is due to its many advantages when compared to a traditional literature review because the former are "more systematic, more explicit, more exhaustive, and more quantitative" (Rosenthal, 1991, p. 17).

As noted by Losel (1995), 13 meta-analyses were published on the effectiveness of correctional treatment between 1985 and 1995, a number that continues to rise. Although recent meta-analyses still explore offender rehabilitation from a more generic perspective (see Andrews, Dowden, & Gendreau, 1999; Cleland, Pearson, & Lipton, 1996; Redondo, Sanchez-Meca, & Garrido, 1999), this literature has matured to such an extent that others have explored specific questions of interest within the "what works" arena. More specifically, meta-analyses have focused on effective correctional treatment for female (Dowden & Andrews, 1999a), young (Dowden & Andrews, 1999b; Lipsey, 1999; Lipsey & Wilson, 1998), and sexual offenders (Hall, 1995; Hanson et al., 2002), while others have focused on specific program modalities such as relapse prevention (Dowden, Antonowicz, & Andrews, 2003), substance abuse (Pearson & Lipton, 1999), academic/vocational (Wilson, Gallagher, & MacKenzie, 2000), cognitive-behavioral (Pearson, Lipton, Cleland, & Yee, 2002) and family-based (Dowden & Andrews, 2003; Farrington & Welsh, 2004; Latimer, 2001) approaches to offender treatment.

In fact, family-based interventions represent one of the most frequently used and evaluated forms of correctional treatment (Andrews & Bonta, 2002). This is not overly surprising as several recent studies have shown that familial problems are highly predictive of criminal activity for both young (Cottle, Lee, & Heilbrun, 2001; Lipsey & Derzon, 1998; Simourd & Andrews, 1994) and adult (Gendreau, Little, & Goggin, 1996) populations. Positive familial aspects, on the other hand, have also demonstrated utility as protective factors for youth at risk for criminal activity (Hoge, Andrews, & Leschied, 1996; Kliewer, Lepore, Oskin, & Johnson, 1998; Leventhal & Brooks-Gunn, 2000).

Despite its intuitive appeal, however, the effectiveness of this program modality is not clear-cut. More specifically, although several earlier meta-analyses of the broader correctional treatment literature for delinquents provided preliminary indications of the effectiveness of this approach (Garrett, 1985; Lipsey, 1989; Roberts & Camasso, 1991), Latimer (2001) pointed out that there is considerable variability in the results of the individual studies, with some boding neutral or negative findings. In fact, he argued that the previous positive findings for family programs may have been an artifact of the methodological rigor of the study design rather than the therapeutic effectiveness of the program. More specifically, in his meta-analysis, he found that under the strictest of methodological conditions, the effect size for family programs exhibited a null effect on recidivism.

In response to this finding, Dowden and Andrews (2003) presented meta-analytic evidence documenting that while methodological rigor did have an impact on the magnitude of the effect size associated with the family treatment program, those that followed the clinically relevant and psychologically informed principles of effective correctional treatment (e.g., risk, need, and responsivity) continued to yield significant mean reductions in reoffending regardless of methodological quality. Thus, the actual programmatic components were more important for postprogram success than was the rigor of the evaluation design.

WHAT ARE THE PRINCIPLES OF RISK, NEED, AND GENERAL RESPONSIVITY?

Considerable meta-analytic evidence has been gathered demonstrating the importance of appropriately adhering to the principles of risk, need, and responsivity to ensure maximum program effectiveness. As these principles of effective correctional intervention have been discussed at length elsewhere, only a brief summary is provided below.

The risk principle states that the level of treatment services must be appropriately matched to the risk level of the offender. More specifically, higher-risk offenders (e.g., those with a prior offense) should receive more intensive and extensive services whereas lower-risk clients (e.g., first-time offenders) should receive minimal or no intervention.

The need principle, on the other hand, focuses specifically on offender needs and classifies them into two categories. Criminogenic needs are defined as dynamic risk factors that, when changed, are associated with reduced levels of criminal activity (Andrews & Bonta, 2002; Andrews, Bonta, & Hoge, 1990; Andrews, Zinger et al., 1990). Noncriminogenic needs, on the other hand, are also dynamic, but changes in these areas are not associated with subsequent reductions in criminal activity. The need principle illustrates the types of treatment targets that should be selected within correctional interventions. More specifically, in order to effectively reduce recidivism, criminogenic needs must be targeted. However, it should be noted that targeting noncriminogenic needs may be important for reasons other than reducing recidivism (e.g., increasing subjective well-being). A list of criminogenic and noncriminogenic needs is presented in Table 1.

Finally, the general responsivity principle is concerned with the strategies used to deliver the program content. More specifically, it states that in order for correctional treatment to be effective, the styles and modes of program delivery must match the learning styles of the clients (Andrews & Bonta, 2002). In particular, the most effective types of service for inducing positive behavioral change are based on cognitive-behavioral and social learning approaches which include the use of modeling, graduated practice, rehearsal, role playing, reinforcement, resource provision, and detailed verbal guidance and explanations (Andrews, Zinger et al., 1990).

GOALS OF THE CHAPTER

The meta-analyses of Latimer (2001) and Dowden and Andrews (2003) demonstrate the value of digging deeper to provide a more specific answer to the question of what works when delivering family treatment to delinquents. In particular, the review by Dowden and

TABLE 1   List of Criminogenic and Noncriminogenic Needs (Andrews & Bonta, 2003)

Criminogenic Needs	Noncriminogenic Needs
Anger/Negative affect	Vague/Emotional personal
Other needs	Physical activity
Self-control	Fear of official punishment
Prosocial model	Increase conventional ambition
Antisocial attitudes	Family: Other interventions
Vocational skills	Increase cohesive antisocial peers
Family: Affection	Increase self-esteem
Information: Substance abuse	Physical activity
Substance abuse treatment	Fear of official punishment
Reduce Antisocial peers	Respect criminal thinking
Relapse Prevention	Improve living conditions
Family: Supervision	
Barriers to treatment	
Vocational skills + Job	
MDO: Medication	

Andrews (2003) provides a framework within which effective family interventions may be delivered (e.g., adherence to the principles of risk, need, and responsivity). However, one of the major shortcomings of these and other reviews is that they have not explored other potentially important treatment factors that may be impacting program effectiveness. Therefore, it is important to take the next step forward and identify the combination of factors one should consider when developing such a program so that best practices can be identified, a suggestion which has been tabled previously (Wilson et al., 2000).

Thus, the goal of the present chapter is to provide a more in-depth review of the family intervention literature than has been provided previously to identify "what else works" by looking inside the "black box" of treatment. This analysis will not only focus on treatment targets, an area which has received increasing interest to date, but also will examine several other issues that have been largely ignored within the family treatment realm, including program integrity, staff characteristics, and demographic considerations. The chapter concludes with a series of recommendations regarding future research agendas and a compilation of best practices for program developers/administrators.[1]

---

[1] For those readers interested in broader meta-analytic reviews of this literature, they are strongly encouraged to read any of the following outstanding works (Farrington & Welsh, 2004; Garrett, 1985; Latimer, 2001; Lipsey, 1995; Lipsey & Wilson, 1998).

TREATMENT TARGETS—THE NEED PRINCIPLE

Although past meta-analytic reviews of the correctional treatment literature have included family treatment as one of their programmatic targets, none have explored the specific focus of the family program.[2] This type of breakdown is crucial as it provides additional insight into the black box of treatment and allows investigators the opportunity to identify what aspects of the program are most effective (or if they are all equally as effective).

For example, in terms of family treatment, one possible explanation for the disparate findings discussed by Latimer (2001) may be due to the programmatic targets. More specifically, according to the need principle, "appropriate family targets" would include increasing communication/affection within the family as well as improving their supervision techniques. Nondescript programs that did not provide any elaboration of the focus of the program (e.g., used the generic term *family counseling* without any further explanation) would be classified as noncriminogenic. Thus, based on this information, one would expect that programs that included family treatment targets that are criminogenic needs would yield significantly better results than those that are classified as noncriminogenic.

To find an answer to this question, the Carleton University meta-analytic databank was consulted. In all, 38 primary studies involving 53 effect sizes were included in the analyses.[3] The results of our meta-analysis supported the above hypothesis as we found that programs that targeted enhancing communication/affection and/or supervision yielded a significantly higher mean effect size than those that were labeled "family counseling" programs. This result was clinically interesting as it provided a caveat to the widely held notion that all family interventions are effective. In fact, it highlighted that programs should be precise about their therapeutic goals in order to be maximally effective and that they must predominantly target criminogenic needs.

However, there is more to the need principle than just the family issues targeted within treatment. More specifically, as noted by Farrington and Welsh (2004), one of the problems researchers face when exploring the effectiveness of family-based programs is that multiple treatment targets are included within the program milieu. For example, one of the most effective forms of family treatment, multisystemic therapy (see Henggeler, 2004; Henggeler, Schoenwald, Borduin, Rowland, & Cunningham, 1998) targets the intervention at the individual, familial, peer, school, and community level (see Curtis, Ronan, & Borduin, 2004; Henggeler, 2004; Henggeler et al., 1998). Thus, to address this important observation, we decided to break down the results of the programs within our database according to the co-occurring targets within treatment.

The percentage distributions for each of the more and less promising targets for intervention are listed in Tables 2 and 3, respectively.[4] The mean effect size for each need, when

---

[2] Although Farrington and Welsh (2004) separated their sample of family programs into different types, they were concerned with interventions offered to antisocial youth, a component of which would be offender-based. As our study is exclusively concerned with offender populations, we feel this statement is justifiable.

[3] Interested readers are directed to Dowden and Andrews (2003) for a summary of the overall findings.

[4] Given the relatively small number of effect sizes, the criminogenic and non-criminogenic needs were aggregated into larger categories that have been used successfully in several meta-analyses conducted by the authors (see Andrews, Dowden, & Gendreau, 1999; Dowden & Andrews, 1999a, 2000).

TABLE 2   Criminogenic Needs and their Magnitude of Correlation with Effect
Size: Percentage of Tests with Need Targeted, Mean Effect Size When and
When Not Targeted, and Correlation with Effect Size

Criminogenic Need Area Targeted	%	Mean Phi[†] (k)		Corr. with Phi
		Not a Target	Targeted	
Antisocial Cognition	26	.18 (39)	.30 (14)	.23
Self-Control Deficits	21	.17 (42)	.38 (11)	.35**
Family Affection	53	.09 (25)	.32 (28)	.48***
Family Monitoring	40	.10 (32)	.38 (21)	.56***
Antisocial Associates	26	.09 (36)	.35 (9)	.45**
School/Work	30	.18 (37)	.30 (16)	.23
Substance Abuse	11	.14 (40)	.14 (5)	−.01
Remove Barriers	25	.17 (40)	.41 (13)	.47**

Notes: (a) Components of Antisocial Cognition: Antisocial attitudes (k = 14, r = .03ns), Anger (k = 13, r = .31). (b) Components of Antisocial Associates: Increase contact with prosocial (k = 9, r = .31). Decrease contact with antisocial (k = 1, r = N/A). (c) Components of School/Work: School (k = 16, r = .23ns), Vocational Skills (k = 3, r = .07ns, f). (d) Components of Substance Abuse: Treatment (k = 1, r = N/A), Information (k = −.12ns).

[†]k refers to the number of studies that contributed to the mean effect size of interest.

TABLE 3   Noncriminogenic Needs: Percentage of Tests with Need Targeted,
Mean Effect Size When and When Not Targeted, and Correlation with
Effect Size

Noncriminogenic Need Area Targeted	%	Mean Phi (k)		Corr. with Phi
		Not a Target	Targeted	
Vague Emotional/Personal Problems	32	.28 (36)	.08 (17)	−.39**
Family: Other	36	.32 (34)	.02 (19)	−.60***

it was and was not targeted, and the magnitude of the association with effect size is presented in these tables.

Not surprisingly, given that the present meta-analysis focused on family treatment programs, Table 4 reveals that the most frequently targeted criminogenic needs were increasing familial affection/communication skills (53%) as well as improving familial monitoring practices (40%). More importantly, the majority of the criminogenic needs were significantly correlated with effect size. For the noncriminogenic needs, on the other hand, both were significantly but negatively correlated with effect size. In other words, targeting vague emotional/personal problems (r = −.39, p < .001) and/or nondescriptive forms of family intervention (e.g., stating that the program included a family counseling component but did not specify exactly what was the goal of the program, r = −.60, p < .001), yielded significant mean increases in recidivism for the treatment as opposed to the comparison group. Clearly, the specific targets of family intervention were important indicators of the therapeutic potential of these particular programs.[5]

Overall, the results confirm that it is inappropriate to conclude that family programs are equally effective. In fact, if crimogenic needs do not predominate the therapeutic milieu, the results from our meta-analysis suggest this may lead to significantly worse levels of postprogram performance for participants. Thus, the majority of treatment targets included in family treatment programs should be criminogenic needs.

DEMOGRAPHIC INFORMATION

The criminological literature is replete with articles dealing with issues surrounding gender (Bloom, 1999; Bloom & Covington, 1998, 2000; Covington, 1998; Koons, Burrow, Morash, & Bynum, 1997) and race (King, Holmes, Henderson, & Latessa, 2001) and their impact on the criminal justice system. This attention certainly is warranted, especially considering the fact that our review of the meta-analytic literature uncovered only one meta-analysis (Dowden & Andrews, 1999a; Wilson, Lipsey, & Soydan, 2003) that examined effective correctional treatment for each of these populations. Thus, it is not surprising that little knowledge is available regarding what works for these offender groups within the family treatment literature.

To provide a preliminary answer to this question, once again, the Carleton University meta-analytic database was consulted to determine whether programmatic results were differentially affected by gender and race. In terms of the former, the findings reflected those reported in the broader family treatment meta-analysis (Dowden & Andrews, 2003) in that stronger effects were identified in programs that targeted family affection/communication and/or supervision. Generic family counselling programs (e.g., those without any specific family-based targets), on the other hand, yielded weak (boys) or negative (girls) effects. Interestingly, however, the mean effect size for females was higher for both criminogenic needs, and in the case of family supervision, significantly so. Thus, although family intervention programs are appropriate for both groups, the preliminary evidence suggests that these programs are particularly effective for female offenders (see Table 4).

It should be noted that the effectiveness of family interventions with this population was not surprising given Dowden and Andrews (1999) reported this in their meta-analysis examining what works for female offenders. This result also falls in line with the theoretical developments made in the field of feminist criminology as many of its leading scholars have stressed the importance of familial variables in the etiology of female criminality (Blanchette & Brown, 2006; Bloom & Covington, 1998, 2000)

---

[5] One of the major criticisms lodged against meta-analytic techniques is that studies can contribute multiple effect sizes to the analysis, thereby potentially biasing the overall results by overrepresentation. To control for this possibility, we conducted the analysis, only allowing one effect size per program to be contributed to the final result. The results were identical in both cases, with the same variables achieving statistical significance or nonsignificance. This eliminates study bias as a possible explanation for these findings and removes concerns of nonindependence of data. This analysis was not conducted within the gender and racial subanalyses given the low numbers of effect sizes.

TABLE 4   Mean Effect Size, Number of Tests (*k*), and Correlation (*r*) with Effect Size by Criminogenic and Noncriminogenic Needs within Gender

	No	Yes	*r*
Affection	.09 (25)	.32 (28)	.48**
Male	.12 (21)	.27 (17)	.37*
Female	−.04 (4)	.40 (11)	.66**
r	−.29ns	.28ns	
Monitoring	.10 (32)	.38 (21)	.56***
Male	.11 (23)	.30 (15)	.46**
Female	.09 (9)	.57 (6)	.79***
r	−.04ns	.56**	
Family: Other	.32 (34)	.02 (19)	−.60***
Male	.28 (23)	.03 (15)	−.59***
Female	.40 (11)	−.04 (4) −.66**	
r	.25ns	−.25ns	

*p < .05, **p < .01, ***p < .001

TABLE 5   Mean Effect Size, Number of Tests (*k*) and Correlation (*r*) with Effect Size by Criminogenic and Noncriminogenic Needs within Racial Groups

	No	Yes	*r*
Affection	.09 (25)	.32 (28)	.48**
Caucasian	.08 (17)	.32 (24)	.49**
Non-Caucasian	.10 (8)	.33 (4)	.44ns
r	.05ns	.02ns	
Monitoring	.10 (32)	.38 (21)	.56***
Caucasian	.13 (27)	.40 (14)	.56***
Non-Caucasian	−.02 (5)	.32 (7)	.69*
r	−.29ns	−.17ns	
Family: Other	.32 (34)	.02 (19)	−.60***
Caucasian	.32 (27)	.03 (14)	−.58***
Non-Caucasian	.32 (7)	−.02 (5)	−.69*
r	.01ns	−.20ns	

    In terms of race, the same pattern of findings emerges. More specifically, programs that target family factors classified as criminogenic needs yielded significantly higher mean effect sizes (in the range of .32−.40) than those generic, nonspecific forms of family therapy (range = −.02−.03). However, in this case the mean effect sizes were statistically indistinguishable (e.g., the program was equally effective for both populations). Thus, what works for delinquents is consistent regardless of the racial composition of the treatment population (see Table 5).

The previous set of findings regarding race should not be surprising, especially considering Wilson et al. (2003) have already reported in their comprehensive meta-analytic review of the broader offender rehabilitation literature that 'what works' for Caucasian offenders applies equally well with minority offenders. Although issues as important as race and gender must be continually reevaluated and explored (Sue, 1999), certainly the preliminary evidence to date suggests the framework within which effective family-based correctional services can be successfully offered are virtually the same regardless of gender/race.

Although these results comment on the differential effectiveness of family intervention programs based on gender and racial consideration, our coding procedures did not allow us to explore either variable as a specific responsivity issue. More specifically, the present meta-analysis did not examine whether modifying the treatment program to the specific learning styles of women (i.e., relationship-oriented treatment) or minority (e.g., culturally senstitive) offenders had any impact on recidivism. Exploring the effects of gender and race as a specific responsivity consideration should be the focus of future family-based program evaluations.

One final point must also be made before we proceed to the next section. Unfortunately, our meta-analytic database indicates that the knowledge accumulation that has occurred in the areas of gender- and racially responsive treatment has been seriously hampered by the way in which the results in these evaluations have been reported rather than from a lack of female or minority participants. For example, of the 53 effect sizes included in our aforementioned meta-analysis, only 18.5 percent (n = 10) were based on solely male or female program clients. In other words, when evaluators were faced with situations in which both males and females composed the treatment group, they chose to aggregate the data when reporting the results of the program evaluation (n = 43). In other words, if the authors chose to disaggregate the data by gender, there would have been an additional 86 *direct* tests of the differential effectiveness of treatment for males and females (e.g., they could have determined program effectiveness for both males and female offenders separately). Clearly, this is a missed opportunity to explore differential programmatic effects for family treatment programs by gender.

The situation is equally discouraging when client race is considered. More specifically, for 40.7 percent of the effect sizes in our review, the racial profile of the offenders exposed to treatment was not provided! Furthermore, even our coding for client race had to be adjusted where predominant racial group membership was determined by a majority approach (e.g., more than 60%). Once again, by failing to separate the results by race, this precludes the identification of racially responsive differences to correctional rehabilitation. More specifically, it is possible that a program that has yielded statistically significant reductions in recidivism for Caucasian offenders, may yield minimal or no effects for minority offenders. Clearly, better reporting practices will be required in order to lead to improved knowledge construction within this field.

STAFF CHARACTERISTICS AND PRACTICES

Although considerable focus has been placed on determining what constitutes an effective family program, very little research has focused on the impact of staff characteristics or the practices they use to deliver the program (Dowden & Andrews, 2004). This is especially surprising when one considers the plethora of articles published in the psychotherapy literature that focus on these critical clinical issues (Lambert & Barley, 2001).

Andrews and Carvell (1998) tackled this issue by highlighting the characteristics/ practices of effective correctional staff and developing a program outlining the ways in which staff could be trained to achieve these objectives. Termed *core correctional practice* (CCP), this perspective emphasizes the importance of staff characteristics (such was warmth, humor, approachability, etc.) along with the actual skills used to deliver the program (see Appendix A for a detailed description of each of the elements of CCP). Although their approach was developed specifically for offenders, other experts have acknowledged the importance of these skills in general clinical settings (e.g., Trotter, 1999).

To test the impact of CCP on family treatment effectiveness, once again, the Carleton University database was consulted (see Table 6). It should be noted that each element of CCP yielded a strong positive effect, with the most effective element being appropriate modeling of desired behaviours for clients. Even the least effective element, utilizing a problem-solving model, yielded a large mean effect size ($M = .24$).

Analyses were also conducted on the additive effect of the number of CCP components on programmatic outcomes. The simple correlation between the number of elements of CCP and recidivism was .43 ($p < .01$). The mean score was 0.85 ($SD = 1.23$) with a mean inter-item correlation of .24 and an alpha coefficient of .67. The number of CCP elements present within a program was categorized using a three-level composite measure (0 = the program did not utilize any elements of CCP; 1 = the program targeted and identified only one or two elements of the model; 2 = the program used three or more elements) as a frequency analysis revealed this would be the most appropriate splitting of the data to achieve an approximate equal number of effect sizes in each group. An analysis of variance revealed that significant differences existed, [$F(2, 51) = 6.86$, $p < .01$], with follow-up contrasts using the LSD[6] correction revealing that programs that overtly identified three or more elements of CCP were associated with a significantly higher mean effect size

TABLE 6   Elements of CCP: Mean Effect Size When and When Not Targeted and Correlation with Effect Size

Variable Label	Adheres to Principle		
	No	Yes	Eta
Modeling	.16 (47)	.53 (7)	.52***
Effective Reinforcement	.18 (49)	.43 (5)	.30*
Effective Disapproval	.19 (51)	.40 (3)	.20ns
Problem-Solving	.19 (38)	.24 (16)	.08ns
Learning	.16 (41)	.35 (13)	.34**

*$p < .05$. **$p < .01$. ***$p < .001$

[6] As this was an exploratory study and given the relatively low number of effect sizes, the LSD corrections was used to maximize the probability of finding a significant difference.

(0.47, $n = 7$) than programs that identified one or two elements (0.24, $n = 13$) or did not utilize any of these techniques (0.14, $n = 33$) ($p < .01$).

The fact that staff characteristics and practices impact program outcome should not be overly surprising. However, what is surprising is that the vast majority of the evaluations do not report anything whatsoever about these critical clinical issues or discuss virtually anything about the program staff for that matter. Clearly, future primary research must ensure that attention is paid to the characteristics/practices of the staff when writing up the results of the program evaluation.

PROGRAM INTEGRITY

Program integrity is evident when the original program theory and design are appropriately captured in the way in which the services are ultimately delivered (Hollin, 1995). This issue has recently gained increasing attention in the field of correctional treatment (Gendreau, Goggin, & Smith, 1999) and the meta-analytic results thus far have been encouraging. For example, meta-analyses of the effectiveness literature have linked enhanced reductions in recidivism to higher levels of program integrity (Andrews & Bonta, 2002; Andrews, Dowden, & Gendreau, 1999; Hill, Andrews, & Hoge, 1991; Lipsey, 1995). Some have even suggested that enhanced integrity not only increases the positive effects of reduced reoffending when the program is psychologically appropriate, but also increases reoffending when the program is inappropriate (Hill et al., 1991). More recently, Andrews and Dowden (2005) found that several indicators of integrity were significantly and positively linked with effect size. Some of the indicators reviewed in their study included:

- Training of therapists and/or supervisors in treatment model applied
- Supervision of therapists
- Systematic monitoring of in-program activities
- Dosage (e.g., number of treatment hours)[7]
- Presence of printed materials (e.g., printed/taped manuals; printed treatment scripts, guidelines for skill training)

However, one of the limitations of their review was that it was conducted on the broader correctional treatment literature and not the family intervention literature proper. Thus, we wanted to explore whether these variables would be equally as important when the analyses solely focused on family programs.

Not surprisingly, exploring these variables within the context of family treatment yielded equally impressive results. More specifically, five of the six indicators of integrity that were examined in our meta-analytic database yielded significant between-group differences (see Table 7). As we did with CCP, the additive effect of the number of elements of program integrity on programmatic outcomes was examined. The simple correlation between the number of indicators of integrity and effect size was .51 ($p < .01$). The mean score was 3.11 ($SD = 2.20$) with a mean inter-item correlation of .46 and an alpha coefficient of .84. Thus, these results suggest that researchers within the family intervention literature

---

[7] Too few studies in the present meta-analysis reported on this variable to make analyses appropriate.

TABLE 7   Indicators of Program Integrity: Mean Effect Size When
and When Not Targeted and Correlation with Effect Size

| | Adheres to Principle | | |
Variable Label	No	Yes	Eta
Specific Model	.08 (20)	.29 (33)	.44***
Trained Workers	.04 (17)	.29 (36)	.48***
Clinical Supervision	.14 (31)	.32 (22)	.38**
Trained Supervisor	.13 (31)	.33 (22)	.43***
Printed Program Materials	.14 (31)	.32 (22)	.37**
Monitoring Process/Change	.17 (23)	.24 (30)	.16ns

*$p < .05$, **$p < .01$, ***$p < .001$

are paying more attention to these variables than they are to issues surrounding staff practices/characteristics, although a more concerted effort is still required.

The number of elements of program integrity present within a program was categorized using a three-level composite measure (0 = the program did not utilize any elements of program integrity; 1 = the program evidenced 1–3 indicators of program integrity; 2 = the program used 4–6 indicators) as a frequency analysis revealed this would be the most appropriate splitting of the data to balance the theoretical and statistical considerations arising from this type of analysis. An analysis of variance revealed that significant differences existed, $F(2, 51) = 6.06$, $p < .01$. Follow-up contrasts using the LSD correction revealed that programs that incorporated four or more indicators of program integrity were associated with a significantly higher mean effect size (0.32, $n = 23$) than programs that identified one to three indicators (0.16, $n = 24$) or did not have any of these techniques within their program (0.01, $n = 6$) ($p < .01$). Clearly, issues surrounding program integrity are crucial to delivering effective correctional treatment within a family-based program.

CONCLUSION

In conclusion, this chapter has highlighted that there are many factors to consider when developing a family-based program for youthful offenders. Clearly, the principles of risk, need, and responsivity are crucial building blocks of any correctional intervention, regardless of modality or population. However, our review demonstrated that other variables are also important for maximizing the therapeutic potential of the program. More specifically, the co-occurring targets selected, degree of program integrity, and staff characteristics/practices all play a role. Although the research implications of some of these issues are surely in their infancy, it is our hope that future evaluations will address these areas more systematically so that future reviews of this literature may provide even stronger evidence reflecting the issues to consider when developing and implementing an effective family treatment for correctional populations. Nonetheless, the following provides an overview of the issues that we feel are empirically supported and clinically relevant at present.

Checklist for Delivering Effective Family Treatment with Young Offenders

Client Characteristics

- Ensure high-risk individuals receive the most intensive treatment services
- Ensure program content and delivery style take into consideration the demographics of the treatment group including gender, age, and race/ethnicity
- Identify and target protective or strength factors
- Assess client motivation and develop strategies to minimize the probability of program attrition through linking clear and observable rewards with program participation
- Identify and target family problems for intervention as early as possible

Program Development

- Target multiple need areas within the treatment strategy including familial relationships (e.g., affection, communication), structural familial variables (e.g., monitoring and supervision practices of the parents), academic and vocational performance, anger management issues, and antisocial peer group involvement
- Ensure the program utilizes cognitive-behavioral/social learning strategies to impart course content
- Ensure attention is paid to program integrity variables (i.e., ensure that: the program is based on a specific, theoretical model; workers are trained in program delivery and are supervised by a trained supervisor; printed program materials are available describing program goals and content; in-program monitoring of key performance behaviours is conducted; and staff are selected on key interpersonal or skill factors)
- Ensure clients are matched to the appropriate program
- Ensure staff variables are appropriately considered and that these issues are noted during the formal evaluation

REFERENCES

Andrews, D. A., & Bonta, J. (2003). *The psychology of criminal conduct* (3rd ed.). Cincinnati, OH: Anderson.

Andrews, D. A., Bonta, J., & Hoge, R. D. (1990). Classification for effective rehabilitation: Rediscovering psychology. *Criminal Justice and Behavior, 17,* 19–52.

Andrews, D. A., & Carvell, C. (1998). *Core correctional training–core correctional supervision and counseling: Theory, research, assessment and practice.* Unpublished training manual, Carleton University, Ottawa, Canada.

Andrews, D. A., & Dowden, C. (2005). Managing correctional treatment for reduced recidivism. A meta-analytic review of program integrity. *Legal and Criminological Psychology, 10,* 173–187.

Andrews, D. A., Dowden, C., & Gendreau, P. (1999, November). *New meta-analytic tests of the principles of human service, risk, need and general responsivity.* Symposium presented at the annual meeting of the American Society of Criminology, Toronto, Ontario.

Andrews, D. A., Zinger, I., Hoge, R., Bonta, J., Gendreau, P., & Cullen, F. (1990). Does correctional treatment work? A clinically relevant and psychologically informed meta-analysis. *Criminology, 28,* 369–404.

Blanchette, K., & Brown, S. L. (2006). *The assessment and treatment of women offenders: An integrated perspective.* Wiley.

Bloom, B. (1999). Gender-responsive programming for women offenders: Guiding principles and practices. *Forum on Corrections Research, 11,* 22–27.

Bloom, B., & Covington, S. (1998). *Gender-specific programming for female offenders: What is it and why is it Important?* Paper presented at the 50th annual meeting of the American Society of Criminology, Washington, DC.

Bloom, B., & Covington, S. (2000). *Gendered justice: Programming for women in correctional settings.* Paper presented at the 52nd annual meeting of the American Society of Criminology, San Francisco, CA.

Cleland, C. M., Pearson, F., & Lipton, D. S. (1996, November). *A meta-analytic approach to the link between needs-targeted treatment and reductions in criminal offending.* American Society of Criminology annual meeting (Chicago, IL).

Covington, S. (1998). Creating gender-specific treatment for substance-abusing women and girls in community correctional settings. *The ICCA Journal, December,* 24–29.

Cottle, C. C., Lee, R. J., & Heilbrun, K. (2001). The prediction of criminal recidivism in juveniles: A meta-analysis. *Criminal Justice & Behavior, 28,* 367–394.

Curtis, N. M., Ronan, K. R., & Borduin, C. M. (2004). Multisystemic treatment: A meta-analysis of outcome studies. *Journal of Family Psychology, 18,* 411–419.

Dowden, C., & Andrews, D. A. (1999a). What works for female offenders: A meta-analytic review. *Crime and Delinquency, 45,* 438–452.

Dowden, C., & Andrews, D. A. (1999b). What works in young offender treatment: A meta-analysis. *Forum on Corrections Research, 11*(2), 21–24.

Dowden, C., & Andrews, D. A. (2000). Effective correctional treatment and violent recidivism: A meta-analysis. *Canadian Journal of Criminology, 42,* 449–476.

Dowden, C., & Andrews, D. A. (2003). Does family intervention work for delinquents? Results of a meta-analysis. *Canadian Journal of Criminology and Criminal Justice, 45,* 327–342.

Dowden, C., Antonowicz, D. H., & Andrews, D. A. (2003). The effectiveness of relapse prevention with offenders: A meta-analysis. *International Journal of Offender Therapy and Comparative Criminology, 47,* 516–528.

Farrington, D. P., & Welsh, B. C. (2004). Family-based prevention of offending: A meta-analysis. *Australian and New Zealand Journal of Criminology, 36*(2), 127–151.

Garrett, C. (1985). Effects of residential treatment of adjudicated delinquents: A meta-analysis. *Journal of Research in Crime and Delinquency, 22,* 287–308.

Gendreau, P., Little, T., & Goggin, C. (1996). A meta-analysis of the predictors of adult recidivism: What works! *Criminology, 34,* 575–607.

Gendreau, P., Goggin, C., & Smith, P. (1999). The forgotten issue in effective correctional treatment: Program implementation. *International Journal of Offender Therapy and Comparative Criminology*

Hall, G. C. N. (1995). Sex offender recidivism revisited: A meta-analysis of recent treatment studies. *Journal of Consulting and Clinical Psychology, 63,* 802–809.

Hanson, R. K., Gordon, A., Harris, A. J. R., Marques, J. K., Murphy, W., Quinsey, V. L., & Seto, M. C. (2002). First report of the Collaborative Outcome Data Project on the effectiveness of psychological treatment for sex offenders. *Sexual Abuse: A Journal of Research and Treatment, 14,* 167–192.

Henggeler (2004). Decreasing effect sizes for effectiveness studies—Implications for the transport of evidence-based treatments: Comment on Curtis, Ronan, and Borduin (2004). *Journal of Family Psychology, 18,* 420–423.

Henggeler, S. W., Schoenwald, S. K., Borduin, C. M., Rowland, M. D., & Cunningham, P. B. (1998). *Multisystemic treatment of antisocial behavior in children and adolescents.* New York: Guilford Press.

Hill, J. K., Andrews, D. A., & Hoge, R. D. (1991). Meta-analysis of treatment programs for young offenders: The effect of clinically relevant treatment on recidivism, with controls introduced for various methodological variables. *Canadian Journal of Program Evaluation, 6,* 97–109.

Hoge, R. D., Andrews, D. A., & Leschied, A. W. (1996). An investigation of risk and protective factors in a sample of youthful offenders. *Journal of Child Psychology and Psychiatry, 37,* 419–424.

Hollin, C. (1995). The meaning and implications of "programme integrity." In J. McGuine (Ed.), *What works: Reducing reoffending–Guidelines from research and practice* (pp. 193–206). Chichester, England: John Wiley & Sons.

King, W. R., Holmes, S. T., Henderson, M. L., & Latessa, E. J. (2001). The Community Corrections Partnership: Examining the long-term effects of youth participation in an Afrocentric diversion program. *Crime and Delinquency, 47,* 558–572.

Kliewer, W., Lepore, S. J., Oskin, D., & Johnson, P. D. (1998). The role of social and cognitive processes in children's adjustment to community violence. *Journal of Consulting and Clinical Psychology, 60,* 199–209.

Koons, B. A., Burrow, J. D., Morash M. M., & Bynum, T. (1997). Expert and offender perceptions of program elements linked to successful outcomes for incarcerated women. *Crime and Delinquency, 43,* 512–532.

Lambert, M. J., & Barley, D. E. (2001). Research summary on the therapeutic relationship and psychotherapy outcome. *Psychotherapy, 38,* 357–361.

Latimer, J. W. (2001). A meta-analytic examination of youth delinquency, family treatment, and recidivism. *Canadian Journal of Criminology, 43,* 237–254.

Leventhal, T., & Brooks-Gunn, J. (2000). The neighborhoods they live in: The effects of neighborhood residence on child and adolescent outcomes. *Psychological Bulletin, 126,* 309–337.

Lipsey, M. W. (1989). *The efficacy of intervention for juvenile delinquency: Results from 400 studies.* Paper presented at the 41st annual meeting of the American Society of Criminology, Reno, NV.

Lipsey, M. W. (1995). What do we learn from 400 research studies on the effectiveness of treatment with juvenile delinquents? In J. McGuire (Ed.), *What works: Reducing reoffending: Guidelines from research and practice* (pp. 63–78). Chichester, England: Wiley.

Lipsey, M. W. (1999). Can rehabilitative programs reduce the recidivism of juvenile offenders? An inquiry into the effectiveness of practical programs. *Virginia Journal of Social Policy and Law, 6,* 611–641.

Lipsey, M. W., & Derzon, J. (1998). Predictors of violent or serious delinquency in adolescence and early adulthood: A synthesis of longitudinal research. In R. Loeber and D. P. Farrington (Eds.), *Serious and violent juvenile offenders: Risk factors and successful interventions* (pp. 85–105). London: Sage.

Lipsey, M. W., & Wilson, D. B. (1998). Effective intervention for serious juvenile offenders: A synthesis of research. In R. Loeber & D. P. Farrington (Eds.), *Serious and violent juvenile offenders: Risk factors and successful interventions.* (pp. 313–345). London: Sage.

Losel, F. (1995). The efficacy of correctional treatment: A review and synthesis of meta-evaluations. In J. McGuire (Ed.), *What works: Reducing reoffending: Guidelines from research and practice* (pp. 79–111). Chichester, England: Wiley.

Pearson, F. S., & Lipton, D. S. (1999). A meta-analytic review of the effectiveness of corrections-based treatments for drug abuse. *The Prison Journal, 79,* 384–410.

Pearson, F. S., Lipton, D. S., Cleland, C. M., & Yee, D. S. (2002). The effects of behavioral/cognitive-behavioral programs on recidivism. *Crime and Delinquency, 48,* 476–496.

Redondo, S., Sanchez-Meca, J., & Garrido, V. (1999). The influence of treatment programmes on the recidivism of juvenile and adult offenders: An European meta-analytic review. *Psychology, Crime & Law, 5,* 251–278.

Roberts, A. R., & Camasso, M. J. (1991). The effect of juvenile offender treatment programs on recidivism: A meta-analysis of 46 studies. *Notre Dame Journal of Law, Ethics, and Public Policy, 5,* 421–441.

Rosenthal, R. (1991). *Meta-analytic procedures for social research* (Rev. ed.). Newbury Park, CA: Sage.

Simourd, L., & Andrews, D.A. (1994). Correlates of delinquency: A look at gender differences. *Forum on Corrections Research, 6(1),* 26–31.

Sue, S. (1999). Science, ethnicity, and bias: Where have we gone wrong? *American Psychologist, 54,* 1070–1077.

Trotter, C. (1999). Working with involuntary clients: A guide to practice. Australia: Allen & Unwin.

Wilson, D. B., Gallagher, C. A., & MacKenzie, D. L. (2000). A meta-analysis of corrections-based education, vocation, and work programs for adult offenders. *Journal of Research in Crime and Delinquency, 37,* 347–368.

Wilson, S. J., Lipsey, M. W., & Soydan, H. (2003). Are mainstream programs for juvenile delinquency less effective with minority youth than majority youth? A meta-analysis of outcomes research. *Research on Social Work Practice, 13,* 3–26.

APPENDIX A: DESCRIPTION OF CCP ELEMENTS

Effective use of authority: A "firm but fair" approach to interacting with offenders. Correctional treatment providers should explicate the formal rules associated within the correctional setting such that they are made more visible, understandable, and unambiguous in application. In addition, treatment providers should seek compliance with these rules through positive reinforcement while avoiding interpersonal domination or abuse.

Appropriate modeling and reinforcing of anticriminal attitudes and behaviors through directive positive and/or negative reinforcement: The underlying goal of this approach is that offenders will learn prosocial and anticriminal attitudinal, cognitive, and behavioral patterns from their regular interactions with front-line staff.

Employing a problem-solving model: This involves capitalizing on the knowledge and skills of the treatment provider to engage the offender in resolving the key obstacles that are resulting in reduced levels of satisfaction and rewards for noncriminal pursuits.

Effective use of community resources: This has also been commonly referred to as advocacy/brokerage and is viewed as a special subset of the problem-solving component of CCP. The treatment provider (or probation officer more commonly) should be actively involved in arranging the most appropriate correctional services (e.g., job referrals, medical referrals) for the client. However, it should be noted that the value of these services is contingent upon the degree to which they are available in the surrounding community.

Relationship factors: The interpersonal influence exerted by the correctional staff member is maximized under conditions characterized by open, warm, and enthusiastic communication. An equally important consideration is the development of mutual respect and regard between the offender and correctional staff member. This approach asserts that correctional interventions will be most effective when these types of relationships exist within the treatment program.

6

Juvenile Offender Suicide

Prevalence, Risk Factors, Assessment, and Crisis Intervention Protocols

Albert R. Roberts and Kimberly Bender

Suicide is the leading cause of death in juvenile detention and correctional facilities. Moreover, incarcerated juvenile offenders have an estimated suicide risk four times greater than adolescents in the general population. To address the problem of juvenile offender suicide, this article describes the extent of the problem and protocols for intervening with this high-risk population. Procedures for crisis intervention are recommended, and we delineate and discuss Roberts's step-by-step, sequential seven-stage crisis assessment and crisis intervention model. The article concludes with an examination of the extent to which suicide assessment and prevention protocols are currently being implemented in juvenile justice facilities. The implementation of suicide prevention programs has been shown to decrease risk of suicide in juvenile offenders; however, much work is still needed to encourage facilities to implement comprehensive assessment and prevention programs nationwide.

INTRODUCTION

Suicide is the leading cause of death in juvenile justice facilities (Gallagher & Dobrin, 2006). Moreover, incarcerated juvenile offenders have an estimated suicide risk four times greater than adolescents in the general population (Memory, 1989). Researchers have pondered the reason behind elevated suicide risk in juvenile offenders. Plausible explanations include (1) juvenile justice facilities simply house extremely high-risk youth who are likely to attempt suicide whether in a facility or outside; (2) the act of living in the facility environment increases youths' risks for suicide; or (3) youth may be at extreme mental health or health crises at the time they enter juvenile justice facilities, increasing their risk of suicide (Gallagher & Dobrin, 2006). Most likely the high suicide risk of incarcerated juvenile offenders is due to a combination of individual, environmental, and situational factors. Researchers have identified specific individual risk factors as well as particular facility environments and crisis situations that are associated with suicide risk in this vulnerable population. Juvenile justice administrators and policy makers have then utilized this research to develop protocols for suicide prevention programs and crisis intervention in juvenile justice facilities.

One of the most traumatic events for an adolescent is being incarcerated for the first time and for an indeterminate period of time. This crisis is further compounded when juvenile offenders lack money to hire an attorney, are housed in isolation, and are removed from support networks of close friends and family.

For those who value the lives of all members of society, including high-risk juvenile offenders, the scientific and systematic evidence-based study of suicide and suicide prevention is both challenging and critically needed. The primary goals of this article are to identify diagnostic clues and suicide risk factors as well as step-by-step suicide prevention protocols that seem to be effective in saving lives. Specifically, this article describes the prevalence of suicide for juvenile offenders, a variety of risk factors shown to be associated with suicidal behavior in incarcerated juvenile offenders, empirically supported methods for assessing suicide risk, and current protocols for crisis intervention and suicide prevention programs in juvenile justice facilities.

Adolescents in general have heightened risk for suicidal gestures and attempts (Centers for Disease Control and Prevention, 2000). As many as 3 million youth are estimated to be at risk for suicide in a given year (Substance Abuse and Mental Health Services Administration, 2001). However, of all adolescents, those incarcerated in juvenile justice facilities are most at risk (Gray et al., 2002). Although the behavior of incarcerated juveniles is more strictly controlled and thus suicide completions may be low, suicidal behaviors are markedly high compared to adolescents in the general population. Wasserman et al. (2002) report that over 3 percent of incarcerated juveniles report attempting suicide in the previous year. Of particular concern is that adolescents in juvenile justice facilities tend to use more violent and more successful means of suicide than adolescents in the general population (Penn, Esposito, Schaeffer, Fritz, & Spirito, 2003). Due in part to this severity, it is estimated that 19 percent of juvenile offenders will be suicidal while involved in the juvenile justice system (Galloucis & Francek, 2002).

SELF-INJURIOUS BEHAVIOR

Often researchers group together self-injurious behaviors and suicidal behaviors when reporting risk. A multitude of behaviors involving harm to self such as cutting, head banging, ingesting foreign objects, and foreign substance ingestion (Cox, 2003) occur in juvenile justice settings. However, it should be noted that there is debated as to whether these behaviors have different underlying motivations than suicidal acts and should thus be categorized as behaviors distinctly different from suicidal gestures or attempts that have the potential to end one's life. Some argue that these self-injurious behaviors are indications of more serious suicidal risk in the future (Apter et al., 1995). Evans, Albers, Macari, and Mason (1996) describe a continuum with self-harming behaviors at one end, suicidal gestures and attempts in the middle, and suicide completion at the other. Research indicates that these behaviors are related; Cox (2003) found 86 percent of prisoners who completed suicide in a five-year period had histories of self-harming behaviors.

Making this distinction is of particular concern in juvenile populations as correctional staff are confronted with youth who may exhibit self-harming behaviors that are manipulative rather than suicidal. Whether expressing thoughts of harming oneself or engaging in self-harming behaviors, some juvenile offenders may be motivated by underlying efforts to avoid incarceration or to be placed in medical or psychiatric settings, perceived to be less restrictive by the youth (AACAP, 2005).

While youth in these situations may have different motivations and risks than truly suicidal youth, it is important for correctional staff to promptly report these behaviors to clinical staff and for clinical staff to thoroughly assess suicide risk. Staff should not make assumptions about the nature of self-injurious behaviors or take responsibility for distinguishing suicidal behaviors from manipulative self-harming. Mental health professionals should thoroughly assess youths' risk using collateral information in the form of staff observations, chart histories, and family reports, thereby clarifying true risk from manipulative behaviors (Hayes, 2004).

RISK FACTORS

Researchers have posited that juvenile offenders' elevated suicide risk is due to a combination of individual, environmental, and crisis situation factors (Gallagher & Dobrin, 2006). Several of these individual and environmental risk factors have been identified in empirical studies.

Individual Risk Factors.   Elevated suicide risk among detained or incarcerated juveniles has most consistently been associated with depressive symptoms and/or diagnosis (Penn et al., 2003; Rohde, Secly, & Macc, 1997; Sanislow, Grillo, Fehon, Axelrod, & McGlashan, 2003). Less consistent research has shown juvenile offenders' increased suicide risk is associated with substance abuse (Sanislow et al., 2003), young age, female gender, sexual abuse history (Morris et al., 1995), psychiatric history, living without at least one biological parent (Penn et al., 2003), impulsivity, and social impairment (Rohde et al., 1997). One particularly strong predictor for risk in both juveniles and adults, assessed in most suicide screenings, is past suicide attempts (Rohde et al., 1997; Wasserman & McReynolds, 2006).

Environmental Risk Factors.   Fear of violence and danger within juvenile justice facilities coupled with separation from support networks further heighten youths' vulnerability to suicidal ideation and behaviors (Correia, 2000). Detainees at certain types of facilities are at increased risk for suicide, including facilities responsible for screening youth for further placement such as detention centers and reception/diagnostic centers, facilities that lock doors to sleeping rooms, and facilities housing large African American populations (Gallagher & Dobrin, 2006).

Crisis Situations.   Researchers propose one final explanation for elevated rates of suicide among incarcerated juveniles beyond individual and environmental factors—that youth may be at extreme mental health or health crisis at the time they enter juvenile justice facilities, increasing their risk of suicide (Gallagher & Dobrin, 2006). The nature of arriving for intake at juvenile justice facilities may very well constitute a crisis situation for many youth. This is supported by research that indicates facilities with the role of assessment and referral have higher incidences of suicidal behavior, as described above (Gallagher & Dobrin, 2006). Evidence further supports that suicide risk further increases when juvenile detainees/offenders are held in detention centers or lockups with no way to post bail (Hayes, 1995). It is in these situations that juvenile offenders are faced with several compounded stressors. Being confronted with eventual transfer to a juvenile justice facility elicits feelings of fear, distrust, lack of control, isolation, and shame, and can often be dehumanizing. Coping with entering this environment, juvenile offenders often feel overwhelmed and hopeless, increasing their risk of suicidal behaviors (Yeager & Roberts, in press).

GUIDELINES FOR SUICIDE ASSESSMENT AND INTERVENTION IN JUVENILE JUSTICE FACILITIES

Recognizing the elevated risk of suicide in juvenile justice facilities, national organizations have come forward supporting systematic suicide prevention programs. For example, in 2005, the American Academy of Child and Adolescent Psychiatry (AACAP) developed guidelines for working with adolescents in juvenile justice settings. In this Official Action Statement, the AACAP stated that minimal standards of care in juvenile justice facilities should include: (1) screening of all youths entering a detention or correctional facility for suicide risk factors; (2) continued monitoring of juveniles identified as potential suicide risks; and (3) providing thorough mental health assessments by qualified mental health clinicians for all youth at risk (AACAP, 2005). Staff training and communication between correctional staff and clinical staff were identified as essential components of effective monitoring in suicide prevention protocol (AACAP, 2005).

COMPONENTS OF SUICIDE PREVENTION PROGRAMS

Training Correctional Staff

Although mental health professionals are responsible for thorough assessments, it is correctional staff who spend the most time with juvenile offenders. Therefore staff are in the best position to recognize behavior changes or hear comments that might warn of suicidal thoughts or behaviors and to then refer youth to mental health professionals. If a potential risk is identified by mental health professionals, staff are primarily responsible for following up, monitoring, and observing youth, thus ensuring their safety. Furthermore, in cases in which a juvenile makes a suicide attempt, staff are usually the first to respond and intervene. For all of these reasons, it is essential that correctional staff be trained as to the risk factors, crisis response procedures, and proper monitoring of potentially suicidal youth (Hayes, 1995).

Coordinating Suicide Screening and Comprehensive Suicide Assessments

There are two primary types of suicide assessments utilized in juvenile justice facilities. First, brief suicide screenings are usually implemented at a juvenile detention center by bachelor-level intake workers; this intake includes psychosocial, educational, and criminal history background and usually takes about 30 to 60 minutes. If there are any red flags such as prior suicide attempts or the presence of psychiatric disorders like bipolar or major depression, then the youth should immediately be referred for more comprehensive suicide assessment.

A more thorough assessment of youths' suicide risk should be conducted by a competent mental health professional. This critical step should begin with conducting a lethality and biopsychosocial risk assessment. This involves a relatively standard assessment of the number and duration of risk factors, including imminent danger and availability of lethal weapons, verbalization of suicide or homicide risk, need for immediate medical attention, positive and negative coping strategies, lack of family or social supports, and current drug or alcohol use (Eaton and Roberts, 2002; Roberts, 2005).

If possible, a medical assessment should include a brief summary of the presenting problem, any ongoing medical conditions, and current medications (names, dosages, and time of last dose). More specifically, suicide risk assessment examines the following: whether the youth expresses suicidal ideation, thoughts, or gestures; whether the youth has a specific suicide plan; whether he exhibits poor judgment and impulsivity; whether the youth has access to lethal means; whether the youth is exhibiting command hallucinations or delusions; and whether the youth seems high on illegal drugs and/or alcohol. Following is a list of important factors to consider in conducting a suicide assessment.

Suicide Assessment Checklist

Does client have a definite suicide plan, other than vague statement?

Has specific method been chosen?

Is method readily available?

Current or previous psychiatric history

Drug or alcohol use

Prior suicide attempts

Recent major stressors such as incarceration in dormitory with rival gang members

Rate sense of worthlessness

Rate sense of hopelessness

Rate degree of social isolation

Rate degree of depression

Rate degree of impulsivity

Rate degree of anger and hostility

Rate intent or determination to die

Overwhelming or humiliating environmental stress

To what extent is client able to focus on positive future events?

There are several useful evidence-based measures of suicide risk that accurately measure the magnitude of a client's specific psychiatric symptoms, level of depression, level of hopelessness, beliefs, behaviors, attitudes, and/or plans to commit suicide at specific times. We are listing the most commonly used suicide assessment measures that have been found to be reliable and valid with thousands of clients (Beck, Brown, & Steer, 1997; Beck, Brown, Steer, Dahlsgaard, & Grisham, 1999; Beck, Steer, Beck, & Newman, 1993; Brown, 2002; Linehan, Goodstein, Nielsen, & Chiles, 1983; Roberts & Grau, 1970; and Roberts & Yeager, 2005). It is our firm belief that all crisis counselors, correctional counselors, psychiatric screeners, forensic social workers, psychiatric mental health nurses, probation officers, and psychiatrists be trained in the use of the following suicide assessment tools:

- Beck Hopelessness Scales (Beck, Weissman, Lester, & Trexler, 1974)
- Beck Depression Inventory (Beck, Ward, Mendelson, Mock, & Erbaugh, 1961)
- Rosenberg Self-Esteem (Rosenberg, 1965)
- Buss-Durkee Hostility-Guilt Inventory (Buss & Durkee, 1957)
- Linehan Reasons for Living Inventory (Linehan, Goodstein, Nielsen, & Chiles, 1983)
- Brief Reasons for Living Inventory (Ivanoff, Jang, Smyth, & Linehan, 1994)
- The Suicidal Ideation Scale (Rudd, 1989)
- Suicide Status Form (Jobes, Jacoby, Cimbolic, & Hustead, 1997)
- Scale for Suicide Ideation-Worst Point in Time (Beck et al., 1999)
- The Parasuicide History Interview (Linehan, Wagner, & Cox, 1983)
- The Juvenile Suicide Assessment (Gallousis & Francek, 2002)
- Suicide Intent Scale (Beck, Schuyler, & Herman, 1974)
- Personality Assessment Schedule (Tryrer, Alexander, Cicchetti, Cohen, & Remington, 1979)

While standardized assessment tools have great utility to mental health professionals working in juvenile justice facilities, it should be mentioned that there are critics of relying solely on these tools in conducting assessments Correia (2000) strongly suggests that a certain level of clinical judgment is an essential part of conducting a comprehensive suicide assessment. Mental health professionals should use standardized tools for guidance to make sure they are considering all relevant factors and as support in the case that they need to defend their assessment in court. However, they are warned against using assessments merely for a cutoff score without supplementing results with clinical judgment.

Supervision and Housing

The ability of correctional staff to prevent self-harming behaviors and to respond promptly in suicide attempts is dependent on the level of supervision imposed by the suicide prevention protocol. Supervision of youth can range from one-on-one continuous observation in very serious cases to more standard frequent checking. Roving staff should make continuous but intermittent/unpredictable rounds, observing not only the youth under supervision but also the cell for slight changes in content (presence of sheets, blankets, shoelaces) and alterations to the safety features (altered room fixtures) (Hayes, 1995; Yeager & Roberts, in press).

In addition to supervision, youth at risk should be housed with other offenders to reduce alienation and improve staff's ability to monitor them (Correia, 2000). Living spaces should be carefully selected; all dangerous objects should be removed, and dormitory rooms or cells should be located close to staff (Hayes, 1995). Further, removal of prisoner's clothing (excluding belts and shoelaces) as well as physical restraints should be avoided and used as a last resort (Hayes, 1995).

Documentation and Review

Mental health professionals should document not only their final determination after an assessment and their recommendations for precautions to be taken but also the information used to make that determination (Correia, 2000). This documentation serves the purpose of protecting the professional and the institution in case of lawsuits. It is also essential that this documentation be reviewed by administrators in cases when suicides are completed to determine if the appropriate prevention and intervention procedures were taken, any factors that could have further indicated suicide risk, and make recommendations for changes in policy/procedures as needed (Hayes, 1995).

CRISIS INTERVENTION

One particularly important component of suicide prevention planning is establishing crisis intervention procedures for situations in which youth are at risk. Crisis intervention, also known as emotional "first aid," focuses on rapid assessment, "stabilizing the individual, and resolving acute crisis episodes and emotionally volatile conflicts with a minimum number of sessions" (Roberts, 2005; p. 779).

The circumstances and situations warranting crisis intervention are as endless and diverse as the population served. For some individuals dealing with ambivalence, thoughts of self-harm and of immediate gratification/satisfaction constitute a sporadic event. For some, the thought of suicide mistakenly appears to be an immediate fix to an emotionally painful, intensely fearful, or acutely embarrassing situation that seems insurmountable. For the chemically dependent individual, suicide may be the easy way out of a cycle of substance dependence and withdrawal.

Crisis intervention generally refers to a counselor, behavioral clinician or therapist entering into the life situation of an individual to alleviate the impact of a crisis episode in order to facilitate and mobilize the resources of those directly affected. Rapid assessment and timely intervention on the part of crisis counselors, social workers, psychologists, or child psychiatrists are of paramount importance (Roberts, 2005).

Crisis workers should be active and directive while displaying a nonjudgmental, accepting, hopeful, and positive attitude. Crisis workers need to help crisis clients to identify protective factors, inner strengths, psychological hardiness, or resiliency factors that can be utilized for ego bolstering. Effective crisis workers are able to gauge the seven stages of crisis intervention described in Figure 1, while being flexible and realizing that several stages of intervention may overlap. Crisis intervention should culminate with a restoration of cognitive functioning, crisis resolution, and cognitive mastery (Roberts, 2005).

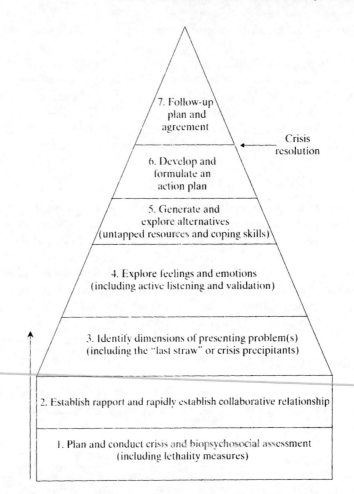

FIGURE 1
Roberts' Seven Stage Crisis Intervention Model
Source: Copyright © Albert R. Roberts. 1991. Reprinted by permission of the author.

DECISION MAKING ACCORDING TO CLASSIFICATION OF RISK LEVEL

According to the *Crisis Intervention Handbook* (Roberts & Yeager, 2005), all practitioners should be required to determine imminent, moderate, and low suicide risk among impulsive, depressed, and/or psychotic adolescents and young adults. In doing so the individual practitioner should be required to assign the youth to the most appropriate level of care. Ideally, the vital role of crisis clinician in correctional settings should be held by professionals with graduate degrees in a mental health field. The implementation of Roberts's seven-stage model provides appropriate interventions for resolution of moderate and low suicidal ideation immediately after an individual seeks assistance. Application of the seven-stage model for low- and moderate-risk youth can provide insight in a nonthreatening manner to assist the youth in development of cognitive stabilization. However, practitioners must decide when and with whom it is appropriate to use the seven-stage model. For imminent-risk youth, more secure levels of care are necessary. Making this decision is often the first stage of crisis intervention. Ideally there should be coverage in large facilities 24 hours, 7 days per week. If budget constraints prevent this, then mental health clinicians should be on-call on a rotating basis evenings and weekends. The following flowchart describes the clinical pathways used in classifying a potentially suicidal youth and determining a course of action.

In essence crisis intervention and suicide prevention includes certain primary steps in an attempt to prevent suicide. A trained mental health clinician working with juvenile offenders should:

1.   Conduct a rapid lethality and biopsychosocial assessment.

2.   Attempt to establish rapport, and at the same time communicate a willingness to help the person in an acute suicidal crisis.

3.   Help the person in crisis to develop a plan of action, which links him or her to hospital-based or mental health based continuum of care. The most frequent outcome for depressed or suicidal individuals in immediate danger in the community is that they are transported to psychiatric screening and intake at a forensic psychiatric facility or inpatient hospital psychiatric unit or residential addictions treatment program (Roberts & Yeager, 2005). In juvenile and adult correctional facilities depressed and/or suicidal individuals often go undetected until they have made a serious suicide attempt.

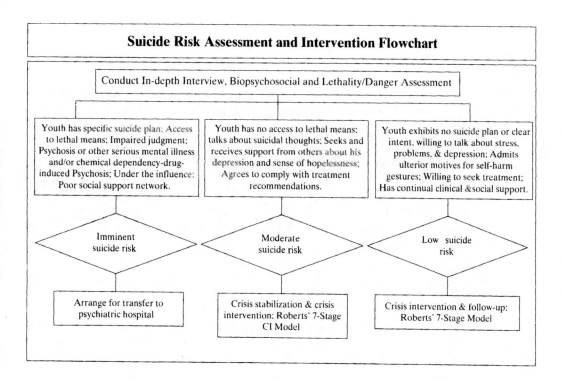

Suicide Risk Assessment and Intervention Flowchart

Conduct In-depth Interview, Biopsychosocial and Lethality/Danger Assessment

| Youth has specific suicide plan; Access to lethal means; Impaired judgment; Psychosis or other serious mental illness and/or chemical dependency-drug-induced Psychosis; Under the influence; Poor social support network. | Youth has no access to lethal means; talks about suicidal thoughts; Seeks and receives support from others about his depression and sense of hopelessness; Agrees to comply with treatment recommendations. | Youth exhibits no suicide plan or clear intent, willing to talk about stress, problems, & depression; Admits ulterior motives for self-harm gestures; Willing to seek treatment; Has continual clinical & social support. |

| Imminent suicide risk | Moderate suicide risk | Low suicide risk |

| Arrange for transfer to psychiatric hospital | Crisis stabilization & crisis intervention: Roberts' 7-Stage CI Model | Crisis intervention & follow-up: Roberts' 7-Stage Model |

The crisis mental health clinician assumes full responsibility for the case when a correctional officer or correctional administrator notifies them. The youth cannot be rushed and handled simply by quick referral to a hospital forensic unit. Crisis clinicians should follow the case until complete transfer of responsibility has been accomplished by some other agency/facility assuming the responsibility. The crisis worker should complete the state-mandated mental health and psychiatric screening report, which makes an initial determination as to whether the youth is a danger to him/herself or others. If the youth is being transported, this report should be given to the ambulance driver and faxed to the intake worker on duty at the receiving forensic unit or hospital. In other cases when there is low suicide risk and a correctional officer, supervisor, or case manager is taking responsibility for the youth in crisis, it is important to give the juvenile offender the names of the person to contact in an emergency. The ultimate goal of all crisis and suicide prevention services is to strive to relieve intense emotional pain and acute crisis episodes, while helping the youth to find positive ways to cope with life.

It is imperative for all crisis clinicians to establish rapport with the youth in crisis by listening in a patient, hopeful, self-assured, interested, and knowledgeable manner. The skilled crisis clinician tries to communicate an attitude that the person has done the right thing by asking for help and also conveys a willingness and an ability to help. An empathetic ear is provided to the youth in crisis in order to relieve his or her intense stress through active listening (Yeager & Gregiore, 2005)

After listening to the youth's story and asking several key questions the mental health clinician makes a determination as to whether the juvenile has a high suicide risk. If the youth has a lethal method (sharp instrument or means to hang themselves) still readily available and a specific plan for suicide, or has previously attempted suicide, then he or she is considered as having a high suicide risk. In sharp contrast, youths evaluated as low suicide risk still need help but they are primarily manipulative, or depressed and expressing ambivalent thoughts about what it's like to be in heaven verses hell. They have not yet planned the specific details of suicide. Other youths may need emergency medical attention (Roberts & Yeager, 2005).

With regard to transferring the juvenile offender to an inpatient forensic hospital unit versus a mental health secure unit within a juvenile correctional facility, the most important determinant should be imminent danger and lethal means to suicide. It is also extremely important for crisis clinicians to make a multiaxial differential diagnosis, which determines acute or chronic psychosocial stressors, dysfunctional relationships, decreased self esteem or hopelessness, severe or unremitting anxiety, recent fights and violent outbursts, personality disorders (particularly borderline personality disorders), major depressive disorders, bipolar disorders, and comorbidity (APA, 2003) Making accurate assessments and predicting short-term risk of suicide (one to three days) has been found to be much more reliable than predicting long-term risk (Simon, 1992).

CASE STUDY AND PSYCHOLOGICAL CASE AUTOPSY

The following case study illustrates a juvenile suicide act and the precipitating factors. We outline a typical clinical response and crisis intervention procedures used to respond to suicide attempts and self-injurious behaviors in juvenile justice facilities. While graphic in nature, this case is based on the true experiences of a suicidal juvenile. Identifying information has been removed to ensure confidentiality.

CASE #1: VANESSA

Vanessa is a 17-year-old African American female being held on charges of attempted murder, as she allegedly shot another woman whom she found in bed with her boyfriend. At the time of her arrest Vanessa had screamed to her boyfriend that "she would never go to trial for this crime" and that he would "have to live the rest of his life with the piss poor decision he had made." Vanessa was insistent that this was going to be his problem in the long run, that this was not going to be her problem, and that she was not going to spend the remainder of her life paying for his mistake.

On the third day of her incarceration in the detention facility, Vanessa noticed she was being stuck by a sharp piece of steal on the bottom edge of the table in the lunchroom. Vanessa began to bend the metal back and forth until it broke free from the table. She cautiously cupped the small piece of metal and slipped it into her shoe. She then walked compliantly with the other young women back to her cell block. Once in her cell Vanessa sat quietly in her bunk sharpening the small piece of metal by rubbing it against the concrete wall of the cell. Within a one-hour time period the metal had become sharp as a result of the friction against the concrete, later examination would indicate cuts on Vanessa's thumb and index finger from the period of time that she worked the piece of metal sharpening the edge.

That night after lights went out Vanessa began to cut. She first cut her left arm vertically beginning at the wrist and stopping at the bend of the elbow. She then cut a half-moon from each ear forward to the clavicle at the connection to the sternum. She then pulled her bed sheet to her chin and waited. A correctional officer making routine rounds identified blood on the sheet near Vanessa's left arm. At the time of intervention Vanessa was unconscious. Pressure was applied to the wounds and she was transported to a local emergency department. Vanessa's blood loss was so severe she has experienced brain damage. She has lost coordination of her left side and now has difficulty articulating when she speaks.

Case Autopsy

Once stabilized Vanessa was seen by a psychiatric social worker. She denied being suicidal until the point when the opportunity presented for self-harm. She reports, "I remember sitting in the lunch area thinking 'this is it; this is the way out.'" The establishment of rapport required a significant period of time as Vanessa has experienced numerous abusive relationships throughout her life. Working with the same psychiatric social worker over a four-week period of time provided the opportunity to identify crisis precipitants. Lethality did not subside immediately, in fact Vanessa remained on suicide precautions with one-to-one sitters round the clock for two weeks. Typically stage three of Roberts' seven-stage model is to identify major problems and crisis precipitants, including the last straw. However, in this case, the focus was not on the precipitating factor, instead this stage examined the impulsive act of self-harm and developing self-protective skills. In this case, stage four, examining feelings and emotions focused primarily on issues of hurt, loss, and fear of the unknown. Vanessa was able to begin examining the issues. She progressed into stage five of Roberts' model in week three of her treatment when she began to examine alternative behaviors to self-harm and began cooperating with authorities seeking a reduced sentence. By the fourth week of her hospitalization Vanessa had developed a plan of action and appeared to have a more realistic grasp of the nature of her legal issues including a targeted approach toward resolution of her pending legal problems.

Vanessa returned to the county facility and completed the trial. She was sentenced to two years. She completed her sentence. While incarcerated Vanessa was maintained on an antidepressant medication. She attended support groups to address issues of abandonment, anger, and impulse control. Vanessa transitioned to a women's halfway house following 18 months and was later released on parole. Following the initial rocky start, Vanessa appears to have benefited from her experience. She verbalizes having a clear understanding of where she needs to be in her life and what she will need to do to accomplish her goals. Vanessa is seeking admission to the local community college in the fall and hopes to attend a nursing program as a long-term goal.

There are some cases in which suicide is not the intention; in fact, nearly half of all suicides are preceded by an attempt at suicide that does not end in death. Those with a history of such attempts are 23 times more likely to eventually end their own lives than those without a history of previous suicide attempt. Some engage in actions best described as acts of deliberate self-harm, frequently referred to in the literature as parasuicide. Vanessa's case also demonstrates the acute need for corrections staff and clinical professionals in the juvenile justice system to be cognizant of the risk level of juveniles in their custody. When levels of desperation combine with means for self-harm, effective crisis response requires knowledgeable, competent, and keenly aware staff members. Establishing protocols for crisis intervention, such as those described in this article, can aid staff in systematically responding to a suicidal crisis.

THE STATE OF JUVENILE JUSTICE CENTERS' SUICIDE ASSESSMENT AND PREVENTION

While clear protocols and guidelines exist for preventing juvenile offender suicide, juvenile justice facilities vary greatly in the degree to which guidelines for suicide prevention and crisis intervention are currently implemented. Many juvenile justice facilities fail to follow basic guidelines necessary to comprehensively assess suicide risk and mental health needs in incarcerated youth, whereas others invest great time and effort in developing and implementing comprehensive prevention programs (Coalition for Juvenile Justice, 2000).

The OJJDP recently released findings from the 2002 Juvenile Residential Facility Census (JRFC; Sickmund, 2006). After polling 3,534 juvenile facilities, the JRFC survey results indicated that 68 percent of facilities screen all youth for suicide risk, 17 percent screen some youth, and 15 percent didn't evaluate any youth. These findings indicate both concern and improvement. It is disconcerting that a substantial percentage of facilities in self-reports are not screening youth for suicide risk at all. On the other hand, from 2000 to 2002 the percentage of facilities that reported that they do screen all youth for suicide risk increased 6 percent, a noted improvement.

In 2002 the majority of facilities screening all youth did so by the end of their first day in custody (66%) or by the end of the first week (15%). Furthermore, 56 percent of facilities that screened all or some youth used mental health professionals with masters degrees in psychology or social work to conduct screenings. Most other facilities relied on counselors trained by mental health professionals in the screening process. Smaller institutions were more likely than larger ones to not have a suicide assessment process in place. Detention centers, diagnostic centers, and training schools were more likely than shelters, group homes, boot camps and wilderness camps to screen for suicide (Sickmund, 2006).

Even more important than the rate of screening, is evaluating the benefit screening can have on reducing juveniles' suicide attempts and completions. An analysis of the JRFC data (Gallagher & Dobrin, 2005) shows that facilities that screened youth within the first 24 hours significantly reduced the odds of youth making serious suicide attempts while in their facilities. This is true even for facilities more at risk for suicide due to size or type. Furthermore, facilities that systematically screened all youth rather than selecting some youth to screen as necessary significantly reduced risk of serious suicide attempts (Gallagher & Dobrin, 2005). These findings justify the recent investment in establishing thorough suicide screening plans that has taken place across many large facilities and argue for this trend to be implemented in smaller, private institutions across the country.

CONCLUSION AND RECOMMENDATIONS FOR THE FUTURE

There is an increasing critical need for mental health professionals to be recruited and hired to work in juvenile justice and adult correctional settings. It is important to find straightforward, realistic approaches to crisis intervention with increasingly complex populations. Our goal in this article has been to provide evidence-based suicide assessment guidelines, suicide risk factors and suicide screening procedures, and a step-by-step framework for crisis intervention and suicide prevention. Correctional treatment specialists and mental health practitioners working within complex crisis-oriented juvenile justice settings should consistently consider the utility of instruments to assess and reassess juvenile offender suicide ideation, and cost and potential outcomes of chosen interventions. The application of best practices and systematic protocols such as the Roberts' seven stage crisis intervention model will assist practitioners by providing a systematic framework for addressing suicidal crises within an institutional and sometimes volatile environment. The challenge for all mental health practitioners is to fully develop their knowledge and skills in rapid assessment, suicide prevention, and treatment alternatives.

REFERENCES

AACAP. (2005). Practical parameter for the assessment and treatment of youth in juvenile detention and correctional facilities. *Journal of the American Academy of Child and Adolescent Psychiatry, 44*(10), 1085–1098.

American Psychiatric Association Steering Committee on Practice Guidelines (APA). (2003). *Practice Guideline for the Assessment and Treatment of Patients with Suicidal Behavior.* Washington, DC: American Psychiatric Association.

Apter, A., Gothele, D., Orbach, I., Weizman, R., Ratzoni, G., Hareven, D., & Tyano, S. (1995). Correlation of suicidal and violent behavior in different diagnostic categories of hospitalized adolescent patients. *Journal of the American Academy of Child and Adolescent Psychiatry, 34*, 912–918.

Beck, A. T., Brown, G., & Steer, R. (1997). Psychometric characteristics of the scale for suicide ideation with psychiatric outpatients. *Behavior Research and Therapy, 11*, 1039–1046.

Beck, A. T., Brown, G., Steer, R., Dahlsgaard, K., & J. Grisham. (1999). Suicide ideation at its worst point: A predictor of eventual suicide in psychiatric outpatients. *Suicide and Life-Threatening Behavior, 29*(1), 1–9.

Beck, A. T., & Lester, D. (1976). Components of suicidal intent in completed and attempted suicides. *Journal of Psychology: Interdisciplinary & Applied 92*(1), 35–38.

Beck, A. T., Steer, R. A., Beck, J. S., & Newman, C.F. (1993). Hopelessness, depression, suicidal ideation, and clinical diagnosis of depression. *Suicide and Life-Threatening Behavior, 23*, 139–145.

Beck, A. T., Schuyler, D., & Herman, I. (1974). Development of suicidal intent scales. In A. T. Beck, H. L. P. Resnick, & D. J. Lettieri (Eds). *The Prediction of Suicide* (pp. 45–56). Bowie, MD: Charles Press.

Beck, A. T., Ward, C. H., Mendelson, M., Mock, J., & Erbaugh, J. (1961). An inventory for measuring depression. *Archive of General Psychiatry, 4*, 561–571.

Beck, A. T., Weissman, A., Lester, D., & Trexler, L. (1974). The measurement of pessimism: The Hopelessness Scale. *Journal of Consulting and Clinical Psychology, 42*(6), 861–865.

Berman, A. L. (1975). Self-destructive behavior and suicide: Epidemiology and taxonomy. In A. R. Roberts, (Ed.), *Self-Destructive Behavior* (pp. 5–20). Springfield, IL: Charles C. Thomas.

Brown, G. (2002). A review of suicide assessment measures for intervention research with adults and older adults. Unpublished manuscript. Department of Psychiatry, University of Pennsylvania.

Burgess, A. W., & Roberts, A. R. (2000). Crisis intervention for persons diagnosed with clinical disorders based on the Stress-Crisis Continuum. In A. R. Roberts (Ed.), *Crisis intervention handbook: Assessment, treatment and research*, (2nd ed. pp. 56–76). New York: Oxford University Press.

Buss, A. H., & Durkee, A., (1957). An inventory for assessing different kinds of hostility. *Journal of Consulting Psychology, 21*, 343–349.

Centers for Disease Control and Prevention. (2000). Youth risk behavior surveillance—United States, 1999. MMWR Publication No. 49 (No.SS-05), 1-96, Atlanta, GA: Centers for Disease Control and Prevention.

Coalition for Juvenile Justice. (2000). *Handle with care: Surviving the mental health needs of young offenders*. Washington, DC: Coalition for Juvenile Justice.

Correia, K. M. (2000). Suicide assessment in a prison environment: A proposed protocol. *Criminal Justice and Behavior, 27*(5), 581–599.

Cox, G. (2003). Screening inmates for suicide using static risk factors. *The Behavior Therapist, 26*, 212–214.

Eaton, Y., & Roberts, A. R. (2002). Frontline crisis intervention: Step-by-step practice guidelines with case applications. In A. R. Roberts & G. J. Greene (Eds)., *Social workers' desk reference* (pp. 89–96). New York: Oxford University Press.

Evans, W., Albers, E., Macari, D., & Mason, A. (1996). Suicide ideation, attempts and abuse among incarcerated gang and nongang delinquents. *Child and Adolescent Social Work Journal, 13*, 115–126.

Gallagher, C. A., & Dobrin, A. (2006). Deaths in juvenile justice residential facilities. *Journal of Adolescent Health, 38*, 662–668.

Gallagher, C. A., & Dobrin, A. (2005). The association between suicide screening practices and attempts requiring emergency care in juvenile justice facilities. *Journal of the American Academy of Child and Adolescent Psychiatry, 44*(5), 485–493.

Galloucis, M., & Francek, H. (2002). The Juvenile Suicide Assessment: An instrument for the assessment and management of suicide risk with incarcerated juveniles. *International Journal of Emergency Mental Health, 4*(3), 181–199.

Gray, D., Achilles, J., Keller, T. et al. (2002). Utah youth suicide study, phase I: Government agency contact before death. *Journal of the American Academy of Child and Adolescent Psychiatry, 412,* 427–434.

Hayes, L. (2000). Suicide prevention in juvenile facilities. *Juvenile Justice, 7*(1), 40–53.

Hayes, L. (1995). *Prison suicide: An overview and guide to prevention.* Alexandria, VA: National Center on Institutions and Alternatives.

Hayes, L. M. (2004). *Juvenile Suicide Confinement: A National Survey. Office of Juvenile Justice and Delinquency Prevention.* Alexandria, VA: National Center on Institutions and Alternatives.

Ivanoff, A., Jang, S. J., Smyth, N. F., & Linehan, M. M. (1994). Fewer reasons for staying alive when you are thinking of killing yourself: The Brief Resons for Living Inventory. *Journal of Psychopathology and Behavioral Assessment, 16*(1), 1–13.

Jobes, D. A., Jacoby, A., Cimbolic, P., & Hustead, L.A. (1997). Assessment and treatment of suicidal clients in a university counseling center. *Journal of Counseling Psychology, 44*(4), 368–377.

Kovacs, M., Beck, Aaron, T., & Weissman, A., (1976). The communication of suicidal intent: A reexamination. *Archives of General Psychiatry, 33*(2), 198–201.

Linehan, M. M., Goodstein, J. L., Nielsen, S. L., & Chiles, J. (1983). Reasons for staying alive when you are thinking of killing yourself: The Reasons for Living Inventory. *Journal of Consulting and Clinical Psychology, 51*(2), 276–286.

Linehan, M. M., Wagner, A. W., & Cox, G. (1983). Parasuicide history interview: Comprehensive assessment of parasuicidal behavior. Unpublished manuscript. University of Washington, Seattle.

Memory, J. (1989). Juvenile suicides in secure detention facilities: Correction of published rates. *Death Studies, 13,* 455–463.

Morris, R. E., Harrison, E. A., Knox, G. W., Tromanhauser, E., Marquis, D. K., & Watts, L. L. (1995). Health risk behavioral survey from 39 juvenile correctional facilities in the United States. *Journal of Adolescent Health, 17,* 334–344.

Penn, J. V., Esposito, C. L., Schaeffer, L. E., Fritz, G. K., & Spirito, A. (2003). Suicide attempts and self-mutilative behavior in a juvenile correctional facility. *Journal of the American Academy of Child and Adolescent Psychiatry, 42,* 762–769.

Roberts, A. R. (2005). Bridging the past and present to the future of crisis intervention and crisis management. In A. Roberts (Ed.), *Crisis intervention handbook: Assessment, treatment and research.* (pp. 3–34; and glossary, pp. 775–791). New York: Oxford University Press.

Roberts, A. R., & Grau, J. J. (1970). Procedures used in crisis intervention by suicide prevention agencies. *Public Health Reports, 85*(8), 691–697.

Roberts, A. R., & Yeager, K. R. (2005). Lethality assessment and crisis intervention with persons presenting with suicidal ideation. In A. Roberts (Ed.), *Crisis intervention handbook: Assessment, treatment and research,* (pp. 35–63). New York: Oxford University Press.

Roberts, A. R., Yeager, K. R., & Streiner, D. L. (2004). Evidence-based practice with comorbid substance abuse, mental illness and suicidality: Can the evidence be found? *Brief Treatment and Crisis Intervention, 4*(2), 123–136.

Roberts, R. E., Chen, Y., & Roberts, C. R. (1997). Ethnocultural differences in prevalence of adolescent suicidal behaviors. *Suicide and Life-Threatening Behavior, 27,* 208–217.

Rohde, P., Seeley, J. R., & Mace, D. E. (1997). Correlates of suicidal behavior in a juvenile detention population. *Suicide and Life-Threatening Behavior, 27,* 164–175.

Rosenberg, M. (1965). *Society and the adolescent self-image.* Princeton, NJ: Princeton University Press.

Rudd, M. (1989). The prevalence of suicidal ideation among college students. *Suicide and Life-Threatening Behavior, 19*(2), 173–183.

Rudd, M., & Joiner, T. (1998). The assessment, management, and treatment of suicidality: Toward clinically informed and balanced standards of care. *Clinical Psychology: Science and Practice, 5,* 135–150.

Simon, R. I. (1992). *Psychiatry and Law for Clinicians*. Washington, DC: American Psychiatric Press.

Sanislow, C. A., Grillo, C. M., Fehon, D. C., Axelrod, S. R., & McGlashan, T. H. (2003). Correlates of suicide risk in juvenile detainees and adolescent inpatients. *Journal of the American Academy of Child and Adolescent Psychiatry, 42*, 234–240.

Sickmund, M. (June 2006). *Juvenile Residential Facility Census, 2002: Selected findings*. Juvenile Offenders and Victims National Report Serious Bulletin.

Substance Abuse and Mental Health Services Administration. (2001). *Summary of findings from the 2000 National Household Survey on Drug Abuse* (NHSDA Series: H-13, DHHS Publication No. SMA 01–3549) Rockville, MD: Author.

Tyrer, P., Alexander, M., Cicchetti, D., Cohen, M., & Remington, M. (1979). Reliability of a schedule for rating personality disorders. *British Journal of Psychiatry, 135*, 168–174.

U.S. Department of Health and Human Services. (2001). *National strategy for suicide prevention: Goals and objectives for action*. Rockville, Md.: author.

Wasserman, G. A., & McReynolds, L. S. (2006). Suicide risk at juvenile justice intake. *Suicide and Life-Threatening Behavior, 36*(2), 239–249.

Weishaar, M. E. (2004). A cognitive-behavioral approach to suicide risk reduction in crisis intervention. In A. R. Roberts, & K. Yeager (Eds.). *Evidence-based practice manual: Research and outcome measures in health and human services* (pp. 749–757). New York: Oxford University Press.

Yeager, K. R., & Gregoire, T. K. (2005). Crisis intervention application of brief solution-focused therapy in addictions. In A. R. Roberts (Ed.), *Crisis intervention handbook: Assessment, treatment and research* (2nd ed., pp. 566–601). New York: Oxford University Press.

Yeager, K. R., & Roberts, A. R., (2004). Mental illness, substance dependence and suicidality: Secondary data analysis. In A. R. Roberts and K. R. Yeager (Eds.), *Evidence-based practice manual: Research and outcome measures in health and human services* (pp. 70–75). New York, Oxford University Press.

Yeager, K. R., & Roberts, A. R. (In Press). Prevention of prisoner sudden deaths by asphyxiation, hanging, and taser induced 50,000 volt shocks: Emerging safety guidelines and suicide screening protocols. *Brief Treatment and Crisis Intervention*.

7

Finding Evidence-Based Juvenile Offender Treatment Programs
A National Survey

Albert R. Roberts and Kimberly Bender

❖

Systematic evaluation of juvenile offender treatment programs is essential to ensuring that juvenile offenders are rehabilitated and returned to the community with reduced risk of recidivism. Unfortunately very few treatment programs have the funding or staff designated to systematically study their treatment outcomes. This national survey assessed program administrators' rationales for designating certain programs as model offender treatment programs worthy of replication. Findings indicate that less than 15 percent of administrators responding to the survey based their program implementation decisions on systematic research or program evaluations. Additionally, this study uses outcome data provided from program administrators to identify current programs with reduced recidivism 12 months postrelease. Results highlight nine model programs, discussing featured components of each program and describing program outcomes. Across offender treatment programs, individualized flexible treatment plans, multifaceted education/occupational skill building, and supportive aftercare services appear to be important components of successful programs. Implications for evidence-based practice in juvenile offender treatment programs are discussed.

INTRODUCTION

Some progress has been made in identifying juvenile offender treatment programs that demonstrate success in reducing recidivism. In 1987, the first national survey of empirically based treatment programs for juvenile offenders, published in the *Juvenile and Family Court Journal*, found only five programs with six-month postrelease success (Roberts, 1987). The current replicated survey, almost two decades later, found nine programs with outcome measures demonstrating at least 12-months postrelease success (Roberts, 2004). The aim of this study is twofold: (1) to examine administrators' rationale for recommending their programs as successful enough to be worthy of replication in other jurisdictions, and (2) to identify programs with reduced recidivism 12 months postrelease; including common program components that seem to lead to positive outcomes.

Over the past century, criminologists and correctional researchers have demonstrated that large juvenile prisons, also known as state training schools, are usually ineffective sanctions for rehabilitating delinquents. Most studies of juvenile offenders released from large state training schools during the past three decades have reported consistently high rates of recidivism. In fact, past research indicates that between 55 percent and 91 percent of juvenile offenders are rearrested within two years of release from a juvenile institution (Roberts, 2004).

Despite fervent interest with juvenile offender treatment, there is concern about the future of juvenile justice and the quality of treatment and rehabilitation services. Criminal justice practitioners, forensic social workers, and psychologists must be considerably more than well-intentioned, caring people who want to help troubled youth. Practitioners in juvenile justice must learn how to become active producers and consumers of evidence-based studies. Evidence-based practice (EBP) is a systematic process that integrates the best research evidence with intervention or treatment methods most likely to change the lawbreaking behavior of juvenile offenders. Evidence-based decision making requires treatment staff to identify and understand the psychosocial needs of juvenile offenders under their supervision and how to determine the ways in which the evidence applies to their clients.

In the past, too many program administrators have relied on intuition, rather then on standardized outcome measures, to determine effectiveness. It is imperative that the results of systematic program evaluations and research guide state and local juvenile justice agency decisions about which interventions to adopt and implement. The following review of the literature highlights treatments with empirical support for decreasing delinquency and recidivism among juvenile offenders.

LITERATURE REVIEW

In a study of general delinquency, Lipsey (1995) concluded that some delinquency treatment does work; in a meta-analysis of 400 studies, juvenile delinquents receiving treatment reduced recidivism at a rate 10 percent higher than untreated youth. Furthermore, Lipsey (1995) found juveniles receiving treatment improved more relative to untreated youth in psychological outcomes (28% relative improvement), interpersonal adjustment (12% relative improvement), and school participation (12% relative improvement). However, there was great variation in effect sizes reported in the studies reviewed by Lipsey. Some deterrence programs such as shock incarceration actually resulted in increasing delinquent behaviors. Programs aimed at supervision and casework had moderate effects, and programs with structured behavioral and skill-building orientations had large effects in reducing delinquent behavior. Lipsey (1995) concluded that effective treatment programs target behavioral, training and skills issues, are implemented with high quality, and are provided intensively.

One concern with taking such a broad approach to studying effectiveness is that it may not capture the diversity in severity of offenses committed by offenders. Lipsey and Wilson (1998) narrowed his focus slightly when he conducted another meta-analysis of effective interventions with serious juvenile offenders. Results from this study confirmed that interventions are indeed effective with serious offender populations. With serious offenders, as with general delinquents, treatment results varied greatly across treatment type; however, the most effective treatments reduced recidivism by about 40 percent compared to untreated youth. Positive treatment effects were shown for interpersonal skills training, behavioral programs, and programs that offered multiple services at once. Moderate but generally positive effects were found for employment training, academic programs, casework, and family/group therapy. Again, deterrence programs were shown to have negative effects, resulting in increased recidivism compared to control groups.

More narrowly focused studies have recently examined the effectiveness of specific treatments, resulting in varying degrees of positive outcomes for juvenile offenders. In their meta-analysis examining the effects of cognitive-behavioral (CBT) programs for offenders, Landenberger and Lipsey (2005) found CBT to be equally effective with both adult offenders and juveniles. CBT was especially useful in reducing recidivism in high-risk offenders and was effective across secure and community settings. Two particular facets of CBT, the anger control and interpersonal problem-solving components, were associated with much larger effect sizes than were victim impact and behavior modification components (Landenberger & Lipsey, 2005). Other meta-analyses have found similar support for cognitive-behavioral interventions with juvenile and adult offenders (Wilson, Bouffard, & MacKenzie, 2005), with some studies citing particular support for cognitive-behavioral rather than purely behavior modification treatment (Pearson, Lipton, Cleland, & Yee, 2002).

Wilderness challenge programs have also been examined through meta-analysis for their effectiveness in changing outcomes for delinquent youth. Wilson and Lipsey (2000) found that wilderness challenge programs, particularly short-term programs of six weeks or less, resulted in mean recidivism (29%) significantly lower than comparison participants (37%). Programs that offered individual, family, or group therapy sessions in the evenings after strenuous backpacking expeditions were most effective, suggesting that therapeutic components aid youth in processing the defining experiences of the wilderness challenge programs (Wilson & Lipsey, 2000).

Wilson, Lipsey, and Soydan (2003) addressed the gap in effectiveness research with ethnic minority juvenile offenders in their meta-analysis comparing mainstream offender treatment programs' effectiveness for minority and majority youth. Examining mainstream interventions such as institutional and noninstitutional counseling, casework, and service brokerage–type services, the authors found these interventions to be equally effective for minority and majority youth. Results also indicated that these mainstream programs produced modest effect sizes as compared to specialized educational, psychological, and behavioral programs. Key elements associated with effectiveness for both minority and majority youth included a focus on engaging youth, treatment integrity, and service delivery by counselors rather than juvenile justice personnel (Wilson & Lipsey, 2000; Wilson et al., 2003).

Just as studies of effectiveness should focus on adjudicated youth, examining effective prevention programs for youth in early stages of delinquency is equally important. Through a meta-analysis of 165 studies of school-based prevention programs, Wilson, Gottfredson, and Najaka (2001) found that school-based prevention programs are effective in decreasing substance use, truancy, and some conduct problems but did not significantly reduce delinquency. Furthermore, even significant results yielded small effect sizes and varied widely across intervention types. Programs consistently showing effectiveness were those that promoted self-control and social competency using cognitive-behavioral and behavioral instructional methods while non-cognitive-behavioral counseling did not have positive effects.

The state of research has evolved in the past two decades in rigorously identifying treatment modalities successful in working with juvenile offenders. A brief review of the literature reveals support for several treatment modalities including cognitive-behavioral treatment, behavior modification, academic/occupational skills training, and interpersonal skill building. Furthermore research suggests that multimodal treatment programs may best target the multiple needs of offenders.

The current study builds on this knowledge by surveying current juvenile justice programs in order to identify juvenile offender treatment programs currently being implemented nationwide that seem to be successful in reducing recidivism. By identifying current model programs, we are better able to discern what is working in the field and how programs currently being implemented fit into the context of empirical knowledge regarding treatment effectiveness with juvenile offenders. Furthermore, by contacting program administrators directly, we are able to examine the rationale by which juvenile justice administrators justify their labeling of a program as a model for the nation and worthy of replication by other jurisdictions.

METHODOLOGY

Participants

A listing of state and county juvenile justice administrators was developed by cross-listing several address lists compiled from the latest *American Correctional Association Directory of Institutions and Agencies*, the Office of Juvenile Justice and Delinquency Prevention (OJJDP) Web site, NCJRS, and the Google search engine. Administrators who chose to participate in the study represented a cross-section of juvenile justice programs located in urban, suburban, and rural areas in all parts of the United States.

Procedure

A national survey was conducted, surveying all juvenile justice program administrators to identify evidence-based model programs currently being implemented. Those programs identified as evidence-based model programs were reviewed to determine key components of each program, evidence of each program's outcomes, and finally to identify common themes across model programs.

To begin, a detailed two-page questionnaire was developed and pretested with three administrators of large state juvenile justice departments. The questionnaire contained open-ended questions asking administrators about their perceptions of the programs they ran. For example, administrators were first asked, "What program do you consider to be most worthy of replication by other juvenile justice agencies?" and then were asked to "please discuss the rationale for your selection." Finally, those administrators who identified one of their programs as a model program were asked to "please discuss the most promising features of this program as it is now constituted." Administrators were further questioned about whether they had a descriptive report or an evaluation outcome report to support their program's effectiveness, and if so to include that report with their returned survey.

This survey instrument was mailed with a cover letter to all 145 identified state and county juvenile justice administrators. The post office returned fifteen of the envelopes stamped "address unknown" or "moved with no forwarding address." Five months after the questionnaires were mailed out, 69 participants responded with information about their juvenile justice programs, resulting in a 53 percent response rate.

The authors reviewed responses (N = 69) with particular attention to the evidence program administrators used to justify their program as a model program. Ten programs met our criteria for model programs. These programs had three things in common:

1. Demonstrated success by operationally defining recidivism in terms of rearrest rates, technical probation, or court order violations or new adjudications.
2. Conducted systematic research, measuring outcomes including recidivism data 12 months or more after completing the program.
3. Reported recidivism rates significantly lower than traditional training schools after completing program (12 months postrelease to 36 months postrelease).

After identifying model programs, the authors then contacted the administrators of the ten selected programs via follow-up letters and phone calls to obtain the most recent recidivism data measuring program effectiveness.

RESULTS

Lack of Evidence-Based Evaluation

All of the administrators indicated that they direct one or more model juvenile offender treatment programs. Surprisingly, less than 15 percent of the administrators responding to the survey based their program implementation decisions on systematic research or program evaluations. Unfortunately, the majority based their decisions on arbitrary, intuition-based, capricious, or undocumented conclusions. The overwhelming majority of responding programs gave, as their rationale for selecting their program as a model, the following types of responses:

"People like our program."

"We have the best program in the state because the juveniles tell us they like it."

"We have a fine program because it is interesting."

"Our program bolsters self-esteem."

"Values clarification and forcing responsibility is the key to success."

"Our program is widely considered to be the nation's oldest juvenile correction program, and therefore the most successful."

"Our program is best because it has spirit on top of the mechanics of the program."

"Our program should be replicated because none of the juveniles have committed suicide in the past six months."

These responses raise concerns about the ways in which administrators are informing their programmatic decisions. Decisions based on subjective or arbitrary sources of information appear to be guiding administrators not only to implement unevaluated programs but also to encourage replication of these programs in other settings. This flawed decision-making process, evident in 86 percent of administrators' responses, underscores a lack of resources and knowledge necessary to adequately evaluate today's juvenile offender treatment programs. It is clear that funding and training are required to improve juvenile offender programs' abilities to evaluate the effectiveness of the services they are providing (Roberts, 2004).

Model Programs

In sharp contrast to the above selected non-evidence-based rationales, the 10 programs selected as model programs were much more rigorous in the evaluation of their programs. Model programs developed clear definitions of success by operationally defining recidivism in terms of rearrest rates, technical probation, court order violations, or new adjudications. They sought objectivity in their evaluation by systematically collecting outcome data for youth in their programs and did so at follow-up intervals of 12 months to 36 months after completing the program. As a result, administrators of model programs had empirical evidence indicating that youth who completed their programs had significantly lower recidivism rates than youth in traditional institutional programs.

The 10 model programs identified in our study are described below. Programs are categorized according to the severity of the offenders they aim to treat, with programs treating serious offenders described first, followed by programs treating adjudicated offenders of moderate severity, and wrapping up with those programs aimed at treating juveniles with more minor offenses. The key features of each program are described, followed by recidivism rates and other outcomes for each program. Table 1 presents a matrix comparing the 10 evidence-based, model, juvenile treatment programs in more detail.

Model Programs for Serious Offenders

A select group of programs are challenged with the aim of treating the most severe juvenile offenders, including those accused of felonies such as violent personal crimes, capital murder, and sex crimes. The three programs described here were selected for their success in treating serious offenders and are described in more detail in Table 1.

Last Chance Ranch. This program provides high staff-to-participant ratio that allows the program to be tailored to the individual's unique needs. This is accomplished by keeping programs small and intensive. The program is unique in that is a working ranch with no iron bars, handcuffs, or locked cells. With a behavior management regimen, participants work through a three-phase program. Successful progression in the program is based on points earned for behavior, being on time, appearance, attitude, leadership, participation, enthusiasm,

TABLE 1 Model Programs for Treating Serious Offenders

Program	Location	Program Goals	Treatment	Duration	Population	Outcome	Sample Size
AMI's Last Chance Ranch	Florida Everglades	• Behavior management • To improve academic level	• Behavior modification program based on a point system • Education 22 juv at a time • Physical labor on the ranch • Community service and involvement in environmental projects	Minimum 1 year (Ongoing)	Adjudicated youth with felony offenses	• 15.8% recidivism rate (12 months) as defined as new adjudication. Most common recidivating offense burglary & car theft	• 57
Texas Youth Commission	Texas	• Community protection • Education • Resocialization • Competency-based phase research-based system in academic behavior Correctional tx.	• Capital and serious violent offenders program • Sex Offenders program • Chemical Dependency Program • Emotionally Disturbed Program • ABC Resocialization program	17–21 months	Adjudicated, avg. age 16, 4–5 years below grade level, IQ: 75% are below 90	• 32.2% reincarceration rate for any offense (1 year) • 28.9% reincarceration rate for felony offense (3 years)	• 5,524

(continued)

TABLE 1 Model Programs for Treating Serious Offenders (*Continued*)

Program	Location	Program Goals	Treatment	Duration	Population	Outcome	Sample Size
Missouri State-wide system of residential facilities and group homes	Five regions throughout Missouri	• Address education, treatment, and rehabilitation needs • Small residential facilities and group home • Family tx. and aftercare	• Residential and community day treatment, and aftercare by trackers and case managers • Intensive family treatment • 90-minute group therapy sessions 5 days a week	Ongoing	Juveniles with felony adjudications as well as juvenile status offenders	• Recidivism rate of 11% to 29% within 3 years post-release; only 8% recidivism rate–sentenced to adult prisons within 3 yrs release	• Based on 1,386 juvenile offenders released from custody in 1999

and manners. This personalized system allows youth to work through the program at different rates. As youth move through phases, they graduate to more-accommodating housing and gain more privileges. Individualized education and progress toward a GED or diploma are early goals. Youth also perform physical labor on the ranch through basic chores, and community service and environmental projects are integrated midway through the program. Toward completion of the program, participants can earn the right to go back to their hometowns. During the month prior to leaving the ranch, youth work closely with counselors to develop plans for their return. Staff members accompany youth back into their communities in order to help them begin the process of rebuilding their lives. Once home, the youth receive five visits per week from a community coordinator, plus frequent calls from the case manager on staff at the ranch. Community coordinators may return youth to the ranch if their behavior lapses. The youth receive intensive support at home for six months before they graduate from the program.

During 1997–1998, the average youth from Last Chance Ranch had an average of 32.7 overall charges and 11.8 felony charges. However, during the four-year period from 1997 to 2000, only 15.8 percent (9 out of 57) of the serious juvenile offenders released from the ranch were found guilty of a new offense in their first 12 months following program completion. This compares to an average reconviction rate of more than 40 percent for all Florida institutions serving serious juvenile offenders.

Texas Youth Commission (TYC) Capital Offender Treatment Program. This program stands out because it is innovative, intensive, and based on cognitive-behavioral and empathy training skills. All groups are led by Ph.D.-level psychologists, and master's-level cotherapists. According to Dr. Charles R. Jeffords, Director of Research and Planning at TYC, "The program is experientially based in order to facilitate access to emotions typically buried by cognitive defense mechanisms such as denial, avoidance, projection, and blocking. It often proves to be a very powerful and moving experience for participants, and helps connect actions to consequences for these youths." Youths are required to role-play many aspects of their life stories, including family relationships and the violent offense. The reenactment of the crime is done first as the perpetrator, and then from the perspective of the offender's own victim, with other treatment group members participating in the reenactment. The purpose of these experiential sessions is to facilitate the offender's awareness of his or her underlying emotions, and to facilitate empathy toward the victim and learning about prosocial choices and nonviolent coping strategies. In addition, written and verbal exercises and video demonstrations of societal reactions help to explore personal, cultural, and societal value systems. Another unique component to treatment are the periodic progress evaluations and monitoring of treatment effectiveness through assessment tools that measure empathy, hostility, aggression levels, and the sense of internal versus external locus of control. Group leaders and staff psychologists also conduct period assessments.

Based on recidivism rates from 1996 to 2000, it is clear that the Capital and Serious Violent Offender program is successful in reducing recidivism. In Figure 1, the rearrest rates of treated and nontreated offenders diverge over the 36-month period measured. Rearrest rates for felonies showed an average of a 25.8 percent difference between the treated and nontreated groups, violent offences showed a 31 percent difference. There was a 41.1 percent difference between the groups for reincarceration.

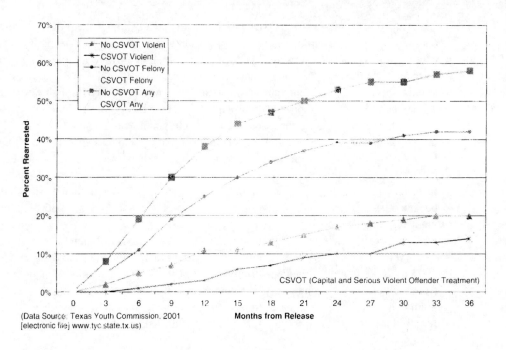

(Data Source: Texas Youth Commission, 2001
[electronic file] www.tyc.state.tx.us)

FIGURE 1
Capital and Serious Violent Offender Rearrest Rates

Missouri Division of Youth (DYS).   Missouri's DYS system stands out for its ability to provide successful intensive treatment across residential facilities, group homes, and aftercare services. The extensive services provided appear to be a result of keeping programs small in size and involving family members throughout the treatment process. Highly trained staff are available 24 hours a day and M.S.W family therapists promote family involvement throughout residential treatment and home-based aftercare. The residential facility, targeting adjudicated youth with felony charges, and the group home programs, targeting status offenders, share a focus on treatment and rehabilitation in small settings as opposed to a focus on punishment in large institutions. Residential treatment facilities offer extensive group therapy as well as multisystemic family therapy. A strength of this program is the use of day treatment transitional programs to bridge the residential setting to returning to the community. These transitional programs offer support through mentoring and monitoring of youth in daily community supervision by either a "tracker" college senior usually majoring in social work or criminal justice or by the same case manager who initially took their case when they entered custody. For less serious offenders receiving group home services, treatment is both therapeutic and involves academic/occupational training. Group home treatment consists of spending considerable time in academic classes, individual and group therapy, computer learning lab, group projects, employment, field trips, pet therapy, and so on.

According to a study by DYS in 2003, approximately 11 percent to 29 percent of youths released from DYS custody in 1999 had recidivated within the following three years. Furthermore, only 8 percent of those released were sentenced to adult prisons or short-term 120-day adult confinement programs during the following three years. DYS's recidivism rates are extremely low compared to reported rates in Maryland (82%) and Washington state (68%) two years after release.

Model Programs for Moderate Offenders

Three treatment programs that we reviewed aimed to treat moderate offenders. This moderate category includes adjudicated youth who have committed property crimes, drug offenses, and/or personal crimes but who are not the serious violent and capital offenders described in the previous section. These programs often treat a range of behaviors by offering varying degrees of services. See Table 2 for more detailed descriptions of programs.

AMI. This program, comprising a network of autonomous, nonprofit, in community non-institutional programs for delinquent youths, stands out for its comprehensive core training programs. This program focuses on involving adjudicated youth in marine research projects with an emphasis on vocational training and gaining of aquatic knowledge. AMI also aims for youth to obtain a GED or high school diploma and provides counseling to encourage core values. Upon release, youth may be placed in work environments, school programs, or combinations of work-school programs. The results are indicators of the success of the programs as a whole with the highest success rate for those who were placed in a work environment.

A study of program participants (N = 2,741) in AMI programs between 1997 and 2001 reports the following recidivism rates at one year posttreatment:

- The overall recidivism rate was 28.5 percent (based on a convicted law violation).
- Over half of the program participants had received a felony conviction before enrollment in the program, and the recidivism rate for these program participants was 28.7 percent.
- Program participants who were placed in some type of work environment upon release from the program had the lowest recidivism rate of 22.1 percent, while participants released into a combined school-work program had a recidivism rate of 25.6 percent, and those released to a school program had a recidivism rate of 35.8 percent.
- Those who had been placed into the program as a condition of juvenile probation recidivated at a rate of 32.4 percent, while those who were directly committed (those who were in legal custody of the state) recidivated at a rate of 27.2 percent.

Gulf Coast Trades Center. This program comprehensively provides intense in-community supervision, occupational/academic skills, basic behavioral modification techniques and the possibility for low-wage employment with an aftercare program. On a basic level, the program serves to "ground" the youth, monitoring the youth's location and activities in the community. A key component, however, is that the program offers realistic vocational trades training in combination with deterrence through threat of harsher regulations or imprisonment. Youth attend school and work, spend hours every day in Gulf Coast's Learning Resource Center where they work on basic skills, and study for the GED or earn high school credits. Students work at their own pace using individualized plans developed and updated using extensive pretesting and ongoing assessments. Vocational skills are

TABLE 2   Model Programs for Treating Serious Offenders

Program	Location	Program Goals	Treatment	Duration	Population	Outcome	Sample Size
Associated Marine Institutes (AMI)	Seven states and the Cayman Islands	• Vocational training • Improve academic level • Emphasizing core values	• Involvement in marine research projects, such as aquatics, diving, ocean-ography, seaman ship, marine biology Education	Ongoing	Adjudicated youth. 14–18 yrs of age Average of 8–12 offenses before coming to AMI	• 28.5% new adjud recidivism rate (1 year after release); most common recid. car theft	• 2741 • 54% of the 782 youths that recidivated did so within 4 months
Eckerd Wilderness Educational System	18 Facilities (7 States)	• Improve academic level, vocational, and social Skills • Avoid secure confinement costs • Community reintegration	• Group activities • Education • Therapy • Community service	1 year (Ongoing)	Adjudicated, Nonadjudicated Avg. intake age: 14.5 (11–17 yrs) Below grade level Avg. IQ: 91.2	• 85.1% graduation rate • 1.3-Year grade-level increase • 26.7% recidivism rate (21 months)	• 820 eligible • 418 graduates
Gulf Coast Trades Center (TYC)Trades Center (TYC)	New Waverly. TX	• Occupational training, 9 trades. • Academic skills training	• Work placement • Location monitoring (community-based) • Intensive aftercare and job placement	6–9 Months	Adjudicated. 13–17 yrs. of age: 65% of program graduates find employment in their chosen trade	• 15.7% recidivism rate, 12-month (rein-carceration)	249 in 2000 311 in 2001 262 in 2002

| Community Intensive Supervision Project (CISP) | Pittsburgh, PA | • Lower Recidivism Rates
 • Low Cost Operation
 • Restitution | • Electronic location monitoring
 • Drug counseling
 • Community service
 • Recreation
 • Counseling service | Ongoing | Adjudicated 10–18 yrs "High-risk" delinquent youth (repeat offenders) Below grade level | • 45% recidivism rate |

acquired through work placement at nonprofit organizations and government agencies. In each vocational track, program participants must demonstrate a mastery of several dozen competencies in order to earn a vocational certificate. After completion of the training programs and obtaining on-the-job work experience, Gulf Coast provides extensive aftercare support including job search and job placement assistance and staff advocates and mentors who visit the home regularly.

Recidivism data show that only 15.7 percent of the youth who graduated from Gulf Coast from 1995 through 1999 were incarcerated within one year of release. This compares to a 37.6 percent recidivism rate for Texas youth released from other medium security residential facilities during this same period. The three-year recidivism rate for Gulf Coast youth for the same time period is 18.2 percent versus 27.4 percent for other Texas youth in medium-security facilities.

Eckerd Wilderness Educational System.   This program stands out for its comprehensive emphasis on education, vocation, emotional and social functioning, and reintegration into family and community. Serving both adjudicated and voluntary youth, the program offers group therapy, educational training, and therapy, but also requires youth to participate in camp-specific projects (beautification/expansion) and public service projects (Adopt-a-Highway).

Eckerd's North Carolina site has been especially successful in evaluating its outcomes. The program saw an 84 percent graduation rate over the 2000–2001 year. After graduation, youth originally adjudicated into the program had an 8.2 percent recidivism rate within 6 months and 15.3 percent within 12 months.

Juvenile Status Postgraduation	6 months	12 months
Residential mental health treatment	1.8%	3.1%
Nonresidential mental health treatment	13.8%	19.1%
Enrolled in school and/or employed	93.7%	87.2%

Outcomes for Eckerd's North Carolina Wilderness Education Program (2000–2001).

Community Intensive Supervision Project (Pittsburgh, PA).   This program stands out as a unique alternative to secure confinement for repeat (high-risk) offenders. The program consists of intensive supervision via electronic monitoring as well as drug screening. While living at home, youth participate in drug and alcohol education as well as individual and peer-group counseling. Parents are encouraged to actively support the program through participation in family counseling. Beyond education and therapeutic components, participants are expected to attend school or work, repay restitution, and develop positive social behaviors. Breaking rules of the program can result in home removal for short periods.

According to administrator reports, the program had a 45 percent recidivism rate for those who fully completed the program. In 1996, only 10 of the 209 juveniles were convicted on new criminal acts and 28 were discharged before completing the program. The 45 percent recidivism rate is a hindrance in rating this program as fully successful.

Model Programs for Status Offenders and Troubled Youth

Prevention is the key to reducing crime and changing the direction of youths' lives. Three programs reviewed here aim to serve youth at the earlier stages of delinquency. These programs target populations of troubled youth who have committed status offenses such as truancy, running away, and incorrigibility or who have committed minor property crimes such as theft. Rehabilitation at these earlier stages of crime is critical because without intervention, many of these youths are likely to become more serious offenders. See Table 3 for more detailed program descriptions.

Bethesda Day Treatment Center.   This program stands out for its ability to assist youth of all troubled circumstances, whether adjudicated delinquents, status offenders, or child abuse dependency cases. The flexibility of the program allows it to serve a variety of hard-to-treat youth. Youth may participate in residential treatment, day treatment, or home-based treatment services. Across settings, 17 different treatment modules are combined and customized to meet the needs of the individual youth. The modules range from psychological counseling, to social counseling, to educational and vocational training. A majority of the youth receive group, individual, family, academic, life skills, and substance abuse counseling. The diversity of treatment options appears to be a strength of the program, offering solutions that other programs frequently overlook. An interesting aspect to the program is how intensive it is. The program involves the whole family and is integrated into the home, school, community, and peer groups. It may require 55 hours or more per week. The program does not suspend or expel any youth, allowing the youth to move beyond hostility and aggression, and making it unlikely that counselors will give up on any youth.

The client recidivism rate was reported to be 10.4 percent. This is impressive considering that two-thirds of the youth are below grade level in reading and many of the program's youths have prior offences at early ages.

Earn-It Program for Status Offenders and Adjudicated Property Offenders.   This program stands out as a model program because it includes an intensive community-based component. The program innovatively focuses on law-related education, prosocial group bonding, highly structured restitution and community service, and teaching job-seeking and job-keeping skills. Whether youths are at a day-care or senior citizen work site, clear and consistent adherence to rules and work schedules are required. At the beginning, youths are responsible for calling prospective employers, scheduling an interview, and starting their community service work assignments. Youths can be terminated from job sites if they fail to follow their work schedule or call their supervisor if they are going to be late. The Earn-It diversion program allows young offenders to remain in the community, with structured supervision and appropriate intervention. Youths usually work after school each day and on the weekends. Thus, the juvenile offender has very limited free time to just hang out, making this program very different from traditional probation.

Performance-based outcome measures demonstrate significantly reduced reoffense rates for youths completing the restitution/community service program. The program had a 14 percent recidivism rate over the observed six-year period (based on the youth that completed the program). In 1996, 72 percent of the participants completed the program. The

TABLE 3 Model Programs for Treating Troubled Youth and Status Offenders

Program	Location	Program Goals	Treatment	Duration	Population	Outcome	Sample Size
Earn-It	Keene, NH	• Restitution • Low-cost operation	• Employment for Restitution (Community Based) Court ordered monthly restitution; arranging work placement & community service	Ongoing	Adjudicated. avg. Age 15.3 (12–18 yrs). "low-risk" youth, below grade level	• 5 to 14% recidivism rate after 12 mos.: Only 5% reoffense rate in all of 2000 • 72% program completion	• 105
Bethesda Day Treatment Center	West Milton, PA	• Positive socialization	• Alternative Education • Drug Counseling • Family Systems Counseling • Short-Term Foster Care (Community Based)	55+ hours a week (Ongoing)	Adjudicated. Nonadjudicated. avg. intake age: 14.1 (10–17 yrs), "high-risk" status offenders referred for truancy. incorrigibility. running away from home. or theft. IQ: 82% below avg.	• 10.4% Recidivism Rate within the first 12 months post discharge-new status offense	• NA

Wraparound Milwaukee	Milwaukee, WI	• Address mental health, substance abuse, emotional and behavioral needs • Provide support in a nonresidential setting	• Community-based care • Family services • Ongoing evaluations • Team-driven servicing for the child and family • Strengths based treatment approach	Ongoing	Children and adolescents who have a serious emotional, behavioral or mental health disturbance that must have persisted for 6 months and who are at an immediate risk of residential treatment, psychiatric hospitalization or juvenile correctional placement.	• 15% Property Offenses, 5% Assault, 3% Weapons 2% Sex Offenses, 6% for Drug Offenses— One yr. Recidivism Rates	• 490 (based on program participants referred by probation

program is successful in meeting its goal of a 30 percent or less recidivism rate. In 1996, the program collected $4,940.95 and paid victims $2,430.89.

Wraparound Milwaukee.   As the name implies, a standout feature of this program is its ability to provide "wraparound" services, defined as care involving the child and family in a planning process resulting in a set of community services and natural supports individualized for each child to obtain a set of positive outcomes. The client-centered program emphasizes developing and delivering strength-based, highly individualized, and community-focused services to the children and their families. Multiple service systems are combined into a single system of care for the program participants and their families. The care coordinators are the cornerstone of this flexible program. They facilitate the process by conducting strength/needs assessments, by facilitating team planning, by identifying and obtaining treatment resources and supports for the child and family, and by monitoring and evaluating the care plan. They work with small caseloads of up to eight families, and they are intensively trained and certified in the wraparound process. Wraparound services allow for intensive, comprehensive assistance in clients' homes, thus avoiding a residential and not as highly individualized "blanket" treatment programs.

Recidivism rates (rates of legal reoffense) decreased from preenrollment levels (average 2) during enrollment (average 1.1) and continued to decline during the year following completion of the program (average .77). Adjudications also measured prior to enrollment (1.26), decreased during enrollment (.73) and one year following completion (.57). The following is a breakdown of the percentages of number of offenses committed prior to enrollment, during enrollment, and during the one year following enrollment:

	Prior to Enrollment %	During Enrollment %	Following Enrollment %
Property Offenses	40	21	15
Assaults	18	11	5
Weapons Offenses	11	4	3
Sex Offenses	17	4	2
Drug Offenses	9	6	6
Other Offenses	32	18	14

(N = 490 program participants).

CONCLUSION

This study highlights the very low percentage of juvenile justice programs that are systematically evaluated for effectiveness. While most administrators view their programs as model programs worthy of replication, only 10 programs had clear evidence of positive outcomes. The current state of juvenile justice systems operating without systematic evaluation may be due in large part to the very low priority state and county funding agencies give to research and evaluation, and appropriations to hire staff to conduct ongoing empirical evaluations. Many responses from administrators/program managers indicated that current federal, state, and local funding sources may be enabling this lack of accountability further by funding programs without requiring any built-in evaluations and measurement of outcomes. Drastic changes in funding requirements, administrative support, and program priorities are needed in order for juvenile justice programs to collect vital outcome data, thereby enabling confidence in their effectiveness.

The 10 programs that demonstrated empirical success had many positive features in common. They found lower recidivism rates 12 or more months posttreatment completion, and demonstrated evidence of improved reading and math levels, reintegration into the community, and improved social skills. Several of the programs were honest about their limitations and changes they would like to make in the near future with regard to more training of counselors and continuous evaluations. More specifically, the Eckerd Wilderness Educational System evaluation highlighted that the counselors needed additional training on a quarterly basis. The Bethesda Day Treatment Center program is trying to obtain additional funding for ongoing and regular program evaluations. On the positive side, all 10 model programs have provided evidence of attaining short-term, interim, and long-term goals (Roberts, 2004).

As is to be expected, comparing outcomes across programs is challenging and difficult. This is due, in large part, to lack of recommended standardized measures to be implemented across programs. It would be useful if federal and state juvenile justice funding sources could standardize outcome measures similar to the outcome measures recommended by the United Way of America for all child welfare program evaluations. Standardized outcome and performance measures should seek to evaluate goal achievement, demographics of program participants, average treatment lengths, effectiveness of individualized treatment aspects in each program, rate of reoffending and technical parole violations for all youth who enter the program (completed or not) at 6-, 12-, 24-, and 36-month intervals. Such standardized measurements would allow for an accurate comparison between programs and for the components of any one program to be evaluated separately (Roberts, 2004).

On a qualitative level several recurrent themes stood out across model programs. Most model programs offered significant aftercare services to help youth transition successfully into the community. This often required working closely with youths' families in counseling and appointing specific staff caseworkers to consistently supervise and support transitioning youth. Model programs also appear to offer flexible programming, allowing for treatment to meet the individualized needs of each youth. This requires a certain degree of specificity—offering specialized programs for youth with certain problems. At the same time, many of the programs provided youth with a range of services, from skill building, to gaining insight, to strict supervision, and this variety appeared helpful in comprehensively targeting several domains of youths' lives. This balance for comprehensiveness and specificity is of course challenging and requires adequate resources and flexibility. It also requires intense staff involvement, a quality particularly useful in the Last Chance Ranch Program; high staff-to-youth ratios are ideal in causing substantive change. Finally, vocational training was emphasized in most of the model programs reviewed in this study. This speaks to the importance of providing youth with strengths and skills that will aid them in transitioning into the community, providing alternatives to criminal behavior.

It is important to examine how our study of currently implemented model programs fits in the context of prior effectiveness research. The majority of model programs included in this study encompassed both the behavioral components and skills training suggested as most effective by Lipsey (1995). Emphasis on vocation and education training found in most of the model programs has also been well supported in the broader literature (Lipsey Wilson, 1998). Furthermore, three programs reviewed (Bethesda Day Treatment, Earn-It, and Wraparound Milwaukee) found encouraging results for preventing further delinquency among troubled teens, promising findings in light of prior research that has found delinquency a particularly hard behavior to prevent (Wilson et al., 2001). The model programs examined in this study appear to be multifaceted, utilizing several components of empirically supported treatments as well as components still requiring further empirical attention such as aftercare supervision, specialized educational programs, and intensive empathy therapy.

The current study is not without limitations. Sixty-one potential participants declined to answer our survey. While it could be assumed that well-evaluated programs would be more encouraged to respond, it is possible that successful programs exist that were not included in this study. Additionally, the recidivism rates reported by model program administrators are not compared to control or no-treatment comparison groups in experimental designs. Due to lack of randomized control groups, recidivism rates should not be viewed as evidence of effectiveness, but instead examined as rates of success for treated youth. Future studies, including matched comparison or control groups, are needed to test the effectiveness of components of the model programs discussed above.

Despite these limitations, our results find these juvenile offender treatment programs serve a very important function. They provide many youth with a second chance through supportive and caring treatment protocols which can break the cycle of habitual delinquency and criminality. As more juvenile offender treatment models are developed, evaluated, and replicated, the exemplary models will stand out. These programs benefit society by teaching the juvenile offenders an alternative path in life, and provide the youth with the mind-set and skills necessary to avoid repeating their mistakes or escalating their level of offending, which make all of society a safer and more humane place (Roberts, 2004).

REFERENCES

Landenberger, N. A., & Lipsey, M. W. (2005). The positive effects of cognitive-behavioral programs for offenders: A meta-analysis of factors associated with effective treatment. *Journal of Experimental Criminology, 1,* 451–476.

Lipsey, M. W. (1995). What do we learn from 400 research studies on the effectiveness of treatment with juvenile delinquents? In J. McGuire (Ed.), *What works: Reducing reoffending—Guidelines from research and practice* (pp. 63–78). New York: Wiley.

Lipsey, M. W., & Wilson, D. B. (1998). Effective intervention for serious juvenile offenders: A synthesis of research. In R. Loeber and D. P. Farrington (Eds.), *Serious & violent juvenile offenders: Risk factors and successful interventions* (pp. 313–345). London: Sage.

Pearson, F. S., Lipton, D. S., Cleland, C., & Yee, D. S. (2002). The effects of behavioral/cognitive-behavioral programs on recidivism. *Crime and Delinquency, 48*(3), 476–496.

Roberts, A. R. (2004). Epilogue. In A. Roberts (Ed.), *Juvenile justice sourcebook: Past, present, and future.* New York: Oxford University Press.

Wilson, D. B., Bouffard, L. A., & MacKenzie, D. L. (2005). A quantitative review of structured, group-oriented, cognitive-behavioral programs for offenders. *Journal of Criminal Justice and Behavior, 32*(2), 172–204.

Wilson, S. J., Lipsey, M. W., & Soydan, H. (2003). Are mainstream programs for juvenile delinquency less effective with minority youth than majority youth? A meta-analysis of outcomes research. *Research on Social Work Practice, 13*(1), 3–26.

Wilson, D. B., Gottfredson, D. C., & Najaka, S. S. (2001). School-based prevention of problem behaviors: A meta-analysis. *Journal of Quantitative Criminology, 17*(3), 247–272.

Wilson, S. J., & Lipsey, M. W. (2000). Wilderness challenge programs for delinquent youth: A meta-analysis of outcome evaluations. *Evaluation and Program Planning, 23*, 1–12.

PART III

Assessment and Treatment of Adult Offenders

❖

8

Treating the Mentally Ill Offender

An Overview

Kathi R. Trawver

❖

Jails and prisons have become the largest providers of mental health services to individuals who experience serious mental illnesses in the United States. This results from a growing trend toward processing those with serious mental disorders through the criminal justice system instead of community-based treatment or psychiatric hospitals.

There are at least three times more mentally ill people in U.S. jails and prisons than in psychiatric hospitals and the two largest providers of mental health services in the United States are urban jails (Human Rights Watch, 2003). Cook County Jail in Chicago holds approximately 1,100 mentally ill offenders on an average day (C. Alaimo, personal communication, September 13, 2006). The Los Angeles County Jail Twin Tower facilities hold up to 1,800 individuals—260 of which are women—that are receiving some type of mental health services on a daily basis (R. C. Fish, personal communication, September 15, 2006). For the purpose of this chapter, serious mental illness or mental disorder will be defined as schizophrenia, bipolar disorder, or depression.

The landmark 1999 Bureau of Justice Statistics study (Ditton, 1999) found that an estimated 283,800 seriously mentally ill offenders, or 16 percent of all people incarcerated, were confined in U.S. jails or prisons. According to Ditton, these inmates were more likely than non-mentally ill inmates to have been homeless and under the influence of alcohol or drugs at the time of arrest. More than three-quarters had previous criminal history. In 2001, the American Psychiatric Association found the prevalence of serious mental illness within corrections to be slightly higher. They estimated that up to 20 percent of all inmates have a serious mental disorder and at least 5 percent are actively psychotic at any given time.

At mid-year 2005, more than one-half, or 1,255,700, jail and prison inmates had some type of mental health problem (James & Glaze, 2006). These authors found that of those inmates, an estimated 30 percent of jail inmates and 23 percent of state prisoners had symptoms of major depression. Furthermore, they found 15 percent of jail inmates and 24 percent of state prison inmates reported symptoms that met criteria for a psychotic disorder diagnosis.

The number of inmates with serious mental disorders continues to increase. As a result, a higher prevalence of severe mental illness is found in prison populations than in the general community (Hills, Siegfried, & Ickowitz, 2004). Watson, Luchins, Hanrahan, Heyrman, and Lurigio (2000) report that between 1980 and 1992, there was a 154 percent increase in the number of persons with serious mental disorder held in U.S. jails and prisons. This means that each year, approximately 900,000 persons with active symptoms of serious mental illness are entering U.S. jails (Steadman, Scott, Osher, Agnese, & Robbins, 2005). While those numbers are sufficiently alarming, they may underestimate the actual prevalence because previous research has relied on inmates' self-identifying and self-reporting their mental illness rather than basing findings on substantiated diagnosis (Quanbeck, Frye & Atshuler, 2003).

Once incarcerated, properly identifying, treating, and planning for successful discharge of incarcerated mentally ill offenders is extremely complex and creates significant challenges for the criminal justice system. In light of these issues, there are three specific aims to this chapter. The first is to detail some of the causes and resulting problems associated with the high prevalence and overrepresentation of individuals with mental illness and co-occurring substance use disorders in the correctional system. The second is to provide an overview of treatment issues and correctional programs that treat mentally ill offenders. The third is to describe some of the most current diversionary efforts that are attempting to prevent the mentally ill from entering the criminal justice system when possible.

MENTAL DISORDERS IN THE CORRECTIONAL SYSTEM: CAUSES AND RESULTING PROBLEMS

For persons with severe mental disorders, entry into the criminal justice system often begins when disruptive behaviors are brought to the attention of law enforcement officials (Lamberti & Weisman, 2004). All too often people who are in psychiatric distress and are merely publicly acting out the symptoms of their illness are arrested and processed through the criminal justice system rather than diverted to community treatment. Responding to complaints from the community about a mentally ill individual, police may find that the individual is not impaired enough to meet legal standards for involuntary hospitalization yet is far too psychiatrically compromised to be left on the street. Without an alternative place to take a seriously mentally disordered individual, officers often have little recourse other than jail to ensure the safety of both the public and the offender (Reynolds, Dziegielewski, & Shapp, 2004).

As a result, most mentally ill offenders are arrested for low-level misdemeanor charges and held on minor infractions (Borum, 2004), such as trespassing or shoplifting, and are more likely to be arrested than individuals without a mental illness (Teplin, 2000). Of those who remain incarcerated in prison, it is divided fairly evenly between those that are held on violent and nonviolent offenses (Ditton, 1999).

One must consider what factors may have contributed to marked increase and disproportionate numbers of mentally ill entering the criminal justice system. Can it be simply that being mentally ill results in increased arrest and incarceration? Is it that the mentally ill are inherently more criminal? Can it be explained by a perceived failure of social policies, the community mental health movement and a fragmented mental health system? Or is it merely the fear and stigma our society holds for its mentally ill members? While there are several theories, there is not yet one definitive explanation to answer these questions.

One of the earliest theories to explain the increased incarceration of the mentally ill is referred to as the "Penrose effect." During the late 1930s, Penrose theorized that at any one time there are a finite amount of individuals who will either reside in jails or psychiatric hospitals and as the numbers go up in one, the numbers will naturally go down in the other, and visa versa (Draine, 2003).

The phenomenon of mentally ill increasingly facing arrest for minor crimes is often referred to as the "criminalization of the mentally ill," a term first coined by Abramson (1972). Since then, this term has been applied by many authors to generically describe the high numbers of incarcerated mentally ill, including those who have committed serious crimes. However, Lamb & Weinberger (1998) have advocated that this term be used, "primarily in connection with mentally ill persons who are arrested, with or without jail detention, and prosecuted for minor offenses instead of being placed in the mental health system" (p. 485).

Currently, one of the most frequently cited explanations for the increased numbers of incarcerated mentally ill points to the deinstitutionalization movement, the resulting profound reductions in psychiatric beds, and the failure and fragmentation of community mental health programs and their inability to adequately meet the needs of the large numbers of discharged psychiatric hospital patients. Clearly, these shifts have had a significant impact on where, how, and to what degree individuals with mental disorders can receive treatment. According to NASMHPD Research Institute (2004), between 1972 and 1990, psychiatric beds in the United States decreased from 361,765 to 98,647, representing a 70 percent reduction. During this same time period, 14 of 277 state psychiatric hospitals closed. During the 1990s, 44 additional hospitals were closed, resulting in an additional decrease to an estimated 54,000 psychiatric hospital residents. While the community mental health system is often blamed for the overrepresentation of the mentally ill in the correctional system, a study by Fisher, Packer, Simon, and Smith (2000) found that the level of mental health services available in the community did not explain the levels of incarcerated mentally ill adults.

Other promulgated theories are more stringent involuntary commitment standards, a lack of police training (Lamb & Weinberger, 1998), and the public sentiment and resulting shifts in public policy during the Regan era that created the "war on drugs," "tough on crime," and "zero tolerance" mentalities (Landsberg & Smiley, 2001). Furthermore, public stigma, an unfounded fear of dangerousness (Desai, 2003), and a mentally disordered individual's refusal to participate in mental health treatment (Lamb & Weinberger, 1998) are also publicized as factors increasing risk of incarceration for the mentally ill.

Draine (2003) asserts that, "when the reasons people got to jail or return to jail are examined, it becomes clear that the key issue are social difficulties complicated by mental illness, but not caused by mental illness" (p. 9). Fisher, Silver, and Wolff (2006) make an excellent point when they state that, "regardless of the empirical validity of the criminalization hypothesis, the question of whether increased availability of mental health services by itself reduces the 'criminalization' problem, remains unanswered" (p. 547). Junginger, Claypool, Laygo, and Cristianti (2006) reviewed records of 113 mentally ill diversion clients to determine if their offenses were directly or indirectly related to their serious mental illness or substance abuse. They found very little correlation between mental illness and the offense, finding that substance abuse led to more offenses than a mental illness. As a result, these authors assert the criminalization hypothesis should be replaced by known risk factors such as substance abuse, poverty, and homelessness.

Indeed, this issue is complicated and demanding. While there is no one simplistic or definitive empirically based explanation to adequately determine causation of the huge numbers of mentally ill in our jails, it seems likely to stem from the combined and complex configuration of individual and personal attributes, public sentiment toward crime and stigma toward the mentally ill, and multiple social problems resulting from changes in mental health and criminal justice policy.

Problems Associated with Incarceration of the Mentally Ill

Jail can be especially terrorizing when someone is in acute psychiatric distress and it is likely to exacerbate preexisting psychiatric symptoms (Slate, 2003). Hills et al. (2004) describe the effects of incarceration on individuals with serious mental disorders:

> Overcrowding, the lack of privacy, temperature and noise levels, victimization, and other environmental conditions in prisons can easily exacerbate the symptoms of mental illness for some people. In fact, the prison environment itself can contribute to increased suicide and the inability of inmates with serious mental illness to adjust. Environmental factors can also elicit significant adjustment reactions from inmates who may not have had a previous diagnosis but who become ill while incarcerated. (p. 6)

Research has shown that incarcerated mentally disordered individuals experience increased rates of psychiatric decompensation and increased risks of victimization and suicide (Rock, 2001). People in jails experience higher levels of suicide than the general population, and the risk is even higher when someone has a mental illness (APA, 2001). In California prisons the rates of suicide for inmates with mental illnesses are 4.5 times greater than the general population. Another study of one Ohio jail reported that suicide rates were 7 times greater among seriously mentally ill detainees (Council on State Governments, 2005).

Once incarcerated, inmates with serious mental disorders are less likely to be released on bail (Torrey, 1995) and are more apt to serve out their entire sentence than inmates without a mental disorder (Harris & Dagadakis, 2004). Ditton (1999) determined that the mentally ill stayed in jail an average of 15 months longer than other inmates. A sobering example is found in a study of New York City's largest jail, Riker's Island. There the average length of stay for all inmates was 42 days, in comparison to 215 days for an inmate with a serious mental disorder (Butterfield, 1998).

Longer stays may be due to a lack of financial resources and inadequate legal representation (Theuma, 2001), or it may be that mentally disordered offenders tend to get into more trouble and have more violations while incarcerated due to behaviors associated with their disorders (Lamb, Weinberger & Gross, 2004). To illustrate this point, a study of New York prisons found that while inmates with mental illness constituted only 11 percent of the total general prison population, 23 percent of the inmates in disciplinary lockdown were mentally ill (Winn, 2003).

It should come as no surprise that incarcerating the low-level mentally disordered offender is a significantly more expensive use of public funds than providing support to an individual through community-based services. In one 1994 study of California's most severely mentally ill, the most intensive outpatient community services cost between $7,000 and $20,000 per year while just the most basic health care services to inmates within a correctional setting ranged from $20,000 to $30,000 per year (Quanbeck et al., 2003).

As a result of the growing numbers of seriously mentally ill entering jails and prisons, who bring with them a host of complex treatment needs, the criminal justice system is continuing to develop the means for managing and treating people with mental illnesses. The next section of this chapter provides an overview of the presenting treatment issues and correctional programs that attempt to treat mentally ill offenders.

TREATING MENTALLY ILL OFFENDERS IN THE CORRECTIONAL SETTING

Hiday (1999) theorized that there is not one category of mentally ill offender but rather three major types. The first type is the mentally ill offender who commits only misdemeanor crimes, often characterized as "nuisance" crimes (trespassing, loitering, disturbing the peace, etc.), or those that are "survival" crimes, such as shoplifting or failing to pay for meals. These offenders are frequently arrested, in contrast to instances when the "crime" is committed by a non-mentally ill individual who do not face the same incidence of arrest. For example, a homeless mentally ill man who comes into a downtown hotel to wash up in the public restroom is arrested for trespassing, while a non-mentally ill person is free to use the facilities without question. The second type of mentally ill offenders includes those with significant character, personality, or substance abuse disorders. Typically, these individuals easily become belligerent and aggressive, making arrest more likely. The third category is made up of those few offenders that have significant hallucinations and delusions that drive their criminal activity. Such was the circumstance in the recently overturned tragic case of Andrea Yates. In 2000, responding to her delusions, she drowned her five children to save them from Satan.

Complex Treatment Needs of the Mentally Ill Offender

The fact that there is not a single type of mentally disordered offender who presents with one problem is especially challenging to correctional facilities. Instead, mentally disordered inmates differ not only from inmates without mental disorders but they also differ among themselves on several characteristics, complexity of presenting problems, and the intensity of treatment needs.

Wolff, Maschi, and Bjerklie (2004) compared characteristics of inmates with mental disorders to those having no mental disorder. They found that individuals with mental disorders were more likely than their non-mentally ill counterparts to have been homeless, had previous psychiatric hospitalizations, reported harming themselves during the six months prior to arrest, and reported drinking more regularly. Nearly one-third (32.5%) had been prescribed psychotropic medications, but reported forgetting to take them six months prior to arrest. Further, they found that 54.5 percent of the mentally disordered inmates had a history of some type of physical or sexual abuse. Even though mentally disordered offenders reported a history of more than a one-year involvement with a mental health program (37.5%), only 20 percent were engaged in treatment at the time of their arrest.

Similar to those findings, Young (2003) identified clinical variables that were correlated with receipt of correctional mental health services among male and female inmates. These factors include prior psychiatric treatment, use of greater numbers of illegal drugs, more days in jail, and being female were significantly associated with placement on the mental health unit. Overall, women of all races/ethnicities had greater health and mental health problems as measured by the clinical variables than men of all races/ethnicities.

Co-Occurring Mental Health and Substance Use Disorders in Correctional Settings

A 2006 Bureau of Justice Statistics report found that 74 percent of state prisoners and 76 percent of jail inmates who had mental health problems also met criteria for a co-occurring substance abuse or dependence disorder (James & Glaze, 2006). Individuals with co-occurring mental health and substance use disorders have been found to have more frequent contact with the criminal justice system (Corrigan & Watson, 2005). They are at higher risk for arrest, to be arrested for less serious offenses (Alemagno, Shaffer-King, Tonkin & Hammel, 2004), and are disproportionately overrepresented in correctional systems (Chandler, Peters, Field, & Juliano-Bult, 2004). As a result, increased numbers of individuals with co-occurring disorders have become involved in the criminal justice system. In fact, nearly all inmates with a mental disorder also have a substance use disorder (Miller & Bakalar, 2003), with prevalence estimates within correctional settings reaching as high as 72 percent (SAMHSA, 2003).

It stands to reason that among probationers, the rates of co-occurring disorders will also run high. In a study of over 600 randomly selected adult probationers, findings showed significantly higher rates of psychiatric disorders, substance use disorders, and co-occurring disorders among offenders when compared to persons in the general population (Lurigio et al., 2003).

Co-occurring substance use disorders significantly intensify a variety of risk factors and increase the treatment needs of the mentally ill offender. Experts agree that the combination of mental health and substance use disorders create a more serious impact on individuals than would either disorder alone (Watkins, Lewellen, & Barrett, 2001) as the co-occurrence of both disorders significantly exacerbate accompanying problems of each individual disorder (Evans & Sullivan, 2001).

Research suggests that co-occurring disorders are also associated with higher levels of violence (Corrigan & Watson, 2005) and other criminal behaviors (Wright, Gournay, Glorney, & Thornicroft, 2002). It is widely known that for individuals with psychosis, abuse of drugs and alcohol increases psychotic symptoms, reduces treatment compliance, and is associated with higher relapse rates (Lambert et al., 2005). Hartwell (2004) compared characteristics of inmates who had mental illness to those with both a mental illness and a co-occurring substance use disorder. Those with both disorders were more likely to have a history of violence, homelessness, prior legal involvement, and use of probation services, and had returned to jail more often following release.

Within the correctional setting, co-occurring disorders are associated with increased risks of suicide and victimization. For example, in a study examining the characteristics of incarcerated individuals who committed suicide in New York prisons between 1993 and 2001, 95 percent of the victims had a history of substance abuse and 84 percent had a mental health disorder (Way, Miraglia, Sawyer, Beer, & Eddy, 2005). Also troubling is the fact that detainees with co-occurring disorders are more frequently subjected to violent victimization than those with a psychiatric or a substance use disorder alone (Sells, Rowe, Fisk, & Davidson, 2003).

Coupled with impulsive and unpredictable behaviors (Chandler et al., 2004) and significantly increased risks and treatment needs, detainees with both mental health and substance use disorders represent one of the most challenging groups to treat within the entire criminal justice system. Because co-occurring disorders among the mentally ill offender population appears to be "the rule, rather than the exception" (Miller & Bakalar, 2003, p. 1), treatment targeted at mentally ill offenders must include integrated mental health and substance abuse treatment. However, these inmates present an especially unique challenge to correctional facilities to treat because while, "these offenders represent a small portion of the total incarcerated population, they demand disproportionate attention and fiscal resources due to increased medical needs and security risk" (Van Stelle & Moberg, 2004, p. 39).

Female Inmates with Serious Mental Disorders

Since 1995, the adult female jail population has continued to grow at rates greater than those of male inmates. According to Harrison and Beck (2006), between the years of 1995 and 2004, the population of incarcerated females increased by about 53 percent, compared to a 31 percent increase of men. These authors further report that the numbers of female inmates is growing each year by over 6 percent (6.2% annual growth rate), while the population of male inmates continues to grow more slowly (3.7% annual growth rate).

The Bureau of Justice Statistics estimated in 2000 that 11 out 1,000 U.S. women were at risk of incarceration in federal or state prisons at least once during their lifetime (Grenfeld & Snell, 2000). By mid-year 2005, women accounted for 7 percent of all inmates in U.S. jails (Harrison & Beck, 2006). Female inmates are estimated to be twice as likely to have a current severe mental disorder (15%) than male detainees (6.1%) (Abram, Teplin, & McClelland, 2003).

Historically, treatment within jails and prisons has largely been geared toward meeting the needs of male prisoners (Green, Miranda, Daroowalla, & Siddique, 2005), even though the treatment needs of female prisoners are unique. Most female prisoners are disproportionally minority (Harrison & Beck, 2006), socioeconomically disadvantaged, and have minor children in the home at the time of arrest (Lewis, 2005). Many female inmates have experienced physical and/or sexual abuse or exploitation, and have a high incidence of substance abuse disorders as well as higher rates of psychiatric disorders (Salasin, 2002). Early research about women in jails and prisons found that nearly 1 in 20 detained women experienced a severe psychiatric disorder, double the rate of nonincarcerated women in the general U.S. population (Teplin, Abram, & McCelland, 1996).

Female mentally ill offenders have unique treatment needs that require specialized treatment. One of the most significant treatment needs of incarcerated women involves the high incidence of trauma history, such as childhood abuse, domestic partner violence or other exploitation that results in high rates of post traumatic stress disorder (PTSD). Research has shown a strong correlation between all forms of childhood abuse and neglect and adult arrests. Over 44 percent of women under some type of correctional authority report experiencing either physical or sexual abuse at some time during their lifetimes (Grenfeld & Snell, 2000).

In 2000, about one-half of women detained in state prisons had been using drugs, alcohol, or both at arrest (Genfeld & Snell, 2000). Substance abuse among female offenders has been linked to more severe psychopathology and more lifetime arrests, arrests related to substance use, and arrests related to their mental health (Brems, Johnson, Neal, & Freeman, 2004).

Female inmates have significantly higher rates of mental disorders and co-occurring substance use disorders than male inmates or compared to females in the general population (Weinstein, Kim, Mack, Malavade, & Saraiya, 2005). A study of 1,272 female arrestees awaiting trial at the Cook County Department of Corrections in Chicago found that 8 percent had both a current severe mental disorder and a current substance use disorder (Abram et al., 2003). Nearly three-quarters (72%) of those with a severe mental disorder also met criteria for one or more substance use disorders during some time in their life. These women were found to be 1.5 to 4.9 times more likely than women without a severe mental disorder to have a co-occurring substance use disorder. Like men, women with mental illness often are unable to adapt to and cope with prison life, resulting in accumulating histories of disciplinary infractions (Human Rights Watch, 2003).

Given the distinct clinical, social, and health needs of incarcerated women, both clinical and correctional staff needs specialized training on appropriate gender-specific interventions, treatment and behavior management. Ideally, correctional facilities offer, in conjunction with psychiatric interventions, integrated treatment for co-occurring mental and substance use disorders, medication treatment, education and management, treatment targeted toward relief of trauma-related symptoms, and other treatment linked to the vocational, health, and family needs of this group of incarcerated women (APA, 2000).

Other variables that influence treatment within jails and prisons include treatment history; motivation for treatment; co-morbid disorders such as brain injury, prolonged substance abuse, or other health related problems; side effects from psychotropic medications; and peer pressure to refrain from treatment (Holton, 2003). Of concern too is the fact that individuals within the correctional setting are often disproportionally minority and have been found to have been at greater risk for arrest and incarceration than non-minority detainees (Greenfeld & Snell, 2000). While there is a beginning body of knowledge around culturally competent mental health services, there is surprisingly little to no work yet done on its implications in the effective treatment of mentally ill minority offenders.

Mentally ill offenders rarely enter jail or prison with a singular mental disorder to treat. Women and minority offenders also bring unique treatment needs that extend beyond their mental illness to the correctional setting. The staggering number of inmates with severe mental disorders, compounded by co-occurring health and behavioral disorders, and other social disadvantages serve to highlight the unique treatment needs and the importance of providing effective treatment to mentally ill offenders. Following is an overview of treatment for such offenders in the correctional setting.

Treating the Mentally Disordered Offender

As recently as the late 1980s many jails and prisons did not routinely screen detainees for mental illness. While facilities reported providing psychotropic medications, few provided psychotherapy or counseling, or any coordination for inmates returning to the community (Steadman, McCarthy, & Morrisey, 1989).

While screening and treatment for the mentally disordered incarcerated offender appears to have improved, a significant number of facilities do not treat the mentally ill. According to data collected by the Bureau of Justice Statistics on mental health treatment provided in state public and private adult correctional facilities, 89 percent report that they provide some type of mental health services to their inmates, 78 percent screen inmates at intake, 83 percent provide psychotropic medications, 79 percent conduct psychiatric assessments, and 84 percent provide some type of therapy or counseling (Beck & Maruschack, 2001).

It has become widely accepted that untreated inmates with a serious mental disorder are more violent than the general population (Junginger, 2006). However, there is substantial evidence that appropriate correctional mental health and related interventions can help prevent mental deterioration that could result in a loss of impulse control and lead to violent behavior toward self and others (Lovell, Allen, Johnson, & Jemelka, 2001). Treatment has been shown to reduce disciplinary problems and the need for behavior management, as well as facility liability (Hills et al., 2004). Additionally, treatment and services for offenders can help to reduce their recidivism to the criminal justice system (Chandler et al., 2004).

Correctional facilities face several challenges in attempting to treat mentally disordered inmates. Probably the most significant challenges are the high costs associated with providing treatment (Human Rights Watch, 2003) coupled with a general lack of resources earmarked for correctional mental health services (Holton, 2003). Even when a budget allows for correctional mental services, facilities still struggle with programmatic factors and other clinical decisions such as: (1) determining whom and how to effectively treat; (2) managing serious behaviors and symptoms; (3) recognizing and attempting to minimize the negative effects of the prison environment; (4) understanding and responding to the difficulty mentally ill inmates have in adjusting to institutional life; and (5) determining the need for special services (Hills et al., 2004). Staff training and diversity are both added variables influencing offender treatment. Educating staff about mental illness, its symptoms, and effective intervention and de-escalation techniques is critical. Programs must also consider how the lack of cultural or ethnic diversity among staff may negatively impact the motivation of inmates to engage in treatment (Holton, 2003).

Legal Mandates to Provide Treatment

Prior to the civil rights movement, there was little scrutiny of how mentally ill offenders were arrested or detained. Moreover, if facilities offered treatment for offenders' mental disorders, it received little attention or scrutiny (Hafemeister, 1998). Improvements to the treatment of mentally disordered offenders coincide with 1970s, when each state made changes to their civil commitment laws that that increased civil liberty protections to individuals.

At present, treatment for the incarcerated mentally ill offender is considered a constitutional right. One of the first court rulings regarding the general treatment of offenders was the U.S. Supreme Court's 1976 ruling in *Estelle v. Gamble*. This case held that once a government deprives a person of liberty, those who are holding them become responsible for providing the means for fulfillment of basic human needs (McLearen & Ryba, 2003). This case affirmed all prisoners' right to basic health care. The following year, *Bowring v. Godwin* (1977) extended those rights to include psychiatric care. In 1980, *Vitek v. Jones* provided that mentally ill offenders have a right to a hearing—similar to a civil commitment hearing—before being transferred to a mental health facility (Lurigio, 2001). Today, much of the treatment provided to mentally ill offenders in the correctional setting is available due to the landmark case of *Ruiz v. Estelle* (1980), which established minimal standards for the provision of adequate mental health care to inmates with mental illnesses (Lurigio, 2001).

More recently, the case of *Washington v. Harper* (1990) confirmed inmates' rights to refuse treatment while incarcerated (McLearen & Ryba, 2003). Most often this involves forced medications, but can include other treatment as well. However, when an inmate poses a threat to themselves or others, treatment may be provided without informed consent (Hills et al., 2004).

The Mentally Disordered Offender Treatment and Crime Reduction Act of 2004 (S.1194) supports collaborative efforts between local mental health, criminal justice, and juvenile justice agencies to develop jail diversion, mental health courts, and other programs to divert nonviolent offenders with mental health problems from the criminal justice to the mental health system.

While legal protections have been awarded mentally ill detainees, the case law and statutes do not provide a universally clear or agreed-upon definition of what correctional services and interventions constitute "adequate" mental health care (Steadman et al., 2005). The American Psychiatric Association (2000), the National Commission on Correctional Health Care (NCCHC) (2003), the American Correctional Association (1991), and the American Jail Association all provide correctional systems with standards of care in the delivery of mental health services to its inmates. These standards, while not mandated, recommend minimum services and set guidelines for the following services: (1) identification, including screening, referral, and evaluation of mental health disorders and treatment needs; (2) treatment; and (3) discharge planning within correctional mental health services. The following sections will describe these three service areas within the correctional setting and how they relate and impact the seriously mentally ill offender.

IDENTIFYING MENTAL DISORDERS AMONG JAIL AND PRISON DETAINEES

When an inmate is received into a correctional institution, they are usually fingerprinted, and receive a medical exam and other assessments that allow staff to make decisions about classification, housing, and other programmatic or special needs (Council on State Governments, 2002). This identification process can also include some sort of screening for mental health disorders needing treatment and to identify risk factors, such as a suicide or violence toward others. Many city jails process up to 300 individuals a day (Grisso, 2006).

The 2006 National Mental Health Association (NMHA) Policy Position on Mental Health Treatment in Correctional Facilities clearly describes how facilities should screen for mental health disorders:

All prisoners should be screened upon admission by trained personnel for mental health and substance abuse problems. When the screening detects possible mental health problems, prisoners should be referred for further evaluation, assessment and treatment by mental health professionals. Prisoners who are already receiving treatment before they enter should be assisted in continuing treatment. All prisoners who are not released within one week should have behavioral, mental health and substance abuse evaluations completed by qualified mental health staff by such date. (p. 10)

Screening can range from one or two questions about previous mental health treatment to an extensive, structured mental health evaluation (Steadman et al., 2005). Early and accurate identification of individuals' mental health disorders is essential to fully assess if they pose a danger to themselves or others, or are taking psychotropic medications. Identification is equally important in establishing the proper placement and level of supervision for offenders. Early detection and assessment of mental disorders helps prevent injuries to offenders, other inmates, and staff, as well as unnecessary mental decompensation and symptom exacerbation, medication interruptions, abuse by other inmates and suicide.

However important this screening may be to the early identification and classification of mentally ill offenders, it can be difficult and does not consistently occur (NCCHC, 2002). Early inquiry into the effectiveness of correctional screening in detecting mental disorders found nearly 63 percent of inmates with serious mental illness were not properly identified (Teplin, 1990). Further studies ensued. In one study of over 1,700 U.S. jails, Steadman and Veysey (1997) found that while 83 percent provided some type of initial mental health screening, the procedures were highly variable. More recently, a concern was raised when Peters, LeVasseur, and Chandler (2004) found that in many cases, co-occurring disorders are not detected in correctional settings, which leads to misdiagnosis, and can lead to a lack of treatment services or diminished treatment results.

There are several factors that impact attainment of consistent and accurate screening of mentally ill offenders. A primary problem is the lack of a standardized and validated screening tool (Osher, Steadman, & Barr, 2003) and screening tools that have high rates of false positives or false negatives (Steadman et al., 2005). For instance, in one study, jail screening detected less than half of the inmates diagnosed with a serious mental illness (McLearen & Ryba, 2003). Additionally, there seems to be an over reliance on self-reports to identify disorders and the presence of drug or alcohol use at arrest that masks symptoms (Swartz & Lurigio, 2005a). While some mental disorders manifest themselves with obvious symptoms, others are more subtle and require skilled clinicians to detect (Human Rights Watch, 2003). The sheer volume of incoming detainees and a lack of correctional staff expertise and training create barriers to having better screening outcomes (Swartz & Lurigio, 2005a).

Initial Screening and Assessment Tools

Steadman et al. (2005) provide an overview of the most commonly used mental health screening tools, which includes identifying their strengths and weaknesses. For example they found that the Symptom Checklist 90, created by Derogatis in 1977, and the Brief Symptom Inventory, also designed by Derogatis in 1993, are both long, focus on the self-rated experience of specific symptoms within the past week, and are expensive. The use of the Brief Psychiatric Rating Scale and the Schedule of Affective Disorders and Schizophrenia–Change Version require an independent clinical rating. The authors find that these may be useful in a more in-depth follow-up assessment but are not practical at the initial, time-sensitive, screening stage. Another commonly used instrument within corrections is the Referral Decision Scale (RDS), created by Teplin and Swartz in 1989. The RDS was designed for use by correctional staff to identify serious mental disorders among inmates. Studies have been mixed in establishing levels of this instrument's measurement validity.

Promising Innovations

Several innovative screening tools have been evaluated for use in jails to quickly identify individuals with serious mental disorders and co-occurring substance use disorders.

Brief Jail Mental Health Screen (BJMHS).   The BJMHS, developed by Veysey, Beckstead and Deane in 1999 (Steadman et al., 2005), is an eight-item screening tool used to identify incoming detainees in jails and detentions centers who require additional mental health evaluation. The BJMHS was validated in a study of over 10,000 detainees (Steadman et al., 2005), which found that this tool correctly identified 73 percent of the males and 62 percent of the females needing treatment. However, while this tool appears reliable with males, it had an unacceptably high rate of false negatives for female detainees.

K6 Screening Tool.   The K6 Screening Tool (Kessler et al., 2002) is well-validated for use in the general population. The six-question scale measures symptom severity and level of functioning. Until recently, the use of this scale had not been validated for use among detainees. Swartz and Lurigio (2005b) found the K6 Screening Tool promising for use in identifying both male and female seriously mentally ill detainees. The scale is easy to administer and score, and appropriate for use by staff with limited mental health training.

Jail Screening Assessment Tool (JAST).   The JAST is a semi-structured interview intended to provide jails and pretrial facilities with an initial screen of incoming detainees for mental health disorders, as well as assessing risk of victimization, violence, and suicide and other self-harming behaviors (Nicholls, Roesch, Olley, Ogloff, & Henepin, 2005). Comparing evaluation results using the JAST with independent assessments on a sample of incarcerated females, the authors found that assessments using the JAST significantly agreed with independent assessments in detecting mental disorders.

Considering the exceptionally high incidence of co-occurring substance use disorders among mentally ill offenders, it seems screening should routinely include assessment for a dual disorder. Yet there is little empirical evaluation of screening for co-occurring disorders in correctional settings, and we must look to studies in the alcohol and drug abuse field to inform future advancements in developing co-occurring disorder screening tools for use in correctional settings. For example, Peters et al., (2000) conducted a study comparing the accuracy of several well-established scales used to detect alcohol or drug dependence and their effectiveness among incoming detainees. These researchers found the Addiction Severity Index–Drug Use (ASI), Texas Christian University Drug Screen (TCUDS), and the Simple Screening Instrument (SSI) to be most accurate among all evaluated screening tools for use with detainees.

While there are promising developments in screening for behavioral health disorders among detainees, there remains a considerable need for continued development and evaluation of valid and reliable screening tools that will accurately identify mental health and substance abuse disorders and risk of harm to self or others. When choosing mental health screening tools, correctional programs should look for those that are brief, easy to administer, and contain explicit decision criteria. Additionally, they should be empirically validated and provide low rates of false negatives (miss detainees with a mental disorder) or false positives (incorrectly identify a mental disorder), and screen for co-occurring substance use disorders (Steadman et al., 2005). Moreover, screening tools must be designed for use by non-mental health professionals, as most screening is conducted by staff other than trained psychiatrists or psychologists (Grisso, 2006).

Screening, identifying, and determining the treatment needs of mentally disordered offenders is indeed a challenge. However, that challenge may significantly pale when comparing it to the task of providing mental health treatment for individuals within the correctional setting. Knowing there is a need and meeting it are clearly two different propositions. Attempting to meet the diverse and complex treatment needs of inmates with serious mental disorders—who more likely than not have co-occurring substance use disorders—in a setting that is designed to detain and maintain order and safety under conditions of understaffing, overcrowding, and budget constraints presents unique challenges to correctional systems. The following section reviews treatment within correctional settings.

TREATMENT PROGRAMS IN JAILS AND PRISONS

According to Young (2002), the primary purpose of correctional treatment "has been to ensure the safety of the individual, other inmates, and staff by identifying and stabilizing those at most immediate risk. Thus, underlying conditions are not routinely treated" (p. 62). Mental health services provided in correctional settings may be provided by jail staff, through private contract, or provided by staff from an outside publicly funded mental health agency (Young, 2002).

Because jails must rapidly process and receive large numbers of detainees who have shorter length of stays, mental health services primarily focus on suicide prevention and stabilizing acute conditions (Veysey & Bichler-Robertson, 2002). Though some level of mental health care is provided to most mentally ill individuals while incarcerated, the most common types are screening and evaluation, suicide prevention, crisis intervention, the prescription and management of psychotropic medications (Young, 2002), and short-term treatment (Veysey & Bichler-Robertson, 2002).

Veysey & Bichler-Robertson (2002) identify minimum principles that should guide treatment to detained mentally disordered offenders: "(1) persons in detention should not leave the facility in worse condition than when they arrived and (2) persons should not be punished for being identified as having a need (i.e., the identification of a mental illness should not affect access to other services or the length of time spent in jail)" (p. 158).

Prisons provide a greater range of services emphasizing long-term support, including residential units for individuals with stable conditions who cannot be placed in general population, psychopharmacological treatment, case management, group therapy, counseling, and other rehabilitation services (Veysey & Bichler-Robertson, 2002). While recreational therapy, cognitive-behavioral therapy, Dialectical Behavior Therapy, therapeutic communities, faith-based services, and behavioral incentive programs are offered within correctional settings, not all of these options work equally well, or are made available to the seriously mentally ill inmate (Chaiken, Thompson, & Shoemaker, 2005).

Crisis Intervention and Suicide Prevention

Because suicide is a leading cause of death among prison inmates, suicide prevention efforts are a primary concern within correctional facilities. The mentally ill offender is statistically at an especially high risk for suicide. Research has shown that serious mental illness, a history of past suicide attempts, a lengthy sentence, problems within the facility, being housed in segregation or in an isolated unit, and being between 31 and 40 years old and male all are factors associated with increased risk of inmate suicide (Hills et al., 2004).

When inmates' mental disorders make them a danger to themselves and/or others, or render them acutely psychotic and unable to care for themselves, crisis intervention is required. Detecting and monitoring inmates in acute psychiatric crisis also requires providing a safe environment. Commonly, suicide prevention includes emergency evaluations, close observation in a special housing area, physical or chemical restraints, or moving the individual to an inpatient psychiatric unit that may be either inside or outside the facility (Veysey & Bichler-Robertson, 2002). The common procedure of isolating and removing the clothing of a suicidal individual has been determined to exacerbate problems (Veysey & Bichler-Robertson, 2002).

NCCHC (2003) standards suggest any program targeted toward suicide prevention should incorporate specific policies and procedures that include the following: (1) identification procedures; (2) training for all staff; (3) suicide assessment by a trained mental health professional; (4) developed procedures for monitoring at-risk inmates that includes regular and documented supervision; (5) a housing plan that allows suicidal inmates to remain out of isolation unless under constant supervision; (6) a referral process for suicidal inmates to be seen by a mental health professional for treatment; (7) clear procedures for staff to follow in the event of a suicide attempt; and (8) a family notification policy if there is an attempted or completed suicide.

Psychopharmacological Treatment

Many mentally ill offenders are routinely provided psychotropic medications during their incarceration. However, Veysey and Bichler-Robertson (2002) report that some correctional facilities do not provide access to all available classes of psychotropic medications, particularly "new generation" medications that have higher costs. New generation, or atypical, psychotropic medications cause less intrusive side effects such as involuntary movement or tremors, and in turn do not need side effect medications that can be abused (Roskes, 2000). As a result, individuals entering the correctional setting can have their medications switched from ones they may have adjusted to, only to be replaced by medications that may not work as well or produce greater side effects, which can have a most undesired effect. As Hills et al. (2004) point out, inmates may be more likely to refuse or discontinue medications altogether if they produce undesirable side effects. In fact, the noncompliance rate for inmates taking older medications is nearly double that of inmates taking new generation medications (Roskes, 2000).

A study conducted in the Texas prison system to evaluate prescribing practices found that Black males and females were prescribed new generation antipsychotic agents less frequently than their counterparts (Baillargeon & Contreras, 2001). This is of particular concern given that African Americans are more susceptible to the development of tardive dyskinesia or dystonia than other ethnic groups (Hills et al., 2004).

According to Hills et al. (2004), forced medication of adult inmates is allowed under NCCHC standards in emergency situations that pose an immediate threat to the inmates or others and when other less-intrusive interventions have been tried and failed. In nonemergency situations, inmates are entitled to a procedural review process if they refuse medications; however, they can still be given medications in most cases. This is of concern due to the tendency to overprescribe medication for the purpose of sedation, and has been identified as a significant treatment and civil rights issue within jails and prisons (Veysey & - Bichler-Robertson, 2002).

Co-Occurring Disorder Treatment in the Correctional Setting

Inmates with severe mental disorders with co-occurring substance use disorders are often excluded from alcohol or drug treatment programs offered in correctional settings. Programs can exclude inmates who are taking psychotropic medications. Programs that use highly confrontational treatment methods can trigger or aggravate individuals' psychiatric symptoms (Hills, 2000).

An integrated treatment approach is necessary to effectively treat inmates with co-occurring disorders. Traditionally, early interventions aimed at treating co-occurring disorders were provided either sequentially—mental health treatment first, then substance abuse treatment, or visa versa. Or, if not sequentially, these services were provided in tandem—treatment was provided by two different programs. Neither of these approaches was successful. In an integrated treatment approach, the mental illness and substance use disorder are considered similar disorders and are treated together with both disorders considered to be of primary importance (DiNitto & Webb, 2005).

The literature suggests several integrated interventions geared toward the effective identification and treatment of offenders with co-occurring disorders within a correctional setting. These interventions include specialized screening and assessment for co-occurring disorders, and motivational and staged interventions based on functioning, impairment, and readiness to engage in treatment. Also recommended are the use of modified therapeutic communities (TCs), assertive community treatment (ACT), and various housing and employment services, all of which show promise in reductions in criminal activity and improved behavioral health outcomes (Chandler et al., 2004; SAMHSA, 2002).

According to Chandler et al. (2004), additional approaches include psychoeducational model interventions, learning contingency management, intensive case-management services, and self-help groups developed for individuals with co-occurring disorders, such as "Double Trouble" groups. In a national survey of 20 treatment programs for co-occurring disorders within correctional settings, Peters, LeVasseur, and Chandler (2004) found commonly provided services included the innovative use of modified therapeutic communities and other services that had been adapted for inmates with co-occurring disorders. These modifications included reduced levels of confrontation, greater staff coordination, and more involvement in program activities. A common approach was providing integrated mental health and substance abuse treatment, and intensive assessment, drug testing, education, therapy and support groups, anger management, and other support services were identified. They also discovered that most of the existing programs were freestanding units located in self-contained housing units that were isolated from the general inmate population.

Specialized Housing and Residential Programs

For inmates with mental disorders who are incarcerated for longer periods of time, a range of housing and residential programs may be offered. These include inpatient care, short-term crisis beds, and long-term residential treatment units, as well as general population housing (Veysey & Bichler-Robertson, 2002).

Inpatient Psychiatric Hospitalization

Inmates who are at risk of harming themselves or others are often removed from the correctional facility to an inpatient psychiatric hospital setting. Services include evaluation, nursing care, assistance with daily living skills, suicide precautions, and medical treatment, as well as individual and group therapy. Because these services may not be provided within correctional facilities, many inmates who require this level of care are sent to state or private inpatient psychiatric hospitals (Chaiken et al., 2005).

Both seclusion and mechanical restraint devices are used at times to protect the mentally ill offender from self-harm or harm directed toward other inmates or staff. However, there is a well-documented potential for misusing these devices to punish or control inmates, rather than as a therapeutic method (Hills et al., 2004). Of special concern is the significant history of trauma and abuse experienced by mentally ill inmates; the use of restraints may only serve to significantly re-traumatize these inmates (APA, 2000).

Some facilities have trained staff and developed protocols to attempt less restrictive alternatives in order to de-escalate a person before implementation of any restraints. This is often referred to as "talking the person down" (APA, 2000). The NCCHA (2003) has established guidelines for the use of restraints in the correctional setting including establishing clear written policies and procedures that outline the use of restraints, and suggests that any use of restraints be ordered by a doctor or other health care provider and not exceed 12 hours. Inmates in seclusion or restraint should be checked at a minimum of every 15 minutes and NCCHA guidelines forbid the use of restraints or seclusion for any disciplinary reason.

"Outpatient" Services

Mentally disordered inmates who live in the general population and are stable may receive individual therapy, group treatment, or psychiatric consultation on an "outpatient" basis or at a drop-in clinic (Chaiken et al., 2005). When available, individual psychotherapy is most often targeted toward the most disturbed mentally disordered inmates, though this treatment approach is often limited by resources (Hills et al., 2004).

Residential Programs

Mentally disordered inmates are often vulnerable to abuse by staff and other inmates. They can be disruptive and have difficulty adjusting to and managing the stresses of prison life. Both short-term and long-term units exist to house the mentally ill offender outside the general population housing. Short-term crisis beds provide 24-hour medical supervision and crisis stabilization as an alternative to inpatient psychiatric hospitalization. Long-term specialized residential units can provide a safe and therapeutic alternative to safely house and treat mentally ill offenders (Veysey & Bichler-Robertson, 2002).

Group Treatment

Group treatment is the most frequently used intervention in correctional settings, in part due to its cost-effectiveness. Groups can help mentally ill inmates gain support and realize others have mental disorders, develop anger management skills, improve interpersonal and communication skills, understand psychotropic medications and their side effects, and learn about mental health and substance use and managing these disorders (Hills et al., 2004).

Support and self-help groups frequently are an organized part of prison life, though not considered a formal treatment intervention. These groups are appealing to correctional program administrators because they can be used in collaboration with other treatment at little or no cost (Hills et al., 2004). However, mentally ill offenders are not always able to meaningfully participate or be welcomed into groups that include general population offenders.

Case Management Services

Case management services are sometimes provided to mentally ill inmates. Prison-based case managers who work with offenders with mental disorders create treatment plans, meet with inmates to monitor their functioning, provide counseling, act as a liaison between offenders and other staff, and help plan for discharge (Hills et al., 2004).

In one study that identified nonpsychiatric social work services provided to over 350 detainees on mental health unit found that housing evaluation (74.4%) and follow-up services, such as checking in with an inmate by a mental health professional (58.5%), were most the most commonly provided support services (Young, 2002).

Modified Therapeutic Communities

Therapeutic communities provide drug and alcohol treatment for those with serious addictive disorders within a residential environment where inmates are usually segregated from the general population for 6 to 24 months (Hills et al., 2004). Modified corrections-based therapeutic communities may have a place in treating incarcerated mentally ill offenders.

Van Stelle, Blumer, and Moberg (2004) evaluated an institutional modified therapeutic community (ITC) offering integrated treatment for male inmates with co-occurring serious mental health and substance use disorders. The Oshkosh, Wisconsin, program is a 25-bed, 9–12 month program that provides a regimented environment, individual therapy, and a variety of treatment groups focusing on mental health and substance use issues, as well as cognitive behavioral treatment, anger management, and relapse prevention. They found that during their incarceration, graduates of this program were released sooner, had less conduct reports, and were more likely to receive mental health and substance abuse treatment when compared to inmates who were terminated from the program and to a comparison group. Postrelease graduates were more likely to be abstinent, taking prescribed medications, and medically stable. However, differences in recidivism rates at 12 months were not significant.

Treating mentally ill offenders with multiple, broad, and complex disorders while attempting to maintain the safety and security of a correctional institution is exceptionally challenging. Even in the most innovative, well-funded, and fully staffed facilities, providing effective treatment remains difficult. While treatment seems to be more prevalent than in the past, there is still significant ground to gain. As Young (2003) cautions, "the reported presence of a service should not be confused with the quality of the service or whether the level of service provision is adequate to the level of need" (p. 65).

RELEASE PLANNING, COMMUNITY REENTRY, AND COMMUNITY CORRECTIONS

Approximately 600,000 people are released from U.S. prisons each year (Beck, 2000), most of whom are not under continued supervision (Hills et al., 2004). At least 96,000 of those who reenter the community have acute to severe mental health problems (Wolff et al., 2005). Persons with mental illness who are released from jails or prisons are at increased risk of rearrest, psychiatric decompensation (McCoy, Roberts, Hanrahan, Clay, & Luchins, 2004), and suicide (Pratt, Piper, Appleby, Webb, & Shaw, 2006).

Expecting a seriously mentally disordered offender will leave a correctional system prepared to locate and navigate a complex community mental health and social service system alone and able to find psychiatric treatment, obtain prescribed medications, arrange for housing, and other needed social services without encountering significant problems is improbable. Even when efforts are made to help coordinate treatment, follow-up appointments are often missed due to a lack of reliable transportation, interagency miscommunication, or stable housing, or due to interrupted support services (Weisman, Lamberti, & Price, 2004).

Community Reentry

Correctional facilities have historically maintained a primary focus on the health care of inmates only while they remain incarcerated (Wolff, Plammons, Veysey, & Brandli, 2002). Reentry planning secures coordinated and continued treatment after incarceration for the mentally disordered offender (Petersilia, 2003) and is essential in ensuring continuity in mental health care. It serves not only as a "diversion" from the correctional system, but also as a "linkage" to treatment, rehabilitation, social services, and other support services (Rock, 2001). While reentry planning and coordination are critical, they are one the least frequently provided mental health service in correctional settings (Osher et al., 2003).

It is unfortunate that in practice inmates with mental health disorders are released to the community with little or no reentry planning (Wolff et al., 2005). Schaefer and Stefanacnic (2003) describe the worst case scenario among Riker's Island inmates upon release:

> All inmates, including the mentally ill ones, are discharged from Riker's Island without money, medications, insurance (insurance is generally lost to those incarcerated), prescriptions or treatment plans. Furthermore, New York City inmates only receive three subway tokens at time of discharge, which is between 2–4 a.m. in the middle of Queens. Without proper care, medication and support, the unavoidable happens: The mentally ill person decompensates, becomes violent and returns to jail again. (p. 45)

Failure to provide discharging mentally ill offenders with comprehensive reentry planning and linkages to necessary mental health care and other social services should be of concern to all. The outcomes of inadequate transition planning include the compromise of public safety, an increased incidence of psychiatric symptoms, psychiatric hospitalization, relapse to substance abuse, suicide, homelessness, and rearrest (Osher et al., 2003).

Little empirical evidence is available to guide development of reentry services (Wilson & Draine, 2006), though its success rests heavily on the collaboration of the corrections and community mental health systems (Reynolds, Dziegielewski, & Shapp, 2004). This collaboration should include defined and clear role expectations, cross-training, good communications, and formalized agreements between the two systems, as well as a means for evaluating the effectiveness of the services arranged (Rock, 2001).

Successful reentry for parolees with mental disorders and co-occurring substance use disorders must start with a plan that outlines assessed psychiatric and substance abuse treatment needs and financial supports, as well as housing and other social or family supports. Hartwell (2001) found that females are more likely to engage in community services and have slightly lower recidivism rates than males. Hartwell (2003b) also found that in addition to community mental health services, mentally ill offenders needed substance abuse treatment (76%), assistance with housing (30%), violence risk assessment (26%), and sex offender treatment (16%).

These reentry planning efforts should, at minimum, include a prerelease treatment plan, medication supply or prescription, and referrals and linkages to community-based mental health and other social services (APA, 2000). Wolff et al., (2005) explains the importance of reentry services:

> Reentry planning, from a social investment perspective, is a mechanism that protects the health outcomes produced by investments in correctional health care and, by extension, produces justice outcomes to the extent that the public is protected from future criminal behavior associated with untreated mental illness. (p. 22)

Another reason to emphasize comprehensive reentry planning is that mentally ill prisoners often serve longer prison terms because of a lack of an approved and viable discharge plan that includes solid arrangements for treatment and housing (Lurigio, Rollins, & Fallon, 2004).

Community-Based Treatment

Even when mentally ill offenders reenter the community with a coordinated referral to treatment, nothing ensures that the services will be comprehensive, meet their treatment needs, or prevent rearrest. A study by Lovell, Gagliardi, and Peterson (2002) compared community-based treatment and recidivism rates of over 300 Washington state mentally ill offenders released to the community. They found that while 73 percent of those released were referred and received some type of community-based mental health or social services, few received comprehensive care. While completely counterintuitive, those offenders who had committed more serious crimes were not engaged in services until much later after release and received fewer services than those who committed less serious crimes. As a result, 77 percent of those studied recidivated during the first year of release.

The mentally ill offender leaving the correctional facility will have a host of unmet needs and other factors that potentially complicate and impact successful reentry and reintegration into the community. These include complex treatment needs, stigma, and statutory restrictions that may impact community reintegration.

Preventing the reincarceration of mentally ill offenders is the primary goal of community corrections programs. Certain risk factors, other than mental illness, have been identified that indicate a greater likelihood of reoffending. Gagliardi, Lovell, Peterson, and Jemelka (2004) evaluated 333 mentally ill offenders (30% female) released from Washington state prisons and found that of the 77 percent who were either arrested or charged with a new crime, younger offenders with more lengthy criminal histories were highly correlated with new felony or violence-related charges. Conversely, those who had low infraction rates and were housed in a mental health unit during incarceration and were older at the time of their first offense were less likely to reoffend. Phillips et al. (2005) examined the ability of demographic, criminal history, and clinical variables to predict recidivism in offenders with serious mental illness, finding that diagnosis was not predictive of reoffending. These results show that reconviction in offenders with mental disorders can be predicted using the same criminogenic variables that are predictive in offenders without mental disorders.

Mentally ill offenders present community-based treatment providers with a set of complex treatment needs and concerns for public safety. These concerns are valid, as these offenders are often more treatment-resistant and have poorer compliance with antipsychotic medications, high rates of co-occurring substance abuse disorders, and a need for structure, all of which can be further complicated by the real or perceived dangerousness of the offender (Lamb & Weinberger, 1998). As a result, community mental health providers often feel ill-equipped to adequately serve the reentering mentally ill offender and their reluctance to serve this population is common (Haimowitz, 2004).

Along these same lines, a one-year follow-up study of the transitional success of offenders with severe mental illness released from an intermediate care facility found that 89 percent were released with discharge plans including referral to mental health services and psychopharmacology (Lamb & Weinberger, 2005). However, during the follow-up period, over half were reincarcerated or had numerous psychiatric hospitalizations. Their treatment professionals characterized them as leading chaotic lives, having severe interpersonal conflicts, and experiencing serious problems in treatment. The earlier works of these authors argued that treatment and services designed for mentally ill offenders "should not treat them as if they were compliant, cooperative, and in need of a minimum of controls" (p. 497).

The double—or triple—stigma of being an offender, mentally ill, and an addict can create serious barriers in accessing community-based treatment. In response, postrelease treatment should integrate comprehensive criminal justice, mental health treatment, medical care, and other support services (Veysey & Bichler-Robertson, 2002) that are intensive, ongoing, and long-term (Lurigio et al., 2004).

In 2005, the Second Chance Act (HR 1704) was passed, calling for correctional systems to improve and strengthen community reentry efforts for offenders. Yet, factors that are outside the control of either the criminal justice or mental health systems impact the ability to create positive reform. Statutory restrictions prevent many released offenders from obtaining a driver's license and those convicted of drug offenses are ineligible for federal student loans. Offenders are ineligible for public housing, public assistance, and food stamps, and are ineligible to apply for certain jobs, all of which mitigate meaningful efforts toward "second chances" and successful reentry (Pogorelski, Wolff, Pan, & Blitz, 2005).

As characterized by Haimowitz (2004), "the initial successes of reentry programs suggest that the revolving door of reincarceration can be slowed, although how much and in what ways remain to be determined" (p. 375). There is still a great deal more to be done to improve reentry efforts and to empirically evaluate programs and successful approaches.

Community Corrections

While the number of people with mental disorders in U.S. jails and prisons is substantial, it does not begin to account for all the other people with mental illness who are under the supervision of probation or parole (Rock, 2001). Ditton (1999) indicates that during 1998, nearly 16 percent of all probationers were mentally ill. Like jails and prisons, probation and parole programs have experienced explosive growth over the past decade (Veysey & Bichler-Robertson, 2002).

Community corrections is a generic term used to describe the authorities responsible for supervising offenders in the community, including traditional probation or parole departments and pretrial services (Veysey & Bichler-Robertson, 2002). Individuals may be given probation by the court that includes a condition of mandatory outpatient treatment, or referral for treatment by their parole officer, with the understanding that failure with treatment, and other conditions, can result in probation or parole revocation and a return to custody (Lamb & Weinberger, 1998).

Advocates for the mentally ill question the use of involuntary treatment and characterize some aspects of mandated treatment as "coercive." However, compliance with treatment has been shown to increase when mentally ill offenders are required to undergo involuntary treatment (Lamb & Weinberger, 1998). Draine (2003) suggests that using jail for noncompliance is more effective in reducing recidivism when it is balanced with supportive services.

To effectively treat individuals with severe mental health and co-occurring substance abuse disorders and criminal justice histories, models that integrate criminal justice, community behavioral health-care, and support services are necessary (Veysey & Bichler-Robertson, 2002). Several innovative programs have been developed to help ease transitioning mentally ill offenders from the correctional setting to the community. They include specialized probation and parole services, specialized case management and other hybrid programs that specialize in transitioning and serving mentally ill offenders in the community setting.

Specialized Probation & Parole Services.   Societal and legal mandates to be "tough on crime" have also affected the services and supervision of postrelease offenders. Like U.S. criminal laws, traditional parole and probation supervision have become increasingly more punitive, moving away from their former focus of assisting with offender reentry and rehabilitation (Petersilia, 1998). This has resulted in making efforts to serve the mentally ill more challenging. However, to better meet the needs of probationers or parolees, some community correction programs have created specialized units or designated caseloads concentrating on providing supervision and services to the mentally ill.

Specialized probation or parole officers, "attempt to balance the monitoring and control of offenders, which is in the interest of public safety and the administration of justice, with the brokerage of social services, which is in the interest of offender rehabilitation and reintegration into the community" (Lurigio et al., 2004, p. 47). Skeem, Emke-Francis, and Louden (2006) conducted a national survey to identify specialized probation services serving the mentally ill and to compare them to traditional probation service agencies. They found that the probation/parole office (PO) staff in the programs that specialized in serving the mentally ill had obtained expertise and training in the field of mental health and maintained an exclusively mental health caseload. These POs were more highly involved with service providers, often attending treatment team meetings or helping to secure other needed services than POs in traditional programs. They tended to employ a problem-solving approach to violations, viewing jail as a last resort. This type of specialized supervision can help deliver needed services while exercising the authority of the criminal justice system to increase medication compliance and other treatment conditions of release, which should be enforceable, reasonable, and tailored to the risk and needs of the offender (Lurigio et al., 2004).

Whether mandated treatment under the supervision of specialized probation targeting mentally ill probationers actually reduces recidivism remains unclear. While probation officers may promote treatment compliance, they can be limited by large caseloads (Lamberti & Weisman, 2004) or an inability to access or secure needed community-based treatment.

In the case of a mentally ill probationer or parolee, providing increased supervision may result in a greater incarceration rate. Solomon, Draine, and Marcus (2002) followed 250 mentally ill probationers for over a year, finding that individuals under specialized and close supervision experienced an increased risk for incarceration. However, they found that increasing motivation to participate in treatment and actual involvement in treatment appears to help mitigate the risk of reincarceration.

Specialized Case Management.   Recent innovations to case management services include development of intensive case management (ICM) or Forensic Assertive Community Treatment (FACT) collaborative case management programs that serve mentally ill probationers or parolees. Both approaches are characterized by the following program elements: they are (1) client centered; (2) provide comprehensive continuity of care; (3) are available 24-hours, 7-days a week; (4) employ small caseloads; and (5) deliver services in the community and involve the offender's natural environment. These programs may use one assigned case manager or employ a team approach to provide or arrange for services that include mental health, substance abuse, daily living skill development, housing, money management, and other support or social services (Veysey & Bichler-Robertson, 2002).

Specialized case management programs have been found helpful in transitioning inmates with mental illness to the community (Fisher, Wolff, & Roy-Bujnowski, 2003), reducing psychiatric hospitalization, and maintaining stable housing (Bond, Drake, Muser & Latner, 1995). However, long-term legal recidivism outcomes have been mixed (Solomon, 2003) and more study is needed to evaluate these innovative and promising programs (Lamberti, Weisman, & Faden, 2004).

Hybrid Programs.   Hybrid programs target mentally ill offenders transitioning to the community and provide a variety of transitional, ongoing, and community supervision services. Project Link is one such program. Based out of the University of Rochester, this program serves the severely mentally ill, most of whom have co-occurring substance use isorders (90%) and a history of active criminal justice involvement. The primary goals of Project Link are to prevent jail and psychiatric hospital recidivism while promoting community reintegration of individuals with severe mental disorders who are involved in the criminal justice system. This program allows referrals from multiple sources and points of contact, combines Assertive Community Treatment, a modified therapeutic community, and jail diversion. An evaluation of their first 60 enrollees found that the 44 individuals who completed the program experienced significant decreases in arrests and days hospitalized or jailed, as well as improvements in community adjustment factors (Weisman et al., 2004).

JAIL DIVERSION PROGRAMS

One of the most significant and promising developments in the criminal justice system in the last decade has been the expansion of initiatives to divert people with mental disorders from the criminal justice system and into treatment (Petrila, 2005). The growing recognition of the human, social, and financial costs of incarceration of the mentally ill has prompted increased efforts to stop the influx of mentally ill into the criminal justice system by developing efforts that divert low-level offenders from the criminal justice system, before they have fully entered the system (Human Rights Watch, 2003). These programs are collectively referred to as jail diversion programs.

Diversion programs attempt to quickly identify and divert people with mental disorders from the criminal justice system to community-based treatment (Lamberti & Weisman, 2004). Participants in a diversion program may avoid incarceration, spend significantly less time in jail on criminal charges (National GAINS Center, 2005), and/or receive a less severe sentence (Draine & Solomon, 1999).

In an early survey of jail diversion programs, Steadman, Barbera, and Dennis (1994) identified 52 jail diversion programs for offenders with mental illness in the United States. By 2005, there were an estimated 300 jail diversion programs for mentally disordered offenders operating nationwide (Steadman & Naples, 2005).

There are two principle types of diversion programs: prebooking and postbooking diversion programs. Prebooking programs involve identification and diversion of people with mental disorders prior to arrest. Postbooking programs identify and divert individuals either from jail or court following their arrest and booking (Crowell, Broner, & Dupont, 2004).

Prebooking Diversion Programs

Prebooking jail diversion programs provide direct access to psychiatric treatment prior to an arrest or criminal incarceration (Draine & Solomon, 1999). Police are able to avoid arrests for low-level crimes committed by mentally ill individuals by making direct referrals to community-based treatment programs (Steadman, Deane, Borum, & Morrissey, 2000). According to the TAPA Technical Assistance and Policy Analysis Center (2007), most prebooking programs include some form of specialized training for police officers, mobile psychiatric crisis intervention teams consisting of law enforcement and mental health professionals, and 24-hour psychiatric drop-off centers to receive persons brought in by the police. All of these responses are designed to respond to potential mental health crises without forcing an officer to turn to the use of incarceration as a treatment alternative.

Police and Crisis Intervention Teams (CIT).   Police are often the first and primary responders called when there are public disturbances involving people with mental disorders (Rock, 2001). As gatekeepers to the criminal justice system, they have, by default, assumed a role coined "street corner psychiatrist" (Lamb, Weinberger, & DeCuir, Jr., 2002, p. 1266).

Police departments across the United States are adopting diversion strategies that are designed to provide improved responses by law enforcement for people with mental disorders at the prearrest phase. One of the most widely known and used is the crisis intervention team (CIT) program model, also referred to as the "Memphis Model." According to Lamberti and Weisman (2003), the CIT model is a police-based prebooking diversion model that provides officers, who volunteer for the program, a 40-hour training program about psychiatric and substance use disorders, sensitization training from people who have mental disorders, and an introduction to community treatment resources and de-escalation techniques. Police are able to avoid arrests of low-level crimes committed by mentally ill individuals by making direct referrals to community-based treatment programs.

Initial studies have shown that the CIT model is most effective in diverting individuals at the prearrest level (Steadman, Deane, Borum, & Morrissey, 2000). CIT programs have shown to be effective in decreasing the number of mentally ill people taken to jail, as well as decreasing injuries to both the mentally ill person and responding police officers (Lamberti & Weisman, 2003).

Psychiatric Crisis Intervention/Mobile Crisis Teams.   Crisis intervention or mobile crisis team models team trained police officers with mental health workers to conduct joint emergency responses in the community. Mental health professionals may accompany police officers to provide an immediate link to treatment, or may be on call to police for immediate psychiatric consultation (Rock, 2001). Frequently, these collaborative teams work with diversion programs, community-based treatment providers, and the courts to find a diversionary therapeutic case disposition instead of resorting to incarceration (Roberts & Yeager, in press).

An example of this model is found in Los Angeles County, California, where the Department of Mental Health has partnered with county, city, and other municipal law enforcement agencies to provide immediate field response to situations involving mentally ill, violent, or high-risk individuals. These teams respond to 911 calls for assistance whenever mental illness is reported or suspected, and are available to patrol officers requesting assistance.

Psychiatric Emergency Rooms and Psychiatric Crisis Centers.   An increasing number of 24-hour crisis psychiatric drop-off centers or psychiatric emergency rooms (PER) with a policy of no-refusal have become available for police to divert individuals from jail (TAPA Center, 2005). King County, Washington, has had a crisis center that allows police to drop off mentally ill nonviolent misdemeanor offenders since 1991 (Shcaefer & Stefancic, 2003).

In a study of police-based diversion programs, researchers found that the availability of a crisis drop-off center for people with mental illnesses increased the number of specialized diversion responses by law enforcement (Steadman et al., 2000). This reinforces the idea that a critical component of a successful diversion program is having a place to divert mentally ill individuals to and may begin to highlight the importance of PER programs in the continuum of diversion efforts.

Prebooking diversion programs have been shown to be effective in reducing arrests and increasing contacts with community mental health treatment for low-level offenders with serious mental disorder (Borum, Deane, Steadman, & Morrissey, 1998). Further research is needed to determine what program components most effectively produce improved diversion results and better outcomes for diverted individuals.

Postbooking Diversion Programs

In contrast to prebooking diversion programs that keep individuals out of jail altogether, postbooking programs identify and divert individuals from either jail or court following arrest and booking (Crowell, Broner, & Dupont, 2004). In the cases of low-risk offenders who have mental illnesses, program staff negotiates with the prosecuting and defense attorneys in terms of legal case disposition and work closely with mental health providers to secure treatment as an alternative to prosecution or for a reduction in charges (Steadman, Deane, Morrissey, Westcott, Salasin, & Shapiro, 1999). Most programs provide some type of ongoing supervision or monitoring of compliance with treatment (National GAINS Center, 2005). The outcomes for the individuals who are diverted generally include a dismissal of charges in return for agreement for participation in a negotiated set of services, deferred prosecution with requirements for treatment participation, or postsentence release in which conditions of probation include requirements for mental health and substance abuse treatment (Lamberti & Weisman, 2003).

Postbooking programs are showing mixed results. Lamberti et al. (2004) evaluated an institution-based diversion program, Project Link based in Rochester, New York, with positive findings. Conducting a one-year follow-up, they found reductions in mean jail days and the number of arrests. Additionally, client functioning improved. A study by Godley et al. (2000) showed that case management services for offenders with co-occurring disorders resulted in fewer legal problems and improved symptom relief.

Less compelling were the findings of recent research conducted on the nine original SAMSHA jail diversion projects, conducted by Naples and Steadman (2003). They found that while diverted individuals spent more days in the community, they did not differ in number of overall jail days or improvements in mental health symptoms. In this same vein, Crowell, Broner, and Dupont (2004) assessed the cost-effectiveness of four diversion programs and found mixed results.

Lattimore, Broner, Sherman, Frisman, and Shafer (2003) studied 100 prebooking and postbooking diversion participants to determine if they differed at baseline on a number of variables. These researchers found that postbooking participants scored significantly worse on social functioning, and reported more serious histories of substance use and criminal activity.

Mental Health Courts.   Mental health courts, a relatively new type of "problem-solving" or "therapeutic" court, seek to quickly identify and divert mentally ill offenders from the criminal justice system to community-based treatment, in lieu of traditional court processing and sentencing. Criminal charges are often reduced or dropped following the individual's successful program completion. These courts are rapidly increasing in number. The first mental health court was established in 1998 in Broward County, Florida. As of 2005, there were over 110 established programs (Council on State Governments, 2005) in 34 states (Redlich, Steadman, Petrila, Monahan, & Griffin, 2005). Early mental health courts focused primarily on serving low-level offenders, but in a survey of 90 mental health courts, researchers found that 14 percent are now accepting felony cases as well (Redlich et al., 2005).

There are few uniform definitions or program requirements for mental health courts and many of the courts have established themselves independently. Programs vary widely and have distinct differences in eligibility, the types of charges that will be accepted, diagnostic criteria, services and monitoring the court will provide, and legal requirements to participate (Watson, Hanrahan, Luchins, & Lurigio, 2001). This variability makes comparisons across courts difficult.

Mental health courts are touted by proponents as providing program participants with better legal outcomes, improved access to services, and reduced recidivism rates, while saving public dollars. Critics say the courts are paternalistic and coercive and may inadvertently encourage the continued arrest of people in order to access needed mental health treatment. As of 2006, many of these claims remain unstudied and there simply is not empirical evidence to support or refute these assertions.

While mental health courts appear promising, there is little professional literature published that goes beyond basic program descriptions or policy commentary and analysis. Some studies have looked at more important issues of program effectiveness (Teller, Ritter, Salupo-Rodriquez, Munetz, & Gil, 2004; Turpin & Richards, 2003); ethical concerns, such as perceived coercion (Poythress, Petrila, McGaha, & Boothroyd, 2002); or clinical outcomes (Boothroyd, Mercado, Poythress, Christy, & Petrila, 2005) that all provided promising results. One of the more rigorous studies (Cosden, Ellens, Schnell, Ymaini, & Wolfe, 2003) compared mentally ill offenders who participated in a mental health court that provided intensive case management, finding significant reductions in substance abuse and criminal activity.

Yet, further research is essential to evaluate these courts' efficacy. If these courts are found to be effective, it is important to identify what factors contribute to their effectiveness and why they work, and to tease out for whom these courts produce the best outcomes.

While a postbooking approach is most common among diversion programs, mental health advocates are calling for a greater emphasis on preventing the problems before they start and focusing available funding and program planning efforts on prebooking efforts, believing that avoiding incarceration should be the goal whenever possible. Although postbooking programs may provide participants with some improved outcomes, critics assert that by default these programs continue to encourage arrest to secure needed, and often scarce, mental health and integrated co-occurring substance abuse treatment.

In summary, due to the high prevalence of mentally ill offenders, most of whom have co-occurring substance use disorders, in the U.S. criminal justice system, continued efforts to identify, treat, and link them to necessary community treatment and supports upon release is critical. Yet, adequately treating incarcerated mentally ill offenders is difficult because correctional facilities must balance institutional security and safety and staff needs, while facing a highly complex set of behavioral health issues that require specialized interventions. As a growing number of individuals who need mental health and substance abuse treatment are being incarcerated in jails and prisons every day, considerable efforts must focus on improving access and quality of interventions and treatments for the inmates, facilitating strong links with community services at discharge, and improving diversion efforts to prevent mentally ill offenders from entering the front door when possible.

REFERENCES

Abram, K. M., Teplin, L. A., & McClelland, G. M. (2003). Co-morbidity of severe psychiatric disorders and substance use disorders among women in jail. *American Journal of Psychiatry, 160*, 1007–1010.

Abramson, M. F. (1972). The criminalization of mentally disordered behavior: Possible side-effect of a new mental health law. *Hospital and Community Psychiatry, 23*, 101–105.

Alemango, S. A., Shaffer-King, E., Tonkin, P., & Hammel, R. (2004). *Characteristics of arrestees at risk for co-existing substance abuse and mental disorder* (No. 207142). Washington, DC: Bureau of Justice.

American Correctional Association. (1991). *Guidelines for the development of policies and procedures: Adult correctional institutions*. Washington, DC: American Correctional Association.

American Psychiatric Association (APA). (2000). *Psychiatric services in jails and prisons: A task force report of the American Psychiatric Association* (2nd ed.). Washington, DC: American Psychiatric Association.

Baillargeon, J., & Contreras, S. A. (2001). Antipsychotic prescribing practices in the Texas prison system. *Journal of the American Academy of Psychiatry and the Law, 29*(1), 48–53.

Beck, A. J. (2000). *State and federal prisoners returning to the community: Findings from the Bureau of Justice Statistics*. Washington, DC: U.S. Department of Justice.

Beck, A. J., & Maruschak, L. M. (2001). *Mental health treatment in state prisons, 2000*. Washington, DC: U.S. Department of Justice, Bureau of Justice Statistics.

Bond, G., Drake, R., Mueser, K. T., & Latiner, E. (1995). Assertive community treatment: An update on randomized trials. *Psychiatric Services, 46*(7), 669–675.

Boothroyd, R. A., Mercado, C. C., Poythress, N. G., Christy, A., & Petrila, J. (2005). Clinical outcomes of defendants in mental health court. *Psychiatric Services, 56*(7), 829–834.

Borum, R. (2004). Mental health issues in the criminal justice system: A public health perspective. In B. L. Leven, J. Petrila, & K. D. Hennesssy (Eds.), *Mental Health Services* (2nd ed.). New York: Oxford University Press.

Borum, R., Deane, M. W., Steadman, H. J., & Morrissey, J. (1998). Police perspectives on responding to mentally ill people in crisis: Perceptions of program effectiveness. *Behavioral Science and the Law, 16*, 393–405.

Brems, C., Johnson, M. E., Neal, P., & Freeman, M. (2004). Childhood abuse history and substance abuse among men and women receiving detoxification services. *The American Journal of Drug and Alcohol Abuse, 30*(4), 799–821.

Butterfield, F. (1998). Prisons replace hospitals for the nation's mentally ill. *New York Times*, March 5, 1998, A1.

Chaiken, S. B., Thompson, C. R., & Shoemaker, W. E. (2005). Mental health interventions in correctional settings. In C. L. Scott & J. B. Gerbasi (Eds.), *Handbook of correctional mental health* (pp. 109–131). Washington, DC: American Psychiatric Publishing, Inc.

Chandler, R. K., Peters, R. H., Field, C., & Juliano-Bult, D. (2004). Challenges in implementing evidence-based treatment practices for co-occurring disorders in the criminal justice system. *Behavioral Sciences and the Law, 22*, 431–448.

Corrigan, P. W., & Watson, A. C. (2005). Findings from the national comorbidity survey on the frequency of violent behavior in individuals with psychiatric disorders. *Psychiatry Research, 136*, 153–162.

Cosden, M., Ellens, J. K., Schnell, J. L., Yamini-Diouf, Y., & Wolfe, M. M. (2003). Evaluation of a mental health treatment court with assertive community treatment. *Behavioral Sciences and the Law, 21*, 415–427.

Council on State Governments. (2005). *Mental health/criminal justice consensus project*. New York: Council on State Governments.

Crowell, A. J., Broner, N., & Dupont, R. (2004). The cost-effectiveness of criminal justice diversion programs for people with serious mental illness co-occurring with substance abuse: Four case studies. *Journal of Contemporary Criminal Justice, 20*(3), 292–315.

Desai, R. A. (2003). Jail diversion services for people with mental illness: What do we really know? In W. H. Fisher (Ed.), *Community-based interventions for criminal offenders with severe mental illness* (Vol. 12, pp. 99–121). Kidlington, Oxford: Elsevier Sciences.

DiNitto, D. M., & Webb, D. K. (2005). Substance use disorders and co-occurring disabilities. In C. A. McNeece & D. M. DiNitto (Eds.), *Chemical dependency: A systems approach* (3rd ed., pp. 423–483). Boston: Allyn & Bacon.

Ditton, P. M. (1999). *Mental health and treatment of inmates and probationers: Special report.* Washington, DC: U.S. Department of Justice, Bureau of Justice Statistics.

Draine, J. (2003). Where is the "illness" in the criminalization of mental illness? In W. H. Fisher (Ed.), *Community-based interventions for criminal offenders with severe mental illness* (Vol. 12, pp. 9–21). Kindlington, Oxford: Elsevier Science.

Draine, J., & Solomon, P. (1999). Describing and evaluating diversion services for persons with severe mental illness. *Psychiatric Services, 50*(1), 56–61.

Evans, K., & Sullivan, J. M. (2001). *Dual diagnosis: Counseling the mentally ill substance abuser* (2nd ed.). New York: Guilford Press.

Fisher, W. H., Packer, I. K., Banks, S. M., Smith, D., Simon, L. J., & Roy-Bujnowski, K. (2002). Self-reported lifetime psychiatric hospitalization histories of jail detainees with mental disorders: Comparison with a non-incarcerated sample. *Journal of Behavioral Health Services & Research, 29*(4), 458–465.

Fisher, W. H., Packer, I. K., Simon, L. J., & Smith, D. (2000). Community mental health services and the prevalence of severe mental illness in local jails: Are they related? *Administration & Policy in Mental Health, 27*(3), 371–382.

Fisher, W. H., Silver, E., & Wolff, N. (2006). Beyond criminalization: Toward a criminologically informed framework for mental health policy and services research. *Administrative Policy in Mental Health & Mental Health Services Research, 33,* 544–577.

Fisher, W. H., Wolff, N., & Roy-Bujowski, K. (2003). Community mental health services and criminal justice involvement among persons with mental illness. In W. H. Fisher (Ed.), *Community-based interventions for criminal offenders with severe mental illness* (Vol. 12, pp. 25–51). Kindlington, Oxford: Elsevier Science.

Gagliardi, G. T., Lovell, D., Peterson, P. D., & Jemelka, R. (2004). Forecasting recidivism in mentally ill offenders released from prison. *Law and Human Behavior, 28*(2), 133–155.

Godley, S. H., Finch, M., Dougan, L., McDonnell, M., McDermeit, M., & Carey, A. (2000). Case management for dually diagnosed individuals involved in the criminal justice system. *Journal of Substance Abuse Treatment, 18,* 137–148.

Green, B. L., Miranda, J., Daroowalla, J., & Siddique, J. (2005). Trauma experience, mental health functioning, and program needs of women in jail. *Crime and Delinquency, 51*(1), 133–151.

Greenfeld, L. A., & Snell, T. L. (2000). Women offenders (No. NCJ 175688). *Bureau of Justice Statistics Special Report.* Washington, DC: Bureau of Justice Statistics.

Grisso, T. (2006). Jail Screening Assessment Tool (JSAT): Guidelines for mental health screening in jails. *Psychiatric Services, 57*(7), 1049–1050.

Hafemeister, T. L. (1998). Legal aspects of the treatment of offenders with mental disorders. In R. M. Wettstein (Ed.), *Treatment of offenders with mental disorders* (pp. 44–125). New York: Guilford Press.

Haimowitz, S. (2004). Slowing the revolving door: Community reentry of offenders with mental illness. *Psychiatric Services, 55*(4), 373–375.

Harris, V., & Dagadakis, C. (2004). Length of incarceration: Was there parity for mentally ill offenders? *International Journal of Law and Psychiatry, 27,* 387–393.

Harrison, P. M., & Beck, A. J. (2006). *Prisons and jails at mid-year 2005* (No. NCJ213133). Washington, DC: Bureau of Justice Statistics.

Hartwell, S. W. (2001). Female mentally ill offenders and their community reintegration needs: An initial examination. *International Journal of Law and Psychiatry, 24*, 1–11.

Hartwell, S. W. (2003a). Prison, hospital or community re-entry and mentally ill offenders. In W. H. Fisher (Ed.), *Community-based interventions for criminal offenders with severe mental illness* (Vol. 12, pp. 199–220). Kidlington, Oxford: Elsevier Science.

Hartwell, S. W. (2003b). Short-term outcomes for offenders with mental illness released from incarceration. *International Journal of Offender Therapy & Comparative Criminology, 47*(2), 145–158.

Hartwell, S. W. (2004). Comparison of offenders with mental illness only and offenders with dual diagnoses. *Psychiatric Services, 55*(2), 145–150.

Hiday, V. A. (1999). Mental illness and the criminal justice system. In A. Horowitz & T. Scheid (Eds.), *The handbook for the study of mental health: Social contexts, theories, and systems* (pp. 508–525). Cambridge, MA: Cambridge University Press.

Hills, H. A. (2000). *Creating effective treatment programs for persons with co-occurring disorders in the justice system.* Delmar, NY: The National GAINS Center.

Hills, H., Seigfried, C., & Ickowitz, A. (2004). *Effective mental health services: Guidelines to expand and improve treatment* (No. 018604). Washington, DC: U.S. Department of Justice, National Institute of Corrections.

Holton, S. M. (2003). Managing and treating mentally disordered offenders in jails and prisons. In T. J. Fagen & R. K. Ax (Eds.), *Correctional mental health handbook* (pp. 101–122). Thousand Oaks, CA: Sage.

Human Rights Watch. (2003). *Ill-equipped: U.S. prisons and offenders with mental illness.* New York: Human Rights Watch.

James, D. J., & Glaze, L. E. (2006). Mental health problems of prison and jail inmates. *Bureau of Justice Statistics: Special Report.* NCJ 213600. Washington, DC: Bureau of Justice Statistics.

Junginger, J. (2006). "Stereotypic" delusional offending. *Behavioral Sciences and the Law, 24*, 295–311.

Junginger, J., Claypool, K., Laygo, R., & Cristianti, A. (2006). Effects of serious mental illness on substance abuse on criminal offenses. *Psychiatric Services, 57*(6), 879–882.

Kessler, R. C., Anderws, G., Colpe, L. J., Hiripi, E., Mroezek, D. K., & Normand, S. L. T. (2002). Short screening scales to monitor population prevelences and trends in non-specific psychological distress. *Psychological Medicine, 32*, 959–976.

Lamb, H. R., & Weinberger, L. E. (1998). Persons with severe mental illness in jails and prisons: A review. *Psychiatric Services, 49*(4), 483–492.

Lamb, H. R., & Weinberger, L. E. (2005). One-year follow-up of persons discharged from a locked intermediate care facility. *Psychiatric Services, 56*(2), 198–201.

Lamb, H. R., Weinberger, L. E., & DeCuir, Jr., W. T. (2002). The police and mental health. *Psychiatric Services, 53*(10), 1266–1271.

Lamb, H. R., Weinberger, L. E., & Gross, B. H. (1999). Community treatment of severely mentally ill offenders under the jurisdiction of the criminal justice system: A review. *Psychiatric Services, 50*(7), 907–913.

Lambert, M., Conus, P., Lubman, D. I., Wade, D., Yuen, H., Moritz, et al. (2005). The impact of substance use disorders on clinical outcome in 643 patients with first-episode psychosis. *ACTA Psychiatrica Scandanavica, 112*, 141–148.

Lamberti, J. S., & Weisman, R. L. (2004). Persons with severe mental disorders in the criminal justice system: Challenges and opportunities, *Psychiatric Quarterly, 75*(2), 151–165.

Lamberti, J. S., Weisman, R., & Faden, D. I. (2004). Forensic Assertive Community Treatment: Preventing incarceration of adults with severe mental illness. *Psychiatric Services, 55*(11), 1285–1293.

Landsberg, C. C., & Smiley, A. (2001). *Forensic mental health: Working with offenders with mental illness*. Kingston, NJ: Civic Research Institute.

Lattimore, P. K., Broner, N., Sherman, R., Frisman, L., & Shafer, M. S. (2003). A comparison of pre-booking and postbooking diversion programs for mentally ill substance-using individuals with justice involvement. *Journal of Contemporary Criminal Justice, 19*(1), 30–64.

Lewis, C. F. (2005). Female offenders in correctional settings. In C. L. Scott & F. B. Gerbasi (Eds.), *Handbook of Correctional Mental Health* (pp. 155–185). Washington, DC: American Psychiatric Publishing.

Lovell, D., Allen, D., Johnson, C., & Jemelka, R. (2001). Evaluating the effectiveness of residential treatment for prisoners with mental illness. *Criminal Justice and Behavior, 28*(1), 83–104.

Lovell, D., Gagliardi, G. J., & Peterson, P. D. (2002). Recidivism and use of services among persons with mental illness after release from prison. *Psychiatric Services, 53*(10), 1290–1296.

Lurigio, A. J. (2001). Effective services for parolees with mental illness. *Crime and Delinquency, 47*(3), 446–461.

Lurigio, A. J., Cho, Y. I., Swartz, J. A., Johnson, T. P., Graf, I., & Pickup, L. (2003). Standardized assessment of substance-related, other psychiatric, and comorbid disorders among probationers. *International Journal of Offender Therapy and Comparative Criminology, 47*(6), 630–651.

Lurigio, A. J., Rollins, A., & Fallon, J. (2004). The effects of serious mental illness on offender reentry. *Federal Probation, 68*(2), 45–52.

McCoy, M. L., Roberts, D. L., Hanrahan, P., Clay, R., & Luchins, D. L. (2004). Jail linkage assertive community treatment services for individuals with mental illness. *Psychiatric Rehabilitation Journal, 27*(3), 243–250.

McLearen, A. M., & Ryba, N. L. (2003). Identifying severely mentally ill inmates: Can small jails comply with detection standards? *Journal of Offender Rehabilitation, 37*(1), 25–40.

Mentally Ill Offender Treatment and Crime Reduction Act of 2004. (2004). Pub L 108-732. U.S. Congress, 2004.

Miller, M. C., & Bakalar, J. B. (2003). Dual diagnosis: Part I. *Harvard Mental Health Letter, 20*(2). Cambridge, MA: Harvard College.

Naples, M., & Steadman, H. J. (2003). Can persons with co-occurring disorders and violent charges be successfully diverted? *International Journal of Forensic Mental Health, 2*(2), 137–143.

National Association of State Mental Health Program Directors (NASMHPD) Research Institute. (2004). State profile update. Retrieved August 16, 2006 from www.nri-inc.org/Profiles02/13Hospitals.pdf#search=%22nasmhpd%20psychiatric%20beds%22

National Commission on Correctional Health Care (NCCHC). (2003). *The health status of soon-to-be-released inmates: A report to Congress* (Vol. 1 & 2). Chicago, IL: National Commission on Correctional Health Care.

National GAINS Center. (2005). Retrieved July 2, 2005 from http://gainscenter.samhsa.gov/html/tapa/default.asp

National Mental Health Association. (2006). *Policy position on mental health treatment in correctional facilities*. Retrieved August 29, 2006 from http://www.nmha.org/position/ps55.cfm

Nicholls, T. L., Lee, Z., Corrado, R. R., & Ogloff, J. R. (2004). Women inmates' mental health needs: Evidence of the validity of the Jail Screening Assessment Tool (JSAT). *International Journal of Forensic Mental Health, 3*(2), 167–184.

Nicholls, T. L., Roesch, R., Olley, M., Ogloff, J. R. P., & Hemphill, J. (2005). *Jail Screening Assessment Tool (JSAT): A guide for conducting mental health screening in jails and pretrial centres*. Burnaby, Canada: Mental Health, Law, and Policy Institute, Simon Fraser University.

Osher, F., Steadman, H. J., & Barr, H. (2003). A best practice approach to community re-entry from jails for inmates with co-occurring disorders: The APIC model. *Crime and Delinquency, 49*(1), 79–96.

Pandiani, J. A., Banks, S. M., & Pomeroy, S. M. (2003). The impact of "new-generation" anti-psychotic medication on criminal justice outcomes. In W. H. Fisher (Ed.), *Community-based interventions for criminal offenders with severe mental illness* (Vol. 12, pp. 73–96). Kidlington, Oxford: Elsevier Science.

Petersilia, J. (2003). *When prisoners come home: Parole and prisoner reentry*. New York: Oxford University Press.

Peters, R. H., Greenbaum, P. E., Steinberg, M. L., Carter, C. R., Ortiz, M. M., Fry, B. C., et al. (2000). Effectiveness of screening instruments in detecting substance abuse disorders among prisoners. *Journal of Substance Abuse Treatment, 18*, 349–358.

Peters, R. H., LeVasseur, M. E., & Chandler, R. K. (2004). Correctional treatment for co-occurring disorders: Results of a national survey. *Behavioral Sciences and the Law, 22*(4), 563–584.

Petrila, J. (2005). Introduction to this issue: Diversion from the criminal justice system. *Behavioral Sciences and the Law, 23*, 161–162.

Phillips, H. K., Gray, N. S., MacCulloch, S. I., Taylor, J., Moore, S. C., Huckle, P., et al. (2005). Risk assessment in offenders with mental disorders: Relative efficacy of personal demographic, criminal history, and clinical variables. *Journal of Interpersonal Violence, 20*(7), 833–847.

Pogorelski, W., Wolff, N., Pan, K. Y., & Blitz, C. L. (2005). Behavioral health problems, ex-offender reentry process, and the "Second Chance Act." *American Journal of Public Health, 95*(10), 1718–1724.

Poythress, N. G., Petrila, J., McGaha, A., & Boothroyd, N. (2002). Perceived coercion and procedural justice in the Broward mental health court. *International Journal of Law and Psychiatry, 25*, 517–533.

Pratt, D., Piper, M., Appleby, L., Webb, R., & Shaw, J. (2006). Suicide in recently released prisoners: A population-based cohort study. *Lancet, 368*, 119–123.

Quanbeck, C., Frye, M., & Atshuler, L. (2003). Mania and the law in California: Understanding the criminalization of the mentally ill. *American Journal of Psychiatry, 160*(7), 1245–1250.

Redlich, A. D., Steadman, H. J., Petrila, J., Monahan, J., & Griffin, P. A. (2005). Patterns of practice in mental health courts: A national survey. *Psychology, Public Policy, and Law, 11*(4), 527–538.

Reynolds, K. M., Dziegielewski, S. F., & Shapp, C. (2004). Serving mentally ill offenders through community corrections: Joining two disciplines. *Journal of Offender Rehabilitation, 40*(2), 185–198.

Roberts, A. R., & Yeager, K. R. (in press). Crisis intervention with victims of violence. In A. R. Roberts & D. W. Springer (Eds.), *Social work in juvenile and criminal justice settings* (3rd ed.). Springfield, IL: Charles C. Thomas.

Rock, M. (2001). Emerging issues with mentally ill offenders: Causes and social consequences. *Administration and Policy in Mental Health, 28*(5), 165–180.

Roskes, E. (2000).Treatment compliance with atypical psychotropic medications. *Correctional Mental Health Report, 2*(1), 1.

Rotter, M., McQuiston, H. L., Broner, N., & Steinbacher, M. A. (2005). The impact of the "incarceration culture" on reentry for adults with mental illness. *Psychiatric Services, 56*(3), 265–267.

Salasin, S. (2002). Working with women in jails: Developing a gender-based network of services for strengthening women and their families. In G. Landsberg, M. Rock, K. W. Berg, & A. Smiley (Eds.), *Serving mentally ill offenders: challenges and opportunities for mental health professionals* (pp. 159–190). New York: Springer.

Schaefer, N. J., & Stefancic, A. (2003). "Alternative to prison" programs for the mentally ill offender. *Journal of Offender Rehabilitation, 38*(2), 41–55.

Sells, D. J., Rowe, M., Fisk, D., & Davidson, L. (2003). Violent victimization of persons with co-occurring psychiatric and substance use disorders. *Psychiatric Services, 54*(9), 1253–1257.

Skeem, J. L., Emke-Francis, P., & Louden, J. E. (2006). Probation, mental health, and mandated treatment: A national survey. *Criminal Justice and Behavior, 33*(2), 158–184.

Slate, R. N. (2003). From the jailhouse to Capitol Hill: Impacting mental health court legislation and defining what constitutes a mental health court. *Crime and Delinquency, 49*(1), 6–29.

Solomon, P. (2003). Case management and the forensic client. In W. H. Fisher (Ed.), *Community-based interventions for criminal offenders with severe mental illness* (Vol. 12, pp. 53–72). Kidlington, Oxford: Elsevier Science.

Solomon, P., Draine, J., & Marcus, S. C. (2004). Predicting incarceration of clients of a psychiatric probation and parole services. *Psychiatric Services, 53*(1), 50–56.

Steadman, H. J., Barbera, S., & Dennis, D. L. (1994). A national survey of jail diversion programs for mentally ill detainees. *Hospital and Community Psychiatry, 45,* 1109–1113.

Steadman, H. J., Deane, M. W., Borum, R., & Morrissey, J. C. (2000). Comparing outcomes of major models of police responses to mental health emergencies. *Psychiatric Services, 51*(5), 645–649.

Steadman, H. J., Deane, M. W., Morrissey, J. P., Westcott, M. J., Salasin, S., & Shapiro, S. (1999). A SAMHSA research initiative assessing the effectiveness of jail diversion programs for mentally ill offenders. *Psychiatric Services, 50*(12), 1620–1623.

Steadman, H. J., McCarthy, D., & Morrisey, J. (1989). *The mentally ill in jail: Planning for essential services.* New York: Guilford Press.

Steadman, H. J., & Naples, M. (2005). Accessing the effectiveness of jail diversion programs for persons with severe mental illness and co-occurring substance use disorders. *Behavioral Sciences and the Law, 23,* 163–170.

Steadman, H. J., Scott, J. E., Osher, F., Agnese, T. K., & Robbins, P. C. (2005). Validation of the Brief Jail Mental Health Screen. *Psychiatric Services, 56*(7), 816–822.

Steadman, H. J., & Veysey, B. M. (1997). *Providing services for jail inmates with mental disorders: Research in brief* (No. NCJ-1622-07). Washington, DC: U.S. Department of Justice, National Institute of Justice.

Substance Abuse and Mental Health Services Administration (SAMHSA). (2003). Report to Congress on the Prevention and Treatment of Co-Occurring Substance Abuse Disorders and Mental Disorders. Washington, DC: U.S. Department of Health and Human Services.

Swartz, J. A., & Lurigio, A. J. (2005a). Screening for serious mental illness among criminal offenders. *Research in Social Problems and Public Policy, 12,* 137–161.

Swartz, J. A., & Lurigio, A. J. (2005b). Detecting serious mental illness among substance abusers: Use of the K6 screening scale. *Journal of Evidence-Based Social Work, 2*(1–2), 133–135.

Technical Assistance and Policy Analysis Center (TAPA) for Jail Diversion. (2007). *Types of jail diversion programs.* Retrieved February 17, 2007 from www.gainscenter. Samhsa.gov/html/tapa/jail%20diversion/types.asp

Teller, L. S., Ritter, C., Salupo-Rodriquez, M., Munetz, M. R., & Gil, K. M. (2004). Akron Mental Health Court: Comparison of incarcerations and hospitalizations for successful and unsuccessful participants in the first cohort. *The Stormer Report.* Akron, OH: Ohio Department of Mental Health and Ohio Criminal Justice Services.

Teplin, L. A. (1990). Detection disorder: The treatment of mental illness among jail detainees. *Journal of Counseling and Clinical Psychology, 58*(2), 233–236.

Teplin, L. A. (2000). Keeping the peace: Police discretion and mentally ill persons. *National Institute of Justice Journal, July,* 9–15.

Teplin, L. A., Abram, K. M., & McClelland, G. M. (1996). Prevalence of psychiatric disorders among incarcerated women: Pretrial jail detainees. *Archives of General Psychiatry, 53,* 505–512.

Theuma, C. (2001). Community mental health services for offenders with mental disorders—Recent innovations in the United States. In G. Landsberg & A. Smiley (Eds.), *Forensic mental health: Working with offenders with mental illness.* Kingston, NJ: Civic Research Institute.

Torrey, E. F. (1995). Editorial: Jails and prisons—America's new mental hospitals. *American Journal of Public Health, 85*(12), 1611–1613.

Turpin, E., & Richards, H. (2003). Seattle's mental health courts: Early indicators of effectiveness. *International Journal of Law and Psychiatry, 26,* 33–53.

Van Stelle, K. R., Blumer, C., & Moberg, D. P. (2004). Treatment retention of dually diagnosed offenders in an institutional therapeutic community. *Behavioral Sciences and the Law, 2,* 585–597.

Van Stelle, K. R., & Moberg, D. P. (2004). Outcome data for MICA clients after participation in an institutional therapeutic community. *Journal of Offender Rehabilitation, 39*(1), 37–62.

Veysey, B. M., & Bichler-Robertson, G. (2002). Providing psychiatric services in correctional settings. *Health status of soon-to-be-released inmates: A report to Congress* (pp. 157–165). Chicago, IL: National Commission on Correctional Health Care.

Veysey, B. M., Steadman, H. J., Morrissey, J. P., & Johnsen, M. (1997). In search of the missing linkages: Continuity of care in U.S. jails. *Behavioral Sciences and the Law, 15*(4), 383–397.

Watkins, T. R., Lewellen, A., & Barrett, M. C. (2001). *Dual diagnosis: An integrated approach to treatment.* Thousand Oaks, CA: Sage.

Watson, A., Hanrahan, P., Luchins, D., & Lurigio, A. (2001). Mental health courts and the complex issue of mentally ill offenders. *Psychiatric Services, 52,* 477–481.

Watson, A., Luchins, D., Hanrahan, P., Heyrman, M. J., & Lurigio, A. (2000). Mental health court: Promises and limitations. *Journal of the American Academy of Psychiatry and the Law, 28,* 476–482.

Way, B. B., Miraglia, R., Sawyer, D. A., Beer, R., & Eddy, J. (2005). Factors related to suicide in New York state prisons. *International Journal of Law and Psychiatry, 28,* 207–221.

Weinstein, H. C., Kim, D., Mack, A. H., Malavade, K. E., & Saraiya, A. U. (2005). Prevalence and assessment of mental disorders in correctional settings. In C. L. Scott & F. D. Gerbasi (Eds.), *Handbook of correctional mental health* (pp. 43–68). Washington, DC: American Psychiatric Publishing.

Weisman, R. L., Lamberti, J. S., & Price, N. (2004). Integrating criminal justice, community health care, and support services for adults with mental disorders. *Psychiatric Quarterly, 75*(1), 71–85.

Wilson, A. B., & Draine, J. (2006). Collaborations between criminal justices and mental health systems for prison reentry. *Psychiatric Services, 57*(6), 875–878.

Winn, J. (2003). Testimony before the Correctional Committee of the New York State Assembly, November 18, 2003.

Wolff, N., Bjerklie, J. R., & Machi, T. (2005). Reentry planning for mentally disordered inmates: A social investment perspective. *Journal of Offender Rehabilitation, 41*(2), 21–42.

Wolff, N., Maschi, T., & Bjerklie, J. R. (2004). Profiling mentally disordered prison inmates: A case study in New Jersey. *Journal of Correctional Health Care, 11*(1), 5–29.

Wolff, N., Plemmons, D., Veysey, B., & Brandli, A. (2002). Release planning for inmates with mental illness compared with those who have other chronic illnesses. *Psychiatric Services, 53*(11), 1469–1471.

Wright, S., Gournay, K., Glorney, E., & Thornicroft, G. (2002). Mental illness, substance abuse, demographics and offending: Dual diagnosis in the suburbs. *The Journal of Forensic Psychiatry, 13*(1), 35–52.

Young, D. S. (2002). Non-psychiatric services provided in a mental heath unit in a county jail. *Journal of Offender Rehabilitation, 35*(2), 63–82.

Young, D. S. (2003). Predictors of placement on a jail mental health unit: Assessing equitable access to care. *Journal of Correctional Health Care, 9*(4), 399–423.

9

Prison Group Counseling

Sabrina R. Haugebrook and Kristen M. Zgoba

The authors would like to thank Dr. H. Kaldany, New Jersey Department of Corrections, Dr. J. Dickert, Vice President, UMDNJ–University Correctional HealthCare, and Commissioner G. Hayman, New Jersey Department of Corrections for their assistance.

INTRODUCTION

The advent of group counseling, which helps offenders acclimate back into society, is not a new development. In the correctional setting, one component used by treatment staff is group counseling to adjust offenders to the outside community after institutionalization. How best to do that is of primary concern today, particularly with the influx of reentry initiatives throughout the corrections field in the late 1990s. The scope of correctional counseling is wide and with it comes a great deal of accountability.

Group counseling in prisons presents the counselor with many challenges, including protecting the safety and security of staff (custody and civilian) and dealing with the demands of the treatment needs of the offender population. Counseling in a prison setting is generally composed of education, treatment, casework (social work), and recreation (arts/ craft, sports). In this chapter, correctional group counseling is discussed and compared with numerous correctional facilities throughout the United States to see what types of services the offender population receives.

INSTITUTIONAL GROUP COUNSELING

Group counseling began during World War II; it was designed to rehabilitate military prisoners of the armed forces convicted of committing crimes. One of the earliest known structures of group therapy for treating offenders termed the "guided group interaction," was practiced and developed by McCorkle and Wolf in the mid-1940s (as cited in Kratcoski, 2000, p. 483). In this form of counseling, military offenders at Fort Knox in Kentucky met in group sessions daily for treatment under the assumption that they could be restored to active duty once they completed the counseling groups (as cited in Lester & Braswell, 1987, p. 176).

McCorkle & Bixby (1951) developed a similar form of guided group interaction with juvenile offenders (as cited in Kratcoski, 2000, p. 483). In the Highfields Experiment in New Jersey, the criminologists (McCorkle, Elias, & Bixby, 1958) investigated their hypothesis that an established group treatment setting was ideal to treat youthful delinquents in training schools (as cited in Bennett, Rosenbaum, & McCullough, 1978, p. 41). The Highfields project, which was set up as a five-year experiment, began operating in 1950 with financial assistance from the New York Foundation and other donors. After the initial two-year joint venture between the State of New Jersey and the New York Foundation, the State of New Jersey's Department of Institutions and Agencies implemented the project into the New Jersey Correctional system (McCorkle et al., 1958, p. 12). The State of New Jersey assumed full control of the project on July 1, 1952. The aim of McCorkle and Bixby in creating Highfields was to change the attitudes and behavior of the juveniles to effect their rehabilitation, and the authors outlined four key features of the project design (Weeks, 1958, p. viii).

The features of the highfields experience are:

1. The informal and intimate living for a short period in a small group in a non-custodial residential center.
2. The experience of a regular routine of supervised work.
3. Evening GGI sessions designed to give the boys insight into the motivations for their conduct and incentive to change their attitudes.
4. To continue the group discussion during leisure time.

Boys in a certain age group were sent to Highfields as a diversion to avoid jail time. For admittance into Highfields, the average age was 16 years, with no prior correctional institutionalization or reform. When Highfields originated, the majority of the juvenile boys came from the most populated counties of the state. The counties of Bergen, Essex, Hudson, and Union sent boys to reroute them away from prison. The program could accommodate up to 20 boys in a four-month residency period. Usually a judge sentenced the boys to the program as a form of probation. The boys would arrive at the Highfields site in central New Jersey with their probation officer. There was no formal orientation, but the juveniles would receive further instructions once they arrived into the facility.

Guided group interaction began the same day the juveniles arrived at Highfields. The youth met five times a week (two separate groups) in the guided group interaction exercises and assumed responsibility for each other's actions. The facilitator (director of Highfields) stressed problem solving and often confrontation solving between the groups. The formal guided group interaction took place in the evenings, but the entire time the juveniles were in the program they participated in group interaction exercises. Anything could be brought up and discussed at the nightly group sessions. Emphasis was placed on creating situations in which the boys made choices about how to behave and then felt secure enough to discuss their choices with the group (McCorkle et al., 1958, p. 70).

The Highfields Experiment received broad attention as a innovative mechanism for counseling troubled juveniles. The program was evaluated after five years of operation. The evaluation conducted by Weeks (1958) compared Highfields with another New Jersey state–run facility, the Annandale Reformatory for Boys. Weeks concluded that the Highfields project worked because for every 100 boys sent to Highfields and Annandale, 63 Highfields residents completed their treatment and did not recidivate compared to 47 Annandale boys (Smith & Berlin, 1988, p. 396). Weeks (1958) sought to answer two other questions as well. He evaluated whether the juvenile boys changed their attitudes after treatment and whether short-term treatment changed the basic personality of the youthful offenders.

The highly favorable results of the Highfields Experiment spawned other programs throughout the State of New Jersey and the United States. Other state correctional systems replicated Highfields and guided group interaction for juvenile offenders. The Provo experiment on juvenile rehabilitation project in Utah, Essexfields group rehabilitation project in New Jersey and Southfields in Kentucky were three programs that adopted the Highfields model. In these projects, juvenile boys were sent to residential programs in the community instead of training schools. These experiments produced similar results in lowering recidivism through group peer counseling.

After World War II, the public was more sympathetic to the needs of offenders and desired reformation therapy that could correct the bad choices criminals made. Gone was the punitive era of locking a lawbreaker away from society. The practice of group counseling or guided group interaction spread and was adapted to fit the correctional institutional model. Group counseling at the time involved group activity generally led by a treating therapist or counselor. Group counseling placed a strong emphasis on many aspects of an offender's life such as job training and education. At the outset, most group counseling dealt with helping lawbreakers resolve or deal with the emotional troubles in their lives.

Group therapy continued to grow in the corrections field with other group rehabilitations, such as psychodrama (Moreno, 1957) and role-playing used by Slavson (1950). Both therapy sessions are somewhat similar, as all members of the group share and act out various parts of the community (family, peers, etc.) in the life of the offender. One aspect of the group counseling process was the therapeutic community (TC) model. The TC philosophy grew out of the works of Glasser (1965). He created a community based on reality therapy at the Ventura School for Girls in California (Bennett et al., 1978, p. 31). Glasser believed clients needed to be responsible for their actions, establish an identity, and learn to manage later actions with a realistic approach (as cited in Bennett et al., 1978, p. 31). He used the structure of the guided group interaction (GGI), in conjunction with other forms of group treatment in prison facilities. Glasser believed that anyone who seeks therapy suffers from an inability to realize his or her fundamental requirement in life.

Group counseling began in the correctional setting in the 1940s as a way to boost competence with prisoners. Group counseling may help with the inmate code. Offenders are open to counseling with others and the inmate code usually meant inmates mistrusted authority and other offenders. They include inmates trying to discuss their grievances with the prison administration by "conning" the treatment staff. Therefore, staff should be careful and recognize the characteristics of an offender who is trying to gain sympathy from treatment personnel.

Correctional counseling is progressing from a punitive focus to one in which inmates who are in counseling discover how to alter their behavior with support from the treatment staff, family, and fellow offenders. A counseling model that encompasses all levels of an offender's life is ideal because it may help deter the offender from returning to prison.

Therapeutic Community Counseling

In the therapeutic community, offenders who are imprisoned for a drug-related offense usually obtain treatment from specialized counselors with a background in substance abuse and addictions treatment. As designed, the therapeutic community makes inmates more amenable to treatment and less intimidating to staff. A treatment staff of professionals usually leads the group-counseling portion of the therapeutic community, but increasingly in many instances, inmates facilitate and direct many of the group sessions. In many prison sites, such as in the therapeutic community (TC), the offenders may lead some of the counseling sessions under the supervision of the treatment staff. In the TC setting, each participant is given the opportunity to correct deficiencies that hold them back. Correcting the deficient behavior in a familiar group setting with other compatible participants obliges individuals to be honest with themselves and other group members.

Some professionals in the field argue that the TC better prepares inmates for release than other treatment programs. Group counseling of a large number of offenders is economical because treatment is given to the entire group simultaneously. The public may be more accepting to the treatment of offenders in a prison, especially when outcome studies show that counseling may aid in reducing recidivism and repetitious criminal conduct.

After Martinson (1974) in his research in the early 1970s said that nothing works in corrections, the public started to turn against the level of correctional treatment for the inmate populace. Rehabilitation programs were seen as failures according to Martinson and his colleagues. Martinson and his colleagues evaluated correctional treatment programs from 1945 to 1967 (Martinson, 1974) and could not find one treatment program that reduced recidivism. Since Martinson and others assumed that treatment does not work, the public began to doubt anecdotal evidence that treatment programs rehabilitated offenders.

Mental Health Counseling in Prisons

According to the U.S. Bureau of Justice Statistics (BJS) report, *Provision of Mental Health Care in Prisons* (2001), 16 percent of the inmate population in U.S. prisons had or were known to have a mental related illness. Many inmates enter or leave the correctional system with mental health needs. Some offenders who enter prison have mental health needs that were never recognized or diagnosed until they became involved with the justice system. When an offender is branded as abnormal or unruly, treatment counseling along with medication management may provide the offender an outlet to manage their illness. The treatment of the mentally ill offender, while under the care of the criminal justice institution, is important to many stakeholders. Policy makers, mental health advocates, prison operations, treatment staff, the media and the community at large all have a vested interest in the treatment that mentally ill inmates receive.

The National Institute of Corrections (NIC) surveyed prison facilities in the United States in 1999 (*Provision of Mental Health Care in Prisons*, 2001). Initial identification of mentally challenged ill inmates generally occurs with initial classification during the intake process. Under the current system, offenders are usually placed in treatment program with other offenders categorized as having a similar mental condition. However, many offenders are asymptomatic, displaying no warning signs or unusual behavior that could alarm prison custody staff. Some argue that placing severely mentally impaired offenders in segregation/isolation is not ideal for their treatment as it could make the offender more disruptive once the inmate returns to general population in the penitentiary (as cited in Kratcoski, 2000, p. 634). An ideal rehabilitation program (Coulson & Nutbrown, 1992) for mental offenders is more sensible.

In the assessment conducted by NIC under the guidance of BJS, most state departments of corrections mandate that custody staff who work around mentally challenged offenders receive preservice training. The number of service hours varies per institution in each state. Most states now have a cognitive-behavioral agenda in which mentally ill offenders receive some level of group counseling. Usually, this is completed because many offenders have co-occurring disorders (mental and substance abuse). One fundamental element in helping mentally ill offenders is the level of aftercare the inmates receive once they reenter the community (community can be general custody in the prison or the community the offender will return to once the sentence is served). The aftercare component is vital to helping offenders sustain their well-being.

CROSS-STATE COMPARISON

There are several correctional agencies around the United States with admirable models of counseling for the prisoner population. Although there are two systems working, criminal justice and treatment counseling, many state correctional departments have formed programs that show benefits to offenders in terms of solid treatment, which thereby could possibly reduce recidivism. The majority of counseling services for the inmate population throughout the country involve mental health, substance abuse, and sex offender group counseling. Texas, North Carolina, Ohio, and New Jersey correctional counseling and treatment systems are presented in this chapter.

Texas

In 1997 the Texas legislature selected many correctional facilities in the state to provide treatment and rehabilitation. According to a Criminal Justice Policy Council (CJPC) report on the performance of rehabilitation programs (2003), as of 2002, the "tier of rehabilitation facilities," as they were called, served up to 9,200 offenders in Texas. In the state of Texas, the Division of Rehabilitation and Reentry manages programs and services for treating the inmate population. The first treatment and therapy programs for substance abuse in Texas became operational in 1992 (Eisenberg, 2003). The in-prison TC and substance abuse programs for probationers are both tracked by the CJPC to ascertain success and failure. In addition to the substance abuse programs, the Texas Department of Criminal Justice (TDCJ) offers treatment counseling to sex offenders and inmates designated with mental impairments. Additionally, the Inner Change Freedom Initiative is a voluntary program for inmates.

TDCJ integrated all treatment delivery programs into a tier system so the department could better address the treatment and therapy needs of offenders in a holistic mode

(Eisenberg, 2003). The TDCJ labeled six rehabilitation treatment plans useful in reducing recidivism and treating offenders in group/individual counseling (Eisenberg, 2003). Four of the six programs use some level of the TC model approach for offenders who will be released into the community. In these four programs, the offenders receive group and individual counseling, substance abuse treatment, anger management, life skills, and vocational and educational instruction. The remaining stages of therapy (sex offender and inner change) programming consists of intensive group and individual counseling, relapse prevention, cognitive skills exercises, community service, and reintegration. With the exception of the Inner Change Freedom Initiative (ICFI), five of the six programs are funded by the State of Texas. The Inner Change Freedom Initiative receives funding from Prison Fellowship Ministries. Each program targets a specific group within the prison system.

The average length of rehabilitation treatment sessions could last from 3 to 30 months before parole or release into the community. Once offenders are released from the programs, they are tracked for two years for recidivism outcomes. The biggest drawbacks to most programs are whether the treatment goals are achieved and are considered adequate for participants in the program.

In Texas TCs, all offenders actively participate in the group process. In the TC, offenders learn cognitive skills in groups; the skills assist the offender to recognize the errant choices made and the offender starts to make positive changes in overcoming the cycle of prison return. According to the Texas Rehabilitation and Reentry Division Web site (2006), the TC treatment group plan in Texas embraces positive ways of thinking, acceptance of oneself through positive criticism, being accountable and responsible for your actions, developing a self-view that is realistic and attainable, setting goals that are achievable, and analyzing performance with the group through counseling. In Texas, most participants enter TC treatment programs as a condition of parole or usually when he/she is within 18 months of release (parole, probation, and max out).

In 1987, the TDCJ recognized mental treatment counseling for offenders classified as mentally challenged. The legislature created a service delivery program, which addresses the specific medical needs of offenders in the prison system (the prison system could be state jails, state prisons, and private jails and prisons). Because of this action, the Texas structure is recognized nationally as a system that tackles all aspects of mental treatment for offenders. The Texas legislature is committed to mental service delivery; the government appropriates a budget each fiscal year to enhance mental health services. The legislature also established the Texas Correctional Office on Offenders with Medical or Mental Impairments (TCOOMMI). Texas merged all mental health counseling for incarcerated offenders in prisons/jails or within the community on parole and still under the jurisdiction of TDCJ. The linkage between the community and institutions in providing mental health offenders' access to medical, psychiatric, and other rehabilitative services significantly benefits offenders.

The TDCJ classifies inmates as mentally deficient through medical diagnosis, often using the Diagnostic and Statistical Manual of Mental Disorders--Fourth Edition (DSM-IV) Axis 1. Offenders are also classified if they score 50 or less on the Global Assessment Functioning (GAF) scale, which shows a serious emotional impairment (Biennial report, Texas Council on Offenders with Mental Impairments, 2003). Once classified, offenders have 32 mental health programs offering a range of services. Some services offered include rehabilitation through group therapy, case management, and medication monitoring. Although Texas is a model for other state correctional systems to follow for delivery of services to the mentally impaired inmate population, it still needs improvement. The state does not follow one particular curriculum or structured delivery service to help offenders diagnosed as mentally deficient.

North Carolina

The North Carolina Department of Correction has a rehabilitation system that balances the treatment counseling needs of the inmate population. One of the newest treatment plans for offenders commenced in 1998. The department uses the cognitive-behavioral intervention (CBI) approach as the foundation for all programs and services. According to research, among rehabilitation programs CBI reduces recidivism through the techniques used, which have an impact on the offender's thinking. CBI is based on the principle that thinking (internal) controls your actions (external) (Price, 2004). Offenders learn new skills and receive training that leads to changes in behavior and action, which could affect the criminals' conduct.

The North Carolina Department of Correction uses CBI effectively in the group counseling process with both substance-abusing and mentally ill offenders. The department followed the research of Ross and Gendreau (1987) on revivification and rehabilitation, which analyzed effective programs that reduced recidivism (as cited in Price, 2004, p. 5) and cited CBI as a valuable technique for offenders. CBI is available to all North Carolina offenders both in correctional facilities and in the community.

The NC DOC approved four CBI curricula for use with the offender population; they include thinking for a change, problem-solving skills in action, reasoning and rehabilitation, and choices and changes (Price, 2004). The majority (85%) of prison facilities use thinking for a change. Problem-solving is the core in the thinking for a change program. Cognitive reform is emphasized in groups and participants learn social skill development and self-change. Problem-solving skills in action (PSSA) instructs offenders in basic social skills for successful problem solving. PSSA is a short-term program usually taught over four weeks to a larger group in interval periods of four days. Each aspect of this program is scripted to allow for greater skill application in groups. The NC DOC uses the reasoning and rehabilitation course developed by Ross, Fabiano, and Diemer-Ewies (1989) in Canada (Price, 2004, p. 6). This program uses a psychoeducational approach with role-playing and demonstration in the groups. The choices and changes curriculum is based on the Wisconsin THINK program. Interactive exercises through role-playing give offenders insight about their thinking and an opportunity to practice social skills with each other.

In addition to offering cognitive behavioral intervention groups to the inmate population, the NC DOC provides substance abuse treatment sessions, which also may use CBI techniques. In 1985, the NC Legislative Research Commission reported that over 67 percent of criminal offenses are connected to alcohol and drug use (North Carolina DOC, Division of Alcoholism & Chemical Dependency Web site, 2006). Thereafter, the department created the Department of Correction Substance Abuse & Chemical Dependency Program. Statewide, there are about 1,500 beds allocated for treating substance abusers in a group setting.

The department has prison-based, community, and residential treatment programs. The department uses the therapeutic community (TC) model approach based on NY DOC's "Stay 'N Out" TC (North Carolina DOC, Division of Alcoholism & Chemical Dependency Web site, 2006). The three programs currently under North Carolina's Department of Correction authority are the prison-based Drug Alcohol Recovery Treatment (DART), Driving While Impaired DART (DWI DART), and Residential Substance Abuse Treatment (RSAT), in addition to other outpatient community programs with various agencies operated by the NC DOC. Offenders in prison, probation, or parole may be required to attend and complete a TC substance abuse program and most inmates should have no more than 24 months remaining on their conviction sentence.

The DART program became operational in North Carolina in January 1988. Offenders receive counseling in a traditional TC with a structured community hierarchy, one of the foundations of a therapeutic community. Since the majority of program lessons are conducted and acted out in a group (family) style, all offenders participate in the counseling of their peers.

Another counseling modality the North Carolina DOC offers the offender population is mental health group service. The department offers inpatient, outpatient, day treatment, and sex offender treatment programs. According to the Division of Prison Mental Health Web site, the mission of mental health services in NC is to protect, control, reduce, or eliminate conditions, which contribute to the inmate's mental impairment. Under North Carolina statute, the corrections system should provide "preventive, diagnostic, and therapeutic measures for outpatient and hospitalization for all types of patients."

The Department of Correction in North Carolina provides about a 600-bed capacity in numerous facilities to treat mentally ill offenders. In addition, outpatient services are provided to over 30,000 inmates. Offenders are first classified as mentally deficient through a variety of testing instruments (North Carolina DOC, Division of Mental Health Services, 2006). After the testing, inmates classified as mentally handicapped/impaired are tracked through the mental health tracking system. Some offenders are transferred to day treatment centers where they live with like-minded offenders in a dormitory style facility such as Brown Creek Correctional Institution (Brown Creek and Pender Correctional Institutions house offenders in day treatment centers). The offenders receive treatment together. Treatment consists of group counseling, art therapy, social and coping skills, and community reentry. Day treatment programs in NC DOC are effective because offenders interact more with the treatment staff with more freedom set aside for groups, which may help these offenders reintegrate into the general prison population or the community.

The North Carolina Department of Correction uses various techniques for group counseling offenders. Programs target the inmate populace and increase inmate participation awareness by offering reasonable problem-solving skills, which further enhances the outlook for many offenders. Since the 1990s, cognitive and other treatment programs have produced positive outcomes for offenders released from North Carolina prisons, thereby reducing recidivism.

Ohio

The Ohio Department of Rehabilitation and Correction (DRC) have similar counseling models to Texas and North Carolina for inmates. The department cooperates with numerous other state agencies and community partners to deliver counseling services. Ohio took the approach of the Corrections Service of Canada and organized programming into seven domains (Ohio Dept. of Rehabilitation and Correction—IPP. 2006). Ohio classifies inmates to see which domains fit the offender's programming plan. All interested stakeholders provide substance abuse treatment counseling, and cognitive-behavioral programs for offenders in the prison system, probation, and parole.

One program model the department uses is the "corrective thinking" principle based on the research of Yochelson and Samenow (1976, 1977), called corrective thinking or truthought (Hubbard & Latessa, 2004, p. 3). The corrective thinking approach theorizes why someone commits a crime. The authors surmised that most people recognize dangers in their thinking; criminals tend to exaggerate errors in their thinking and choose to commit crimes.

Rogie Spoon (1999) developed the truthought concept. This concept teaches inmates how to recognize thinking barriers and correct them with positives. Spoon enhanced the original model of Yochelson and Samenow (1976, 1977) with exercises for offenders. Through this training, offenders learn to take responsibility for choices and actions. The core course in Ohio is offered in a group arrangement at five treatment sites. Offenders receive a battery of tests, including sexual abuse history, personality profiles, intelligence testing, and depression scale testing. Although cognitive thinking groups are one form of treatment program in the Ohio Department of Rehabilitation and Correction, researchers from University of Cincinnati, Center for Criminal Justice Research did not find the treatment counseling to be more effective than other group treatment programs (i.e., therapeutic community).

Just like all the other state correctional programs referred to previously, the Ohio DRC provides other forms of group treatment to the inmate population. One such group is the TC. The process of treating substance-abusing offenders begins during the intake process at reception facilities in Ohio. If an offender's criminogenic compulsion is substance abuse, the offender may receive treatment, which helps them abstain from abusing substances.

Ohio operates several alcohol and other drugs (AOD) group treatment programs. Two of the intensive programs are located at North Coast Correctional Treatment Facility, a private facility, and Pickaway Correctional Facility, a state-run therapeutic community facility. Both facilities provide alcohol and other drug treatment for a 90-day period in many forums. The department uses an AOD instrument, PII (Prison Inmate Inventory) method, to screen potential applicants who may benefit from intensive group treatment. Offenders receive primary and secondary programming treatment. Some primary alcohol and other drug treatment consists of group and individual counseling, support/fellowship meetings, AOD education, and biopsychosocial assessment. The Pickaway facility provides these primary services as well as detailed TC programming. After completion of either treatment module, offenders are closely supervised for up to a year and may be required to continue AOD treatment once in the community for a stated time. After completion of each Intensive Program Prisons (IPP) cycle, staff and inmates evaluate the program for effectiveness and both programs conduct monthly quality assurance activities.

The State of Ohio provides the inmate population with many counseling resources to help improve offender's outlook on life once they leave prison. The cognitive behavioral program the state utilizes has worked for most offenders who receive the treatment. However, the state should continue to develop the process with more staff training to ensure all offenders get the best level of counseling available while incarcerated. Ohio should also assess the risk and needs of future offenders through evaluation so that the programs (cognitive behavior and substance abuse) operate more efficiently to improve inmate service delivery.

New Jersey

In New Jersey, the number of treatment services available to the inmate population is substantial. Offenders can receive treatment for mental health, substance abuse, parenting skills, sexual offenses, adaptation/reentry, and so on. Some treatment focuses on cognitive reasoning, which increases offenders' self-esteem and thought processing, while others such as substance abuse focus on promising treatment. New Jersey has dual systems of group counseling delivery for offenders, mental health, and substance abuse groups in the therapeutic community. Sometimes these services can overlap as well.

Mental health offenders in New Jersey now have enhanced counseling services available to them with the creation of University Correctional HealthCare (UCHC). This collaboration between NJ DOC and University of Medicine and Dentistry of New Jersey (UMDNJ) implemented in January 2005 provides mental health care services for inmates in the state's 14 prisons and 26 residential community release (halfway house) facilities. The State of New Jersey was mandated to provide mental group as a requirement under the *CF v. Terhune* settlement in 1999. *CF v. Terhune* was a class action lawsuit originated by inmates to address the lack of support and services accessible for mentally ill prisoners. At the time, mental health services and treatment available to mental inmates was considered the worst in the country.

In accordance with the contract reached between the State of New Jersey and the University of Medicine and Dentistry of New Jersey, the current mission of mental health services in NJ is to provide inmates services that meet the UMDNJ-University Behavioral Healthcare's community standard of excellence (J. Dickert, Ph.D, personal communication, August 11, 2006). The treatment staff at UCHC thoroughly evaluate offenders to determine who needs treatment services. The goal of the mental treatment program is to help offenders minimize symptoms and maximize their functioning, which may improve the chances of completing their convicted incarceration term. To do this, UCHC, the treatment provider, developed the Secure Environment Clinical Treatment (SECT) modality to react to problems unique to a correctional facility. The working standards of SECT comprise 10 basic understandings:

1. Inmates with mental health needs have a right to treatment.
2. Custody officers are allies in the treatment process.
3. Inmates will always be treated respectfully.
4. Effective screening is the beginning of all treatment.
5. Inmates are continually assessed for the appropriate level of mental health care.
6. Inmates are to be treated in the least intensive level of care.
7. Psychoeducation is an important intervention.
8. Clinical supervision is essential.
9. By measuring outcomes, quality of care can be improved.
10. Timely planning for reentry is essential for inmates with mental health needs (J. Dickert, Ph.D, personal communication, August 16, 2006).

In New Jersey, about 3,000 inmates require special mental health services. Another 350 of these offenders need specialized secure housing treatment placement. There are three inpatient unit settings, stabilization units (SU), residential treatment units (RTU), and transitional care units (TCU). Mental health staff use two group modules for mental health offenders. One program is the neuroscience treatment team partner (NTTP) program, a modular for recovery and wellness through a psychosocial program. Eli Lily and Company developed NTTP and the Department of Corrections treatment supplier, University Corrections HealthCare employs the service with offenders in mental health. In this component, offenders receive treatment in a structured educational program that encourages a healthy lifestyle. This is transferred over to mentally challenged offenders in prison who receive instruction on understanding their illness and symptoms and learning to apply principles, which will be an asset for the offender once he returns to his neighborhood.

The NJ Department of Corrections also adopted the New Direction curriculum developed by the Hazeldon Foundation. New Direction is a cognitive-behavior therapy (CBT) treatment program that addresses offenders with multiple needs (mental illness and substance abuse history). Offenders are challenged to change their criminal and addictive patterns in a group session. New Direction and NTTP serve a small number of offenders. The department has expanded group counseling treatment for other general population offenders as well. In the first year of the partnership between NJ DOC and UMDNJ-UCHC, group treatment increased from 13.6 to 20.2 percent at the conclusion of 2005. Overall, the levels of mental health groups for offenders in the State of New Jersey have improved. The treatment provider, UMDNJ-UCHC surveyed inmates who receive treatment to determine their level of satisfaction with the services. Out of 3,000 mental offenders, 23 percent (709) responded to the surveys. The survey results were favorable, providing cautious optimism that the groups are working. The strategic two-year plan is progressing as expected.

In addition to providing group counseling services to offenders with mental challenges, the NJ Department of Corrections provides counseling for inmates in the therapeutic community. New Jersey contracts 1,414 beds currently in eight prisons throughout the state. The NJ Department of Corrections receives federal funding under the Residential Substance Abuse Treatment (RSAT) grant for state prisoners. About a third of the available allocated beds are funded through RSAT and other federal funding sources. The NJ Department of Corrections contracts out programming to a substance abuse provider. The selected provider, Gateway Foundation Inc., commenced operation of the inpatient prison TC treatment in October 2002.

The therapeutic community inpatient treatment in New Jersey prisons is one structured for a specific inmate population group. Eligibility for therapeutic community placement is based on several factors; the primary one being the assessment severity index (ASI) instrument (NJ Department of Corrections, Office of Drug Programs fact sheet, 2006). Incoming inmates into the jurisdiction of the state prison system are screened on intake by trained social workers who evaluate the offenders' need for substance abuse treatment. Once identified as needing addiction treatment with an ASI score of five and above, offenders should meet time frame criterion and be able to achieve community corrections minimum custody status for continued treatment beyond the therapeutic community.

The therapeutic communities in the eight New Jersey prisons all have prison-based treatment where the offenders live in the same housing unit and receive program treatment every day. Living on the same housing unit increases the chance for success because all offenders in the family structure are there for the same reason, to receive treatment together. The therapeutic community is planned to address the multitude of socialization and psychological needs of the participating offenders in the community. All program activities and instruction are preplanned to inspire members of the community. While in the therapeutic community, offenders usually attend daily seminars that focus on anger management, conflict resolution, decision making, and academic teaching. In addition, the program offers group treatment counseling through encounter group sessions. Encounter groups maximize the probability that all offenders will participate in the group sessions and gain insight and perspective, which may help offenders once they are released into the community. The therapeutic communities in New Jersey prisons also provide cognitive skills development. Cognitive skills are utilized to help offenders understand the triggers that cause the addictive behaviors and that may change the thinking process.

The NJ Department of Corrections has taken an enhanced approach to dealing with treatment of the offender population. Diverse group counseling programs are used to gain results that will benefit and possibly avert offenders from returning to prison. It is hoped that the correctional counseling offenders receive will help with the continuum of care component offenders will contact neighborhood providers to continue treatment once released into the community.

Other states in the vicinity of New Jersey provide group counseling services for the inmate population as well. The State of Delaware Department of Correction has an excellent substance abuse program, which is recognized worldwide as being effective in rehabilitating drug offenders. Offenders are tracked through incarceration, work release, and aftercare into the community. The multilevel components of the program are called Key, Crest, and Aftercare. The Key component is a traditional prison therapeutic community setting, while Crest is a work release program. The final module, Aftercare, follows offenders once they leave prison and remain on probation in the community. In all three components, offenders continue to meet at least weekly for group counseling in the continuum of treatment plan (Delaware DOC Substance Abuse Treatment, 2005).

Another neighboring state that provides enhanced group counseling services to a targeted inmate population is the Connecticut Department of Correction (DOC). The comprehensive programs for adult offenders include mental health and substance abuse treatment under the department's health and addiction services office. The Connecticut DOC collaborated with the University of Connecticut Health Center in 1997 to provide managed health care to the offender population. One component is the level of mental health services offenders can receive while incarcerated. All of the state's correctional facilities provide mental health services and four facilities (Garner, Manson Youth, Osborn, and York Correctional Facilities) provide comprehensive care. Offenders can receive individual and group counseling as well as cognitive behavior treatment plans.

In addition to providing mental health services, the Department of Correction in Connecticut has a graduated substance abuse system similar to the tier system of the Texas Department of Criminal Justice. According to the Connecticut Department of Correction, 85 percent of incoming offenders have a substance abuse history. After a formal assessment through the objective classification system, which determines an offender's need for treatment, an offender can be placed in substance-abuse education program in four separate levels. The tier system ranges from six sessions to a 12-month aftercare program. Most of the programs in the tier system focus on substance abuse treatment using the therapeutic community model. Offenders usually receive group counseling, education instruction, relapse prevention, and cognitive development. The tier system was evaluated for effectiveness in 2002 by Brown University's Center for Alcoholism and Addiction Services and the Schneider Institutes for

Health Policy at Brandeis University. The principal investigator, Dr. Daley, and her colleagues found that the tier structure worked favorably. Inmates who attended any tier program of the Department of Correction were less likely to recidivate.

CORRECTIONAL COUNSELING EFFECTIVENESS

According to Lipsey (1992), when he looked at all evaluation studies regardless of their nature, 64 percent of correctional counseling/treatment studies indicated a reduction in recidivism. The average reduction across these studies was 10 percent, an acceptable level according to Van Voorhis, Braswell, and Lester (2004). It has also been indicated that programs that share certain characteristics deemed "appropriate interventions" can produce reductions in antisocial behavior that are correlated with recidivism (Andrews, Bonta, & Hoge, 1990; Lipsey & Wilson, 2001; Van Voorhis et al., 2004).

Specifically, two types of group correctional counseling programs researched and evaluated a great deal are drug/alcohol treatment programs and sex offender treatment programs. The findings from the evaluation studies of these two types of treatment programs have yielded cautiously positive findings. A description of these two types of programs and a brief review of their effectiveness follows.

Sex Offender Group Counseling/Treatment

The group treatment offered to sex offenders at the Adult Diagnostic Treatment Center (ADTC hereafter) in Avenel, New Jersey, is consistent with other North American treatment programs; both cognitive-behavioral treatment and relapse prevention are offered to offenders (Freeman-Longo, Bird, Stevenson, & Fiske, 1994; Zgoba, Sager, & Witt, 2003). Group cognitive-behavioral treatment focuses on reconstructing an offender's cognitive distortions, while relapse prevention programs teach offenders to recognize the patterns that lead up to their eventual offending (Cornwell, Jacobi, and Witt, 1999; Zgoba et al., 2003). This treatment combination is offered to offenders under a hierarchy of five-levels, with each level building on the level before it. Within this five-level context, patients undergo a standard set of psychoeducational modules where they also receive increased responsibilities and therapeutic tasks. Once offenders graduate to the fifth level of involvement, they procure additional responsibilities and make an effort at maintaining the gains they have made in treatment (Zgoba et al., 2003). The levels of the group counseling for sex offenders at the ADTC are as follows (Cornwell et al., 1999; Zgoba et al., 2003):

> *Level I:* Patients receive basic information about sex offending, receive an orientation to treatment, and begin to acquire the skills needed to participate fully in more advanced psychotherapy. Level I treatment is provided in structured, didactic groups.
>
> *Level II:* Patients begin to use a sex-offender-specific workbook and begin applying knowledge acquired in Level I to their own lives. Treatment focuses primarily on the acknowledgement of responsibility and victim empathy.
>
> *Level III:* Patients focus on acquiring comprehensive cognitive mastery of information gained at earlier levels. Psychoeducational modules are heavily supplemented

by a core treatment group with less structure. Relapse prevention exercises begin during this level.

Level IV: This level focuses on a more detailed relapse prevention plan and release preparation.

Level V: Patients begin a maintenance program to help them maintain earlier gains. Patients may be placed in a therapeutic community within the walls of the ADTC with additional responsibilities, such as limited self-government.

While the topic of sex offender treatment is often complicated with controversy, the evaluation of many treatment programs and various meta-analyses report positive results to the counseling. Hall's findings (1995) concluded that treatment did result in a small improvement relative to comparison conditions (Hall, 1995; Nicholaichuk, Gordon, Gu, & Wong, 2000). While the effect size for treatment versus comparison groups was small ($r = 12$), it was robust. Additionally, 19 percent of the treated sex offenders committed a sexual reoffense, while 27 percent of the comparison group, the untreated offenders, recommitted a sexual offense (Hall, 1995).

A follow-up meta-analysis conducted by Hanson and Bussiere (1998) contained 61 treatment evaluation studies with an overall sample size of 23,393 sexual offenders. On average, the sexual offense recidivism rate was found to be low with 13.4 percent of the sample recommitting a sexual offense. Particular subgroups of sexual offenders, as well as offenders who prematurely terminated treatment, recidivated at higher levels. The results of this analysis suggest that there are different predictors for non-sexual and sexual recidivism among offenders (Hanson & Bussiere, 1998).

A subsequent and more recent meta-analysis conducted by Hanson, Gordon, and Harris (2002) examined the effectiveness of psychological treatment for sexual offenders by summarizing 43 studies, resulting in a sample size of 9,454. Similar to the previous meta-analysis, the sexual reoffense rate was lower for the treatment group (12.3%) versus the comparison group (16.8%). Similar patterns were detected for rates of general recidivism, although the rates were predictably higher. Current psychological treatments, namely cognitive behavioral treatment, were associated with reductions in both general and sexual recidivism (Hanson et al., 2002). Overall, as meta-analyses have evolved with an increase in methodological clarity, the picture of sexual offender treatment evaluation studies looks more optimistic.

Substance Abuse Group Counseling

Addiction to drugs and/or alcohol is an issue that affects individuals across all sections of society. As such, it is not surprising that it has such a severe impact on the prison population. Moreover, substance abuse is believed to place offenders at an elevated likelihood of reoffending. It has been estimated that substance abuse problems affect as many as 75 percent of incarcerated offenders (Mumala, 1999; Van Voorhis et al., 2004). NJ Department of Corrections findings indicate similar numbers; recent assessments reveal that nearly 60 percent of incoming inmates have moderate to extreme drug/alcohol addictions and 72 percent have some level of drug/alcohol disorder. In response to the magnitude and pervasiveness of the substance abuse problem, many programs focusing on drug and alcohol abuse have been the subject of increased scrutiny and evaluation. The wide variety of substance abuse interventions that developed over the years has fueled the desire to evaluate correctional substance abuse programs. Gone are the days of recovery aided only by 12-step programs. Substance abuse interventions have evolved considerably and now follow different approaches and philosophies, including psychodynamic approaches, radical behavior approaches (i.e., classical conditioning, aversion therapies, and covert sensitization), social learning and cognitive-behavioral approaches (therapeutic communities, social skills training, relapse prevention training), drug courts, family therapy approaches, support groups, and pharmacological approaches (Van Voorhis et al., 2004).

Early research on correctional substance abuse programs was not as optimistic as it has now become. Previous studies indicated high relapse rates with little effect from the treatment components. As programs have evolved and treatment techniques have advanced, outcome studies and meta-analyses concerning drug and alcohol counseling for inmates have shown an increased benefit. Meta-analyses now show support for behavioral, social learning, and cognitive-behavioral approaches to treating substance abusers (Miller et al., 1995; Van Voorhis et al., 2004). More specifically, Miller et al. (1995) indicated that programs utilizing behavioral or cognitive-behavioral components were the most effective. Examples of these approaches include social skills training, relapse prevention, motivational enhancement, and community reinforcement (Van Voorhis et al., 2004).

PATHWAY TO IMPROVING CORRECTIONAL COUNSELING

Despite the widespread controversy and competing ideologies over the effectiveness of correctional counseling, according to Schrink and Hamm (1989) and Van Voorhis et al. (2004), the following standards should be set regarding effective group counseling and treatment in a correctional setting. They are as follows:

Correctional Counselors

1. The criteria for gaining employment as a counselor in a correctional setting should include an expectation of hiring individuals with advanced degrees in the relevant fields. This should also extend to include those who have extensive fieldwork in counseling.

2. Requiring that all counselors maintain an understanding that working in a correctional setting is a challenging occupation and that the counselors must be committed to rehabilitating the offenders.

3. Continuously providing correctional counselors with training.

4. It is necessary that correctional counselor job descriptions and mission statements are clear, consistent, specific, and relevant to the job expectations.

5. It is important that caseloads in the correctional setting be reasonably small and include offenders who are amenable to treatment and open to rehabilitation.

6. Group counseling sessions should utilize a multimodal approach that focuses on a more specific direction and small groups. For example, specific group sessions should help rapists, child molesters, offenders with drug problems, and/or anger management.

7. Group counseling programs and counselors should feel supported by the correctional communities and administrators.

Correctional Counseling Programs

1. Program evaluations should be completed in order to accomplish three tasks: (1) identify which programs work and why, (2) monitor strengths and weaknesses of effective programs, and (3) identify opportunities for improvement.

2. It is recommended that treatment (Andrews et al., 1990) be based on behavioral and social learning strategies (i.e., cognitive-behavioral treatment).

3. A collaboration between various disciplines will benefit the correctional counseling program by offering components of health care, education, vocation, recreation, mental health, and substance abuse treatment.

4. Practice of a technique referred to as the "principle of responsivity," whereby characteristics of the offender, therapist, and programs are matched is recommended.

5. Relapse prevention strategies should be offered to assist offenders upon release back into the community after receiving treatment while incarcerated.

6. It is also suggested that life skills and treatment experiences that emphasize personal accountability within the prison institution and in the community be offered.

CONCLUSION

An impressive body of literature provides empirical evidence that rehabilitation works to reduce recidivism (i.e., Andrews et al., 1990; Andrews & Bonta, 2003; Cullen & Applegate, 1997). Despite the known benefits of correctional counseling, offenders who receive treatment while in prison but then reoffend in society get negative press. Treatment of the offender is considered ineffective when the offender commits another crime. A goal for offenders should be learning how to gain insight from the environment they lived in and anticipating new beginnings once they leave the jurisdiction of the criminal justice system. Community corrections play a huge part in helping to rehabilitate offenders. Now that reentry policy and the continuum of care theory is recognized as paramount in keeping offenders from recidivating, community corrections (halfway houses, MAP, ISP, halfway back) are recognized as helping with the treatment modality of offenders. Usually in these programs, offenders continue to get cognitive-behavior intervention, work release, group counseling, and quality of life training. With the wide breadth of resources available to offenders, it is hoped that offenders are able to remain crime free.

According to Van Voorhis et al. (2004), the topic of correctional counseling and treatment is one composed of various mental health professionals working with a population of individuals who have been identified as delinquent or criminal. The services that are provided to the inmates are pervasive across a diversity of settings, including correctional facilities, community-based residential treatment communities, probation and parole settings, departments of human services, and specialized court systems (Van Voorhis et al., 2004). Because of the wide array of treatment and group counseling settings, it is common for different programs to have different goals. The primary question becomes whether counseling should focus on preparing an inmate for a successful return to the community or whether it should concentrate on the inmates' adjustment and existence within the confines of the prison world (Van Voorhis et al., 2004). Over time, it has come to be that many programs simultaneously concentrate on both goals, as it is understood that the manner of adjustment to the prison community can be correlated with the way a released inmate reintegrates back into society.

Given monetary constraints and inmate-to-therapist ratios, the majority of correctional counseling programs take place in a group-counseling environment. According to Van Voorhis et al., 2004, correctional group counseling sessions are usually held with 5 to 10 inmates in a session that meets once or twice a week for approximately an hour and a half. It is suggested that the appropriate group size should range from 8 to 10 participants because it is small enough for the group members to develop trust for one another and large enough to ensure that participants will not feel pressured or self-conscious. However, there is some question as to whether group counseling is as effective and beneficial to the recipients as individualized counseling. According to research conducted by Lipsey (1992) and Andrews et al. (1990), group counseling was found to be just as effective during meta-analyses studying decreases in recidivism (Van Voorhis et al., 2004; see also Andrews & Bonta, 2003). Given this lack of a difference between group and individual therapy, group therapy has a number of benefits that make it conducive to utilization in a prison setting. These advantages include: (1) the financial aspect, as it is more economical to conduct group therapy, and (2) the motivation garnered by having other inmates present. In other words, sometimes offenders are not motivated to change and they benefit from other inmates' presence, as they consider it a potential facilitator of change (Van Voorhis et al., 2004). Conducting the therapy in a group setting therefore allows for gentle persuasions or unspoken acceptance by the other inmates.

REFERENCES

Andrews, D., Bonta, J., & Hoge, R. (1990). Classification for effective rehabilitation: Rediscoivering psychology. *Criminal Justice and Behavior, 17,* 19–52.

Andrews, D. A. & Bonta, J. (2003). *Psychology of Criminal Conduct.* Cincinnati, OH: Anderson.

Bennett, L., Rosenbaum, T., & McCullough, W. (1978). *Counseling in Correctional Environments.* New York: Human Sciences Press.

Biennial Report of the Texas Council on Offenders with Mental Impairments. (2003). Retrieved August 7, 2006, from www.tdcj.state.tx.us/publications/tcomi/TCOMI-Biennial-Report-2003.PDF

Connecticut Department of Correction. (2006). *Health and addiction services.* Retrieved September 7, 2006, from www.ct.gov/doc/cwp/

Connecticut Department of Correction. (2005). *University of Connecticut health center correctional managed health care (CMHC) overview.* Retrieved September 6, 2006, from www.ct.gov/doc/lib/doc/pdf/medicalMHProgram.pdf

Cornwell, J., Jacobi, J., & Witt, P. (1999). The New Jersey sexually violent predator act: Analysis and recommendations for the treatment of sexual offenders in New Jersey. *Seton Hall Legislative Journal, 24,* 1–42.

Coulson, G., & Nutbrown, V. (1992). Properties of an ideal rehabilitative program for high-need offenders. *International Journal of Offender Therapy and Comparative Criminology, 36*(3), 203–208.

Cullen, F. T., & B. K. Applegate (1997). *Offender Rehabilitation: Effective Correctional Intervention.* Hampshire, U.K.: Ashgate Puplishing Company.

Daley, M., Love, C. T., Shepard, D. S., Peterson, C. B., White, K. T., & Hall, F. (2004). Cost-effectiveness of Connecticut's in-prison substance abuse treatment. *Journal of Offender Rehabilitation 39*(3), 69–92. Retrieved September 7, 2006, from http://sihp.brandeis.edu/pub_details_69.html

Eisenberg, M. (2003, February). *Second Biennial Report on the Performance of the Texas Department of Criminal Justice Rehabilitation Tier Programs.* (2003). Retrieved August 9, 2006, from www.cjpc.state.tx.us

Freeman-Longo, R., Bird, S., Stevenson, W., & Fiske, J. A. (1995). *1994 Nationwide survey of treatment programs & models: Serving abuse reactive children and adolescent & adult sexual offenders.* Brandon, VT: Safer Society Press.

Glasser, W. (1965). *Reality Therapy.* New York: Harper & Row.

Hall, G. (1995). Sexual offender recidivism revisited: A meta-analysis of recent treatment studies. *Journal of Consulting and Clinical Psychology, 63*(5), 802–809.

Hanson, K., & Bussiere, M. (1998). Predicting relapse: A meta-analysis of sexual offender recidivism studies. *Journal of Consulting and Clinical Psychology, 66*(2), 348–362.

Hanson, K., Gordon, A., & Harris, A. (2002). First report on a collaborative outcome data project on the effectiveness of psychological treatment for sexual offenders. *Sexual Abuse: A Journal of Research and Treatment, 14*(2), 169–194.

Hubbard, D., & Latessa, E. (2004, January). *Evaluation of cognitive-behavioral programs for offenders: A look at outcome and responsivity in five treatment programs.* Ohio: University of Cincinnati, Center for Criminal Justice Research, Division of Criminal Justice. Cincinnati. Retrieved August 10, 2006, from www.uc.edu/criminaljustice/ProjectReports/CogEvaluationFINAL_REPORT.pdf

Kratcoski, P. (2000). *Correctional counseling and treatment.* Prospect Heights, IL: Waveland Press.

Lester, D., & Braswell, M. (1987). *Correctional counseling.* Cincinnati, OH: Anderson.

Lipsey, M. (1992). Juvenile delinquency treatment: A meta-analytic inquiry into the variability of effects. In T. Cook, H. Cooper, D. Cordray, H. Hartmann, R. Hedges, T. Light, & F. Mostelle, (Eds.), *Meta-Analysis for Explanation.* New York: Russell Sage Foundation.

Lipsey, M., & Wilson, D. (2001). *Practical meta-analysis.* Thousand Oaks, CA: Sage.

Marlowe, D. (2006). When "what works" never did: Dodging the "Scarlet M" in correctional rehabilitation. *Criminology & Public Policy, 5*(2), 339–346.

Martinson, R. (1974). What works?: Questions and answers about prison reform. *The Public Interest, 35*, 22–54.

McCorkle, L., Elias, A., & Bixby, F. (1958). *The Highfields story.* New York: Henry Holt.

Miller, W., Brown, J., Simpson, T., Handmaker, N., Bien, T., Luckie, L., Montgomery, H., Hester, R., & Tonigan, J. (1995). What works? A methodological analysis of the alcoholism treatment outcome literature. In Hester & Miller (Eds.), *Handbook of alcoholism treatment approaches* (2nd ed.). Boston: Allyn & Bacon.

Moreno, J. L. (1957). *The First Book on Group Psychotherapy.* New York: Beacon House.

Mumala, C. (1999). *Substance abuse and treatment: State and federal prisoners.* Washington, DC: Bureau of Justice Statistics.

Nicholaichuk, T., Gordon, A., Gu, D., & Wong, S. (2000). Outcome of an institutionalized sexual offender treatment program: A comparison between treated and matched untreated offenders. *Sexual Abuse: A Journal of Research and Treatment, 12*(2), 139–153.

North Carolina Department of Correction-Division of Alcoholism & Chemical Dependency Programs. (n.d.). Retrieved August 18, 2006, from http://www.doc.state.nc.us/substance/aboutus.htm

North Carolina Division of Prisons Mental Health Services. (n.d.). Retrieved August 18, 2006, from www.doc.state.nc.us/dop/health/mhs

Ohio Department of Rehabilitation and Correction. (2005). *Recovery services F.Y. 2005 report: Pathway to recovery.* Retrieved August 10, 2006, from www.drc.state.oh.us/web/Reports/Recovery/Fiscal%20Year%202005.pdf

Ohio Department of Rehabilitation and Correction—Intensive Program Prisons. (n.d.). Retrieved August 11, 2006, from www.drc.state.oh.us/web/ipp.htm

Peters, R., LeVasseur, M., & Chandler, R. (2004). Correctional treatment for co-occurring disorders: Results of a national survey. *Behavioral Sciences and the Law, 22*, 563–584.

Price, C. (2004, June). *Cognitive behavioral interventions process evaluation report.* Retrieved August 14, 2006, from www.doc.state.nc.us/rap/CBI-Process-Evaluation-Report.pdf

Rhine, E., Mawhorr, T., & Parks, E. (2006). Implementation: The bane of effective correctional programs. *Criminology & Public Policy, 5*(2), 347–358.

Schrink, J., & Hamm, M. (1989). Misconceptions concerning correctional counseling. *Journal of Offender Counseling, Services and Rehabilitation, 14*(1), 133–147.

Slavson, S. R. (1950). *An Introduction to Group Therapy.* New York: Commonwealth Fund.

Smith, A., & Berlin, L. (1988). *Treating the criminal offender.* New York: Plenum Press.

Spon, R. (1999). *Corrective Thinking Treatment Manual: Charting a New Course Curriculum.*

State of Delaware Department of Correction. (2005). *Substance abuse treatment.* Retrieved September 5, 2006, from www.state.de.us/correct/Programs/treatmentprograms.shtml

U.S. Department of Justice, National Institute of Corrections. (2001). *Provision of mental health care in prisons.* Washington, DC: LIS, Inc.

Van Voorhis, P., Braswell, M., & Lester D. (2004). *Correctional counseling & rehabilitation* (5th ed.). Cincinnati, OH: Anderson.

Weeks, H. (1958). *Youthful offenders at Highfields: An evaluation of the effects of the short-term treatment of delinquent boys.* Ann Arbor: University of Michigan Press.

Yochelson, S. & Samenow, S. E. (1976). *The Criminal Personality, Volume 1: A Profile for Change.* New York: Jason Aronson.

Yochelson, S. & Samenow, S. E. (1977). *The Criminal Personality, Volume 2: The Change Process.* New York: Jason Aronson.

Zgoba, K., Sager, W., & Witt, P. (2003, Summer). Evaluation of New Jersey's sexual offender treatment program at the Adult Diagnostic Treatment and Treatment Center: Preliminary results. *The Journal of Psychiatry and Law,* (31), 133–165.

10

California's Correctional Drug Treatment System

William M. Burdon, Michael L. Prendergast, and Harry K. Wexler

ACKNOWLEDGEMENTS AND DISCLAIMER

This paper was supported by interagency agreements (Contracts C97.355 & C98.346) between the California Department of Corrections and Rehabilitation, Office of Substance Abuse Programs (CDCR-OSAP) and the UCLA Integrated Substance Abuse Programs (ISAP). Opinions and views expressed herein are those of the authors solely. They do not necessarily represent the opinions or views of the California Department of Corrections and Rehabilitation or its employees. Inquiries should be directed to William M. Burdon, Ph.D., UCLA Integrated Substance Abuse Programs, 1640 S. Sepulveda Blvd., Suite 200, Los Angeles, CA 90025; E-mail address: wburdon@ucla.edu.

ABSTRACT

Since 1997, California has been engaged in the largest expansion of prison-based treatment of its kind in the nation and perhaps even the world. This chapter provides a historical overview of the California correctional drug treatment system, including the current expansion of prison-based treatment programs and the related system of aftercare treatment. Findings from a series of evaluation studies of prison-based treatment programs in California are presented and discussed, as are the findings from continuing analyses that have been performed on data collected from these evaluations. The collective body of findings that have been generated from the California correctional drug treatment system have made a substantial contribution to the literature on corrections-based treatment. However, there remains much to be learned about how to further enhance the effectiveness of treatment for offenders. To that end, the chapter concludes with a discussion of how the expanding and evolving body of literature can be used to inform and advance corrections-based substance abuse treatment, not only in California, but nationwide.

INTRODUCTION

Over the past 40 years, therapeutic communities (TCs) have flourished in many states, primarily in community-based settings. However, it has only been in the past decade that they have emerged as the "treatment of choice" for dealing with substance-abusing offenders in prison settings (Inciardi, 1996; Wexler, 1995). Perhaps nowhere has this been more apparent than in California, which, since 1997, has been engaged in the largest expansion of prison-based substance abuse treatment ever undertaken in the United States; perhaps even the world. This chapter documents the story of the California correctional drug treatment system to date.

The story of the California correctional drug treatment system begins with the opening of the Amity TC at the R. J. Donovan Corrections Center in San Diego in 1989. Early evaluations of this and other prison-based TC programs, which showed the benefits of providing in-prison substance abuse treatment using the TC model, formed the foundation for legislation to expand the number of in-prison TC treatment beds in California prisons. This chapter will describe this expansion of prison-based treatment programs in California and the complementary system of aftercare that was developed and implemented to help ensure positive outcomes by providing continuity of care for paroles choosing to continue treatment in the community following release from prison.

Prendergast and Wexler (2004) provided a historical perspective of prison-based substance abuse treatment programs in California. This chapter seeks to supplement and build upon that historical overview by providing details of the outcomes from the evaluation studies that were performed on the California correctional treatment system, as well as findings from continuing research and analyses performed on the treatment database developed from these evaluations, which contains client-level background, treatment participation, and return to prison data on almost 28,000 inmates who participated in prison-based treatment from 1997 to 2004. The chapter closes with a discussion of how to move the initiative forward and ensure its continued viability and success into the future. This includes broadening the scope of in-prison treatment to include modalities other than TC treatment, the adoption and implementation of a system for assessing and referring drug-involved offenders to the appropriate modality and intensity of in-prison treatment, improving the system of in-prison and aftercare treatment by focusing on assessing and improving the quality of existing treatment programs, and the need for more gender-specific treatment.

Early Prison-Based Treatment in California— The Civil Addict Program

In the 1960s, California pioneered the "civil commitment" approach to the treatment of drug and alcohol addiction among offenders. This approach to treatment allowed judges to designate certain drug-involved offenders facing sentencing before the court as "narcotics addicts" and commit them to serve their sentence at the California Rehabilitation Center, where they were required to undergo a period of in-prison residential treatment in the newly formed Civil Addict Program (CAP), followed by mandatory community-based treatment after release from prison. Entrance into CAP was voluntary, and offenders could refuse the designation and be sentenced as a felon offender to regular state prison.

At its height, CAP proved to be a relatively successful treatment program for drug-involved offenders. An evaluation of the programs conducted in the mid-1970s (McGlothlin, Anglin, & Wilson, 1977) found that, during the seven years after initial commitment, CAP clients reduced their daily opiate use by 22 percent, whereas comparison clients reduced their daily use by only 7 percent. Similarly, criminal activities among the CAP group were reduced by 19 percent, while the comparison group reported a reduction of only 7 percent.

Despite these positive findings, CAP became a victim of a budget reductions and the antirehabilitation ideology of the late 1970s. In 1976, California passed the Uniform Determinate Sentencing Act, which specified defined lengths of time in prison for specific offenses rather than leaving the decision up to the parole board. This act removed a major incentive for inmates to participate in rehabilitation programs, making it difficult to maintain existing programs (e.g., CAP) or initiate new ones. As a result, CAP eventually became little more than a shell of the initial program, and its value as a treatment tool declined. Apart from the much weakened programming at the California Rehabilitation Center and scattered short-term drug education programs in a few prisons, programming for drug-using inmates within the California prison system virtually disappeared in the late 1970s and the 1980s.

A Return to Correctional Treatment in California

Between 1983 and 1988, commitments to prison for drug offenses in California increased from 11.1 percent of all new felon admissions to 35.4 percent. Sharp increases were also observed in the number of parolees returned to prison for drug-related offenses. The contribution of drug and alcohol abuse to the increasing number of offenders entering prison and being returned to prison on parole violations was highlighted by a Blue Ribbon Commission on Inmate Population Management (established in 1987). This commission also pointed out that, despite the increase in drug-involved offenders in state prison, there were few drug and alcohol treatment programs available to California prisoners or parolees. The commission urged the Department of Corrections, the Board of Corrections, and local correctional agencies to "immediately develop and implement a state and local corrections substance abuse strategy to systematically and aggressively deal with substance abusing offenders while they are under correctional supervision, because this is perhaps the most significant contributing factor to prison and jail overcrowding" (Blue Ribbon Commission on Inmate Population Management, 1990, p. 7).

Several other developments that were occurring nationally in the late 1980s also contributed to the revival of treatment programs within California's correctional system. There was growing support nationally for rehabilitation as evidenced by positive reviews of correctional treatment programs (Camp & Camp, 1989; Chaiken, 1989; Gendreau & Ross, 1987), surveys indicating public support for rehabilitation (Cullen, Cullen, & Wozniak, 1988), federal backing of treatment for drug-abusing offenders in Project REFORM (Wexler, Lipton, Blackmore, & Brewington, 1992), and the first National Drug Control Strategy (Office of National Drug Control Policy, 1989).

Also, in 1987, at the same time that the Blue Ribbon Commission was meeting, a task force on prison-based treatment was formed that reported directly to the director of the California Department of Corrections and Rehabilitation (CDCR).[1] At the urging of this task force, CDCR initiated participation in Project REFORM. With the assistance of a grant from the Bureau of Justice Assistance and a technical review of the department's substance abuse treatment needs (Rupp & Beck, 1989), CDCR submitted a plan to the legislature that included the establishment of a demonstration treatment project at the newly opened R. J. Donovan Correctional Facility near San Diego (Winett, Mullen, Lowe, & Missakian, 1992). The plan called for this demonstration project to utilize the therapeutic community (TC) model of treatment, modified for a prison environment, and it called for the formation of the Office of Substance Abuse Program (OSAP) within CDCR to oversee and guide the design and implementation of this and other possible treatment programs in prisons throughout the state.

In 1990, OSAP and the Amity Foundation designed and implemented the Amity program at the R. J. Donovan Correctional Facility near San Diego (Amity-RJD), the first prison-based TC treatment program in the California state prison system. Amity-RJD provided TC treatment services to Level III (medium-maximum security) inmates[2] who *volunteered* for treatment, a characteristic of the program that disappeared with the subsequent expansion of prison-based treatment programs throughout the state's prison system (see below).

As with most prison-based treatment programs that have been implemented in the years since Amity-RJD commenced operations and that use a modified TC treatment model, Amity-RJD utilized a three-phase model. The initial phase (2 to 3 months) included orientation, assessment of needs and problem areas, and planning of treatment goals. During the second phase of treatment (5 to 6 months), residents were provided opportunities to earn positions of increased responsibility by showing greater involvement in the program and by engaging in hard emotional work. Encounter groups and counseling sessions focused on self-discipline, self-worth, self-awareness, respect for authority, and acceptance of guidance for problem areas. During the third reentry phase (1 to 3 months), residents strengthened their planning and decision-making skills and worked with program and parole staff to prepare for their return to the community. Upon release from prison, Amity graduates were given the choice of entering a community-based TC program called Vista for up to one year, also operated by Amity Foundation. The content of the Vista program built on the foundation of the Amity-RJD in-prison TC curriculum and was individualized for each resident based on the progress that was made while in the Amity-RJD program and on individual treatment needs.

The Amity-RJD program was originally designed as a pilot project to determine the effectiveness of a TC within the state's prison system. Under a NIDA-funded grant to the Center for Therapeutic Community Research at National Development and Research Institutes, Inc., Wexler (Wexler, De Leon, Kressel, & Peters, 1999; Wexler, Melnick, Lowe, & Peters, 1999) conducted a 12-month prospective outcome study of the Amity-RJD program using a treatment-control group design with random assignment. Inmates on a waiting list of

---

[1] Previous to 2006 and for most of the period of time covered by the story of the California prison-based treatment initiative, the California Department of Corrections and Rehabilitation (CDCR) was known only as the California Department of Correction (CDCR). However, for simplicity, this chapter will use the new title of the department.
[2] Male inmates in the California state prison system are housed at four different levels of security, ranging from Level I (minimum security) to Level IV (maximum security).

volunteers for the Amity-RJD program were randomly selected and assigned to the treatment condition as beds became available in the program. Those who were still on the waiting list when they had less than nine months to serve on their prison term were removed from the list and became members of the control group. This procedure yielded a final sample for the outcome study that consisted of 715 inmates (425 inmates assigned to the treatment group and 290 assigned to the no-treatment group).

Early unpublished findings from this evaluation, presented at various conferences (Wexler & Graham, 1992, 1993, 1994) and directly to OSAP and policy makers in California (Wexler, Graham, Koronkowski, & Lowe, 1995), found strong support for the effectiveness of the Amity-RJD program. At 12 months postrelease, statistically significant differences in return-to-prison (RTP) rates were found for the treatment and the control subjects (33.9% and 49.7%, respectively).

Subsequent analyses also examined RTP rates at 12, 24, 36, and 60 months among three self-selected subgroups within the treatment group: prison TC dropouts, TC completers, and TC and Vista (aftercare) completers (Wexler, De Leon, et al., 1999; Wexler, Melnick, et al., 1999; Prendergast, Hall, Wexler, Melnick, & Cao, 2004). At 12 months, the RTP rate consistently decreased across these three groups (TC dropouts, 44.9%; TC completers, 40.2%; TC/Vista completers, 8.2%). At 24, 36, and 60 months, the RTP rate for all of the groups increased, but the pattern of results was consistent with the 12-month outcomes (at 60 months: TC dropouts, 87.0%; TC completers, 86.2%; TC/Vista completers, 41.8%).

For inmates who were returned to prison, the published Amity outcome reports also assessed outcomes in terms of the time until return to prison. In general, participation in treatment significantly delayed return to prison compared with no treatment, as did longer exposure to treatment.

In 1991, a year after the Amity program was established, OSAP and Mental Health Systems, Inc., opened California's first in-prison treatment program for women, the Forever Free program at the California Institution for Women, using funds provided by the federal Office of Treatment Improvement (which later became the Center for Substance Abuse Treatment). Unlike Amity-RJD, the original Forever Free program was not a TC. Instead, this program adopted a cognitive-behavioral approach to treatment, using a psychoeducational curriculum combined with a strong 12-step emphasis to treat women for up to six months. Upon release to parole, graduates from the program volunteered to participate in community residential treatment.

The earliest evaluation of the Forever Free program was a retrospective study conducted by OSAP (Jarman, 1993), which found that 90 percent of Forever Free clients who graduated from the program and attended at least 6 months of aftercare were successful on parole (i.e., successful discharge from parole and/or no returns to prison) compared to only 38 percent of Forever Free clients who did not complete the program. In a subsequent restrospective study, Prendergast, Wellisch, and Wong (1996) found that, at 12 months following release to parole, 68 percent of Forever Free clients who graduated from the program and attended aftercare were successful on parole, compared with 52 percent of Forever Free program graduates who did not attend aftercare, and 27 percent of a no-treatment comparison group. This study also found that increased time in treatment was associated with success on parole. Among those women who stayed in aftercare for five or more months, 86 percent were successful on parole, compared with 58 percent of women who stayed less than five months in aftercare. More recently, Hall, Prendergast, Wellisch, Patten, and Cao (2004) examined 12-month recidivism (arrests and/or convictions), drug use, and employment among 119 women who participated in the Forever Free program and 96 women who participated in an 8-week (3 hours per day) substance abuse education course. The results showed that the women who participated in the Forever Free program had significantly fewer arrests or convictions, significantly less drug use, and significantly greater employment.

The Expansion of Prison-Based Treatment

The findings from the early evaluations of the Amity-RJD program, combined with published findings supporting the effectiveness of drug treatment programs in prison settings (Field, 1989; Wexler, 1986; Wexler, Lipton, & Falkin, 1992), laid the foundation for California legislation in 1993 that appropriated funds to build the largest prison dedicated solely to drug treatment program in the world, and for subsequent legislation that embarked California on a large and rapid expansion of TC treatment programs throughout the state's prison system; an expansion that remains ongoing.

In 1997, the Substance Abuse Treatment Facility (SATF) opened. In addition to five facilities that house various levels of general population inmates, SATF has two self-contained treatment facilities that are specifically designed to provide housing and residential substance abuse treatment for 1,056 minimum-security offenders with substance abuse problems. Each treatment facility has three housing units, each containing four 44-bed treatment clusters.[3] Each cluster contains space for inmate housing, treatment-related activities, interviewing, and a staff office. Inmates in these treatment facilities are completely separated from the general prison population. Treatment services were provided by two community-based treatment organizations, under separate contracts with OSAP: Phoenix House and Walden House. However, CDCR retains responsibility for custodial operations at both facilities. Consistent with the Amity and Forever Free programs, graduates of SATF can volunteer for up to six months of residential or outpatient treatment following release to parole (Anglin, Prendergast, & Farabee, 1997).

Shortly after the opening of SATF, two state reports called for the further expansion of prison-based treatment as a way to address the problem of prison overcrowding, reduce the need for enlarging or building new prisons, and enhance public safety and health. In 1997, the Legislative Analyst's Office issued a report titled *Addressing the State's Long-Term Inmate Population Growth* (1997) in which it recommended that substance abuse treatment be provided for 10,000 inmates over a period of seven years. It was estimated that this action would result in significant savings to the state. In 1998, the Little Hoover Commission, an independent state body tasked with improving government efficiency, called for prison-based drug treatment to be greatly expanded, with certain high-level offenders targeted for TC treatment and low-level and medium-level offenders targeted for cognitive-behavioral treatment (Little Hoover Commission, 1998).

This further expansion of prison-based treatment programs commenced in 1998, with a 1,000-bed expansion that added five new TC programs in five prisons. This was followed in 1999 with a 2,000-bed expansion that added nine new TC programs in six prisons,

---

[3] Although designed for only 1,056 offenders, the SATF is capable of providing treatment to as many as 1,476 Inmates.

and subsequent expansions added even more programs and treatment beds. As of 2006, there exist 40 programs totaling 9,557 beds devoted to providing prison-based substance abuse treatment to prisoners throughout California's network of 32 prisons and 33 fire camps. Combined, participants in these programs include both male and female inmates at all levels of security classification (minimum to maximum).

All of the TC substance abuse programs (SAPs) in the California state prison system provide between 6 and 24 months of treatment at the end of inmates' prison terms. With few exceptions, participation in these programs is mandatory for inmates who have a documented history of substance use or abuse (based on a review of inmate files) and who do not meet established exclusionary criteria for entrance into a TC SAP (e.g., documented in-prison gang affiliation, being housed in a Secure Housing Unit within the previous 12 months for assault or weapons possession, Immigration and Naturalization Service holds). Also, with the exception of the treatment beds located at the SATF, the TC SAPs are not fully separated from the general inmate populations of the institutions within which they are located. Rather, inmates enrolled in the programs are housed in a normal inmate housing unit that has been designated as a SAP housing unit. Programming activities generally occur in specially constructed trailers that are located within or near to the facility where the TC SAP inmates are housed. Thus, outside of the time that the TC SAP inmates spend in the designated housing units and 20 hours per week of programming activities, they remain integrated with the general population inmates, that is, they dine, work, attend education classes, and share recreation time with general population inmates.

The average size of the in-prison TC programs (approximately 240 beds per program) was the result of efforts to maintain some level of segregation from general population inmates. This was accomplished by selecting a housing unit that existed on the general population facility and designating it as the housing unit for the TC SAP inmates. Housing units in the state prison system house from 100 to 250 inmates, depending on the institution and level of security. Thus, the average size of the TCs was essentially driven by the capacity of the average housing unit in the state prison system.

Aftercare

As a result of evaluation findings from prison-based TC programs showing the importance of aftercare, the California initiative has included a major aftercare component that allows inmates paroling from the prison-based programs to participate in up to six months of continued treatment (residential or outpatient services) in the community.

The Substance Abuse Services Coordinating Agency (SASCA) network, developed in California in parallel with the expansion of in-prison TC treatment programs, is an aftercare system of interrelated and interdependent components. At the center of this system are four regionally based SASCAs, under contract with OSAP and geographically located in each of the state's four parole regions. The specific tasks that each SASCA is responsible for can be classified into four main areas (Ossmann, 1999): (1) Capacity development: The SASCAs are responsible for ensuring that sufficient treatment capacity exists within their respective regions to satisfy the expected demand. This is accomplished primarily through contracting with community-based service providers to provide treatment services to graduates from prison-based treatment programs. (2) Liaison: Each SASCA serves as a liaison between the (a) prison-based treatment providers, who are responsible for developing the aftercare plan for the parolee; (b) CDCR parole division, which is responsible for supervising the parolee; and (c) community-based providers, with whom the SASCA contracts for services and monitors the parolee's progress through post-release treatment. (3) Transitioning: Each SASCA is responsible for ensuring the smooth, timely, and uninterrupted transition of the parolee from prison to community-based treatment. (4) Monitoring and tracking: Each SASCA is responsible for maintaining contact with graduates of the prison-based treatment programs during their period of eligibility for aftercare (whether they participate in treatment or not), securing access to community-based treatment when necessary during this period, and tracking each parolee's progress and participation in community-based treatment.

Parolees from the prison-based SAPs are eligible to access and participate in up to 6 months of aftercare through the SASCA network during the first 12 months following their release to parole. For felons, participation in aftercare is voluntary, and failure to enter community-based treatment in accordance with the established aftercare plan is not mandated and does not constitute a parole violation. However, for civil addicts, participation in aftercare is a condition of parole.

The SASCA network is an example of a "Third-Party Coordination" model for ensuring continuity of care for individuals transitioning from prison-based to community-based treatment (CSAT, 1998; Field, 1998). This continuity of care model involves the use of a third party who acts as a broker of services and coordinates the parolee's release and transition into aftercare. The model is considered most appropriate when there are dispersed services that make it difficult or impractical for the prison, the prison-based treatment provider, or the community-based provider to offer transitional planning or to coordinate continuing care (CSAT, 1998; Field, 1998). These characteristics make this model uniquely suited to ensuring continuity of care within the California correctional drug treatment system, which consists of a large number of prison-based and community-based treatment providers and a large number of clients who will be receiving services over a large geographic region.

Separate from the SASCA system, CDCR also established the Female Offender Treatment and Employment Project (FOTEP) in 1999. Unlike the SASCA system, which was designed to facilitate the transfer of male and female parolees from prison-based to community-based substance abuse treatment, FOTEP was designed to provide actual treatment and employment services to drug-involved female parolees with dependent minor children. The goal of FOTEP is to enable the successful reintegration of women parolees into the community, particularly with regard to reducing criminal behavior, substance use, and welfare dependence, and to strengthen family relationships and vocational education. To be eligible for FOTEP, women must have participated in an in-prison substance abuse treatment program, must have parental rights to at least one child under the age of 18, and must be paroled to a region of the state where a FOTEP program is available. Participants enroll in FOTEP at the time of parole from prison-based treatment. Females who enroll in FOTEP do not need the transitional and case management services offered by the SASCAs, and thus access and participate in aftercare (FOTEP) outside of the SASCA system.

FOTEP services are provided by three not-for-profit community treatment providers (Walden House, Phoenix House, and Mental Health Systems, Inc.), which provide services under separate contracts with CDCR. Over 400 FOTEP slots are currently available in residential FOTEP programs located in eight counties throughout the state. All FOTEP programs provide comprehensive case management, vocational services, and parenting assistance within the context of community-based residential drug treatment, although program design details vary across the three subcontractors. Planned treatment duration ranges from 6 to 15 months, depending on a participant's assessed needs. Specific characteristics of the FOTEP programs are as follows: (1) Residential drug treatment services for 6 to 15 months using a TC treatment model. Services provided include comprehensive needs assessment, relapse prevention, life skills training, self-help/support groups, "criminal lifestyles" awareness, literacy assessment and training, and individual and group counseling sessions. (2) Comprehensive case management, referral, and transportation services to link individuals with legal, social, medical/dental, and other needed services. (3) Vocational services, provided in both individual and group sessions, include assessments for vocational readiness and employability and behavioral skills training in job-seeking skills. (4) Parenting and family services, which include parent training groups and classes, on-site child care, family reunification assessment and advocacy, family therapy, pre- and postnatal support and referrals, and supervised child visitation. Some programs also provide live-in accommodations for minor children (within age limitations).

Shortly after the expansion of prison-based TC programs began in 1997, OSAP formed the Policy Advisory Committee (PAC). The mission of the PAC is to identify larger issues and problems relevant to the ongoing growth of the network of prison-based TCs and the SASCA system, develop possible solutions, and advise OSAP on the formation of new policy or revision of existing policy. Since it formed, the PAC has met an average of twice each year. The membership of the PAC consists of senior management from OSAP, executives of the major treatment organizations that are contracted to provide in-prison treatment and SASCA services, UCLA ISAP (the contracted evaluators), and the University of California, San Diego, Center for Criminality and Addiction Research, Training, and Application (CCARTA), which has been contracted to perform training and continuing education for treatment counselors. Beyond these core members, various other stakeholders frequently attend the PAC meetings (e.g., treatment program directors, correctional counselors, parole agents). Identified issues are generally assigned to standing subcommittees or ad hoc subcommittees, which are charged with studying an issue in depth and developing a list of recommended solutions. These are then reported back to the full PAC, which makes final recommendations to OSAP for implementation.

UCLA RESEARCH ON THE CALIFORNIA PRISON-BASED TREATMENT SYSTEM

Evaluating the Expansion Initiative

As part of the expansion of prison-based treatment that began in 1997, UCLA Integrated Substance Abuse Programs (ISAP) was contracted by the CDCR's Office of Substance Abuse Programs to conduct a series of five-year nonexperimental process evaluation studies of 17 TC programs located in 10 institutions and totaling approximately 4,900 beds. At six of these programs, outcome evaluations were also conducted, which assessed return-to-prison rates between inmates who participated in the TC programs and matched comparison groups of inmates who did not receive TC treatment.

Process Evaluation Findings: Growing Pains.   The main objectives of the process evaluations were to (1) document the goals and objectives of CDCR's drug treatment programs and any additional goals and objectives of each provider, (2) assess the degree to which the providers were able to implement these goals and objectives in their programs, (3) determine the degree to which the provider conformed to the therapeutic community model of treatment, and (4) collect descriptive data on treatment participants.

Consistent with these objectives, the process evaluations collected both client- and program-level data. Client-level data consisted of quantitative descriptive and treatment participation data on all inmates participating in the prison-based TC programs that were included in the evaluation studies. These data and the analyses performed on them are discussed in more detail below.

Program-level data was largely qualitative in nature and consisted primarily of data drawn from program documents; observations of programming activities; interviews with program administrators, treatment and corrections staff, and OSAP personnel; and periodic focus groups with treatment staff, custody staff, and inmates. Observations of programming activities and interviews with program administrators, treatment and custody staff, and OSAP personnel occurred during frequent site visits by ISAP research personnel to each of the program sites. Observations also included ISAP staff participation in various regularly scheduled meetings attended by institutional, treatment program, and OSAP personnel, which discussed and addressed issues of import to particular programs and/or the entire treatment initiative (e.g., PAC and various PAC subcommittee meetings).

An additional source of qualitative data came from two waves of focus groups that were conducted at five TC programs located at five different institutions covering both male and female inmates at varying levels of security. The first wave of focus groups was conducted in the winter of 2000. The second wave was conducted in the winter of 2002. At each location, focus groups were held with program clients, treatment staff, and custody staff. Each focus group lasted approximately 90 minutes and was recorded on audiotape. Written transcripts were prepared and content analyzed using qualitative software.

At the program level, the process evaluations revealed a number of system- and treatment-related issues that were relevant to the implementation and ongoing operations of the prison-based TC programs. However, given the nature of these issues, we believe that they are not unique to the California correctional drug treatment system. Many, if not most, states that have established or expanded treatment programs for inmates may have faced or are still dealing with the same or similar issues (Farabee et al., 1999; Harrison & Martin, 2000; Moore & Mears, 2001). Thus, these issues are presented in terms of their importance as key elements in developing and sustaining effective substance abuse treatment programs in correctional environments in general. The first three issues (collaboration and communication, supportive organizational culture, sufficient human resources) represent system-related issues, while the remaining four issues (screening, assessment, and referral; treatment integrity, incentives and rewards; and coerced treatment) represent treatment-related issues.

Collaboration and Communication.   Corrections-based treatment programs exist within, and are largely subordinate to, the organizational culture of the larger correctional system, which holds a very different philosophy and mission with respect to substance abuse and the way it should be dealt with. Correctional systems are dedicated to public safety and view drug use as a crime, whereas substance abuse treatment systems are rehabilitative and view drug use as a chronic, but treatable disorder (Prendergast & Burdon, 2002). As a result of this organizational reality, the goals and philosophies of treatment programs have less influence than those of the superordinate correctional system. Because of this, effective and open communication and collaboration between the two systems becomes critical. The separate objectives of ensuring public safety and rehabilitation can coexist, but both systems need to be committed to developing and maintaining an inter-organizational "culture of disclosure" (Prendergast & Burdon, 2002), in which there exists a common set of goals and where system-, program-, and client-level information is shared in an atmosphere of mutual understanding and trust.

Supportive Organizational Culture.   Most departments of corrections are complex bureaucratic organizations that need to emphasize safety, security, and conformance to established policies and procedures. For the most part, such an organizational culture does not easily facilitate or support the presence of client-oriented substance abuse treatment programs. Yet, in order for substance abuse treatment programs to operate effectively, some degree of meaningful coordination needs to exist between the criminal justice and treatment systems. For this to occur, the organizational culture should facilitate the work of treatment programs, while ensuring the continued safety and security of the inmates, staff, and public. While it is not realistic to expect that correctional treatment programs be exempt from departmental and institutional policies and procedures, it is also not realistic to expect treatment programs to operate effectively in a prison environment that does not support the existence and operation of such programs. Without clear and continuing commitment and support from correctional management, the ability of treatment programs to operate effectively will be impeded. Examples of actions and activities that can facilitate the creation of a supportive organizational culture and the overall effectiveness of treatment programs include the development and incorporation of policies and procedures into existing departmental operations manuals that explicitly recognize and reflect the unique nature of substance abuse treatment programs. Such policies and procedures can address sensitive issues such as behavioral guidelines that cover counselor-client interactions and recognize the importance of developing therapeutic bonds, or establishing guidelines that allow treatment staff to initiate disciplinary actions for infractions of treatment program rules of conduct and behavior, which are distinguished from disciplinary actions that are initiated by custody staff for infractions of institutional rules of conduct and behavior.

Sufficient Human Resources.   Most discussions of effective treatment systems address the issue of resources (Field, 1998; Greenley, 1992; Rose, Zweben, & Stoffel, 1999; Taxman, 1998). While departments of corrections understandably need to control costs, the commitment of insufficient financial resources, especially for salaries, often prevents the recruitment and retention of experienced and qualified treatment staff, which in turn results in excessive staff turnover.

Qualitative data from the focus groups with treatment staff suggest that paying frontline counselors salaries that are competitive with the local markets is often not sufficient to ensure long-term retention and avoid turnover. Even with previous experience in substance abuse counseling, many individuals who come to work as counselors in prison-based treatment programs are unprepared for the realities of working in a highly structured prison environment, where they are constantly being "tested" by inmates, struggle to establish personal boundaries of interaction, and are closely monitored to ensure that they do not become overly familiar with the inmates. This often results in stressful working conditions where counselors are likely to "burn-out" and leave within short periods, either as a result of resignation or termination.

Screening, Assessment, and Referral. Therapeutic community treatment is the most intensive form of substance abuse treatment available. It is also the most costly to deliver. As such, it should be reserved for inmates with more severe substance abuse or dependence problems. Simply put, not all substance-using offenders are in need of TC treatment. Given the limited amount of treatment bed space in TC programs relative to the number of inmates who are in need of substance abuse treatment, identifying inmates who are most in need of intensive TC treatment requires the use of valid screening procedures.

The "risk principle" (Andrews, Bonta, & Hoge, 1990; Gendreau, Cullen, & Bonta, 1994) states that treatment services are most effective when offenders receive services based on risk level; high-risk offenders require more intensive services, whereas low-risk offenders require less intensive services. (Risk refers to the likelihood of engaging in subsequent criminal behavior.) Several meta-analyses on offender treatment have consistently found that treatment interventions are more effective when delivered to high-risk offenders (Andrews et al., 1990; Bonta, 1997; Lipsey, 1995; see also Lowenkamp & Latessa, 2004). There also exists empirical support for the risk principle (Bonta et al., 2000; Brown, 1996; Lowenkamp & Latessa, 2003). In a study of 53 residential treatment programs for offenders, Lowenkamp and Latessa (2003) found that among low-risk and low/moderate-risk offenders, there was a 4 percent and 1 percent (respectively) increase in the probability of recidivism, whereas among moderate-risk and high-risk offenders, there was a 3 percent and a 8 percent (respectively) decrease in the probability of recidivism. With respect to prison-based substance abuse treatment, Knight, Simpson, and Hiller (1999) found that intensive in-prison TC treatment was most effective for high-severity inmates. Similarly, using data collected from the original sample of inmates in the evaluation of the Amity-RJD program (Graham & Wexler, 1997), Wexler, Melnick, and Cao (2004) found that risk factors predicted return-to-prison rates at three years and that positive treatment effects were more likely among higher risk treatment participants.

However, even when good assessment and referral procedures exist, many correctional systems often base decisions to place inmates into drug treatment programs less on the severity of their substance abuse problem and more on institutional factors such as management and security concerns. Treatment staff often have little control over which inmates are entering the programs. When this occurs, inmates who could or should be placed into these programs (i.e., those with substance abuse disorders and at highest risk for relapse) may be excluded, whereas inmates who may not be amenable to or appropriate for treatment programs may be included (e.g., those who have severe mental illness or are dangerous sex offenders). This, in turn, directly impacts the treatment providers' ability to provide treatment services to those who are most in need of them.

Treatment Integrity. "Community as method" (De Leon, 2000) refers to that portion of TC philosophy that calls for a full immersion of the client into a community environment and culture that is designed to change (rehabilitate) the "whole person." In correctional environments where treatment programs are not fully segregated from the general inmate population, inmates participating in the treatment curricula remain exposed to the prison subculture and its negative social and environmental forces, which may attenuate treatment benefits. To counteract the dysfunctional influence of the prison subculture on participants in treatment, it is important that treatment curricula be structured, well-defined, and engaging. Wexler and Williams (1986) highlighted several features that help ensure the effectiveness of prison-based TC programs. Among them is program integrity; the perception that the program is strong, coherent, and autonomous while maintaining cooperative and respectful communications with correctional staff and the administration of the host institution. Related to this is the enforcement of TC program rules by treatment staff in a manner that maintains credibility with custody staff and discipline within the treatment program while keeping the primary focus on treatment. Program integrity is especially important in mandated programs, where problem awareness and motivation for change among many treatment participants may be limited.

Incentives and Rewards in Treatment.   Correctional environments generally rely on punishment for rule infractions and seldom offer inmates positive reinforcement for engaging in prosocial behaviors (i.e., complying with institutional rules and codes of conduct). Similarly, within the context of prison-based treatment, inmates are seldom reinforced for *specific* acts of positive behavior (e.g., punctuality, participation, timely completion of tasks). To the extent that they are, the reinforcement "tends to be intermittent and, in contrast to sanctions, less specific, not immediately experienced, and based on a subjective evaluation of a client's progress in treatment" (Burdon, Roll, Prendergast, & Rawson, 2001, p. 78).

Where participation in prison-based TC treatment programs is mandated, the treatment process needs to counteract the resentment and resistance that inmates initially feel and exhibit as a result of being coerced into treatment. This requires that programs and institutions not only reduce disincentives that may exist, but also incorporate incentives that would serve as meaningful inducements to participating in the treatment process. However, at some institutions, the ability of treatment providers to develop and implement incentive or reward systems is limited by departmental and institutional policies and procedures that severely limit the granting of special privileges, rewards, or other incentives to specific groups of inmates (e.g., those participating in a treatment program).

Coerced Treatment.   Much of the growth in criminal justice treatment (both in California and nationally) is based on the widely accepted belief that involuntary substance abuse clients tend to do as well as, or even better than, voluntary clients (Farabee, Prendergast, & Anglin, 1998; Leukefeld & Tims, 1988; Simpson & Friend, 1988). However, the studies supporting this position were based on community-based treatment samples. As mentioned above, mandated referral to prison-based treatment programs often breeds a high degree of resentment and resistance among inmates forced into these programs.

One possible strategy to overcome this resentment and resistance, increase engagement in treatment, and facilitate the development of a therapeutic treatment culture would be to limit admissions during a program's first year or so to a relatively small number of inmates who volunteer for treatment. Ideally, the majority of clients referred to prison-based programs (particularly new programs) should be inmates with at least some desire to change their behavior through the assistance of a treatment program. Once a treatment milieu is established, the presence of involuntary inmates may prove to be less of an impediment to the delivery of effective treatment. Another strategy for overcoming resistance and increasing engagement in treatment is the use of peer mentors for new inmates entering the program. In TCs, peers act as the primary agents of change through the reinforcement of positive norms, values, and beliefs (De Leon, 2000). In prison-based programs, the recruitment of respected "shot-callers" from the general population into the program and their advancement to the role of peer mentors can lend substantial credibility and respect to the program and the inmates participating in it. Indeed, some California prison-based TCs have started mentor programs that involve recruiting inmates who are serving long sentences into the programs. After successfully completing the full curriculum, rather than being released to parole, these inmates remain involved in the TC as peer mentors to new inmates entering the programs.

Outcome Evaluations.   Six of the 17 TC programs evaluated by UCLA ISAP were also selected for more in-depth quantitative outcome evaluations: the SATF and five other TC programs located at five different prisons. These six outcome studies included five male programs covering all levels of security (except maximum security) and one female felon program, which included females at varying levels of security.[4]

The fundamental question addressed by outcome evaluations of prison-based treatment programs, and the one of most interest to policy makers and legislators, is how well a program performed in terms of its ability to reduce criminal recidivism among offenders. Most often this is measured by reincarceration or return-to-prison (RTP) rates.

For these outcome studies, random assignment to treatment and nontreatment conditions was not possible. (Human subjects concerns did not allow inmates to be randomly assigned to a nontreatment condition.) Thus, RTP rates were examined between first admission cohorts of inmates who participated in prison-based TC treatment and a matched comparison group of inmates who did not participate in prison-based TC treatment. To ensure that subjects in the comparison groups were in fact comparable to those in the treatment groups, a one-to-one matching procedure was employed. Lists of similar (nontreatment) inmates were selected from among general population inmates who had not participated in a prison-based TC program. This was accomplished using data from the CDCR Offender-Based Information System (OBIS), which contains demographic, incarceration history and status (i.e., prison admission and release dates, current location, custody level), and conviction offense data on each inmate. Primary matching criteria consisted of age, race/ethnicity, commitment offense, and custody level.

Overall, these studies found no significant differences in RTP rates between the treatment and matched comparison groups in these six studies. Two important factors likely contributed to this finding. First, each of these outcome studies started collecting data in only the second or third year after the program commenced operations. Many of the system- and treatment-related issues identified in the process evaluations (see above) had not been identified or addressed. As a result, it is likely that these issues were having an impact on the ability of each of these programs to deliver optimal treatment services to inmates, thus stunting the impact they could potentially have on reducing RTP rates. Second, each of these outcome studies used an intent-to-treat method when computing RTP rates: computation of RTP rates

---

[4] In California, male inmates are segregated by level of security (Level 1-Minimum to Level IV-Maximum). However, although they are assigned a security classification level, females are housed together; they are not segregated based on security level.

for the treatment group included all inmates who entered a prison-based TC program and agreed to participate in the study. Participation in aftercare was not considered. Analyses of RTP rates among inmates participating in all of the prison-based TC programs (see below) did look at the role of aftercare and highlighted the importance of aftercare in conjunction with prison-based treatment in improving post-treatment outcomes.

UCLA ISAP is currently conducting a further outcome evaluation of RTP rates among successive cohorts of inmates enrolled in the two programs at SATF, which have now been in operation for almost a full decade. It remains to be seen whether the system- and treatment-related issues identified in the process evaluations have been addressed and what if any impact they may still have on RTP rates among inmates now participating in these programs.

Ongoing Analyses of the UCLA Treatment Database

As part of the process evaluations described above, quantitative data on clients and their participation in treatment (both in prison treatment and aftercare) was collected from three sources. First, client-level data were collected by the treatment providers at the time that inmates entered the prison-based TC treatment programs using an Intake Assessment (IA) instrument. The IA was designed to assess a client's pretreatment/preincarceration sociodemographic background, criminality, employment, and substance use, abuse, or dependence. Adapted from the Initial Assessment developed at the Institute of Behavioral Research at Texas Christian University (Broome, Knight, Joe, & Simpson, 1996), the IA has been used extensively with criminal justice populations and provides information that is useful for both clinical and evaluation purposes. Second, aftercare participation data (i.e., admission and discharge dates, treatment modality) were collected from the SASCAs, which obtained these data from the community-based treatment providers. Third, return-to-prison (RTP) data were obtained from CDCR's OBIS database (described above). Data collection started when each of these programs commenced operations (1997–1999) and continued through June 2004.

Collectively, these data were combined into what is perhaps the largest database of prison-based treatment in existence. It contains data on 27,898 inmates (18,676 men and 9,222 women), including individual-level data (i.e., sociodemographics, employment, criminal history, and substance use, abuse, and dependence), treatment participation and retention data relating to both in-prison and community-based treatment, and return-to-prison data and criminal offense history.

Since collection ceased in July 2004, UCLA ISAP has continued to perform quantitative analyses on this treatment database to examine previously unexplored aspects of prison-based treatment. These analyses have generated important findings relating to the influence of aftercare on treatment outcomes, general predictors of outcomes, the need for gender-responsive treatment, and the effectiveness of prison-based TC treatment for maximum security inmates. Some of these findings have been published in peer reviewed journals (cited below). Other findings have been reported in various internal reports submitted to OSAP and/or in response to special requests by OSAP.

The Influence of Aftercare on Treatment Outcomes.   The most consistent finding to emerge from UCLA ISAP's quantitative analyses of participation in prison-based TC treatment and its impact on return-to-prison has been the importance of continuing substance abuse treatment in the community following release from prison-based treatment (i.e., aftercare).

While the initial decision to provide funding for an aftercare component to the prison-based treatment initiative in California was based on findings from the early evaluation study of the Amity-RJD program (Wexler, 1996), evaluations of prison-based substance abuse treatment programs since then have consistently demonstrated the importance of aftercare as a means of reinforcing and consolidating the gains made in prison-based treatment, improving clients' behavior while under parole supervision, and promoting long-term successful outcomes (Burdon, Messina, & Prendergast, 2004; Knight et al., 1999; Martin, Butzin, Saum, & Inciardi, 1999; Prendergast, Wellisch, & Wong, 1996; Prendergast, Hall, & Wellisch, 2002; Wexler, Melnick, et al., 1999). The combined findings of these studies have consistently demonstrated the positive impact that aftercare in combination with prison-based treatment has on reducing relapse to drug use and recidivism. They also highlight the need for making available effective community-based treatment services to parolees exiting prison-based treatment programs and for developing and implementing a structured system to ensure efficient transition from prison- to community-based treatment.

Quantitative analyses of data contained in the treatment database described above further reinforces the robustness of these findings by demonstrating the importance of aftercare for both male and female participants in prison-based treatment and for inmates at all levels of security (minimum to maximum). These analyses have examined two aspects of aftercare treatment: (1) retention or time spent in aftercare and (2) modality of aftercare (residential or outpatient).

These analyses focused on aftercare treatment that occurred subsequent to a subject's first parole date following his/her first admission into a prison-based TC (i.e., first admission cohorts). Participation in aftercare that followed subsequent incarcerations was not considered. This minimized potential confounding factors associated with previous in-prison residential or TC treatment and postprison aftercare. The dependent variable of interest was 12-month return to prison, which was operationalized as the first return to prison that occurred within 12 months of a subject's first parole from prison as defined below (retention in aftercare analyses) or within 12 months of a subject's discharge from his/her first aftercare treatment episode (modality of aftercare analyses).

Retention in Aftercare.   Analyses were performed to determine the 12-month return-to-prison (RTP) rates based on participation and retention in aftercare for varying lengths of time. In order to be eligible to participate in aftercare in California, parolees must have successfully completed participation in a prison-based TC treatment program or must have been in good standing in a prison-based TC treatment program at the time of their parole from prison. Such parolees are referred to as "TC graduates."

Among all TC graduates (male and female), the 12-month RTP rate was 39.1 percent. This included TC graduates who chose to enter aftercare and those who chose not to enter aftercare. However, the 12-month RTP rate among TC graduates who chose not to participate in aftercare was 45.1 percent; among those who did participate in aftercare, the RTP rate was 29.1 percent; and among those who participated in more than 90 days of aftercare, the RTP rate was 16.5 percent. While these rates differed substantially between males and females and among males classified at different levels of security (Level I-Minimum to Level IV-Maximum), the noted decreasing trend in RTP rates remained consistent across these groups.

Although this trend reinforces the significant contribution of aftercare to successful postprison outcomes as measured by RTP, it masks an important phenomenon relating to time spent in aftercare and its impact on RTP. The varying groups described above are not mutually exclusive. The RTP statistics reported for TC graduates who participated in any aftercare included those who participated in less than 90 days and those who participated in more than 90 days. Analyses of mutually exclusive groups of TC graduates (i.e., no after-care, less than 90 days of aftercare, and more than 90 days of aftercare) showed that the highest rate of return to prison occurred among TC graduates who participated in less than 90 days of aftercare (48.8%). This trend was consistent among both genders at all levels of security. While this phenomenon has been noted in other studies of prison-based treatment and aftercare (Knight et al., 1999; Martin et al., 1999; Wexler, De Leon, et al., 1999), it has yet to be explained or subjected to further study.

In any event, the data show that retention in aftercare for more than 90 days signifi-cantly improves outcomes as measured by return-to-prison rates. To the extent that after-care is voluntary, this may be at least partly the result of selection bias, that is, systematic differences between parolees who opted for and remained in aftercare and those who did not, although this statistical trend was consistent among both felons (for whom aftercare is voluntary) and civil addicts (for whom aftercare is a mandated condition of parole).

Modality of Aftercare.   While research has been consistent in demonstrating the benefits of substance abuse treatment in terms of more time spent in treatment (Condelli & Hubbard, 1994; Hubbard, Craddock, Flynn, Anderson, & Etheridge, 1997; Hubbard, Craddock, & Anderson, 2003; Simpson, Joe, & Brown, 1997), it has not consistently demonstrated that more intensive substance abuse treatment produces better outcomes than does less intensive treatment. Numerous studies that have examined differences between clients receiving treat-ment in different modalities have found significant improvements among all clients across modalities, while finding no significant differences between modalities on dependent mea-sures of interest. (Gottheil, Weinstein, Sterling, Lundy, & Serota, 1998; Hser, Evans, Huang, & Anglin, 2004; McLellan, Hagen, Meyers, Randall, & Durell, 1997; Weinstein, Gottheil, & Sterling, 1997). However, many studies that have shown no effect of treatment modality did not examine which clients within each modality experienced the best outcomes (Gastfriend & McLellan, 1997). The lack of differences between varying modalities may be due to a failure to match clients to the appropriate modality of treatment, resulting in different modalities having a mix of clients—those who were more appropriate for that particular modality and those who were less appropriate—thus masking the true effectiveness of each modality. There is evidence that matching drug-involved individuals to substance abuse treatment programs based on the severity of their substance abuse problem and the level of need for treatment and ancillary services leads to increased retention in treatment and improved outcomes (Friedmann, Hendrickson, Gerstein, & Zhang, 2004; Melnick, De Leon, Thomas, & Kressel, 2001; Moos, 2003; Thornton, Gottheil, Weinskin, & Kerachsky, 1998).

Burdon, Dang, Prendergast, Messina and Farabee (2006) conducted an analysis of the differential effectiveness of community-based residential and outpatient drug treatment on 12-month RTP rates. This analysis found that type of aftercare (i.e., *only* outpatient ver-sus *only* residential treatment) was not a significant predictor of 12-month RTP rates, even when subjects were matched to treatment modality based on the severity of their substance abuse problem. Subjects who were classified as having a drug/alcohol abuse problem or no diagnosable drug/alcohol problem (low severity) benefited equally from outpatient and residential aftercare. Similarly, those who were classified as being drug/alcohol dependent (high severity) also benefited equally from outpatient and residential aftercare.

Although type of aftercare did not predict 12-month RTP, time spent in aftercare was a significant predictor of 12-month RTP rates for both low-severity and high-severity parolees. These results are consistent with previous research highlighting the importance of aftercare in combination with prison-based treatment as a means of ensuring successful treatment outcomes as measured by return-to-prison rates (e.g., Burdon et al., 2004; Knight et al., 1999; Martin et al., 1999; Prendergast et al., 1996; Wexler, De Leon, et al., 1999; Wexler, Melnick, et al., 1999; Prendergast et al., 2004; Wexler, Burdon, & Prendergast, 2006).

The "continuum of care" construct rests on the notion that the transition of parolees from prison-based treatment to community-based treatment be "seamless" (i.e., uninterrupted; Taxman, 1998). Implicit in the concept of a seamless transition is the belief that treatment in the community will pick up where treatment in prison left off. Prior to the California initiative, research demonstrating the importance of aftercare in conjunction with prison-based treatment was largely limited to situations where only one or very few aftercare programs were available for parolees who completed prison-based treatment (Knight et al., 1999; Martin et al., 1999; Wexler, De Leon, et al., 1999; Wexler et al., 1992; Wexler, Melnick, et al., 1999). These continuity of care situations were characterized by well defined and/or contractual relationships between the in-prison and aftercare treatment programs; in some cases (e.g., Amity and Vista), both programs were operated by the same treatment provider. This ensured that clients experienced a relatively smooth transition into aftercare treatment, participated in aftercare with individuals who were in prison-based treatment with them (i.e., progressed through the treatment continuum in cohorts), and received aftercare treatment that was tailored to their needs and that built upon the progress that parolees made in prison-based treatment.

Due largely to its size, both in terms of geography and the number of offenders being served, the California correctional treatment system (inclusive of prison-based treatment, the SASCA network, and aftercare) has not been able to realize many of these characteristics. The rapid expansion of prison-based TC treatment and aftercare after 1997 resulted in a similar rapid growth in the number of community-based programs providing treatment services to individuals paroling from the many prison-based TC programs. In the analyses examining modality of aftercare, 455 different community-based treatment programs (164 outpatient and 291 residential) delivered treatment services to the 4,165 parolees included in the analyses (an average of 9.2 parolees per program).

Most of the community-based treatment programs where parolees receive aftercare are located at great distances from the prisons where they received treatment and are usually operated by community providers that have no direct relationship or contact with the prison-based treatment providers and little or no experience with prison-based treatment. As a result, parolees who choose to enter aftercare often experience difficulties getting to the designated community-based treatment program and seldom participate in treatment with other parolees from the same prison-based treatment programs they attended, or even with other drug-involved individuals under parole supervision. They are also less likely to receive treatment that builds upon the progress that was made in prison-based treatment.

Any combination of these factors may contribute to increased dissatisfaction with aftercare treatment and increased dropout rates, triggering a perception of failure on behalf of the parolee (who voluntarily entered aftercare treatment), which in turn may lead to a return to criminal activity, drug use, and ultimately reincarceration. In addition, the large number of community-based treatment programs raises the question of variability in the quality of aftercare treatment services provided to parolees by community-based providers, which may also account for the inability of treatment modality to predict outcomes.

In sum, the results of the analyses examining modality of aftercare highlight the need for empirical research that examines more closely the "continuum of care" construct and the assumptions that underlie it and for assessing the quality of community-based treatment services.

General Predictors of Outcomes.   In an analysis examining general predictors in aftercare and 12-month return-to-prison, Burdon et al. (2004) found that motivation for treatment was a significant predictor of participation in aftercare, which in turn was a significant predictor of 12-month RTP. This finding reinforced the findings of previous research that examined the relationship between motivation, continued participation in aftercare, and return-to-prison (De Leon, Melnick Kressel, & Jainchill, 2000; Melnick et al., 2001).

The most consistent theme that emerged from the results of this study was the importance of duration of time spent in treatment—both in-prison treatment and aftercare. With respect to in-prison treatment, subjects who spent more time in prison-based treatment were significantly more likely to participate in aftercare and significantly less likely to be returned to prison within 12 months. This finding is consistent with previous research that has demonstrated a significant relationship between time spent in treatment and treatment outcomes among substance abusers (Gossop, Marsden, Stewart, & Rolfe, 1999; Lipton, 1995; Westhuis, Gwaltney, & Hayashi, 2001; Wexler, Falkin, & Lipton, 1990). Similarly, with respect to aftercare, subjects who spent more time in aftercare were significantly less likely to be returned to prison within 12 months.

The results also showed that Hispanics were significantly less likely to participate in aftercare, but were also significantly less likely to be returned to prison within 12 months following their release. A possible explanation for this finding is that the social and/or familial support systems for Hispanics are stronger, and that they tend to rely on these support systems to a greater degree and with greater success following release to parole. (A significantly greater percentage of Hispanics reported living with family/relatives or friends prior to being incarcerated.) Previous research has found that social support systems (including familial factors) are important in preventing drug abuse among Hispanics (De La Rosa & White, 2001).

Finally, education was also a significant predictor of 12-month RTP, highlighting the importance of this factor in facilitating the process of post-release reintegration and promoting posttreatment successful outcomes.

In sum, the results of Burdon et al. (2006) were consistent with the findings of previous research. Motivation for treatment was a significant predictor of participation in aftercare, which in turn was a significant predictor of 12-month RTP. However, the most consistent theme that emerged from the results of this study was the importance of duration of time spent in treatment. The findings relating to Hispanics and education highlight the unique importance of social and/or familial support systems for Hispanics postrelease and the important role that education plays in facilitating postrelease reintegration and ensuring successful outcomes.

Gender-Responsive Treatment.   Under a separate contract with the CDCR, ISAP conducted an evaluation of the FOTEP programs. An intake assessment was administered upon parole from prison-based treatment and admission into FOTEP treatment, and a follow-up assessment was administered 12 months from the date of parole.

Records-based outcome analyses of RTP rates performed at 12, 24, 36, and 48 months revealed RTP rates of 34 percent at 12 months; 46 percent at 24 months; 50 percent at 36 months, and 54 percent at 48 months. Survival analyses showed that being younger, African American, and a felon offender (versus a civil addict); having a mental disorder; and dropping out of FOTEP treatment were all positively associated with an increased likelihood of being returned to prison.

Longer time in FOTEP treatment significantly reduced the likelihood of RTP; completers averaged significantly more time in treatment than noncompleters (217 versus 128 days, respectively). Women who were older and those who entered into FOTEP immediately upon parole were more likely to complete treatment than their respective counterparts, as were women who had fewer treatment needs in the area of mental health problems (Grella & Greenwell, 2006a). Being African American or Hispanic was associated with lower treatment needs (compared with Whites), but also a lower likelihood of treatment completion (Grella & Greenwell, 2006a).

Additional analyses found direct positive relationships between severe childhood profiles (e.g., adolescent conduct problems and substance abuse) and adult criminal behavior and current psychological distress (Grella, Stein, & Greenwell, 2005), and between exposure to childhood traumatic events and negative health-related outcomes as adults (Messina & Grella, 2006). Risky parental attitudes were found to be indirectly related to self-efficacy, decision-making ability, and social conformity; and directly related to depression and education and being non-White (Grella & Greenwell, 2006b).

The FOTEP programs represent a significant effort and commitment by CDCR to focus resources directly on addressing the unique needs of drug-involved female offenders, albeit in a community treatment setting. In a study that examined differences between men and women offenders entering prison-based TC treatment and the specific treatment needs of drug-involved women offenders, Messina, Burdon, and Prendergast (2003) found that, compared with men, women entering prison-based substance abuse treatment were more likely to have experienced some form of psychological impairment, to be taking prescribed medications, to be using cocaine/crack and heroin on a daily basis, to be poly-drug users prior to their current incarceration, to report being sexually and physically abused as children and as adults, to have less than a high school education; and to be financially dependent on family members and in need of public assistance.

These findings highlight the unique needs and characteristics of female drug-involved offenders (compared to males) and the need to provide gender responsive treatment in both prison- and community-based treatment settings. While the FOTEP programs address this need with respect to community-based treatment, prison-based treatment programs and curricula remain largely male-oriented in their content and approach to treatment.

The Effectiveness of TC Treatment for Maximum Security Inmates.   Based in large part on the success of Amity TC in the medium security R. J. Donovan prison in San Diego (Wexler, 1996), Amity Foundation was contracted in 1998 to operate a maximum security TC at the California State Prison, Los Angeles County (LAC), located in Lancaster, California (hereinafter referred to as Amity-LAC). Drug treatment programs are rarely found in maximum-security prisons, largely because of the generally harsh prison conditions, which are believed to be not supportive of a treatment culture and which result in low expectations for the inmates housed in these institutions, who tend to have extensive criminal histories. The Amity-LAC program commenced operations as part of the 1,000-bed expansion of prison-based TCs that occurred in 1998 (see above), and was one of the 17 TC programs included in the UCLA ISAP evaluations.

In terms of demographics and background differences, compared with male felons who participated in lower security level TCs, the Amity-LAC TC participants had significantly more severe and violent criminal histories, had greater unemployment, and were more likely to suffer from a mental disorder. Amity-LAC participants were also younger, single, more likely to be Black, and more likely to use opiates and other drugs as opposed to methamphetamine and alcohol.

The most important finding of this study was that inmates who participated in prison-based TC treatment and at least 90 days of aftercare had significant reductions in RTP. Security level was not related to differential outcomes, even when controlling for significant background differences (i.e., criminal history, unemployment, and prevalence of mental illness) between the maximum-security Amity participants and other lower security male TC participants. Although the significance of the background differences between maximum-security TC participants and male TC participants at other levels of security highlight the challenges confronting providers of treatment to maximum-security offenders, the findings of this study lend support to the expansion of treatment efforts to maximum-security prison populations.

MOVING THE INITIATIVE FORWARD IN CALIFORNIA AND THE NATION

Since 1997, California has been engaged in the largest expansion of prison-based treatment of its kind in the nation and perhaps even the world. In less than a decade, the state has opened 40 in-prison therapeutic community programs totaling more than 9,500 treatment beds. It is important to highlight that it was in fact a limited body of research on prison-based treatment that was relied on in forming the foundation of this rather large and rapid expansion of in-prison TC programs. However, since then a number of studies have contributed greatly to the evolution of and advancement of knowledge regarding the effectiveness of corrections-based treatment. Much of this research was based on data collected from the California treatment initiative. In particular, the process evaluations performed on the prison-based TC programs in California have yielded valuable system and treatment-related findings that are relevant to the implementation and ongoing operations of prison-based treatment programs in general. The question now should focus on how this expanding and evolving body of literature can be used to inform and advance corrections-based substance abuse treatment, not only in California, but nationwide. Several issues are especially important in accomplishing this task: diversifying treatment, assessment and referral, aftercare, treatment quality, and treatment for women.

Diversifying Treatment: Cognitive Behavioral and Educational programs

Although there exists a variety of approaches to treating substance-abusing inmates, the most common treatment modality still in use in California is the TC as modified for the prison setting. However, a substantial body of research supports the effectiveness of cognitive-behavioral (CB) treatment as a means of reducing criminal recidivism.

Programs that fall under the broad scope of CB treatment have as their underlying theoretical foundation social learning theory (Bandura, 1969), in that they focus on helping clients unlearn behaviors associated with criminal behavior and/or substance abuse through the acquisition of new thinking and acting skills (Langevin, 2001). Research on CB treatment suggests that it is effective at reducing recidivism among offenders. Meta-analyses have concluded that CB treatment programs improve outcomes (Andrews et al., 1990; Garrett, 1985; Izzo & Ross, 1990; Pearson, Lipton, Cleland, & Yee, 2002). Pearson et al. (2002) found that CB treatment approaches have a positive effect on reducing recidivism, with an average effect size (r) of .12.

Since the majority of general offender populations have a substance abuse or dependence disorder, and because of the lower cost of CB programs relative to TC programs, the question of the effectiveness of CB treatment programs in reducing recidivism has significant implications for prison-based substance abuse treatment. CB treatment differs from the modified TC model mainly in terms of the length of time that offenders are engaged in the treatment process and the level of intensity with which treatment services are delivered. And, as mentioned earlier, not all substance-abusing offenders are alike in terms of their characteristics or needs. Depending on the severity of their substance abuse or dependence problem, many drug-involved offenders may benefit equally well or better from less intensive forms of treatment, such as CB treatment.

Assessment and Referral

Effectively assessing and referring drug-dependent individuals to the most appropriate treatment modality and intensity is believed to be essential to ensuring the optimal effectiveness of treatment (DHHS, 1994). Yet, there remains no consistent and effective means of performing these tasks (Hser, 1995; Moos, 2003; Thornton et al., 1998). This is true in the California state prison system, where the task of identifying and classifying inmates into a one of the existing TC treatment programs utilizes CDCR's inmate classification system, which was designed to assess the security risk of inmates entering the prison system and place them in the least restrictive (i.e., least costly) security settings based on their tendency to misbehave while incarcerated (CDCR, 1996). Consistent with this, the current process for identifying inmates with substance abuse problems is limited to a review of their "Central Files" for documentation of drug-related offenses and convictions or a history of substance use (not necessarily abuse). Once potential candidates for treatment have been identified, they are subjected to further review using an established set of exclusionary criteria (e.g., documented gang affiliation, time spent in administrative segregation for violence, Immigration and Naturalization Service hold). In short, the primary objective of this process is to ensure that actual placements into substance abuse treatment are consistent with the objective of the classification system to minimize disruptive behavior. There is no formal systematic process that utilizes validated instrumentation to assess the presence or severity of a substance abuse or dependence disorder and make referrals to treatment based on the results of the assessment.

Similarly, the process of transitioning parolees from prison- to community-based treatment does not include a formal systematic process for assessing parolees' needs and referring them to appropriate community-based treatment programs or services. For the most part, following conventional wisdom, parolees are most often referred to and attend residential treatment in the community (i.e., the more intensive treatment modality).

The ability to properly assess and refer clients to appropriate treatment services is believed to be a key component of any effective system of care for drug-dependent individuals (Wellisch, Prendergast, & Anglin, 1993) and promotes increased retention in treatment and improved outcomes (Friedmann et al., 2004; Moos, 2003; Thornton et al., 1998). Without effective assessment and referral practices, resource allocation and utilization, and ultimately treatment effectiveness, are not optimized (Hser, 1995).

A number of instruments have been developed to assess substance abuse severity and make referrals to treatment. The matching criteria developed by the American Society of Addiction Medicine (ASAM, 1998; Gastfriend, 2003; Melnick et al., 2001) are designed to refer clients to increasingly intensive treatment modalities based on how they are evaluated along six dimensions: acute intoxication and/or withdrawal potential, biomedical conditions and complications, emotional/behavioral conditions and complications, treatment acceptance or resistance, relapse potential, and recovery environment. However, while recent articles have reported on their predictive validity and psychometric properties (Magura et al., 2003; May, 2004), the ASAM criteria have yet to be empirically validated (Gastfriend & McLellan, 1997; Turner et al., 1999). Another validated instrument that uses objective criteria to match clients to residential or outpatient treatment programs is the Client Matching Protocol (CMP; Melnick et al., 2001). The CMP assesses client risk across four domains (pattern of use, previous long-term abstinence, social factors, and habilitation). Also, unlike the ASAM criteria, the CMP collects data relating to clients' past criminal behavior and involvement with the criminal justice system. Although designed for use in community-based treatment settings, there has been recent talk of modifying the CMP for use with offender populations and corrections-based treatment.

Focus on Aftercare

Perhaps no finding has been more consistently reported and supported in the literature on prison-based substance abuse treatment than the impact of aftercare on improving postprison treatment outcomes. So widely accepted is the importance of aftercare, that it forms the foundation of the concept of "continuity of care," which emphasizes the importance of transitioning individuals from prison-based treatment to continued treatment in the community with minimal or no interruption (i.e., a "seamless" transition). Data collected from the California initiative has further reinforced the importance of participation and retention in aftercare, but it has also highlighted some important issues relating to aftercare and the continuity of care construct. This includes the phenomenon of higher RTP rates among parolees who choose to enter aftercare, but drop out within 90 days. As expected, these rates are higher than those of parolees who remain in aftercare for more than 90 days, but they are also higher than the RTP rates of parolees who never entered aftercare. In addition, the apparent lack of differential effectiveness of residential versus outpatient aftercare needs to be explored further. One possible explanation for this finding may be a large variance in the quality of programming across the literally hundreds of residential and outpatient community-based programs that parolees have accessed for aftercare services in California.

Monitoring and Measuring Treatment Quality

Through its Policy Advisory Committee, OSAP has initiated a number of efforts to improve the quality of TC SAP and SASCA programming. The main effort in this regard is the Continuing Quality Improvement (CQI) subcommittee, which consists of a rotating group of representatives from the seven SAP provider organizations, prisons where programs are located, and OSAP. The CQI subcommittee conducts periodic site visits to the prison-based TCs for the purpose of collecting and reporting "best practices" aspects of the individual programs that the CQI group believes contribute to the overall effectiveness of the program and should be shared with other prison-based treatment programs. However, despite the benefits that may be derived from the sharing of best practices, the CQI program does not represent, nor does there exist, a systematic validated process for assessing and ensuring the continuing quality of the prison-based treatment programs.

One means for assessing the quality of corrections-based treatment programs is the Correctional Program Assessment Inventory (CPAI, Gendreau & Andrews, 1996), a validated instrument that assesses how well various aspects of a correctional treatment program correspond with principles of effective programming for offenders (Gendreau & Goggin, 1997). Items on the CPAI cover six domains: program implementation, client pretreatment characteristics, program characteristics, staff characteristics, evaluation and quality assurance procedures, and other. The CPAI has been widely used in Canada to assess program quality and is increasingly being used with correctional programs in the United States.

Of greater concern, however, is the question of variability in the quality of the large number of community-based treatment programs that provide aftercare treatment services provided to parolees from the prison-based treatment programs—a measure that is difficult to capture. In California, residential and nonresidential treatment programs are not required to be *certified* by the state, which would ensure that the program is delivering a minimal level of service quality (California Department of Alcohol and Drug Programs [CDADP], 2004). Only about 70 percent of licensed residential programs in the state are certified, and there were only 903 nonresidential programs that had been certified as of July 2003; nonresidential drug/alcohol programs are not required to be licensed, and so it is not known how many of them are operating in the state (CDADP, 2004).

Related to this (and discussed briefly above) is the type and dosage of treatment parolees receive vis-à-vis the treatment that they received while in prison. For a large percentage of parolees entering aftercare, the treatment programs that they are entering do not build upon the progress made in prison-based treatment. While this hypothesis has not been empirically tested, anecdotal data collected as part of process evaluations suggest that parolees entering community-based treatment programs often feel as though they are not being given credit for the progress that they made in prison-based treatment. Furthermore, the SASCA system, while it represents an efficient model for transferring parolees from the large network of prison-based treatment programs to an even larger network of community-based treatment programs, was not designed to assess or ensure the quality of aftercare treatment services,[5] and it does not ensure that the community-based treatment programs take into account progress that parolees made in prison-based treatment. Nevertheless, given the large number of programs involved, the current state regulations covering licensing and certification for community-based treatment programs, and the costs associated with implementing a comprehensive quality assessment protocol, it is likely that the monitoring of program quality, to the extent that it is possible, will need to be built into the existing SASCA system.

Gender-Responsive Treatment

Findings that drug-dependent women offenders have higher rates of co-occurring mental disorders compared with males and are at higher risk for recidivism (Grella & Greenwell, 2005, Messina et al., 2003) indicate the need to place greater emphasis on promoting integrated services (e.g., FOTEP) for women transitioning from prison-based treatment to community-based aftercare programs. The lack of access to integrated treatment for individuals with co-occurring disorders may be especially detrimental, since offenders with both mental health and substance abuse disorders have higher rates of recidivism compared to offenders with only substance use disorders (Messina et al., 2004). Once in community treatment, the findings from the FOTEP evaluation highlight the need to improve treatment completion rates by more effectively addressing the needs of the women and engaging them more in the treatment process.

With respect to in-prison treatment, there is a need for a comprehensive diagnostic assessment at intake that will inform treatment staff of the diverse substance use disorders and psychological needs of women. There is also a need for specialized treatment curricula that address issues that arise from sexual and physical abuse and the resulting mental health disorders.

There is also the question of whether programs for female offenders should only be staffed by female counselors in order to promote stronger therapeutic alliances between clients and counselors, provide strong female role models and supportive peer networks, and more effectively address patterns of abuse from childhood to adulthood (Morash, Bynum, & Koons, 1998). Findings regarding education and employment (Messina et al., 2003) suggest that basic education, literary skills, and marketable vocational training are particularly important components of treatment for women, as well as men. In addition, the large percentage of drug-dependent offenders, male and female, who have children suggests that parenting programs should also become a critical part of treatment for both men and women.

CONCLUSION

During the 1950s and 1960s, California led the nation in the development and evaluation of rehabilitation programs for offenders (Palmer & Petrosino, 2003). During the 1970s,

---

[5] SASCAs have been known to stop referring clients to community-based treatment programs that they viewed as delivering poor quality services. However, it is not clear how common this was or what criteria were used to determine that the services were of poor quality.

correctional treatment in California, as in other states, experienced severe cutbacks as the result of budget reductions and an anti-rehabilitation ideology. As the pendulum swung back in the late 1980s to a focus on treatment for offenders, California again led the way and has since developed a comprehensive and still growing system of prison and community treatment for substance-abusing offenders. Research findings were influential in the initiation of prison treatment, as well as in its further expansion. Much still remains to be learned about what works, with whom, and under what conditions in order to enhance the effectiveness of treatment for offenders. Continued collaboration between research centers and correctional agencies, in California and other states, will move the field forward, to the benefit of offenders and society.

REFERENCES

American Society of Addiction Medicine (ASAM). (1998). Reviewing ASAM's goals and accomplishments. *Journal of Addictive Diseases, 17*(2), 123–128.

Andrews, D. A., Zinger, I., Hoge, R. D., Bonta, J., Gendreau, P., & Cullen, F. T. (1990). Does correctional treatment work? A clinically relevant and psychologically-informed meta-analysis. *Criminology, 28*(3), 369–404.

Andrews, D. A., Bonta, J., & Hoge, R. D. (1990). Classification for effective rehabilitation—rediscovering psychology. *Criminal Justice and Behavior, 17*(1), 19–52.

Anglin, M. D., Prendergast, M., & Farabee, D. (1997). *First annual report on the substance abuse program at the California Substance Abuse Treatment Facility (SATF) and state prison at corcoran: A report to the California State Legislature.* Project Report, California Department of Corrections Contract C97.243. Los Angeles: UCLA Drug Abuse Research Center.

Bandura, A. (1969). *Principles of behavior modification.* New York: Holt, Rinehart & Winston.

Blue Ribbon Commission on Inmate Population Management. (1990). *Final Report.* Sacramento, CA: Blue Ribbon Commission on Inmate Population Management.

Bonta, J. (1997). *Offender rehabilitation: From research to practice* (User Report No. 1997-01). Ottawa: Department of the Solicitor General of Canada.

Bonta, J., Wallace-Capretta, S., & Rooney, J. (2000). A quasi-experimental evaluation of an intensive rehabilitation supervision program. *Criminal Justice and Behavior, 27*(3), 312–329.

Broome, K. M., Knight, K., Joe, G. W., & Simpson, D. D. (1996). Evaluating the drug-abusing probationer: Clinical interview versus self-administered assessment. *Criminal Justice and Behavior, 23*(4), 593–606.

Brown, M. (1996). Refining the risk concept: Decision context as a factor mediating the relation between risk and program effectiveness. *Crime & Delinquency, 42*(3), 435–455.

Burdon, Dang W. M., Messina, N. P., & Prendergast, M. L. (2004). The California treatment expansion initiative: Aftercare participation, recidivism, and predictors of outcomes. *The Prison Journal, 84*(1), 61–80.

Burdon, W. M., Prendergast, M. L., Messina, N. P., & Farabee, D. (2006). *Differential effectiveness of residential versus outpatient aftercare for parolees from prison-based therapeutic community treatment programs.* Manuscript submitted for publication.

Burdon, W. M., Roll, J. M., Prendergast, M. L., & Rawson, R. (2001). Drug courts and contingency management. *Journal of Drug Issues, 31*(1), 73–90.

Bureau of Justice Statistics. (1999a). *Substance abuse and treatment, state and federal prisoners, 1997* (NCJ 172871). Washington, DC: Bureau of Justice Statistics, U.S. Department of Justice.

California Department of Alcohol and Drug Programs. (2004). *Fact Sheet: Licensing & Certification of Alcoholism or Drug Abuse Recovery or Treatment Programs.* Retrieved August 25, 2005 from www.adp.cahwnet.gov/abt_adp.asp#fact

California Department of Corrections and Rehabilitation. (1996). *A report on the inmate classification system.* Sacramento: Offender Information Branch, California Department of Corrections and Rehabilitation.

California Department of Corrections and Rehabilitation. (2005). *Prisoners & Parolees 2004.* Sacramento: Offender Information Services, California Department of Corrections and Rehabilitation.

California Department of Corrections and Rehabilitation. (2006). *Monthly report of population as of December 31, 2005.* Retrieved April 2, 2006 from www.corr.ca.gov/ReportsResearch/OffenderInfoServices/Monthly/MonthlyTpop1aArchive.asp

Camp, G. M., & Camp, C. G. (1989). *Building on prior experience: Therapeutic communities in prison.* South Salem, NY: Criminal Justice Institute.

Center for Substance Abuse Treatment. (1998). *Continuity of offender treatment for substance use disorders from institution to community* (Treatment Improvement Protocol [TIP] Series 30). Washington, DC: Substance Abuse and Mental Health Services Administration, Department of Health and Human Services.

Chaiken, M. (1989). *In-prison programs for drug-involved offenders.* Washington, DC: National Institute of Justice, U.S. Department of Justice.

Condelli, W. S., & Hubbard, R. L. (1994). Relationship between time spent in treatment and client outcomes from therapeutic communities. *Journal of Substance Abuse Treatment, 11*(1), 25–33.

Cullen, F., Cullen, J., & Wozniak, J. (1988), Is rehabilitation dead? The myth of the punitive public. *Journal of Criminal Justice, 16*(4), 303–317.

De La Rosa, M. R., & White, M. S. (2001). A review of the role of social support systems in the drug use behavior of Hispanics. *Journal of Psychoactive Drugs, 33*(3), 233–240.

De Leon G. (2000). The therapeutic community: Theory, model and method. New York: Springer.

De Leon, G., Melnick, G., Kressel, D., & Jainchill, N. (2000). Circumstance, motivation, readiness, and suitability (the CMRS scales): Predicting retention in therapeutic community treatment. *American Journal of Drug and Alcohol Abuse, 20*(4), 495–515.

Department of Health and Human Services. (1994). *Treatment for alcohol and other drug abuse: Opportunities for coordination.* Technical Assistance Publication Series 11, Publication No. (SMA) 94-2075. Washington, DC: Department of Health and Human Services.

Farabee, D., & Knight, K. (2001). *Final report on the Psychometric Properties of the Inmate Pre-Release Assessment (IPASS).* Los Angeles: Query Research.

Farabee, D., Prendergast, M. L., & Anglin, M. D. (1998). The effectiveness of coerced treatment for drug-abusing offenders. *Federal Probation, 62*(1), 3–10.

Farabee, D., Prendergast, M. L., Cartier, J., Wexler, H., Knight, K., & Anglin, M. D. (1999). Barriers to implementing effective correctional treatment programs. *The Prison Journal, 79*(2), 150–162.

Field, G. (1989). A study of the effects of intensive treatment on reducing the criminal recidivism of addicted offenders. *Federal Probation, 53*(10), 51–56.

Field, G. (1998). From the institution to the community. *Corrections Today, 60* (6), 94–97,113.

Friedmann, P. D., Hendrickson, D. C., Gerstein, D. R., & Zhang, Z. W. (2004). The effect of matching comprehensive services to patients' needs and drug use improvement in addiction treatment. *Addiction, 99*(8), 962–972.

Garrett, C. J. (1985). Effects of residential treatment of adjudicated delinquents. A meta-analysis. *Journal of Research in Crime and Delinquency, 22,* 287–308.

Gastfriend, D. R. (Ed.). (2003). *Addiction treatment matching: Research Foundation of the American Society of Addiction Medicine (ASAM) criteria.* Binghamton, NY: Haworth Medical Press.

Gastfriend, D. R., & McLellan, A. T. (1997). Treatment matching: Theoretical basis and practical implications. *Medical Clinics of North America, 81*(4), 945–966.

Gendreau, P., & Andrews, D. A. (1996). *Correctional Program Assessment Inventory (CPAI)* (6th ed.). Saint John: University of New Brunswick.

Gendreau, P., Cullen, F. T., & Bonta, J. (1994). Intensive rehabilitation supervision: The next generation in community corrections. *Federal Probation, 58*(1), 72–78.

Gendreau, P., & Goggin, C. (1997). Correctional treatment: Accomplishments and realities. In P. Van Voorhis, M. Braswell, & D. Lester (Eds.), *Correctional counseling & rehabilitation* (3rd ed., pp. 271–279). Cincinnati: Anderson.

Gendreau, P., & Ross, R. (1987). Revivification of rehabilitation: Evidence from the 1980s. *Justice Quarterly, 4*(3), 349–407.

Gossop, M., Marsden, J., Stewart, D., & Rolfe, A. (1999). Treatment retention and 1-year outcomes for residential programmes in England. *Drug and Alcohol Dependence, 57*(2), 89–98.

Gottheil, E., Weinstein, S. P., Sterling, R., Lundy, A., & Serota, R. D. (1998). A randomized controlled study of the effectiveness of intensive outpatient treatment for cocaine dependence. *Psychiatric Services, 49*(6), 782–787.

Graham, W. F., & Wexler, H. K. (1997). The Amity therapeutic community at Donovan prison: Program description and approach. In G. De Leon (Ed.), *Community as method: Therapeutic communities for special populations and settings.* New York: Praeger.

Greenley, J. R. (1992). Neglected organizational and management issues in mental health systems development. *Community Mental Health Journal, 28*(5), 371–384.

Grella, C. E., & Greenwell, L. (2006a). *Treatment needs and completion of community-based aftercare among substance-abusing women offenders.* Manuscript under review.

Grella, C. E., & Greenwell, L. (2006b). Correlates of parental status and attitudes toward parenting among substance-abusing women offenders. *The Prison Journal, 86*(1), 89–113.

Grella, C. E., Stein, J. A., & Greenwell, L. (2005). Associations among childhood trauma, adolescent problem behaviors, and adverse adult outcomes in substance-abusing women offenders. *Psychology of Addictive Behaviors, 19*(1), 43–53.

Hall, E. A., Prendergast, M. L., Wellisch, J., Patten, M., & Cao, Y. (2004). Treating drug-abusing women prisoners: An outcomes evaluation of the Forever Free program. *The Prison Journal, 84*(1), 81–105.

Harrison, L. D., & Martin, S. S. (2000). *Residential substance abuse treatment for state prisoners formula grant: Compendium of program implementation and accomplishments. Final report.* Newark, DE: Center for Drug and Alcohol Studies, University of Delaware.

Hser, Y. (1995). A referral system that matches drug users to treatment programs: Existing research and relevant issues. *The Journal of Drug Issues, 25*(1), 209–224.

Hser, Y. I., Evans, E., Huang, D., & Anglin, M. D. (2004). Relationship between drug treatment services, retention, and outcomes. *Psychiatric Services, 55*(7), 767–774.

Hser, Y. I., Polinsky, M. L., Maglione, M., & Anglin, M. D. (1999). Matching clients' needs with drug treatment services. *Journal of Substance Abuse Treatment, 16*(4), 299–305.

Hubbard, R. L., Craddock, S. G., Flynn, P. M., Anderson, J., & Etheridge, R. M. (1997). Overview of 1-year outcomes in the Drug Abuse Treatment Outcome Study (DATOS). *Psychology of Addictive Behaviors, 11*(4), 261–278.

Hubbard, R. L., Craddock, S. G., & Anderson, J. (2003). Overview of 5-year follow-up outcomes in the drug abuse treatment outcome studies (DATOS). *Journal of Substance Abuse Treatment, 25*(3), 125–134.

Inciardi, J. A. (1996). The therapeutic community: An effective model for corrections-based drug abuse treatment. *Drug treatment behind bars: Prison-based strategies for change* (pp. 65–74). Westport, CT: Praeger.

Izzo, R. L., & Ross, R. R. (1990). Meta-analysis of rehabilitation programs for juvenile delinquents. *Criminal Justice & Behavior, 17,* 134–142.

Jarman, E. (1993). *An evaluation of program effectiveness for the Forever Free Substance Abuse Program at the California Institution for Women, Frontera, California.* Sacramento: Office of Substance Abuse Programs, California Department of Corrections.

Knight, K., Simpson, D. D., & Hiller, M. L. (1999). Three-year reincarceration outcomes for in-prison therapeutic community treatment in Texas. *Prison Journal, 79*(3), 337–351.

Langevin, C. M. (2001). An evaluation framework for the Maison decision house substance abuse treatment program. *Canadian Journal of Program Evaluation, 16*(1), 99–129.

Leukefeld, C. G., & Tims, F. M. (1988). *Compulsory treatment of drug abuse: Research and clinical practice* (NIDA Research Monograph 86, Department of Health and Human Services Publication No. ADM 89-1578, pp. 236–249). Washington, DC: U.S. Government Printing Office.

Lipsey, M. W. (1995). What do we learn form 400 research studies on the effectiveness of treatment with juvenile delinquents? In J. McGuire (Ed.), *What works: Reducing reoffending*, Chichester: John Wiley & Sons.

Lipton, D. S. (1995). *The effectiveness of treatment for drug abusers under criminal justice supervision* (NIJ Research report). Washington, DC: National Institute of Justice, U.S. Department of Justice.

Little Hoover Commission. (1998). *Beyond bars: Correctional reforms to lower prison costs and reduce crime*. Sacramento: Little Hoover Commission.

Lowenkamp, C. T., & Latessa, E. J. (2003). *Increasing the effectiveness of correctional programming through the risk principle: Identifying offenders for residential placement*. Retrieved January 25, 2005 from www.uc.edu/criminaljustice/Articles.htm

Lowenkamp, C. T., & Latessa, E. J. (2004). *Residential community corrections and the risk principle: Lessons learned in Ohio*. In Ohio Corrections Research Compendium, Volume II, Columbus, OH: Ohio Department of Rehabilitation and Correction.

Magura, S., Staines, G., Kosanke, N., Rosenblum, A., Foote, J., DeLuca, A., et al. (2003). Predictive validity of the ASAM patient placement criteria for naturalistically matched vs. mismatched alcoholism patients. *The American Journal on Addictions, 12*, 386–397. II,Columbus, OH: Ohio Department of Rehabilitation and Correction.

Martin, S. S., Butzin, C. A., Saum, C. A., & Inciardi, J. A. (1999). Three-year outcomes of therapeutic community treatment for drug-involved offenders in Delaware: From prison to work release to aftercare. *Prison Journal, 79*(3), 294–320.

May, W. W. (2004). A psychometric analysis of the dimension rating system—2nd edition. *Journal of Addictive Diseases, 23*(4), 85–112.

McGlothlin, W. H., Anglin, M. D., & Wilson, B. D. (1977). *An evaluation of the California civil addicts program*. (NIDA Services Research Monograph Series, Department of Health and Human Services Publication No. ADM 78-558). Rockville, MD: National Institute on Drug Abuse.

McLellan, A. T., Hagan, T. A., Meyers, K., Randall, M., & Durell, J. (1997). Intensive outpatient substance abuse treatment" Comparisons with traditional outpatient treatment. *Journal of Addictive Diseases, 16*(2), 57–84.

Melnick, G., De Leon, G., Thomas, G., & Kressel, D. (2001). A client-treatment matching protocol for therapeutic communities: First report. *Journal of Substance Abuse Treatment, 21*(3), 119–1289.

Messina, N., Burdon, W., Hagopian, G., & Prendergast, M. (2004). One year return to custody rates among co-disordered offenders. *Behavioral Sciences and the Law, 22*, 503–518.

Messina, N., Burdon, W., & Prendergast, M. (2003). Assessing the needs of women in institutional therapeutic communities. *Journal of Offender Rehabilitation, 37*(2), 89–106.

Messina, N., & Grella, C. (2006). Childhood trauma and women's health outcomes in a California prison population. *American Journal of Public Health, 96*(10), 1842–1848.

Moore, G. E., & Mears, D. P. (2001). *Strong science for strong practice: Linking research to drug treatment in the criminal justice system. Views of practitioners*. Washington DC: The Urban Institute.

Moos, R. H. (2003). Addictive disorders in context: Principles and puzzles of effective treatment and recovery. *Psychology of Addictive Behaviors, 17*(1), 3–12.

Morash, M., Bynum, T., & Koons, B. (1998). *Women offenders: Programming needs and promising approaches.* Bureau of Justice Statistics Bulletin, Washington, DC: U.S. Department of Justice, Bureau of Justice Statistics.

Office of National Drug Control Policy. (1989). *National drug control strategy.* Washington, DC: The White House.

Ossmann, J. (1999). *Evolution of continuing care in California.* Sacramento: Office of Substance Abuse, California Department of Corrections.

Palmer, T., & Petrosino, A. (2003). The "Experimenting Agency": The California Youth Authority Research Division. *Evaluation Review, 27*(3), 228–266.

Pearson, F. S., Lipton, D. S., Cleland, C. M., & Yee, D. S. (2002). The effects of behavioral/cognitive-behavioral programs on recidivism. *Crime & Delinquency, 48*(3), 476–496.

Prendergast, M., & Burdon, W. (2002). Integrated system of care for substance-abusing offenders. In C. Leukefeld, F. Tims, & D. Farabee (Eds.), *Clinical and policy responses to drug offenders* (pp. 111–127). New York: Springer.

Prendergast, M., Hall, E., & Wellisch, J. (2002). *An outcome evaluation of the Forever Free Substance Abuse Treatment Program: One-year post-release outcomes.* Final Report, National Institute of Justice Grant 99-RT-VX-K003. Los Angeles: UCLA Drug Abuse Research Center.

Prendergast, M., Hall, E. A., Wexler, H. K., Melnick, G., & Cao, Y. (2004). Amity prison-based therapeutic community: Five-year outcomes. *The Prison Journal, 84*(1), 36–60.

Prendergast, M. L., Wellisch, J., & Wong, M. (1996). Residential treatment for women parolees following prison-based drug treatment experiences, needs and services outcomes. *Prison Journal, 76*(3), 253–274.

Prendergast, M., & Wexler, H. K. (2004). Correctional substance abuse treatment programs in california. *The Prison Journal, 84*(1), 8–35.

Rose, S. J., Zweben, A., & Stoffel, V. (1999). Interfaces between substance abuse treatment and other health and social systems. In B. S. McCrady & E. B. Epstein (Eds.), *Addictions: A Comprehensive Guidebook.* New York: Oxford UP.

Rupp, L. G., & Beck, A. R. (1989). *Invited review: California Department of Corrections substance abuse treatment programming.* Washington, DC: Bureau of Justice Assistance, U.S. Department of Justice.

Simpson, D. D., & Friend, H. J. (1988). Legal status and long-term outcomes for addicts in the DARP follow-up project. In C. G. Leukefeld & F. M. Tims (Eds.), *Compulsory treatment of drug abuse: Research and clinical practice* (NIDA Research Monograph 86, Department of Health and Human Services number (ADM)89-1578, pp. 81–98). Washington DC: U.S. Government Printing Office.

Simpson, D. D., Joe, G. W., & Brown, B. S. (1997). Treatment retention and follow-up outcomes in the drug abuse treatment outcome study (DATOS). *Psychology of Addictive Behaviors, 11*(4), 294–307.

Taxman, F. S. (1998). *Reducing recidivism through a seamless system of care: Components of effective treatment, supervision, and transition services in the community.* (Prepared for Office of National Drug Control Policy Treatment and Criminal Justice System Conference). Greenbelt, MD, University of Maryland, College Park.

Thornton, C. C., Gottheil, E., Weinstein, S. P., & Kerachsky, R. S. (1998). Patient-treatment matching in substance abuse: Drug addiction severity. *Journal of Substance Abuse Treatment, 15*(6), 505–511.

Turner, W. M., Turner, K. H., Reif, S., Gutowski, W. F., & Gastfriend, D. R. (1999). Feasibility of multidimensional substance abuse treatment matching: Automating the ASAM patient placement criteria. *Drug and Alcohol Dependence, 55*(1–2), 35–43.

Weinstein, S. P., Gottheil, E., & Sterling, R. (1997). Randomized comparison of intensive outpatient vs. individual therapy for cocaine abusers. *Journal of Addictive Diseases, 16*(2), 41–56.

Wellisch, J., Prendergast, M., & Anglin, M. D. (1993). Criminal justice and drug treatment systems linkage: Federal promotion of interagency collaboration in the 1970s. *Contemporary Drug Problems, 20*(4), 611–650.

Westhuis, D. J., Gwaltney, L., & Hayashi, R. (2001). Outpatient cocaine abuse treatment: Predictors of success. *Journal of Drug Education, 31*(2), 171–183.

Wexler, H. K. (1986). Therapeutic communities within prisons. In G. De Leon & J. T. Ziegenfuss (Eds.), *Therapeutic communities for addictions: Readings in theory, research and practice* (pp. 227–237). Springfield, IL: Charles C. Thomas, Publishers.

Wexler, H. K. (1995). The success of therapeutic communities for substance abusers in American prisons. *Journal of Psychoactive Drugs, 27*(1), 57–66.

Wexler, H. K. (1996, November). *The Amity prison TC evaluation: Inmate profiles and reincarceration outcomes.* Paper presented to the California Department of Corrections, Youth and Adult Correctional Agency, Sacramento, California.

Wexler, H. K., Burdon, W. M., & Prendergast, M. L. (2006). Maximum-security prison therapeutic community and aftercare: First outcomes. *Offender Substance Abuse Report, 5*(6), 81–82, 91–94.

Wexler, H. K., DeLeon, G., Thomas, G., Kressel, D., & Peters, J. (1999). The Amity prison TC evaluation: Reincarceration outcomes. *Criminal Justice and Behavior, 26*(2), 147–167.

Wexler, H. K., Falkin, G. P., & Lipton, D. S. (1990). Outcome evaluation of a prison therapeutic community for substance abuse treatment. *Criminal Justice and Behavior, 17*(1), 71–92.

Wexler, H. K., Falkin, G. P., Lipton, D. S., & Rosenblum, A. B. (1992). Outcome evaluation of a prison therapeutic community for substance abuse treatment. In C. G. Leukefeld & F. M. Tims (Eds.), *Drug abuse treatment in prisons and jails* (NIDA Research Monograph 118, pp. 156–175). Rockville, MD: National Institute on Drug Abuse.

Wexler, H. K., & Graham, W. F. (1992, October). *Evaluation of a prison-based therapeutic community for substance abusers: Preliminary findings.* Paper presented at the World Conference of Therapeutic Communities, Venice, Italy.

Wexler, H. K., & Graham, W. F. (1993, October). *Evaluation of a prison therapeutic community: Relationship between crime and drug histories, psychological profiles and 6-month outcomes.* Paper presented at the American Society of Criminology, Phoenix, Arizona.

Wexler, H. K., & Graham, W. F. (1994, August). *Prison-based therapeutic community for substance abusers: Follow-up outcomes.* Paper presented at the American Psychological Association, Los Angeles, California.

Wexler, H. K., Graham, W. F., Koronkowski, R., & Lowe, L. (1995). *Amity Therapeutic Community Substance Abuse Program preliminary return to custody data: May 1995.* Report to the Office of Substance Abuse Programs, California Department of Corrections.

Wexler, H. K., with Lipton, D. S., & Falkin, G. P. (1992). *Correctional drug abuse treatment in the United States: An overview.* (NIDA Monograph 118, pp. 8–30). Washington DC: National Institute on Drug Abuse.

Wexler, H. K., Lipton, D. S., Blackmore, J., & Brewington, V. (1992) *Comprehensive state department of corrections treatment strategy for drug abuse (Project REFORM). A final report to the Bureau of Justice Assistance.*

Wexler, H. K., Melnick, G., & Cao, Y. (2004). Risk and prison substance abuse treatment outcomes: A replication and challenge. *The Prison Journal, 84*(1), 106–120.

Wexler, H. K., Melnick, G., Lowe, L., & Peters, J. (1999). Three-year reincarceration outcomes for Amity in-prison therapeutic community and aftercare in California. *Prison Journal, 79*(3), 312–336.

Wexler, H. K., & Williams, R. (1986). Therapeutic communities within prisons. In G. De Leon & J. T. Ziegenfuss (Eds.), *Therapeutic communities for addictions: Readings in theory, research, and practice* (pp. 227–237). Springfiled, IL: Charles C. Thomas.

Winett, D. L., Mullen, R., Lowe, L. L., & Missakian, E. A. (1992). Amity Righturn: A demonstration drug abuse treatment program for inmates and parolees. In C. G. Leukefeld & F. M. Tims (Eds.), *Drug abuse treatment in prison and jails* (NIDA Research Monograph Series 118, pp. 84–98). Rockville, MD: National Institute on Drug Abuse, U.S. Department of Health and Human Services.

11

Sex Offenders

Assessment and Treatment

Shahid M. Shahidullah and Diane L. Green

INTRODUCTION

There has been a rapid growth and expansion of correctional institutions in America in the 1980s and 1990s. Between 1982 and 2003, correctional expenditures for all levels of government, including federal, state, and local, increased 573 percent. In 1982, total correctional expenditures were about $9.1 billion. In 2003, they increased to about $60.9 billion (Bureau of Justice Statistics, 2006). This rapid growth in correctional expenditures was accompanied with rapid growth in incarcerated population. In 2004, there were about 7 million people in America who were in prison, or jail, or in probation. Between 1995 and 2005, the incarcerated population in America grew at an annual rate of about 3.4 percent (Bureau of Justice Statistics, 2005). In 2001, about $38.2 billion was spent by the state authorities for corrections, and out of that about $28.4 billion was spent for adult correctional facilities. In 2001, about 59 percent of the justice expenditures of the states were for corrections alone.

This growth and expansion in corrections has brought, particularly for the states, not only new prisons and prison jobs but also new responsibilities and concerns for offender management. In the context of the emerging policy model of prison reentry, correctional institutions are being increasingly asked to build a bridge between prison and communities, particularly through a model of offender management that can reduce recidivism and strengthen reentry and reintegration. A new managerial paradigm is currently growing in American corrections that emphasizes that offender management should be seen in terms of a more holistic and comprehensive perspective—a perspective that can combine risk assessment and treatment with new goals and planning for their reentry and offender management in the communities (MacKenzie, 2001). This new model has expanded particularly in the area of sex offender management, and its expansion is planned and guided nationally by the Center for Sex Offender Management [CSOM]—a federal program established in 1997 by the Office of Justice Programs, U.S. Department of Justice, in collaboration with the National Institute of Justice, National Institute of Corrections, State Justice Institute, and the American Probation and Parole Association.

The core of the CSOM model is that sex offender management must begin with effective assessment and treatment of sex offenders inside the prison. Reentry and recidivism depend on whether the risk of reoffending was effectively assessed, and suitable treatment plans were made and offered. The postincarceration success of sex offender registration, notification, tracking, and management is now seen as intimately connected with effective sex offender assessment and treatment during incarceration in prison. It is because of this emerging comprehensive approach that correctional institutions are reexamining the existing methods of sex offender assessment and treatments. It is with these issues that this chapter is concerned. This chapter describes some of the existing methods of sex offender assessment and treatment, examines some of the new policy directions evolving in these areas of correctional management and counseling, and outlines some of the more evidence-based assessment and treatment approaches used in correctional settings.

SEXUAL OFFENSES AND SEX OFFENDERS UNDER CORRECTIONAL SUPERVISION

The major governmental sources and surveys on sex offense data include the Uniform Crime Reports (UCR), National Crime Victimization Survey (NCVS), National Incidence-Based Reporting System (NIBRS), and the National Corrections Reporting Program (NCRP). Sex crimes data are also collected by many advocacy organizations such as the National Sexual Violence Resource Center (NSVRC), National Violence Against Women Survey, and the National College of Women's Victimization Survey. The NCVS and NIBRS, however, collect and codify more reliable and comprehensive data on sexual offenses.

The Uniform Crime Reports collect sexual offense data in terms of two major categories: forcible rape and sex offences that include sodomy, statutory rape, and offences against chastity, decency, and morals. The National Crime Victimization Survey collects sexual offense data also in terms of two major categories: rape and sexual assault. The National Incidence-Based Reporting System divides sex crimes data into six major categories: forcible rape, statutory rape, forcible sodomy, forcible fondling including indecent liberties and child molestation, incest, and sexual assault. In addition to these national statistical surveys, there are also sex crimes categories defined and described by different state statutes. What is happening today is that law is increasingly defining a wide range of sexual acts, behavior, and sexual expressions as crimes (Table 1).

According to the National Crime Victimization Survey, about 50 percent of all violent crimes are not reported to law enforcement, and of all violent crimes, rape and sexual assaults are less likely to be reported. From 1992 to 2000, on average only 31 percent of rape and sexual assaults were reported to law enforcement (Bureau of Justice Statistics, 2003). Reporting of sexual offenses has increased by about 6 percent in between 1992 and 2000, but on average about 70 percent of cases remain unreported. The National Crime

TABLE 1   Major Categories and Types of Sex Crimes

Sex Crime Categories	Major Types of Sex Crime
Sex Crime Acts	Rape, Male Rape, Forcible Sodomy, Conspiracy to Commit to Forcible Sodomy, Attempt to Commit Forcible Sodomy, Marital Rape, Date Rape, Acquaintance Rape, Child Rape, Object Rape of a Child, Sodomy on a Child, Child Molestation, Forcible Fondling, Incest, Bestiality, Object Sexual Penetration, Adultery, and Prostitution
Sex Crime Behaviors	Sexual Harassment, Stalking, Indecent Exposure to Children, Exhibitionism, Fornication, Custodial Sexual Relations, Custodial Sexual Misconduct, Marital Sexual Assault, Spousal Violence, Lewdness Involving a Child, Enticing a Child Over the Internet, Attempt to Rape a Child, Conspiracy to Rape a Child, Attempt to Commit Object Rape, Conspiracy to Commit Object Rape, Solicitation to Commit Object Rape, Aggravated Kidnapping, Attempt or Conspiracy to Aggravated Kidnapping, Participation in Child Sex Tourism, Participation in Global Trafficking of Children and Women, Financing of Global Sex Tourism and Trafficking, Commercial Sexual Exploitation of Women, and Commercial Sexual Exploitation of Children at Home and Abroad
Sex Crime Expressions	Production and Sale of Child Pornography, Possession of Child Pornography, Financing of Child Pornography, Internet Child Pornography, Videotaping and Filming Minors for Sexual Purposes, Indecent Liberties, and Obscene Phone Calls

Victimization Survey estimated that in 2004 U.S. residents age 12 and over experienced about 5.2 million violent crimes including rape and sexual assault. The average annual number of rape and sexual assault victims in 2003–2004 was 204,370 thousands (rape, 65,510; attempted rape 43,440; and sexual assault, 95,420). During the same period, annual victimization rate for rape and sexual assault was 0.9 per 1,000 households (Bureau of Justice Statistics, 2005).

Majority of the victims of sexual offenses are juveniles. In his analysis of NIBRS data on reported sexual offences in 12 states covering the years 1991 through 1996, Snyder (2000) found that about 67 percent of all victims of sexual assault were juveniles under the age of 18, and 34 percent of all victims of sexual assaults were juveniles under the age of 12. One of every seven victims was under the age of 6.

Another report, funded by the National Institute of Justice and the Centers for Disease Control and Prevention, that analyzed the National Violence Against Women Survey [NVAW] date collected in 1995–1996, presents similar findings. The report finds that "many American women are raped at an early age. Thus, more than half (54 percent) of the female rape victims identified by the survey were younger than age 18 when they experienced their first attempted or completed rape" (Tjaden & Thoennes, 2000, p. iii–iv). The same report also finds that "[w]omen who reported that they were raped before age 18 were twice as likely to report being raped as an adult" (Tjaden & Thoennes, 2000, p. iv).

The Centers for Disease Control and Prevention and the National Center for Injury Prevention and Control analyzed the data provided by the National Violence Against Women Survey in 2004, and estimated that about 5.3 million women become the victims of intimate partner violence (IPV) in the United States every year. "The cost of intimate partner rape, physical assault, and stalking exceed $5.8 billion each year, nearly $4.1 billion of which is for direct medical and mental health care services" (Centers for Disease Control and the National Center for Injury Prevention and Control, 2004, p. 1). The same study also estimated that in the United States "nearly 7.8 million women have been raped by an intimate partner at some point in their lives, and an estimated 201,394 women are raped by an intimate partner each year" (Centers for Disease Control and the National Center for Injury Prevention and Control, 2004, p. 1). It is also estimated that intimate partners kill about 30 percent of female murder victims and 4 percent of male murder victims each year (Bureau of Justice Statistics, 2002, p. 1).

Sexual assaults take place at homes, schools, colleges, work, and a variety of custodial organizations such as day care centers, nursing homes, and prisons. About 70 percent of sexual assaults reported to law enforcement take place in the homes of the victims or the offenders. Snyder's (2000) analysis of NIBRS data revealed that 83.3 percent of rape, 81.5 percent of forcible sodomy, and 82.4 percent of forcible fondling, where victims were ages 6 to 11, occurred within a residence. For juveniles ages 12 to 17, 68.7 percent of forcible rape, 72.7 percent of forcible sodomy, and 68.8 percent of forcible fondling occurred within a residence. Juvenile sexual offending, particularly the victimization of female juveniles ages 6 to 17, is more likely to occur within a residence (Snyder, 2000, p. 6).

The nation's federal prisons house less than 2 percent of convicted sex offenders. In 2004, the number of total inmates sentenced in federal prisons was 169,370. Out of these inmates, only 1.1 percent of inmates were sentenced for sex offenses compared to 53.3 percent of inmates sentenced for drug offenses. However, there is a growing trend, since the middle of the 1990s, for increased federal involvement in prosecuting sex offence cases. Between 1995 and 2004, both sex offenses cases and defendants in federal courts "jumped 24 percent to 1,638 cases and 1,709 defendants. Defendants charged with sexual abuse rose 11 percent, and sexual abuse cases increased 10 percent" (Newsletter of the Federal Court, 2005, p. 4).

Rape and sexual assault comprise about 11 percent of all inmates sentenced for violent crimes in state prisons (Bureau of Justice Statistics, 2005, p. 9). There were about 624,900 inmates in state prisons who were sentenced for violent crimes in 2004. Out of those, 142,000 were sentenced for rape and sexual assault charges. Out of those 142,000 inmates, 140,500 were males, 1500 were females, 73,000 were Whites, 36,600 were Blacks, and 19,200 were Hispanics. However, the number of inmates sentenced for sex offences vary from state to state. In 2002, Montana had the highest percentage of inmates incarcerated (33 percent) for sexual offenses, followed by Vermont (29 percent), New Hampshire (27 percent), and Massachusetts (26 percent). In the same year, New Jersey and the District of Columbia had the lowest percentage (7 percent) of inmates incarcerated for sexual offenses (Table 2).

Since the definition of sexual offense is broadening, more sex offenses today are reported to law enforcement, more sex offenses are prosecuted in federal and state courts, and more sex offenders are sentenced to prison for longer terms. Felony sex offenses are

TABLE 2   **High Rates of Incarceration of Sex Offenders in Selected States, 2000**

States	Number of Incarcerated Sex Offenders	Percentage of Total Incarcerated Offenders
Alaska	496	24%
California	22,720	15%
Colorado	3,391	22%
Hawaii	634	18%
Iowa	1,228	17%
Kansas	2,002	23%
Massachusetts	2,769	26%
Michigan	9,756	21%
Minnesota	1,164	20%
Montana	465	33%
New Hampshire	633	27%
New Mexico	910	18%
North Carolina	5,101	16%
Ohio	9,100	19%
Pennsylvania	6,931	19%
South Dakota	550	22%
Tennessee	3,036	18%
Texas	25,398	17%
Vermont	362	29%
Virginia	5,400	18%
Washington	3,117	22%
West Virginia	518	17%
Wisconsin	4,000	19%
Wyoming	257	18%

Source: West, M., Hromas, C. S., & Wenger, P. (2000). *State Sex Offender Treatment Program: 50-State Surveys.* Colorado Springs: Colorado Department of Corrections.

more likely than other violent and nonviolent felony cases to result in convictions. More than 50 percent of felony sex offenses in state courts result in a prison sentence.

SEXUAL OFFENSES AND SEX OFFENDERS: POLICY AND LEGISLATIVE DEVELOPMENTS

The renewed interest in recent years for more effective sex offender assessment and treatment methods came not just in response to growing sexual crimes and the growth of sexual offenders in correctional population. It came also in response to the growth of a number of federal and state statutes and policy developments. Some of the major federal enactments in this area include the Jacob Wetterling Act of Crimes Against Children and Sexual Violent Offenders Act of 1994 (PL 103-322), Sex Crimes Against Children Prevention Act of 1995 (PL 104-71), Megan's Law of 1996 (PL 104-145), Pam Lychner Sexual Offender Tracking and Identification Act of 1996 (PL 104-236), Children Online Protection Act of 1998 (PL 105-775), Children's Internet Protection Act of 2000 (PL 106-14), Aimee's Law of 2000 (PL 106-386), Federal Campus Sex Crimes Act of 2000 (PL 106-386), DNA Analysis—Debbie Smith Act of 2003 (PL 108-21), Prison Rape Elimination Act of 2003 (PL 108-79), PROTECT Act of 2003 (PL 108-21), and Adam Walsh Child Protection and Safety Act of 2006 (Pl 109-248). Such legislation created new laws for mandatory sex offender registration, mandatory community notification system, a nationwide sex offender database at the FBI, and a National Sex Offender Registry (NSOR). The legislations also created new federal laws for mandatory exchange of sex offender information between federal and state law enforcement agencies, mandatory interstate sharing of sex offender information, mandatory notification of campus sex offenders, expert determination of sex offender classification, the designation of a separate group of sex offenders as sexual predators, and increased sentencing for repeat and violent sex offenders.

All 50 states generally comply with these and other recently enacted federal sex offender laws and guidelines. In response to federal guidelines, the states have enacted their own laws and regulations for sex offender management. In 2005, more than 100 new sex offender laws were enacted by state legislatures. There were over 500,000 registered sex offenders in the nation in 2005. The Department of Justice formally announced the activation of a National Sex Offender Registry (NSOR) Web site in 2005—a requirement mandated by the Pam Lychner Act. The FBI's Crimes Against Children unit is responsible for developing and coordinating the NSOR system. Currently, the NSOR Web site gives real-time access to public sex offender information from about 41 states. These legal and policy developments for the creation of a new national initiative and a model for sex offender management brought new mandates to federal and state correctional authorities for developing more effective methods of assessment, treatment, and management of sex offenders.

SEX OFFENDER RISK ASSESSMENT: CHALLENGES, EXISTING METHODS, AND BEST PRACTICES

Sex offender assessment and treatment methods, which in the past were mostly done by correctional authorities in an isolated and disconnected way, have now become vital components in the whole national effort and a national model for sex offender management. The nature of compliance with sex offender registration, the length of time that an offender is required to remain under registration and notification, the length of sentencing, parole decisions, and planning for effective reentry—all are now seen as largely dependent on the success of risk assessment and treatment methods. Risk assessment and treatment in the past were based mostly on experience and traditional knowledge. They are now becoming issues of important scientific and professional concern in the context of the emerging national effort to control and contain sex crimes. This is evidenced not only by increased reliance of correctional authorities on external scientific and professional communities for evidence-based standards of assessment and treatments methods, but also internally by their own efforts to set up new commissions, agencies, and boards to link the tasks of assessment and treatment to more improved and evidenced-based correctional practices. In recent years, many correctional departments or state criminal justice agencies have created separate boards and commissions for improved scientific advice on correctional assessment and treatment, particularly for sex offenders. Some of these initiatives include the Governor's Commission on Sex Offender Policy in Minnesota, Texas Council of Sex Offenders created within the Texas Department of Health Services, Sex Offender Management Board in Colorado, Correctional Institutions Inspection Committee in Ohio, Washington State Institute for Public Policy, Virginia Criminal Sentencing Commission, Sexual Predator Working Group of Alaska, Sexual Offender Assessment Board of Pennsylvania, and the Commission to Improve Community Safety and Sex Offender Accountability of the State of Maine.

RISK ASSESSMENT CHALLENGES: SEX OFFENDER RECIDIVISM

Given the risk that sex offenders pose to the community, effective tools for assessing the probability of recidivism are crucial. Risk assessment usually refers to an uncertain prediction about a future harmful behavior, and an assessment of the frequency, impact, and likely victim(s) of the behavior (Kemshall, 2001). Reliable means of distinguishing between high- and low-risk individuals and the circumstances under which they are likely to reoffend are crucial for decisions about allocating program and human resources, the best point at which to release offenders, and subsequent supervisory processes (Hudson, Wales, Bakker, & Ward, 2002).

One of the major challenges for effective sex offender assessment is to contain the high rate of recidivism among sex offenders. The key question basic to sex offender assessment is, What is the likelihood that a specific offender will commit sexual offenses again? What are the indicators in the past behavior of a specific offender and in the nature of his or her specific offenses, lifestyle, social and economic status, and childhood socialization that can help predict whether he or she is more likely to commit sex offenses again? The risk of sexual recidivism varies according to offender type. Rapists tend to be more criminally versatile than child molesters and are more likely to reoffend nonsexually than sexually. Among child molesters, the risk of sexual recidivism is higher for homosexual and extrafamilial sex offenders than for heterosexual and incest offenders.

Recidivist sexual offenders exhibit many of these characteristics, but specific predictors of sexual recidivism may include sexual deviancy; a history of sex offending, especially early onset of offending and engaging in a range of sexual crimes; diversity in offending, including violent and general crimes; psychological maladjustment, including substance use or abuse, antisocial attitudes, and personality disorders; childhood sexual victimization; presence of violent sexual fantasies; long-standing social isolation; use of sadomasochistic or pedophilic pornography; and failure to complete treatment (Gordon & Grubin, 2004).

The Bureau of Justice Statistics conducted a major study on sex offender recidivism in 2003 on the basis of a three-year follow-up of 9,692 male sex offenders, including 4,295 child molesters and 3,115 rapists, released from prison in 15 states in 1994. According to this study, which is the "largest follow-up ever conducted of convicted sex offenders following discharge from prison," the released sex offenders, compared to released non-sex offenders, were 4 times more likely to commit sexual offenses. Within three years, 5.3 percent of male sex offenders who committed rape or sexual assault were rearrested for committing sexual offenses. The study found that the rate of recidivism is higher among those who had several prior arrest records. Those who had 7 to 10 prior arrests had the highest rate of recidivism (8%) compared to those who had 1 prior arrest (3%). The study also showed that out of the 9,692 released sex offenders, 67 percent were White, 31.5 percent were Black, and 1.4 percent from other races. "Both the 4,295 child molesters and 443 statutory rapists were predominantly non-Hispanic white males. Nearly three-fourths of the child molesters (73.2%) were age 30 or older" (Bureau of Justice Statistics, 2003, p. 8). And statutory rapists are more likely to reoffend with any type of crime than child molesters. Within three years, 49.9 percent of statutory rapists were rearrested and 32.7 percent of them were reconvicted for any type of crime compared to 39.4 percent of arrests and 20.4 percent of conviction of child molesters.

In 2003, the Washington State Institute for Public Policy conducted a six-year follow-up study of 89 sex offenders who were released from prison between 1990 and 1996 with recommendations for civil commitment by the Washington Department of Corrections. The study found that "high percentage (57 percent) of the subjects were convicted of new felony offenses, with 40 percent re-offending with against-person offenses, including sex offenses. Almost one-third of the group (29 percent) re-offended with a felony sex offense, and 16 percent failed to register as a sex offender" (Washington State Institute for Public Policy, 2003, p. 17). The study concludes that violent sexual offenders "have a high risk of a subsequent conviction for a felony offense, particularly a new against-person (including sex) offense" (Washington State Institute for Public Policy, 2003, p. 17).

It is this phenomenon of sex offender recidivism that is at the core of concern for effective methods of risk assessment. Even though there exists some empirical literature on sex offender recidivism (Center for Sex Offender Management, 2001), there is still a large gap in our understanding of the complexity of this phenomenon. The issues of psychopathology, endocrinology, brain development, and social and behavioral contexts are intertwined with sexual deviance and sexual violence in a hugely complex manners. It is for these multifaceted dimensions of the challenge of recidivism that there is now growing a new generation of sex offender risk assessment methods that are more scientific and more multidimensional in perspectives. The following is an analysis of some of these new generation of sex offender risk assessment methods, and their use and application in selected correctional settings.

Risk Assessment and Sex Offender Classification

Sex offender risk assessment in the correctional setting begins with an evaluation of offender classification. All categories of offenders are classified for custody decisions, risk assessment, treatment, and service delivery, but it is a much more rigorous and statutorily mandated process for sex offenders. Many states in recent years have enacted specific statutes for sex offender classification. Presently, it is particularly guided by two federal laws—Jacob Wetterling Crimes against Children and Sexually Violent Offenders Registration Improvements Act of 1997 and the Adam Walsh Child Protection and Safety Act of 2006. The Jacob Wetterling Act of 1997 created the classification of sexual predators. Sexual predators are defined as violent and high-risk repeat sex offenders who have the characteristics of psychopathic personalities. However, the act requires that the determination of whether a sex offender is in the category of sexual predator be made by a court with the advice of a board composed of mental health and behavioral science experts, representatives from law enforcement agencies, and victim' rights advocates.

The Adam Walsh Child Protection and Safety Act further extended the Wetterling classification provisions and made a three-tier classification mandatory for sex offender sentencing, risk assessment, and treatment services. The act placed the repeat and violent sex offenders, defined as sexual predators by the Jacob Wetterling Act of 1997, in tier III. Tier II offenders are those who are convicted of federal offenses involving a minor such as coercion and enticement, transportation with the intent to engage in sexual activities, abusive sexual conduct, use of a minor in sexual conduct, solicitation of a minor to practice prostitution, and the production and distribution of child pornography. And those who are convicted for aggravated sexual abuse or sexual abuse, and kidnapping of a minor are placed in tier I.

Even before the enactment of the Adam Walsh Child Protection and Safety Act, most states adopted some versions of the three-tier system of classification of sex offenders. The Sex Offender Registration Act (SORA) of New York, for example, classifies sex offenders into three groups: Level I (low-risk), Level II (moderate-risk), and Level III (high-risk). Following the Jacob Wetterling Act of 1997, many states enacted specific legislations to define repeat and violent sex offenders as sexual predators. One of the significant policy developments in this area recently came through the enactment of Jessica Lunsford Act, commonly described as Jessica's Law, in Florida in 2005. Under the Jessica Lunsford Act in Florida, the courts have been given the responsibility to define and classify violent and repeat sex offenders as sexual predators. The Jessica Lunsford Act made a provision of mandatory sentencing of 25 years to life in prison for first-time sex offenders and the molesters of children below the age of 12. The act also requires life-time electronic monitoring of sexual predators.

Alabama, Arkansas, Arizona, Georgia, Iowa, Nevada, Oklahoma, Indiana, Oregon, Virginia, and Wisconsin have laws similar to those of the Jessica Lunsford Act. In 2005, Michigan, following the Jessica Act, enacted a new law which had a provision that violent sex offenders can even be forced to wear GPS electronic devices for life. Following the Jessica's Law, "Iowa mandates life sentence for certain sex crimes against children. Indiana authorized a life sentence for certain repeat sex offenders. Minnesota mandated life without parole for certain violent sex crimes" (National Conference of State Legislatures, 2005, p. 1). In 2006, Wisconsin and Kansas enacted new statutes similar to Jessica's Law. In Georgia, the mandatory sentencing of 25 years in prison statute is applicable also for teen sex offenders, ages 13 through 15, who are tried as adults for forced rape, molestation, and sodomy of children. Jessica's Law thus became a major focus for state policy makers in recent years to classify different categories of sex offenses and different types of sex offenders. Sex offender risk assessment in correctional settings presently thus begins through an evaluation of state-specific sex offender classification system. One of the dominant trends is the identification of high-risk violent sex offenders, and this poses a significant challenge for assessment methodologies.

Sex Offender Risk Assessment Methods: Clinical versus Actuarial Models

Risk assessment in general is one of the major tasks in corrections. *The Report on State and Federal Corrections Information Systems,* published by the Office Justice Programs of the Department of Justice in 1998, showed that the national correctional information system is

TABLE 3   Possible Outcomes of Risk Assessment

		Prediction	
		Yes	No
Outcome	Yes	A True positive prediction	B False negative prediction
	No	C False positive prediction	D True negative prediction

Source: Kemshell. 2001.

composed of 14 core dimensions of corrections processing, and risk assessment is one of the core dimensions. Other core dimensions include demographic information, conviction offenses, sentences imposed, current commitments, classification decisions, confinement characteristics, and data elements related to managing and supervising offenders. Risk assessment elements and decisions belong to the high availability core.

One of the key issues in sex offender risk assessment is avoiding underprediction and overprediction of offending. There are four possible outcomes of risk assessment. (Table 3) The most desirable outcome is an accurate prediction that sexual assault will occur (Box A), or a correct prediction that it will not occur (Box D).

The consequences of a false negative prediction (Box B, when a risk of harm is not identified but does occur) include a heightened risk of harm to future victims, as potential repeat offenders may not receive appropriate treatment or surveillance. Conversely, false positive predictions, (Box C, when harm is predicted but does not occur) wastes resources, impacts on civil liberties, and results in overintervention (Kemshall, 2001). These possibilities make reliance on evidence-based risk assessment methods much more important and significant. Correctional psychologists, counselors, and treatment service specialists increasingly are being demanded by correctional authorities and the court to choose the right methods and to avoid the error of making of false negative predictions.

During the 1990s, there was a rapid growth of literature on risk assessment of sex offenders. As number of sex offenses were growing and more sex offenders were being convicted and incarcerated, public fear of sexual killings and kidnappings was rising. Policy makers increased pressures on correctional authorities to be more accountable for sex offender classification, assessment, custody decisions, parole decisions, and decisions on treatment services (Janus, 2003; Robinson, 2003). This led to the growth of a new movement, from the beginning of the 1990s, to bring more objectivity and empirical analysis in the development of methods for sex offender risk assessment. There began to emerge a new professional community or a "paradigmatic community" of scholars who specialized in sex offender risk assessment. There also emerged many private professional groups of experts, such as Sinclair Seminars and Orange Psychological Services, who specialized in providing risk assessment services to correctional institutions.

There are two key issues that are raised and debated in choosing the right methodology for sex offender risk assessment. The first is that whether the methodology is based on static or dynamic factors. "The assessment of dangerousness among sex offenders is concerned with those characteristics of the offenders that increase or decrease risk" (Craig, Browne, & Stringer, 2003a, p. 46). The core question here is, What factors or characteristics can predict sex offender recidivism with a high degree of validity? The controversy is about the recognition and identification of the core set of factors related to recidivism. Static risk factors are relatively fixed and include variables such as the offender's gender, race/ethnicity, age, offense history, previous and present conviction records, relationship to victim, deviant sexual preference for children, antisocial personality disorder, psychopathic behavior, deviance sexual age preferences, dysfunctional socialization, youth and never-married status, and parental instability. Dynamic risk factors are those that change naturally over time or are open to change through treatment and interventions. They may be situational and intangible factors such as substance use and abuse, motivation, isolation, cognitive distortions, antisocial attitudes, lack of social networks, lack of victim empathy, intimacy deficits, poor self-management strategies, poor sexual self-regulation, and deviant sexual fantasies. The dynamic factors are also defined as criminogenic needs of the offenders. These include a set of attitudes "that appear to support negative attitude toward all forms of official authority/conventional pursuits (education, work, pro-social relationships), deviant values that justify aggression, hostility, substance abuse, and rationalizations for anti-social behavior, free from moral constraints" (Craig, Browne, & Stringer, 2003a, p. 46).

The second is about the method of analysis of the relationship between and among different static and dynamic factors and their impact on recidivism. The core question here is, How are these factors to be examined and analyzed to reach to predictions about recidivism? The concern is whether analysis should be based on clinical judgments, or if it should rely on statistical tools and methods to be more objective in making predictions. The literature on risk assessment of sex offenders is broadly divided into these two approaches—the clinical model and the actuarial model of analysis. Before the 1990s, the clinical model was the dominant form of risk assessment. Risk assessment at that time was generally done on the basis of clinical experience, and psychoanalytic understanding of repressive and neurotic behaviors of the offenders. The clinical model was a means to reach to behavioral predictions through introspections and the subjective understanding of the psychopathic behaviors of offenders.

From the beginning of the 1990s, the risk assessment research community began to move away from the clinical model, and the actuarial approach emerged as a new paradigm for predicting violent behavior in general, and sex offender recidivism in particular. Actuarial risk assessment is "based upon the risk factors which have been researched and demonstrated to be statistically significant in the prediction of re-offense or dangerousness" (Center for Sex Offender Management, 1999, p. 3). The actuarial risk assessment procedure "involves discerning the variables predictive of recidivism and assigning them relative weights to determine low-, medium-, and high-risk cases by score" (Craig, Browne, & Stringer, 2003a, p. 57). "In the clinical method the decision-maker combines information in his or her head. In the actuarial or statistical method the human judge is eliminated and conclusions rest solely on empirically established relations between data and the conditions or event of interests" (Dawes et al. as quoted in Janus & Prentky, 2004, p. 7).

Several actuarial sex offender risk assessment methods or scales are now available within the risk assessment community (Table 4). Some of them include PRASOR (Rapid Risk Assessment for Sex Offense Recidivism), STATIC 99/Static-2002, SVR-20 (Sexual Violence

TABLE 4   Some Selected Actuarial Risk Assessment Methods Used for Predicting Sex offender Recidivism

Actuarial Methods	Description of the Scales
PRASOR (Raid Risk Assessment For Sex Offenders)	Four-item recidivism scale measuring prior sex offenses, unrelated victims, male victims, age less than 25 (Hanson, 2000).
Static-99	Probability of recidivism is measured in terms of 10 static items (Hanson & Thornton, 1999).
SACJ (Structured Anchored Clinical Judgment)	Recidivism is measured in terms of a stage approach. The first stage examines offender's conviction records including current sex offenses, prior sex offenses, current nonsexual offenses, and prior nonsexual offenses (Grubin, 1998).
MnSOST- R (Minnesota Sex Offender Screening Tool–Revised)	The MnSOST is 16-item scale (both static and dynamic factors are used to measure three levels of risk category–high, medium, and low) (Epperson, Kaul, & Hasselton, 1998).
SVR-20 (Sexual Violence Risk-20)	SVR-20 is a 20-item scale including 11 items to measure psychosocial adjustments, 7 items to measure sexual offenses, and 2 items to measure offender's future plans (Boer, Hart, Kropp, & Webster, 1997).
SORAG (Sex Offender Risk Appraisal Guide)	SORAG–a 14-item scale-is a revised version of VORAG [The Violence Risk Appraisal Guide]. It also uses clinical records and Psychopathy Check List (Quinsey, Harris, Rice, & Cormier, 1998).

Source: Hanson, 2000; Craig, Browne, & Stringer, 2003a.

Risk-20), SORAG (Sex Offender Risk Appraisal Guide), VRAG (Violence Risk Appraisal Guide), RRAS (Registrant Risk Assessment Scale), SACJ (Structured Anchored Clinical Judgments Scale), MnSOST-R (Minnesota Sex Offender Screening Tool-Revisited), J-SOAP (Juvenile Sex Offender Assessment Protocol), A-SOAP (Adult Sex Offender Assessment Protocol), MASORR (Multi-Factorial Assessment of Sex Offender Risk for Recidivism), and VASOR (Vermont Assessment of Sex Offender Risk). STATIC-99 and PRASOR are two of the actuarial scales that are extensively used in correctional settings (Hanson & Thornton, 1999–2002).

PRASOR is widely used in the United States and Canada (Hanson, 1997). It is brief four-item actuarial scale designed to measure sex offender recidivism among males who have at least one prior conviction for sex offense (Hanson & Bussiere, 1998). The four items are prior sex offenses, any unrelated victims, any male victims, and age less than 25. One of the unique features of PRASOR is that "it used data from seven different follow-up studies that were then cross-validated on a different sample; thus, not only was the sample size large, but the studies originated from various countries" (Craig, Browne, & Stringer, 2003a, p. 59). In predicting recidivism among sex offenders, PRASOR "showed a moderate level of predictive accuracy across all samples with average correlations significantly better than the best single predictor (prior sexual offenses, $r = .20$)" (Craig, Browne, & Stringer, 2003a, p. 59).

The Static-99 is an actuarial instrument created by Hanson and Thornton (1999) "by adding together the items from the PRASOR and SACJ-Min. The scale is called Static-99 to indicate that it includes only static factors and that the current version is this year's version of work in progress" (Hanson & Thornton, 1999, p. 4). The Static-99 was designed to estimate the probability of sexual and violent recidivism among adult males who have already been convicted of at least one sexual offense against a child or non-consenting adult. The scale contains 10 static items: prior sexual offenses, prior sentencing dates, any convictions for noncontact sex offenses, current convictions for nonsexual violence, prior convictions for nonsexual violence, unrelated victims, stranger victims, male victims, young, and single. When the Static-99 scale is "tested in four diverse samples, the resulting scale predicted sexual offense recidivism (average $r = .33$) better than either original scale PRASOR or SAC-J)" (Hanson, 2000, p. 4).

Actuarial Strategies: Empirical Assessment

There is some consensus among risk assessment researchers that the actuarial methods—the second-generation risk assessment methods—are much more able to produce high-validity predictions about recidivism than those of the first-generation methods of the clinical model. A considerable amount of empirical studies and meta-analysis has been done in recent years to test the reliability and the predictability of different actuarial methods (Bartosh, Garby, Lewis, & Gray, 2003; Craig, Beech, & Browne, 2006; Gottfredson & Moriatry, 2006; Looman, 2006). Janus and Prentky (2004) conducted a major study on the accuracy and reliability of different [a]ctuarial methods, and they conclude that "actuarial methods have proven equal to or superior to clinical judgment" (p. 4). However, within the risk assessment community, there still remain two competing perspectives. One group is for uncontaminated actuarial risk assessment methodology. This group believes that in making predictions for sex offender recidivism, we must rely solely on statistical inference and the mathematical degrees of probability. Risk assessment must be a truly scientific venture, and it should not be contaminated with the subjectivity of clinical judgment. "The 'actuarial only' proponents contend that accurate risk appraisal demands the use of statistically based models omitting clinical judgment" (Craig, Browne, & Stringer, 2003a, p. 62).

Another group within the risk assessment community claims that there should be a bridge of thought between actuarial assessment and clinical judgment (Jhonson, 2006). The actuarial methods are based primarily on the analysis of static factors. A large amount of risk assessment research in recent years has shown the empirical relevance of dynamic factors (Jhonson, 2006). The advocates of this perspective suggest that clinical and professional judgments must also be taken into consideration in making predictions and decisions about the future of incarcerated sex offenders. "By their nature, actuarial models tend to be limited to static or historical variables and are not targeted toward assessing patient treatment potential or management" (Craig, Browne, & Stringer, 2003a, p. 62). The actuarial methods are designed "to make absolute prediction of a specified behavior within a specific time period and tend not to measure dynamic change based on motivation, insight, or intervention, producing estimates of probabilities of reoffence with less emphasis on confidence intervals" (Craig, Browne, & Stringer, 2003a, p. 62). A study from the Center for Sex Offender Management (2001) made the same observation: "Most meta-analysis studies have focused on static factors. It is critical that more research be conducted to identify dynamic factors with sex offender recidivism. These factors will assuredly provide a foundation for developing more effective intervention strategies for sex offender" (p. 15).

In order to address the limitations of the "actuarial assessment alone" approach, there has grown in recent years a third generation of sex offender risk assessment methods described as "structured professional judgment (SPJ)." The SPJ approach combines the first-generation methods of clinical judgment with those of second-generation actuarial assessments. In addition to using probabilities based on statistical inferences, the SPJ methods seek to integrate individual-specific factors and events, make judgments on the basis of case studies, and analyze the relevance of dynamic risk factors related to an offender's life situations. Some of the third-generation sex offender risk assessment methods include SONAR (Sex Offender Need Assessment Rating), SAVRY (Structured Assessment for Violence Risk among Youth), SARA (Spousal Abuse Risk Assessment), PCL-R (Psychopathy Checklist-Revised), LSI-R (Level of Service Inventory-Revised), HCR-20 (Historical, Clinical Risk-20), ERASOR (Estimate of Risk of Adolescent Sexual Offenses Recidivism). MnSOST-R and SVR-20 can also be considered third-generation methods because they incorporate dynamic factors with actuarial assessments (Craig, Browne, & Stringer, 2003a). The general consensus both within the community of correctional practice and risk assessment studies today is that SPJ is more reliable for sex offender risk assessment. "Considering dynamic factors such as treatments effects, motivation, insight, sexual deviance, and general psychological problems, alongside actuarial risk classification may provide a more global and valid assessment of an offender's risk for sexual recidivism" (Craig, Browne, & Stringer, 2003a, p. 63).

The second-generation actuarial assessment methods have generated a considerable amount of empirical studies, and they have made enormous contributions in the understanding of the complexity of sex offending and sex offender recidivism. More importantly, they have established sex offender risk assessment as a separate field of scientific research and professional specialty. But the advocates of the "actuarial assessment alone model" have made some errors. First, they defined the concept of recidivism from a narrow perspective. They failed to make distinctions between "dangerousness" and recidivist behavior. Recidivist behavior is a complex of attitudes and life situations, and it is much broader than the concept of violence or dangerousness. They also failed to see sex offender assessment in the context of correctional management and a comprehensive approach to sex offender management. By relying primarily on static factors, they ignored the social and psychological pathways related to the development of deviant sexual behavior (Craig, Browne, & Stringer, 2003a).

Secondly, the actuarial assessment advocates have also ignored the legal and human implications of their probabilistic assessments. If a sex offender is defined as a sexual predator, in most of the states today, he or she may remain in prison for life, or in civil commitment for life, or registered for life. On the other hand, if a violent sex offender is released into communities, public security will be threatened and comprised. Risk assessment of sex offenders in correctional settings is of high significance. It has legal and ethical considerations. It has humanistic implications as well. Risk assessment of sex offenders, therefore, need to be approached and understood from multidimensional perspectives. Both nomothetic and ideographic approaches need to be combined for developing assessment methods and making assessment decisions. The third-generation assessment methods seem to be moving in the right direction in this regard.

The third issue with the "actuarial assessments alone" model is epistemological in nature. In post-positivist science, there is nothing called certainty in scientific research. In post-positivist science, "the notion of 'observational facts' as brute undeniable givens, wholly independent of our fragile and insecure interpretations of them was all but surrendered, and the idea that there was anything "given" in experience was thrown in jeopardy" (Shapere, 1985, p. 1) One of the critical notions in science today is the idea of uncertainty. The rise of quantum physics and the general acceptance of Hinesburg Uncertainty Principle (HUP) by the contemporary scientific community have permanently changed the notion of truth and certitude in modern science. The prevailing notion is that for any fact or an event at a given point of time, there may exist several probable explanations. In a quantum mechanical world, scientists cannot understand even the behavior of particles with 100 percent certainty. As Noble Laureate Physicist Richard Feynman said, "Philosophers have said that if the same circumstances don't always produce the same results, predictions are impossible, and science will collapse. Here is a circumstance—identical photons are always coming down in the same direction to the same piece of glass—that produces different results. We cannot predict whether a given photon will arrive at A or B" (Feynman, 1983, p. 9). What this suggests is that uncertainties are bound to exist in assessing and predicting human behavior even with the help of high-mathematics. Given the enormous complexity of human sexuality, sex offender risk assessment methods and decisions are more vulnerable to uncertainties and, hence, they should be based on the complementarity of knowledge and experience from different professional groups and communities (Bonta, 2002; Gottfredson & Moriatry, 2006).

Sex Offender Risk Assessment in Corrections and the Court

In most correctional settings, the actuarial assessment approach is applied in combination with clinical and other assessment approaches. Sex offender risk assessment in most states is a legislative mandate, and in many states there are specialized boards, agencies, or commissions, as we mentioned before, responsible for developing evidence-based assessment approaches. One of the best examples can probably be drawn from the Virginia Criminal Sentencing Commission. In 1999, the Virginia General Assembly (Senate Joint Resolution 333) instructed the Virginia Criminal Sentencing Commission to develop evidence-based sex offender risk assessment methods for the purpose of integrating them in sentencing guidelines. In 2001, the Virginia Criminal Sentencing Commission published a report based on both prior research and an independent study conducted by the commission. The commission tracked 579 felony sex offenders, released from prison between 1990 and 1993, on average for eight years. The study defined recidivism specifically to mean a new arrest for a sex offense or against-person offenses. Three independent analyses of the data were done, by applying three statistical techniques: logistic regression, survival analysis, and classification tree analysis. On the basis of three independent analyses, two models emerged that displayed the significance of a similar set of nine static and dynamic factors for recidivism: offender age, offender education, employment, relationship with victim, aggravated sexual battery, location of offenses, criminal history, prior incarceration, and prior treatment (Ostrom, Hansen, & Kauder, 2002; Virginia Criminal Sentencing Commission, 2001).

In Ohio, a separate committee, the Correctional Institutions Inspection Committee (CIIC), is statutorily mandated to study the problem of prison management and improvement. In 2006, the CIIC published a report on sex offender classification and treatment in Ohio prisons. The report documented a study on recidivism of sex offenders done by the Ohio Department of Rehabilitation and Correction (ODRC). The ODRC study is based on a 10-year follow-up of 879 sex offenders released from Ohio prisons in 1989. The study found that the baseline rate of recidivism was 34 percent, and the total sexual offense–related recidivism rate was 11 percent (Correctional Institutions Inspections Committee Report, 2006, p. 16). The ODRC conducted a separate study of 5,045 sex offenders released from Ohio prisons between 1989 and 1993. Based on this study, ODRC developed an eight-item risk assessment method following the actuarial approach of STATIC-99. These items are prior adult-sex related arrests, prior sex-related felony convictions, any evidence of sexual offending without arrest, use of illicit drug and alcohol, victim sex of all adult sex crime convictions, victim under the age of 13, total number of victims of all adult sex crime convictions, and weapons used at the time of the commission of crime. The CIIC report, however, cautioned ODRC about the limitations of STATIC-99. As the report said: "Considering the heavy weight that is given to the risk assessment determined by STATIC-99, including whether or not the inmate is even provided treatment within the institution, an intra-Departmental study should be conducted to determine the accuracy of the STATIC-99 in predicting sexual recidivism." (Correctional Institutions Inspection Committee Report, 2006, p. 23.)

The Vermont Assessment of Sex Offender Risk (VASOR) is based on two scales: a 13-item reoffense scale and a 6-item violence scale. The 13-item scale is designed to measure the rate of sex offender recidivism. A statistical and reflective study of VASOR conducted in 2001 suggests that "[b]ecause the VASOR does not provide a comprehensive survey of all factors relevant to sexual offending, it is best used as a decision aid along with professional judgment and other appropriate tools" (McGrath & Hoke, 2001, p. 1).

In Texas, the Council Sex Offender Treatment has recently undertaken a new Dynamic Risk Assessment Project. The project goal "is to collect data from a variety of assessment tools which in turn can be used when considering deregistration issues. The Council is to provide to the Governor and to the Legislature a project status report by November 6, 2006" (Texas Department of State Health Services, 2006, p. 1).

The Colorado Sex Offender Management Board (SOMB) has legislative mandates to work on the development of sex offender risk assessment tools and management strategies. In 1998, the SOMB, in cooperation with the Colorado Parole Boards (which supplied the clinical criteria) and the Colorado Division of Criminal Justice's Office of Research and Statistics (which offered actuarial research assessments), developed an assessment scale described as Colorado Sexually Violent Predator Assessment Instrument (SVPAS). The SVPAS explicitly recognized the significance of integrating motivational factors in developing sex offender risk assessment scales. The motivational scale of the SVPAS includes such factors as verbalized desire for treatment, compliance to court order for interventions, positive attitudes towards evaluation, and active participation in evaluation. In 2003, the SOMB and the Office of Research and Statistics conducted an evaluation of the SVPAS (Colorado

Sex Offender Management Board, 2003) and concluded that actuarial risk assessment scales have theoretical limitations. "Statistical predictions of behavior sort individual offenders into subgroups which have different rates of repeat offenders. Individual behavior is not being predicted. Individuals falling into a statistically determined high risk group may be considered dangerous, whether or not the person actually reoffends upon release" (Colorado Sex Offender Management Board, 2003, p. 37). Because of the complexity and uncertainty in predicting sex offender recidivism, the SOMB recommends the use of multiple strategies for developing effective assessment tools: use of instruments that have specific relevance to measure sex offender recidivism, instruments that have evidence-based reliability and validity, use of multiple assessment instruments, and use of structured interviews (Colorado Division of Criminal Justice, 2003).

In 2006, the Washington State Institute for Public Policy conducted an evaluation, under a mandate from the Washington State Legislature, of the Washington State Sex Offender Risk Level Classification Tool developed in 1997 by State End of Sentence Review Committee (ESRC). On the basis of an empirical study of 684 sex offenders released from Washington state prisons between 1997 and 1999, the study found that within five years 22 percent recidivated with a felony offense, and 3 percent with a felony sex offense (Washington State Institute for Public Policy, 2006). The study also found that "recidivism rates do not consistently increase when the assessment scores 25 point increase" (Washington State Institute for Public Policy, 2006, p. 3). The study "could not identify sex offenders with a high risk for either violent or felony sex reoffending" (Washington State Institute for Public Policy, 2006, p. 3) In order to develop a new instrument, the study recommended a rigorous assessment of existing risk assessment literature and "involvement of clinicians."

The same trend for the use of multiple risk assessment strategies (Correctional Institutions Inspection Committee Report, 2006) and the inclusion of both actuarial and clinical approaches is observed in a proceeding of the Commission to Improve Community Safety & Sex Offender Accountability of the State Maine. "The evaluation should include a review of the specific factors for each individual. Actuarial and assessment tools must be used, but practitioners must recognize the weakness of these tools. There must be a comprehensive and collaborative approach" (Commission to Improve Community Safety and Sex Offender Accountability, 2003, p. 1).

For correctional institutions to search for and rely on balanced, comprehensive, and evidence-based assessment methods is significant not just for the improvement of sex offender management and treatment. It has legal implications as well. As more states are enacting sexual predator laws, and laws for civil commitment of sexually violent predators [SVP], the methods and tools of sex offender classification and risk assessments are being increasingly challenged in the court. The issues related to scientific evidence in the court today are settled not by scientists and professionals alone. A turning point in the admissibility of scientific evidence in the court in America came in 1993. Before 1993, the acceptance of scientific evidence and methodology was based on the "general acceptance test," described as the "Frye test," which came from the 1923 *Frye v. United States* case. The Frye test is that "expert opinion based on scientific technique is admissible if it is generally accepted as a reliable technique among the scientific community."

In 1993, the Supreme Court, in the case of *Daubert v. Marell Dow Pharmaceuticals,* ruled that it is not the experts but trial judges who should be the gatekeepers of science in the court. *Daubert* brought a fundamental change in the way American courts respond to science today. *Daubert*, in a way, confirmed the post-positivist notion of uncertainty in scientific evidence. Validity of scientific evidence in post-positivist science is based more on common consensus within the scientific and professional community. It is this need for common paradigmatic consensus that demands a bridge of thought between actuarial and clinical approaches to sex offender risk assessment. Federal law clearly suggests that assessment of SVP classification, as we mentioned before, must be "made by a court after a considering the recommendation of a board composed of experts in the behavior and treatment of sex offenders, victims' rights advocates, and representatives of law enforcement agencies" (42 U.S.C. 14071 as quoted in Logan, 2000, p. 601).

In 1997, the U.S. Supreme Court, in *Kansas v. Hendricks*, for the first time made ruling on the constitutionality of civil commitment. The Kansas civil commitment statute requires that sexual offenders who are convicted of violent sex crimes or those who committed violent sex crimes but are found to be not guilty by reason of insanity are placed, with a unanimous jury trial, in secure confinement after their release from prison. A Kansas man, named Leroy Hendricks, was repeatedly convicted for child molestations and taking indecent liberties with minors since 1957. Before he was to be released from prison in 1994, after serving a 10-year prison term for taking indecent liberties with minors, a unanimous jury found him mentally abnormal, and a Kansas court sent him for civil commitment in 1995. Hendricks appealed the lower court decision to send him to civil commitment on the claim that Kansas Act is in violation of the U.S. Constitution's due process clause, double jeopardy, and *ex post facto* clauses.

The Supreme Court of Kansas reversed the lower court decision and invalidated the Kansas Sexually Violent Predator Act on the ground, that "the preeminent condition of 'mental abnormality' did not satisfy what is perceived to be the 'substantive' due process requirement that involuntary civil commitment must be predicated on a 'mental illness' finding." But on appeal, the U.S Supreme Court reversed the decision of the Kansas Supreme Court, and ruled that the Kansas act was not in violation of the due process clause. The majority opinion noted that the "Act's definition of 'mental abnormality' satisfies 'substantive' due process requirements. An individual's constitutionally protected liberty interest in avoiding physical restraint may be overridden even in civil context." The majority opinion also added: "The Act does not violate the Constitution's double jeopardy prohibition or its ban on *ex post facto* lawmaking. The Act does not establish criminal proceedings, and involuntary confinement is not punishment."

In 2002, the U.S. Supreme Court made another ruling about the Kansas Sexually Violent Predator Act. In *Kansas v. Crane* the Supreme Court extended the definition of the concept of "mental abnormality" and argued that for the act to remain within the due process clause, the state must prove that one is suffering not only from "mental abnormality" but also an inability to control his or her behavior. There "must be a 'lack-of-control' determination."

In recent years, number of cases went to the court challenging particularly the admissibility of actuarial risk assessment methods. In *Carlos Ortega-Mantilla v. Florida* in 2005, the District Court of Appeal of Florida held that "We agree with the appellant that the actuarial instruments are scientific evidence, and, therefore, in order for them to be admissible, they must pass the Frye test." In re Simon in 2004, the Illinois Supreme Court held the same view that in order for actuarial assessments to be admissible in the court, they must pass the Frye test. In *Collier v. State*, in 2003, the Fourth District Court of Appeals of Florida held that "Frye requirements were applicable to the SVR-20, the state did not establish the Frye requirements.

and the use of the SVR-20 at trial was a reversible error." The "general acceptability" of actuarial methods of sex offender risk assessment within the scientific and professional community is still a debatable issue. The important point is that these legal issues need to be considered in developing sex offender risk assessment methods and instruments. "Legislatures have mandated that court perform risk assessment in SVP cases, and courts will undoubtedly continue to oblige by admitting clinical judgments of risk even if ARA (Actuarial Risk Assessment) is excluded. The question is not whether courts should assess risk, but rather, how risk assessments that are mandated by law should be undertaken" (Janus & Prentky, 2004, p. 26).

SEX OFFENDER TREATMENT: ISSUES AND EVIDENCE-BASED PRACTICES

State Treatment Statutes and Types

Formal psychiatric treatment for incarcerated sex offenders has long been a policy to combat sex offender recidivism. The advocates of the Progressive Movement in the beginning of the 20th century thought that sexual offending was a sickness that could be treated through the application of biology, psychology, and psychiatry. In the 1940s and 1950, many states enacted psychopathic laws. Psychopathic laws defined sexual offenders as individuals who have psychopathic personalities—a concept currently defined by psychiatry as antisocial personality disorder. The enactment of psychopathic statutes in the 1950s by different states came in the context of increasing public fear of child molesters, and the growth of a movement, particularly in psychiatry, for the medicalization of deviance (Cole, 2000; Galliher, 1985; Sutherland, 1950). In the 1980s and 1990s, however, sex offender policy began to move away from treatment and rehabilitation to incarceration, registration, and community notification. A belief began to emerge among many policy makers that sex offenders cannot be cured, and sex crimes must be controlled and contained though the model of "just deserts." From the late 1990s, treatment again began to be seen as a viable option for dealing with sex offenders, particularly in the context of the rise of a new comprehensive approach to sex offender management advanced by the Center for Sex Offender Management (CSOM). Sex offender treatment currently is not seen as a single approach to sex offender rehabilitation, but as an integral part linked to other components of sex offender management: incarceration, registration, notification, tracking, and civil commitment.

As of 2000, 34 states had formal psychiatric treatment methods available for their sex offenders. Eight states including the District of Columbia—Alabama, California, Delaware, Florida, Mississippi, New Mexico, and Oregon—do not have any formal treatment options available for their incarcerated sex offenders (Colorado Department of Corrections, 2000). In some states, as in Minnesota, incarceration times are extended for failure to participate in treatment programs. As of 2001, only six states had policies for mandatory participation in sex offender treatment: Iowa, Missouri, New York, North Dakota, Rhode Island, and South Carolina. In two states, the court mandates participation: Alaska and New Hampshire.

A number of sex offender treatment methods are now available (Table 5). These methods suggest four broad approaches to treatment: psychological, pharmacological, biological, and sociological. "In practice, these approaches are not mutually exclusive and treatment programs are increasingly utilizing a combination of these techniques" (Center for Sex Offender Management, 2001, p. 16). The most commonly used method in corrections is

TABLE 5　Some Selected Approaches to Sex Offender Treatment and Treatment Methods

Treatment Approaches	Treatment Methods
Psychological	Cognitive-Behavioral Therapy Relapse Prevention Techniques Psychoeducational Methods
Pharmacological	Cyproterone Acetate Treatment (CPA) Medroxyprogesterone Acetate (MPA) Luteinizing Hormone-releasing Hormone (LHRH) Serotonin Re-uptake Inhibitors (SSRIs)
Biological	Stereotoxic Neurosurgery Surgical Castration Electrical Aversion Penile Plethysmograph
Sociological	Family-System Intervention Group Therapy Therapeutic Communities Faith-Based Interventions Morality Training Work-Based Interventions

cognitive behavior therapy (CBT). Producing change in the pattern of thinking related to sexual behavior is the core of the cognitive-behavioral approach. The main goal is to reduce sexual arousal and enhance appropriate sexual responding. Cognitive-behavioral therapy includes a range of treatments from conditioning-based approaches to behavior skills training, empathy, and assertiveness. Cognitive-behavioral interventions focus on changing sexual behaviors and interests, modifying cognitive distortions, and addressing a range of social difficulties (Marshall & Barbaree 1990).

Twenty states—"almost 50% of the programs—offer more intensive forms of this approach through therapeutic communities or residential programs" (Colorado Department of Corrections, 2000, p. 5). In addition to cognitive-behavioral modification, treatment of sex offenders in therapeutic communities is based on a psychoeducational approach aimed at reducing the risk of recidivism through the use of effective self-management. The emphasis is on the need for offenders to take responsibility for their actions recognize the behavioral progression that proceeded and followed sexual offenses, identify situations that place them at risk to reoffend, and assist them to develop strategies to prevent recidivism. Core focus areas of treatment are defining and taking responsibility, victim empathy; social skills, sex education, anger management, arousal reconditioning, overcoming past trauma, and relapse prevention. The general duration of the treatment in 28 states is over one year. North Dakota, Arizona, and Massachusetts provide treatments over five years. The cognitive-behavioral therapy and psychoeducational therapeutic community approaches are primarily based on the theories and concepts of psychology, psychiatry, sociology, social work, and other human sciences.

As an alternative to cognitive behavior therapy and therapeutic community approaches, some states have recently approached treatment of sexual predators and repeat child molesters from a pharmacological approach, and have enacted laws for sex offender castration. In 1996, California became the first state to legalize chemical castration. In 1997, a mandatory chemical castration law Chapter 97–184 was passed in Florida. As of 2006, nine states—California, Florida, Georgia, Louisiana, Montana, Oregon, Texas, Virginia, and Wisconsin—have enacted laws for chemical castration. Options for surgical castration—removal of the testes—are available in California, Florida, and Texas.

The Florida statute mandates that repeat sex offenders are given court-ordered weekly injections of hormones and antiandrogenes drugs, such as Depo-Provera and Depo-Lupron, that reduce sex drives. Under the Florida statute, chemical castration can be a part of sentencing given to sex offenders. Mandatory court-ordered chemical castration is also part of the castration law in Montana. In Montana, a judge can legally require a repeat violent sex offender to undergo chemical castration. In Texas, both chemical and surgical castrations are voluntary, and juvenile sex offenders are not considered for castrations. The Texas statute describes that castrations are legally allowed when the offender is a repeat child molester, and it is recommended through psychiatric evaluations and in combination with offender treatments. The California law mandates chemical castration even for a first-time sex offender if the victim is below 12 years of age (Table 6).

TABLE 6   Methods of Sex Offender Treatment in Selected States

States	Cognitive Therapy	Relapse Prevention	Group Therapy/ Counseling	Therapeutic Community
Alaska	X	X	X	X
Arizona	X	X	X	
Arkansas	X	X	X	X
Colorado	X	X	X	
Connecticut	X	X	X	
Georgia	X	X	X	
Hawaii	X	X	X	
Illinois	X	X	X	
Indiana	X	X	X	X
Iowa	X	X	X	
Kansas	X	X	X	
Kentucky	X	X	X	
Maine	X	X	X	X
Massachusetts	X	X	X	X
Michigan	X	X	X	
Minnesota	X	X	X	X

(continued)

TABLE 6   Methods of Sex Offender Treatment in Selected States   (*Continued*)

States	Cognitive Therapy	Relapse Prevention	Group Therapy/ Counseling	Therapeutic Community
Missouri	X	X	X	
Montana	X	X	X	X
Nebraska	X	X	X	X
Nevada	X	X	X	
New Hampshire	X	X	X	X
New Jersey	X	X	X	X
New York	X	X	X	X
North Carolina	X	X	X	X
North Dakota	X	X	X	
Ohio	X	X	X	
Oklahoma	X	X	X	X
Pennsylvania	X	X	X	X
Rhode Island	X	X	X	
South Carolina	X	X	X	
South Dakota	X	X	X	
Tennessee	X	X	X	X
Texas	X	X	X	X
Vermont	X	X	X	X
Virginia	X	X	X	X
Washington	X	X	X	
West Virginia	X	X	X	X
Wisconsin	X	X	X	X
Wyoming	X	X	X	

Source: Colorado Department of Corrections (2000).

Sex offender Treatment and Recidivism

The field of empirical studies on relations between treatment and sex offender recidivism is still in its infancy (Quinsey, 1998). "There have been very few studies of sufficient rigor (e.g., employing an experimental and quasi-experimental design) to compare treated to untreated sex offenders" (Center for Sex Offender Management, 2001, p. 13). However, as interests are growing on expanding sex offender treatments in corrections in the context of the comprehensive approach to sex offender management model, studies are also currently growing on understanding the relations between treatment and recidivism, particularly through *Sexual Abuse: Journal of Research and Treatment,* published by the Association for the Treatment of Sexual Abusers (ATSA) (Beech & Hamilton-Giachritsis, 2005; Studer, Aylwin, & Reddon, 2005). Many empirical studies are also being done by criminal justice agencies in different states (Alaska Department of Corrections, 1996; Colorado Division of Criminal Justice, 2003; Iowa Department of Corrections, 2006).

On the basis empirical studies, the advocates of pharmacological interventions claim, that antiandrogens and hormonal agents is successful in reducing sex offender recidivism. "There is empirical evidence that CPA and sertraline have a differential effect on the sexual arousal pattern of pedophiles suppressing the pedophilic arousal and enhancing the arousal toward adult consensual sexual activity" (Bradford & Kaye, 2006, p. 3). Studer, Aylwin, and Reddon (2005), in their study on the effect of testosterone treatment on sex offender recidivism, found that "serum testosterone remained significantly predictive of sexual recidivism for the treatment non-completer group" (p. 1).

Among all other psychological and sociological treatment methods, cognitive-behavioral approaches have been found to have positive effects on reducing recidivism. But it has also been found that cognitive-behavioral therapy is more effective if it is combined with psychoeducational and sociological approaches. "Cognitive-behavioral approaches appear most promising and a combination of educational, cognitive-behavioral, and family system interventions can be effective" (Center for Sex Offender Management, 2003, p. 2) McGrath, Cumming, Livingston, and Hoke (2003) conducted a study of the rate recidivism of 195 adult sex offenders, drawn from the Vermont Department of Correction's computerized offender records, who were referred to receive prison-based cognitive-behavioral therapy. Out of 195 referred sex offenders, 56 completed treatments, 49 received some treatments but did not complete the treatment schedule, and 90 refused to participate in treatment services. On the basis of a mean follow-up period of more than six years, the study found that the "number of sexual reoffenders in the completed treatment group (5.4%) was significantly lower than that of the some-treatment group (30.6%) and no-treatment group (30.0%)" (p. 10), and those completed the treatment also had a lower number of violent reoffenders. Similar findings came from the Seager, Jellicoe, and Dhaliwal (2004) study of 177 adult sex offenders recommended for treatment in a Canadian federal prison. Out of 177 offenders, 146 were released into the community, and out of them, 81 completed treatments, 28 were unsuccessful completers, 17 dropped out of treatment, and 19 did not participate in treatment program before they were released. On the basis of a two-year follow-up, the study found that those who did not complete the program had a higher rate of recidivism, "that is 18%, 42%, and 100% of men who dropped out, refused, or were terminated, respectively, incurred a new conviction" (p. 606). A number of major reviews and meta-analytic studies on relations between sex offender recidivism and treatments have shown that treatments reduce the rate of recidivism (Alexander, 1999; Gallagher et al. 1999; Hall, 1995; Hanson et al. 2002; Polizzi et al., 2002). Alexander (1999) reviewed 79 studies [N = 10,988] and found that "sex offenders who participated in relapse treatment programs had a combined rearrest rate of 7.2 percent, compared to 17.6 percent for untreated offenders" (Center for Sex Offender Management, 2001, p. 14) Hanson et al. conducted a meta-analysis of 43 treatment studies (N = 5,078 treated; N = 4,376 untreated), and found that "those who dropped out of treatment had consistently higher rates of sexual recidivism" (Craig, Browne, & Stringer, 2003b).

Positive results of sex offender treatments have also been found by many empirical studies done by many state criminal justice agencies. A study conducted by the Iowa Department of Corrections (2006) reports that the offenders who successfully completed sex offender treatment program "have a lower rate of rearrest for sex offenses than other offenders, particularly those who receive no treatment, refused treatment, or were denied treatment" (p. 7). The Colorado Division of Criminal Justice (2003) conducted a major evaluation study of Colorado's Prison Therapeutic Community. One of the findings of the study was described as follows: "While pull-up system is not perfect, almost all inmates, we spoke with agreed that it works and is essential to treatment" (p. 10). The Alaska Department of Corrections (1996) conducted a treatment evaluation study in collaboration with the Justice Center of the University of Alaska, Anchorage in 1995. The study came up with some important observations: (1) a treatment effect was clearly demonstrated, (2) treatment improved survival in the community without reoffense, (3) rapists and child sexual abusers are equally positively effected by treatment programs, and (4) Alaska's native offenders do no progress as well in the program as nonnative offenders. The overall estimation is that sex offender treatment "reduces sexual recidivism about 10 percent. The generally accepted recidivism rate is about 30 percent for all untreated sex offenders and about 20 percent for treated sex offenders" (Center for Sex Offender Management, 2003, p. 2).

CONCLUSION

Sex offender risk assessment and treatment today are not isolated policy instruments or scientific constructs. They are an integral part of a new comprehensive sex offender management model. The success of all other components of the model—incarceration, registration, community notification, civil commitment, and reentry management—largely depends on risk assessment and treatment success. The sex offender risk assessment methods have evolved through three stages. The first-generation assessment methods of the 1970s and 1980s were mostly clinical in orientations.

From the late 1980s and early 1990s, a second-generation assessment methods—described as actuarial assessment methods—began to emerge. From that time risk assessment began to grow as a separate specialty in scientific research, particularly in psychology, psychiatry, social work, counseling, and other human sciences. Borrowing methodological tools from mathematics and statistics, the advocates of this new movement of actuarial assessment created a new paradigmatic community. The new advocates of the movement firmly belied that risks can be scientifically and objectively measured with a high degree of certainty, and that measurements should not be contaminated with the subjectivity of clinical judgments.

From the late 1990s, however, the paradigm of actuarial assessment began to be questioned. Its assumptions of objectivity began to be challenged, and it its relevance in correctional settings began to be reexamined. From the late 1990s, a third-generation of assessment methods—described as structured professional judgment (SPJ)—began to grow. The third-generation methods seek to combine static with dynamic factors, and actuarial assessments with clinical judgments. The values of actuarial assessments are not ignored but assessments began to be seen also in a broader perspective of clinical experience, and collective institutional knowledge of correction professionals.

Like sex offender risk assessment approaches, sex offender treatment methods have also gone through a process of change and evolution. In the 1940s and 1950s, sex offenders were generally seen as psychopathic personalities, and many states enacted psychopathic laws. Treatments based on Freudian psychoanalysis were generally prescribed for sex offenders. From the 1970s and 1980s, in the context of the growth of biology, neurology, brain research, psychiatry, psychology, sociology and other behavioral sciences, there began to emerge, however, a new notion that sexual behavior and sex offending are much more complex, and that effective sex offender treatments must be multidimensional. There are now four different approaches to sex offender treatments: psychological, pharmacological, biological, and sociological. All 50 states employ some combination of these approaches. A considerable amount of empirical literature has examined the relations between sex offender treatment and recidivism. The general consensus is that treatment helps to reduce recidivism about 10 percent. Effective risk assessment tools and treatment methods are vitally important for meeting the correctional challenges in the 21st century, particularly for the management of sex offenders and the containment of sex crimes. The development of effective assessments and treatments should be based on evidence-based research. They should also be based on evidence-based policies, practices, and correctional innovations. The "two communities" of research and practice should also integrate the issues of law, justice, ethics, and morality into sex offender risk assessment and treatment.

REFERENCES

Alaska Department of Corrections (1996). *Sex offender treatment program: Initial recidivism study.* Anchorage: Justice Center, University of Alaska– Anchorage.

Alexander, M. A. (1999). Sexual offender treatment efficacy revisited. *Sexual Abuse: A Journal of Abuse and Treatment, 11*(2), 101–116.

Bartosh, D. L., Garby, T., Lewis, D., & Gray, S. (2003). Differences in the validity of actuarial risk assessments in relations to sex offender type. *International Journal of Offender Therapy and Comparative Criminology, 47*(2), 422–438.

Beech, A. R., & Hamilton-Giachritsis, C. E. (2005). Relationship between therapeutic climate and treatment outcomes in group-based sexual offender treatment program. *Sexual Abuse: A Journal of Research and Treatment, 14*(4), 127–140.

Boer, D. P., Hart, S. D., Kropp, P. R., & Webster, C. D. (1997). *Manual for the Sexual Violence Risk-20.* Vancouver, Canada: British Columbia Institute against Family Violence.

Bonta, J. (2002). Offender risk assessment: Guidelines for selection and use. *Criminal Justice and Behavior, 24*(4), 355–379.

Bradfrod, M. W., & Kaye, N. S. (2006). The pharmacological treatment of sexual offenders. *Pharmacological Committee Newsletter Column,* 1–5.

Bureau of Justice Statistics. (2006). *Expenditure facts at a glance.* Washington DC: Office of Justice Programs, Department of Justice.

Bureau of Justice Statistics. (2005). *Corrections facts at a glance.* Washington DC: Office of Justice Programs: Department of Justice.

Bureau of Justice Statistics. (2005). *Criminal victimization, 2004* [by S. M. Catalano]. Washington DC: Office of Justice Programs, Department of Justice.

Bureau of Justice Statistics. (2005). *Sexual violence reported by correctional authorities, 2004* [by A. J. Beck]. Washington DC: Office of Justice Programs, Department of Justice.

Bureau of Justice Statistics. (2005). *Prisoners in 2004* [by A. J. Beck]. Washington DC: Office of Justice Statistics, Department of Justice.

Bureau of Justice Statistics. (2003). *Recidivism of sex offenders released from prison in 1994* [by P. A. Langan, L. Schmitt, & M. R. Durose]. Washington DC: Office of Justice Programs: Department of Justice.

Bureau of Justice Statistics. (2003). *Reporting crime to the police, 1992–2000* [by T. C. Hart]. Washington DC: Office of Justice Programs, Department of Justice.

Bureau of Justice Statistics. (2002). *Intimate partner violence* [by C. M. Rennison]. Washington DC: Office of Justice Programs, Department of Justice.

Centers for Disease Control and The National Center for Injury Prevention and Control. (2004). *Costs of intimate partner violence against women in the United States.* Atlanta: CDC.

Center for Sex Offender Management. (2003). *Effectiveness of sex offender treatment.* Washington DC: Office of Justice Programs, Department of Justice.

Center for Sex Offender Management. (2001). *Recidivism of sex offenders.* Washington DC: Office of Justice Programs, Department of Justice.

Center for Sex Offender Management. (1999). *Glossary of terms used in the management and treatment of sex offenders.* Washington DC: Office of Justice Programs: Department of Justice.

Cole, S. A. (2000). From sexual psychopath statute to "Megan Law": Psychiatric knowledge in the diagnosis, treatment, and adjudication of sex criminals in New Jersey, 1949–1999. *Journal of the History of Medicine and Allied Sciences, 55*(3), 292–314.

Colorado Division of Criminal Justice. (2003). *Evaluation of Colorado's prison therapeutic community for sex offenders: A report of findings.* Denver: Office of Research and Statistics, DCJ.

Colorado Division of Criminal Justice. (2003). *Process evaluation of the Colorado sex offender management board standards and guidelines: A report of findings.* Denver, Office of Research and Statistics, DCJ.

Colorado Sex Offender Management Board. (2003). *Handbook: Sexually Violent Predator Assessment Screening Instrument for felons: Background and instruction.* Boulder, Colorado: SOMB.

Colorado Department of Corrections. (2000). *Sex Offender Treatment Program: 50-state survey* (by M. West, C. S. Hromas, & P. Wenger). Colorado Springs: Colorado Department of Corrections.

Commission to Improve Community Safety & Sex Offender Accountability. (September 22, 2003). *Summary of Meeting #1.* Augusta: State of Maine.

Correctional Institutions Inspection Committee Report. (2006). *Sex offender classification and treatment in Ohio.* Cleveland, OH: CIIC.

Craig, L. A., Beech, A., & Browne, K. D. (2006). Cross validation of the risk matrix 2000 Sexual and Violence scales. *Journal of Interpersonal Violence, 21*(5), 612–633.

Craig, L. A., Browne, K. D., & Stringer, I. (2003a). Risk scales and factors predictive of sexual offence recidivism. *Trauma, Violence, & Abuse, 4*(1), 45–69.

Craig, L. A., Browne, K. R., & Stringer, I. (2003b). Treatment and sexual offense recidivism. *Trauma, Violence & Abuse. 4*(1), 70–89.

Epperson, D. L., Kaul, J. D., & Hasselton, D. (1998). *Final report of the Minnesota Sex Offender Screening Tool-Revised (Mn–SOST–R). Paper presented at the 17th Annual Conference of the Association for the Treatment of Sexual Abusers.* Vancouver, Canada.

Feynman, R. P. (1985). *QED: The strange theory of light and matter.* Princeton, NJ: Princeton University Press.

Galliher, J. F. (1985). Edwin Sutherlnd's research on the origins of sexual psychopathic laws: An early case study of the medicalization of deviance. *Social Problems, 33*(2), 100–113.

Gallagher, C. A., et al. (1999). *A quantitative review of the effects of sex offender treatment on sexual reoffending. Corrections Management Quarterly, 3*(4), 19–29.

Gottfredson, S. D., & Moriatry, L. J. (2006). Statistical risk assessment: Old problems and new applications. *Crime and Delinquency, 52*(1), 178–200.

Gordon, H., & Grubin D. (2004). Psychiatric aspects of the assessment and treatment of sex offenders. *Advances in Psychiatric Treatment, 10*, 73–80.

Grubin, D. (1998). Sex offending against children: Understanding the risk. Police Research Series Paper. London: Home Office.

Hall, G. C. N. (1995). Sexual offender recidivism revisited: A meta-analysis of recent treatment studies. *Journal of Consulting and Clinical Psychology, 63,* 802–809.

Hanson, R. K. (1997). *The development of a brief actuarial risk scale for sexual offense recidivism* (User Report 97–04). Ottawa: Department of the Solicitor General of Canada.

Hanson, R. K. (2000). *Risk assessment.* Oregon: Association for the Treatment of Sexual Abusers.

Hanson, R. K., & Bussiere, M. T. (1998). Predicting relapse: A meta-analysis of sexual offender recidivism studies. *Journal of Consulting and Clinical Psychology, 66*(2), 348–362.

Hanson, R. K., & Harris, A. (2000). Where should we intervene? Dynamic predictors of sexual offense recidivism. *Criminal Justice and Behavior, 27*(1), 6–35.

Hanson, R. K., et al. (2002). First report of the collaborative outcome data project on the effectiveness of psychological treatment for sex offenders. *Sexual Abuse: A Journal of Research and Treatment, 14*(2), 199–194.

Hanson R. K., & Thornton. D. (1999). *Static 99: Improving Actuarial Risk Assessment For Sex Offenders* (User Report 99–02). Ottawa: Department of the Solicitor General of Canada.

Hudson, S. M., Wales, D. S., Bakker, L., & Ward, T. (2002). Dynamic risk factors: The Kia Marama Evaluation. *Sexual Abuse: A Journal of Research and Treatment, 14*(2), 103–19.

Iowa Department of Corrections. (2006). *Report to the Board of Corrections: Sex offenders.* Des Moines: State of Iowa.

Janus, E. S. (2003). Legislative response to sexual violence. *Annals of the New York Academy of Sciences, 989,* 247–264.

Janus, E. S., & Prentky, R. A. (2004). *Forensic use of actuarial risk assessment with sex offenders: Accuracy, admissibility, and accountability.* www.forensicexaminers.com/forensicusepdf (December, 2006).

Jhonson, S. H. (2006). *Accuracy of predictions of sexual offense recidivism: A comparison of actuarial and clinical methods. Unpublished Ph.D. dissertation.* Santa Barbara, CA: Fielding Graduate University.

Kemshall, H. (2001). *Risk assessment and management of known sexual and violent offenders: A review of current issues.* Police Research Series Paper 140. Home Office, London.

Logan, W. A. (2000). A study in "actuarial justice": Sex offender classification practice and procedure. *Buffalo Criminal Law Review, 3,* 593–637.

Looman, J. (2006). Comparison of risk assessment instruments for sexual offenders. *Sexual Abuse: A Journal of Research and Treatment, 18,* 193–206.

Lowden, K., English. K., Hetz, N., & Harrison, L. (2003). *Process evaluation of the Colorodo sex offender management board standards and guidelines: A report of findings.* Denver: Office of Research and Statics, Division of Criminal Justice.

MacKenzie, D. L. (2001). Corrections and sentencing in the 21st century: Evidenced-based corrections and sentencing. *The Prison Journal, 81*(3), 299–312.

McGrath, R. J., Cumming. G., Livingston, J. A., & Hoke, S. E. (2003). Outcome of treatment program for adult sex offenders. *Journal of Interpersonal Violence, 18*(1), 3–17.

McGrath, R. J., & Hoke, S. E. (2001). *Vermont assessment of sex offender risk.* Middlebury: Department of Corrections.

Marshall, W. L., & Barbaree, H. E. (1990). Outcome of comprehensive cognitive-behavioral treatment programs. In W. L. Marshall, D. R. Laws & H. E. Barbaree (Eds.), *Handbook of sexual assault: Issues, theories, and treatment of the offender* (pp. 363–385). New York: Plenum Press.

National Conference of State Legislatures. (2005). *State crime legislation.* Washington DC: NCSL.

Newsletter of the Federal Court. (2005). *Filings climbed in federal courts in fiscal year 2004, 37*(3), 1–6.

Ostrom, B. J. Hansen, R. M., & Kauder, N. B. (2002). *Offender risk assessment in Virginia.* Williamsburg: VA: National Center for State Courts.

Polizzi, D. M., Mackenzie, D. L., & Hickman, L. J. (1999). What works in adult sex offender treatment? A review of prison and non-prison-based treatment programs. *International Journal of Offender Therapy and Comparative Criminology, 43*(3), 357–374.

Quinsey, V. L. (1998). Treatment of sex offenders. In M. Tony (Ed.), *The Handbook of Crime and Punishment* (pp. 403–425). New York: Oxford University Press.

Quinsey, V. L., Harris, G.T., Rice, M. E., & Cormier, C. A. (1998). *Violent offenders: Appraising and managing risk.* Washington DC: American Psychological Association.

Robinson, L. O. (2003). Sex offender management: the public policy challenges. *Annals of the New York Academy of Sciences, 989,* 1–7.

Seager, J. A., Jellicoe., & Dhaliwal, G. K. (2004). Refusers, dropouts, and completers: Measuring sex offender treatment efficacy. *International Journal of Offender Therapy and Comparative Criminology, 48*(5), 600–612.

Shapere, D. (1985). External and internal factors in the development of science. *Science and Technology Studies, 4,* 1–9.

Snyder, H. N. (2000). *Sexual assault of young children as reported to law enforcement: Victim, incident, and offender characteristics.* (NIBRS Statistical Report). Washington DC: Office of Justice Programs, Department of Justice.

Studer, L., Aylwin, A., & Reddon, J. (2005). Testosterone, sexual offense recidivism, and treatment effect among adult male sex offenders. *Sexual Abuse: A Journal of Research and Treatment, 17*(2), 171–181.

Sutherland, E. W. (1950). The sexual psychopathic laws. *Journal of Criminal Law and Criminology, 40,* 543–554.

Tjaden, P., & Thoennes, N. (2000). *Prevalence, incidence, and consequences of violence against women.* Washington DC: National Institute of Justice.

Texas Department of State Health Services. (2006). *Council on Sex Offender Treatment: Texas Sex Offender Laws/Registration/Rules—Deregistration.* Austin.

Virginia Criminal Sentencing Commission. (2001). *Assessing risk among sex offenders in Virginia.* Richmond: Criminal Sentencing Commission.

Washington State Institute for Public Policy. (2006). *Sex offender sentencing in Washington State: Sex offender risk level classification tool and recidivism.* Olympia: State of Washington.

Washington State Institute for Public Policy. (2003). *Six-year follow-up of released sex offenders recommended for commitment* [by C. Milloy]. Olympia: State of Washington.

12

Behavioral Management for Community Supervision

The Staff is the Agent of Change

Faye S. Taxman

This paper incorporates material from other papers on the topic including a paper commissioned by the National Research Council (Taxman, 2006b) and one published in Perspectives (Taxman, 2006a).

While community supervision is the most prevalent punishment for criminal behavior, with over 4.8 million adults serving such sentences (Bureau of Justice Statistics, 2006), the effectiveness of supervision is consistently questioned and underresearched (Taxman, 2002). More attention has been given to specialized correctional programs such as drug courts, boot camps, intensive supervision, residential treatment, and so on. Research has failed to examine the degree to which the supervision of the offender varies under different program scenarios. And, more importantly, existing models have not incorporated new theoretical approaches for supervising offenders in the community. This paper will briefly review the existing literature on correctional programs and supervision, identify pertinent theoretical frameworks for applying new models to supervise offenders, and describe a model of behavioral management for offenders.

Our Limited Understanding of "What Works"

A long list of researchers (e.g., Bailey, 1966; Farabee, 2005; Mackenzie, 2000; Martinson, Lipton, & Wilkes, 1974; Sherman et al., 1997; Farrington & Welsh, 2005) have questioned the efficacy of correctional programs. All have generally found that very few correctional programs reduce recidivism. The collective wisdom from meta-analysis studies is that in-prison therapeutic community programs that involve aftercare can reduce recidivism and that there is promise in a broad array of correctional programs that engage offenders in substance abuse treatment services. Intensive supervision, or the increased contact between the offender and an agent of the state, and boot camps have been identified as ineffective in changing offender behavior (Mackenzie, 2000; Sherman et al., 1997). Promising programs are those that involve services such as drug treatment; and there is a small amount of literature that supports intensive supervision when treatment services are included (Byrne, 1990; Petersilia and Turner, 1993). While one can examine the literature on correctional effectiveness and view it as bleak, it can also be enlightening to examine the different models of correctional programs and the similarities in their design and underlying theory (most are formal controls). From this perspective, as will be discussed below, more can be done to advance our programming to incorporate some of the new strategies in changing behavior (Prochaska, DiClemente, & Norcross, 1992).

All of the reviewers have lamented the quality of the existing studies, the lack of rigorous studies, and the inability to measure success. And, while Farabee (2005) and others have focused on the inadequacies in the research design and infrequent experimentation, less attention has been given to the issue that continues to plague correctional programs—implementation. The frequently cited implementation snafus are improper or poorly designed strategies to target the appropriate population for the program, insufficient attention to key programmatic features such as services or supervision strategies, inadequate strategies to address program retention or compliance issues, and unclear expectations as to behavioral objectives for program completion. Martinson and his colleagues, way back in 1974, recognized that most correctional programs were seldom implemented to be different than usual services—and that remains the challenge to the field. These implementation woes imply that more attention is needed to clarify the goals of a correctional programming.

The discussion about implementation is also insightful in that it implies that correctional programs are more likely to be a structured set of activities for the offender than a clinical program. Each activity may have different goals, and the program assumes that by participating in these activities the offender will acquire new information that can assist in the change process. This is in contrast to a clinical intervention which is based on a theoretical foundation as to how to change the person's behavior (e.g., values, attitudes, etc.), and the corresponding activities to reinforce this change process. Programs assume that participation will lead to the offender regrouping his/her own behavior while interventions assume that it is necessary to provide the offender with new skills for the purpose of changing attitudes, values, and/or behaviors. This distinction between a program and an intervention is important in reviewing the correctional literature because it could be that the "no difference" results are primarily due to failed program designs instead of failed offenders and failed implementation. That is, one might argue that if our approach to correctional interventions were more theoretical in their design, some of the implementation issues might be resolved by helping staff to appreciate key components of a program.

One example of correctional programs that are a set of activities, and that tend to lack a theoretical foundation for behavioral change, is intensive supervision. Consider an intensive supervision program that includes substance abuse education, drug testing, and community service. Each has a different goal—to inform the offender about the consequences of substance abuse, to monitor potential drug use, and to repay society. The offender is expected to understand how these pieces fit together in a message about what behavior should be changed. However, the conflicting themes and goals may not be self-evident to the offender. Most of the intensive supervision research has been premised on three main models of delivering supervision that do not address the conflicting goals issue at all: reduce caseload size to allow the officer to individualize the cases, increase the number of contacts and program requirements, and increase the number of contacts to refer offenders to services in the community. These intensive supervision, caseload size, and case management models have been subjected to experimental scrutiny with the conclusion that they are not effective in reducing recidivism (Mackenzie, 2000; Petersilia & Turner, 1993; Taxman, 2002). Each of these models assumes that the community supervision staff will do more with the offender than traditional services by increasing contacts, providing the officer with more time to devote to "work" with the offender, and providing the officer with access to more services in the community. Yet, none of these approaches has been accompanied by giving the supervision officers a strategy of how to "do more" with the offender. Instead, the underlying premise of supervision (e.g., the brokerage model, the service model) is that the officer directs but does not facilitate the offender's referral to services and then monitors the offender's involvement in an array of conditions (e.g., fine payment, drug testing, community services, attendance at services, etc.)

Few studies have directly examined the standard supervision brokerage model, which consists primarily of face-to-face contacts. Standard supervision (brokerage model) is generally seen as treatment as usual in studies of other innovative supervision programs (e.g., intensive supervision, case management, caseload size, drug court, etc.). Overall, one can argue that this model is considered ineffective given the 40 percent of probationers and 54 percent of parolees who fail to successfully complete supervision (Glaze & Palla, 2005). And, more importantly that approximately one-third of the arrests are of people who are currently on supervision at the time of the arrest.

Many of the new innovations in the field depend on the supervision model as a framework, such as drug courts, day reporting centers, case management models, and so on. However, many of these models have adopted the traditional supervision approach and have then added on treatment services. Such program models often result in conflicting goals with each service having its own goals, and the offender is basically left to discern how the goals complement each other. For example, in a recent study of drug courts, the study found that when judges used treatment sanctions (e.g., more services, counseling, etc.) that reinforced the treatment goals, the offenders were more likely to continue participation in the drug court program than when judges used punitive sanctions (and, then offenders tended to drop out or were expelled from the program) (Taxman, Pattavina, & Bouffard, 2005). While efforts to involve treatment have shown promise (some positive results, some neutral results), the models appear to be more focused on layering on services than working on a similar framework for offender change. It appears that the next steps should involve the use of theoretically oriented correctional programs.

MAJOR ADVANCEMENTS IN THE LAST DECADE

A review of the criminal justice, drug treatment, and service literature has identified promising strategies that may be relevant to designing new approaches for the general community supervision model of face-to-face contacts. These approaches could incorporate the growing knowledge about critical issues that affect involvement in criminal behavior and/or factors that affect positive outcomes from offenders. Below is a brief thematic overview with a focus on how these issues are relevant to community supervision.

Informal Social Controls versus Formal Social Controls.   In the criminal justice literature there is an ongoing debate about the role and importance of formal social controls. Recent years have seen a growth in the use of conditions of release that serve to raise the bar for standards of conduct of offenders. Correctional programs for the most part rely on using formal social controls to punish the offender, as well as conditions of release to impose treatment conditions for the purpose of rehabilitating the offender. That is, the state uses external controls on the behavior of the offender through a myriad of liberty restrictions on the offender that can range from verbal commands to physical (e.g., curfew limitations, space limitations, incarceration that removes the offender from the community, global positioning systems, requirements to attend treatment, community service, etc.). Little attention is given to the incorporation of informal social controls (e.g., peers, family, support mechanisms, etc.) as part of the correctional intervention except the pro forma collateral contact (and this is generally for monitoring the offender's progress).

Recent literature in the field has highlighted the role that natural support systems and informal social controls can have on the offender's behavior. Informal social controls can augment and enhance the formal social controls extolled by correctional agencies by providing the needed support for the individual offender in committing to a prosocial lifestyle. And, by enhancing some of these natural support systems, it provides the opportunity for offenders to develop new networks that include lawabiding citizens and enhance the traditional support networks (e.g., employment, spouse or significant other, families, etc.). In some of their most recent literature, Laub and Sampson (2003) have examined the pathways that affect an individual's further involvement with the criminal justice system. Adult transition periods, such as marriage, employment, and other naturally occurring events, can be critical factors in affecting a person's involvement in and desistence from criminal behavior. The substance abuse treatment literature has emphasized the importance of support systems for those in recovery as a means of preventing relapse, as well as assisting the addict to develop new social networks that facilitate a more prosocial role in the community. In the therapeutic literature, family, employment, and other support systems are considered critical in the process of altering behavior and lifestyles as well as assisting the offender to be perceived as a asset in the community (Latkin, Formand, Knowlton, & Sherman, 2003; Latkin, Sherman, & Knowlton, 2003). Based on much of this work, Taxman, Young, and Byrne (2004), in proposing new models of reentry, have identified developing natural support systems as part of the reintegration process. Strengthening the natural support system is theorized as an important step in assisting the offender to assume a citizenship persona as compared to adhering to the outlaw persona (Taxman, 2005). Family case management (see Shapiro, 2006) is another example of a new correctional model that can be used to enhance the natural support systems of offenders.

Procedural Justice.   Tom Tyler (2004) and others have proffered the importance of procedural justice as a tool to increase obedience with the law. The underlying premise of the procedural justice theory is that obedience to the law (or compliance with a correctional program) is best achieved when an individual believes that the state is acting legitimately.

Legitimacy stems from actions by state actors that are consistent and evenly applied to others in like situations. Tyler's work on procedural justice has been tested most recently in numerous police-related studies, and the importance of these concepts on police outcomes has been summarized in the National Research Council's recent work on *Fairness and Effectiveness in Policing: The Effectiveness* (Skogan & Frydl, 2004). Essentially the studies demonstrate that how the police conduct themselves in the community directly affects social order in those communities and cooperation with the police. Some studies have also shown that police use of procedural justice techniques can reduce recidivism of offenders (Paternoster, Bachman, Brame, & Sherman, 1997; Skogan & Frydl, 2004). Other studies have shown that when police misconduct occurs in certain neighborhoods, this increases the social disorder and violence in the community (Kane, 2005). These studies tend to confirm that police actions are perceived as legitimate or illegitimate depending on how the police exercise their authority.

The field of corrections has not benefited from direct testing of the theories of trust, legitimacy, and fairness and the potential impact on compliance with supervision requirements/programs or correctional programs. A few papers have pursued whether these theories have some saliency, and they tend to have positive findings but indicate that more work in this area is warranted. Taxman and Thanner (2003/2004) reported that offenders under supervision had reductions in rearrest, positive drug tests, and warrants for violation of probation when offenders expressed that their probation officer listened to them and treated them with respect. The protocol that was being tested in this scenario was that the officer had to identify the key behavioral objectives that would lead to the offender successfully completing supervision. In a study on clients' and counselors' expectations regarding behavior in treatment situations, an agreement on the expected behavior in treatment is closely associated with a more positive therapeutic alliance (Al-Demarki & Kivlighan, 1993). Conversely, a lack of agreement between expectations is likely to create problems in communication and may ultimately lead to failure or early termination. These scenarios apply to community supervision in which the roles for successful completion are often obtuse, and often depend on the behavior of the individual supervision officer. In fact, applying some of the police literature to the probation scenario illustrates that the same conditions for perceptions of illegitimate action by state actors may exist in the judicial and correctional environments where certain behaviors are not guaranteed to be related to certain outcomes—plea bargaining, conditions of supervision, use of revocation, and so on, are all system decisions that depend significantly on the state actors. And they are often applied differentially to offenders in a public forum where it is often difficult to explain the differential treatment (Taxman, Byrne, & Pattavina, 2005). Creating a supervision environment in which the rules for successful completion are clear and equally applied appears to be important to address the toxic nature of supervision, which has become increasingly stiff based on the rules to complete supervision and the number and types of conditions for release.

SOCIAL LEARNING AND COGNITIVE-BEHAVIORAL THERAPIES

Major advancements have occurred in the delivery of treatment services for substance abusers, offenders with mental health disorders, and other care providers. Traditional therapeutic modalities emphasized an array of strategies from psychodynamic to confrontational to reality therapies. Most of these were designed to focus on individuals developing insight and an understanding into their own behavior as a strategy for self-correction. Newer therapeutic strategies emphasize skill building as a mechanism to affect the cognition, behavior, or attitudes of an individual. Cognitive or behavioral therapies have been developed, experimentally tested, and appear to offer efficacy as a therapeutic technique to address offender behavior (Andrews & Bonta, 1998; Landenberger & Lipsey, 2006; Lipsey & Landenberger, 2006; Sherman et al., 1997). The underlying theory of the cognitive and cognitive-behavioral approaches is that behavior is learned and therefore the environment that the offender is involved in can be part of the change process as long as the mechanisms for learning new behaviors are in place. Most of the meta-analyses identify the use of cognitive-behavioral therapies or behavioral therapies as being effective. These types of therapies are designed around four major components that assist in the change process: self-diagnosis of patterns of behaviors, thoughts, or attitudes that are problematic; skills to modify these troublesome behaviors, thoughts, or attitudes; skills to prevent relapse; and maintenance skills. An added component is that the approach addresses the readiness to change issues regarding ambivalence about change and distrust of the treatment goals. (This issue, although it has not been explored, may be particularly relevant in correctional settings where the overall goals of corrections may be perceived by the offender to conflict with the goals of therapy.) Most of these types of therapies can be delivered in short-term interventions (referred to as *brief interventions*) but some require longer durations.

Meta-analytic studies have confirmed the efficacy of social learning, cognitive, and cognitive-behavioral models for offenders and/or addicts (Andrews & Bonta, 1998; Landenberger & Lipsey, 2006; Lipsey & Landenberger, 2006; Sherman et al., 1997). The techniques that are involved in the cognitive and cognitive-behavioral processes are pertinent, and probably relevant to the handling of offenders from a supervision perspective. That is, they provide guidance on the communication and behavioral tools that can be useful in dealing with offenders who are resistant, noncompliant, and disobedient. The face-to-face contact, which is the traditional vehicle of probation, can be modified by incorporating the principles of these therapeutic strategies particularly in the interactions with the offender. Probation officers can use these techniques to enhance their contacts with offenders. Recent work by Landenberger & Lipsey (2006) has focused on the key components of cognitive-behavioral therapies such as role-playing, content time, and so on, in terms of affecting positive outcomes; this provides guidance on how supervision contacts can be modified to improve offender outcomes.

RISK, NEED, RESPONSIVITY, AND THE SUPERVISION PROCESS

Over the last two decades, researchers have devoted attention to the process by which change occurs. Beginning with the stages of change model developed by Prochaska, DiClemente, and Norcross (1992), a theoretical model exists for how an individual can change. Researchers have contributed to considering how the treatment and/or criminal justice processes should occur to facilitate individual offender change. Several models have been articulated that focus on the key business processes and components to advance the offender commitment to change. Taxman (1998), in a paper on the seamless system, identified 12 programmatic processes that can facilitate offender change, such as goals that are compatible across agencies, use of assessment tools, use of responsivity, use of incentives and sanctions to shape behavior, and so on. In further work on reentry, Taxman, Byrne, and Young (2004) have identified a process for reintegration that incorporates the seamless system principles but works on moving from a reliance on formal social controls to informal social controls to encourage prosocial behavior. In this process, the researchers note that the purpose of reentry should be to assist offenders in learning to manage their own behaviors. Interventions are designed to assist the offenders in developing their own self-management skills or an internal locus of control. Others have noted the importance of key components in the design and implementation of criminal justice services such as the importance of risk and needs assessment (Lowenkamp, Latessa, & Hoslinger, 2006), responsivity (Andrews & Bonta, 1998), assigning higher risk offenders to appropriate treatment programs (Lowenkamp, Latessa, & Hoslinger, 2006; Taxman & Marlowe, 2006; Taxman & Thanner, 2006), and compliance management strategies (Marlowe & Kirby, 1999; Taxman, Soule, Gelb, 1999). Andrews and Bonta (1996) specifically discuss the importance of using rewards in the process as a means of encouraging compliance with program requirements.

In the treatment arena, Simpson (2004) have developed a treatment process that expands on the key components of an effective treatment delivery system. The components of this model are similar to that recommended by researchers in that assessment should drive program placement (responsivity). Treatment processes should consist of several layers to facilitate the individual change process including engagement, intensive treatments addressing client/offender needs, and adequate retention in treatment to affect change. Treatment should be supplemented by support systems that can be used to maintain the recovery of the addict. As identified by Simpson and his colleagues, organizational factors affect the services offered include staff motivation, resources, attributes, and climate issues.

A NEW MODEL OF SUPERVISION

The focus on the organization essentially recognizes that individual outcomes are relative to the processes that the offenders are involved in, whether it is in the criminal justice or treatment systems. Collective processes that have been identified as being key to better offender outcomes include having goals that reinforce the importance of offender change, using assessment information to drive the placement in treatment programs, assigning offenders to programs and services (including external controls or restrictions) based on their level of public safety risk and need for services, using sanctions and incentives to address compliance factors, and modifying services based on the progress of offenders. Taxman (2002) discussed this issue in an article about the effectiveness of supervision and argued that there is a need to move away from the nature of face-to-face contacts to a supervision process with measurable phases. In this model, the role of the supervision agent shifts significantly. The supervision officer does not merely have enforcement responsibilities but also has responsibilities to instruct and model prosocial behavior. This shifts the basic function of the supervision business to goal-directive, face-to-face concepts. Goal-directive, face-to-face concepts recognize that in each interaction (e.g., interviews, collateral contacts, phone contacts, etc.), the purpose of the contact needs to be clear.

Generally there are four main goals of contacts:

- **Engagement:** To assist the offender in taking ownership for his/her supervision contract and behavioral plan. Ownership derives from the offender understanding the rules of supervision (e.g., the criteria for being successful, the rewards for meeting expectations, the behaviors that will end in revocation, etc.), the offender's criminogenic drivers that affect the likelihood of involvement with the criminal justice system, the dynamic criminogenic factors that can be altered to affect the chance that the offender will be likely to change, and the prosocial behaviors that will be rewarded by the community (and criminal justice system).

  • **Early Change:** To assist the offender in addressing dynamic criminogenic factors that are meaningful to both the offender and the criminal justice system. As part of the change process, all individuals have certain interests and needs that can be used to motivate them to commit to a change process. The change process begins by allowing the offender to act on these interests as well as begin to address one dynamic criminogenic driver (which will eventually lead to addressing other criminogenic traits). The trade-off in achieving this goal is that the offender's interests in being a parent or provider, or addressing specific needs (e.g., religious, health, etc.), should be acted on simultaneously to the needs identified in the standardized risk/needs assessment tool as a means to assist the offender in taking ownership to his/her own change process.

  • **Sustained Change:** The goal of supervision is to transfer external controls from the formal government institutions to informal social controls (e.g., parents, peers, community supports, employers, etc.). This is best achieved by allowing the offender, as gains are made in the change process, to help stabilize in the community, and to utilize informal social controls to maintain the changes. Part of the supervision process should be to identify those natural support systems that the offender has or to develop these natural support systems to be a guardian for the offender to provide the support mechanisms.

  • **Reinforcers:** The goal of each contact is to reinforce the change process. Formal contingency management systems assist with this goal by providing supervision staff with the tools to reward positive gains and to address negative progress. The formal process of swift and certain responses provides "protection" for the offender by showing that supervision staff recognizes small incremental steps that facilitate and sustain change.

Model of Supervision Process

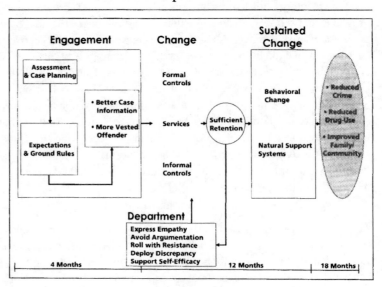

PUTTING THE MODEL INTO PLACE

Many supervision agencies have recognized that to put in place behavioral management systems requires commitment to organizational changes and enhancements. The commitment must involve a strong endorsement of and integration of behavioral management goals, into the fabric of the processes. It also involves new resources to achieve these goals. And as part of the advancements to improve reentry efforts and to change the nature of supervision, a need exists to ensure that supervision system addresses these goals. The first key to advancing the model is the use of motivational interviewing and other strategies to assist the staff in constructive communication with the offender. Many agencies are training their staff on motivational interviewing techniques and other strategies for the purpose of providing a technique to focus on client-centered approaches that build trust and rapport. Communication becomes the key strategy for the behavioral management approach because parole officers must provide consistent feedback to the offender and community to assist the offender in the change process. The manner in which that feedback is provided is critical. And, to be effective in shaping behavior the offender needs to have timely and consistent information about his/her performance to adjust the case plans.

Second, supervision plans should incorporate the constructs of behavioral contracts. In these behavioral contracts, they serve to target goals to address criminogenic needs, conditions of supervision to attend to these needs, and incremental steps to achieve goals. The supervision plan is more than a piece of paper; instead, it is a document that is subject to revision based on the progress of the offender and changing goals of supervision (e.g., engagement, change, sustaining progress). Also, the plan incorporates the agreements that hold both the offender and the system actors accountable. That is the behavioral contract tool translates conditions into short, behavioral steps that are reinforced by incentives and punishments.

The next component is to build on the offender's natural support systems as the protector for the offender. This means the goal of supervision is to assist the offender in the process of identifying and developing a noncriminal, non-substance-abusing natural support system that can be productive in limiting the goals of the offender. More agencies are developing programs and services that include the community in the supervision process. As part of some of the reentry efforts, community guardians (e.g., civic activists, community volunteers, etc.) are being assigned to offenders to assist them in the transition from prison to community; to assist offenders in retention efforts as part of jobs/employment, schooling, or treatment services; and to assist offenders in developing a network that does not involve criminal peers or associates. These efforts are designed both to address retention issues and to lay the groundwork for building those natural support systems.

Another effort is devoted to expanding the service options to accommodate both the offender's interests and a broader array of services that can be used to address criminogenic needs. Many parole agencies have expanded the service providers to include more natural supports in the community such as faith-based organizations, civic associations, educational institutions, employers or local businesses, and so on. Opening the doors of the correctional system has the potential of assisting the offender in the change and maintenance process.

The change process is a difficult one. To advance organization change that moves away from an enforcement-driven process, agencies are using place-based strategies to adopt new innovations and affect the surrounding community in which the offender resides (and the parole officer is located). Place-based strategies allow the parole office to achieve key benchmarks that affect the whole office, and the integration of community-based services are more likely to occur because the parole office is drawing on the community to be part of the supervision process. Place-based strategies can have collateral impact by improving the community well-being, and this assists supervision agencies in becoming a more valued component of the community. Plus, the place based strategie, emphasize the parole office and surrounding community as the unit of change: this is more manageable than a whole agency.

Finally, management controls are needed to assist with the organizational change. As demonstrated in other areas, performance management systems can be used to provide weekly feedback on progress. The old saying, "what gets measured, gets done" is being translated into strategic management sessions in which supervision staff are held account-able for the gains in meeting supervision goals. In some offices these meetings are held weekly, in others monthly. But the goal is to use the performance management system to monitor outcomes (e.g., assessments and case plans completed, employment retention, treatment sessions attended, negative drug test results, rearrests, warrants for violations, etc.), and then to build the organization to achieve these outcomes.

The advancement of this model requires organizations to move slowly but quickly in adapting the core principles. To this end, the authors of this chapter wrote a manual *Tools of the Trade* that was published by the National Institute of Corrections. (Taxman, Shepherdson, & Byrne, 2004). This manual was designed to illustrate how the behavioral management approach operates, as well as to provide the agencies with a guidebook for implementation. Appendix A is a copy of the manual. The manual walks through the key concepts, operational features, tools to assist with the bridging of science to practice (e.g., assessment information, offender interest surveys, behavioral contracts, and typologies), and illustrations of how to administer the model. As discussed in the diffusion literature, this type of manual is a key to operability because it translates to the organization the science into "their" language and business process.

CONCLUSION

With nearly 80 percent of offenders under correctional control in community supervision and prison populations driven by failures on community supervision, new technologies in the supervision field are critical. These new technologies can assist the field to integrat sci-ence into practice. The behavioral management model provides that step forward to change the core practice of supervision—contacts—into a meaningful and potentially powerful tool to achieve the goals of sentencing. While we as researchers have done our job in assist-ing the correctional field in translating research into operational business terms, the next 10 years will be of interest to see how different correctional agencies adopt, adapt, and use this model. If science can provide fruitful information through small incremental steps, the behavioral management approach to supervision will be a giant leap, and small incremental steps will be taken by organizations as they work through the change process. With more than 10 states and many local probation departments adopting this model, the next 10 decade will provide fruitful information as to the viability of the behavioral management approach within correctional environments.

REFERENCES

Al-Darmaki, F., & Kivlighan, D. M. (1993). Congruence in client-counselor expectations for relationship and the working alliance. *Journal of Counseling Psychology, 40,* 379–384.

Andrews, D. A., & Bonta, J. L. (2003). *Level of Service Inventory—Revised (LSI-R): U.S. norms manual supplement.* Tonawanda, NY: Multi-Health Systems.

Andrews, D., & Bonta, J. (1998). *The psychology of criminal conduct* (2nd ed.). Cincinnati, OH: Anderson.

Bailey, W. C. (1966). Correctional outcome: An evaluation of 100 reports. *Journal of Criminal Law, Criminology, and Police Science, 57*(2), 153–160.

Bureau of Justice Statistics. (2006). Correctional surveys: The Annual Probation Survey, National Prisoner Statistics, Survey of Jails, and the Annual Parole Survey as presented in *Correctional Populations in the United States, Annual, Prisoners in 2004 and Probation and Parole in the United States, 2004.* Washington, DC: Office of Justice Programs. Retrieved from www.ojp. usdoj.gov/bjs/glance/corr2.htm

Byrne, J. M., & Taxman, F. S. (2005). Reaction essay: Crime (control) is a choice: Divergent perspectives on the role of treatment in the adult corrections system. *Criminology and Public Policy, 4*(2), 291–310.

Byrne, J. M. (1990). The future of intensive probation supervision and the new intermediate sanctions. *Crime and Delinquency, 36*(1), 6–41.

Byrne, J. M. (1989). Reintegrating the concept of community into community-based corrections. *Crime and Delinquency, 35*(3), 471–499.

Eley, E. (2005). Personnel correspondence. November 29, 2005.

Farabee, D. (2005). *Rethinking rehabilitation: Why can't we reform our criminals?* Washington, DC: AEI Press.

Farrington, D., & Weldon, B. (2005). Randomized experiments in criminology: What have we learned in the last two decades? *Journal of Experimental Criminology, 1,* 1–29.

Glaze, L. E., & Palla, S. (2005). Probation and Parole in the United States, 2004. (Publication No. NCJ-210676), Washington, DC: U.S. Department of Justice, Bureau of Justice Statistics.

Gendreau, P., Little, T., & Goggin, C. (1996). A meta-analysis of the predictions of adult offender recidivism: What works! *Criminology, 34,* 575–607.

Kane, R. (2005). Compromised Police Legitimacy as a Predictor of Violent Crime in Structurally Disadvantaged Communities, *Criminology, 43,* 469–498.

Landenberger, N. A., & Lipsey, M. W. (2005). The positive effects of cognitive-behavioral programs for offenders: A meta-analysis of factors associated with effective treatment. *Journal of Experimental Criminology, 1*(4), 435–450.

Latkin, C. A., Sherman, S., & Knowlton, A. R. (2003). HIV prevention among drug users: Outcome of a network-oriented peer outreach intervention. *Health Psychology, 22*(4), 332–339.

Latkin, C. A., Forman, V., Knowlton, A. K., & Sherman, S. (2003). Norms, social networks, and HIV-related risk behaviors among urban disadvantaged drug users. *Social Science and Medicine, 56*(3), 465–476.

Laub, J., & Sampson, R. (2003). *Shared beginnings, divergent lives: Delinquent boys to age 70.* Boston: Harvard University Press.

Liddle H. A., Rowe, C. L., Quille, T., Dakof, G., Mills, D. S., Sakran, E., & Biaggi, H. (2002). Transporting a research-based adolescent drug treatment into practice. *Journal of Substance Abuse Treatment, 22*(4), 231–243.

Lipsey, M. W., & Landenberger, N. A. (2006). Cognitive-behavioral interventions. In B. C. Welsh & D. P. Farrington (Eds.), *Preventing crime: What works for children, offender, victims, and places.* Great Britain: Springer.

Lowenkamp, C. T., Latessa, E., & Hoslinger, A. (2006). Risk principle in action: What have we learned from 13,676 offenders and 97 correctional programs? *Crime and Delinquency, 52,* 77–93.

MacKenzie, D. L. (2000). Evidence-based corrections: Identifying what works. *Crime and Delinquency, 46*(4), 457–461.

Marlowe, D. B. (2003). Integrating substance abuse treatment and criminal justice supervision. *Science and Practice Perspectives 2*(1), 4–14.

Marlowe, D. B., & Kirby, K. C. (1999). Effective use of sanctions in drug courts: Lessons from behavioral research. *National Drug Court Institute Review, 2,* 1–31.

Martinson, R., & Wilkes, J. (1975). *The effectiveness of correctional treatment.* New York: Praeger.

Paternoster, R., Bachman, R., Brame, R., & Sherman, L. W. (1997). Do fair procedures matter? The effect of procedural justice on spouse assault. *Law and Society Review, 31,* 163–204.

Petersilia, J. (2000). *When prisoners return to the community: Political, economic, and social consequences.* Washington, DC: U.S. Dept. of Justice, National Institute of Justice.

Petersilia, J., & Turner, S. (1993). *Evaluating intensive supervision probation/parole: Results of a nationwide experiment.* Washington, DC: U.S. Dept. of Justice, National Institute of Justice.

Prochaska, J., DiClemente, R., & Norcross, J. (1992). In search of how people change. *American Psychologist, 47*(9), 1102–1114.

Reinventing Probation Council. (2000). *Transforming probation through leadership: The "Broken Windows" Model.* New York: Manhattan Institute, Center for Civic Innovation.

Sampson, R. J., & Laub, J. H. (2004). A general age-graded theory of crime: Lessons learned and the future of life-course criminology. In D. Farrington (Ed.), *Advances in Criminological Theory: Testing Integrated Developmental/Life Course Theories of Offending.* Vol. 13. New Brunswick, NJ: Transaction Press.

Sampson, R. J., & Laub, J. H. (2001) Understanding variability in lives through time: Contributions of life-course criminology. In A. Piquero & P. Mazerolle (Eds.), *Life-course criminology: Contemporary and classic readings* (pp. 242–258). Belmont, CA: Wadsworth/Thomson Learning.

Sampson, R. J., & Raudenbush, S. W. (2001, February). Disorder in urban neighborhoods—Does it lead to crime? *Research in Brief,* 1–5.

Shapiro, C. (2006). Family Justice Organization. www.familyjustice.org

Sherman, L. W., Gottfredson, D., MacKenzie, D., Eck, J., Reuter, P., & Bushway, S. (1997). *Preventing crime: What works, what doesn't, what's promising: A report to the United States Congress.* Washington, DC: U.S. Dept. of Justice, National Institute of Justice.

Simpson, D. D. (2004). A conceptual framework for drug treatment process and outcomes. Journal of Substance Abuse Treatment, *27,* 99–121.

Skogan, W., & Frydl, K. (2004). *Fairness and effectiveness in policing: The evidence.* Washington, DC: National Academies Press.

Taxman, F. (1998). *Reducing recidivism through a seamless system of care: Components of effective treatment, supervision, and transition services in the community.* Washington, DC: Office of National Drug Control Policy, Treatment and Criminal Justice System Conference, February 1998.

Taxman, F., & Bouffard, J. (2000). The importance of systems in improving offender outcomes: New frontiers in treatment integrity. *Justice Policy Journal, 2*(2), 37–58.

Taxman, F., Soule, D., & Gelb, A. (1999). Graduated sanctions: Stepping into accountable systems and offenders. *Prison Journal, 79*(2), 182–204.

Taxman, F. S. (2006a). "What should we expect from parole (and probation) under a behavioral management approach?" *Perspectives, 30*(2), 38–45.

Taxman, F. S. (2006b). A behavioral management approach to supervision: *Preliminary findings from Maryland's Proactive Community Supervision (PCS) pilot program.* Commissioned paper by the National Research Council, semi-annual meeting of the Committee on Law and Justice and Workshop on community supervision and desistance from crime.

Taxman, F. S. (2005). Facing brick walls: Offenders reintegration issues. *International Journal of Comparative and Applied Criminal Justice, 29*(1), 5–16.

Taxman, F. S. (2002). Supervision—Exploring the dimensions of effectiveness. *Federal Probation, 66*(2), 14–27.

Taxman, F. S., & Bouffard, J. (2005). Explaining drug treatment completion in drug court courts. *Journal of Offender Rehabilitation, 42*(1), 23–50.

Taxman, F. S., Byrne, J. M., & Pattavina, A. (2005). Racial disparity and the legitimacy of the criminal justice system: Exploring impacts on deterrence. *Journal of Health Care for the Poor and Underserved, 16*(4, Supplement B), 57–76.

Taxman, F. S., & Marlowe, D. B. (2006). Risk, needs, responsivity: In action or inaction? *Crime & Delinquency, 52*, 3–6.

Taxman, F. S., Shepardson, E. S., & Byrne, J. M. (2004). *Tools of the trade: A guide to incorporating science into practice.* Washington, DC: U.S. Dept. of Justice, National Institute of Corrections. www.nicic.org/Library/020095

Taxman, F. S., & Thanner, M. (2006). Risk, need, & responsivity: It all depends. *Crime and Delinquency, 52*(1), 28–52.

Taxman, F. S., Young, O. W., & Byrne, J. M. (2004). "Transforming Offender Reentry into Public Safety: Lessons from OJP's Reentry Partnership Initialise," Justice Policy and Research, *5*(2), 101–128.

Taxman, F. S., Byrne, J. M., & Pattavina, A. (2005). "Racial Disparity and the Legitimacy of the Criminal Justice System; Exploring Impacts on Deterrence," Journal of Health Care for the Poor and Undeserved, *16*(4), 57–76.

Taxman, F. S., Pattavina, A., & Bouffard, J. (2005) Treatment in Drug Courts in Maine: An Examination of the Impact Virginia: Virginia Commonwealth University.

Taxman, F. S., & Thanner, M. (2003/2004). Probation from a Therapeutic Perspective: Results from the Field. *Contemporary Issues in Law, 7*(1), 39–63.

Tyler, T. R. (2004). Enhancing Police Legitimacy. *The ANNALS of the American Academy of Political and Social Science*, 593: 84–99.

Tyler, T. R. (2006). Legitimacy and legitimation. *Annual Review of Psychology, 57*, 375–400.

Weisburd, D., Mastrofski, S. D., McNally, A. N., Greenspan, R., & Willis, J. J. (2003). Reforming to Preserve: Compstat and Strategic Problem Solving in American Policing. *Criminology & Public Policy, 2*(3), 421–456.

13

Inmate Suicide

Prevalence, Assessment, and Protocols

Stephen J. Tripodi and Kimberly Bender

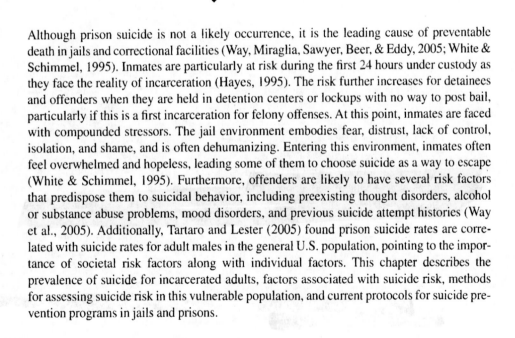

Although prison suicide is not a likely occurrence, it is the leading cause of preventable death in jails and correctional facilities (Way, Miraglia, Sawyer, Beer, & Eddy, 2005; White & Schimmel, 1995). Inmates are particularly at risk during the first 24 hours under custody as they face the reality of incarceration (Hayes, 1995). The risk further increases for detainees and offenders when they are held in detention centers or lockups with no way to post bail, particularly if this is a first incarceration for felony offenses. At this point, inmates are faced with compounded stressors. The jail environment embodies fear, distrust, lack of control, isolation, and shame, and is often dehumanizing. Entering this environment, inmates often feel overwhelmed and hopeless, leading some of them to choose suicide as a way to escape (White & Schimmel, 1995). Furthermore, offenders are likely to have several risk factors that predispose them to suicidal behavior, including preexisting thought disorders, alcohol or substance abuse problems, mood disorders, and previous suicide attempt histories (Way et al., 2005). Additionally, Tartaro and Lester (2005) found prison suicide rates are correlated with suicide rates for adult males in the general U.S. population, pointing to the importance of societal risk factors along with individual factors. This chapter describes the prevalence of suicide for incarcerated adults, factors associated with suicide risk, methods for assessing suicide risk in this vulnerable population, and current protocols for suicide prevention programs in jails and prisons.

DEFINING THE PROBLEM

While the definition of suicide may seem fairly straightforward, the concept deserves some clarification as it can describe a range of thoughts and behaviors from suicidal ideation (thoughts and planning), to suicidal gestures (self-harming behaviors), to suicide attempts (serious harm to self that could result in death with no intervention), and finally completions (harm to self resulting in death). Furthermore, certain means of suicide are particular to the prisoner population as they live in very restricted and tightly controlled environments.

Inmates use several methods to kill themselves, including gas inhalation, drug overdose (Cox, 2003), and hanging (Cox, 2003; Tatarelli, Mancinelli, Taggi, & Polidori, 1999). In a comprehensive evaluation of suicide prevention programs in prison, White and Schimmel (1995) found that hanging was the most common method of suicide, constituting approximately 80 percent of all prison suicides. Cox (2003) conducted case reviews of suicides in one particular correctional facility and found that, along with hangings, prisoners overdosed on Tylenol, Deepen, and Elavil, similar to drugs reported in other correctional facilities.

Closely related to suicide are inmate reports of a multitude of self-injurious behaviors, including cutting, head banging, ingesting foreign objects, and foreign substance ingestion (Cox, 2003). However, researchers and criminologists debate whether these behaviors have different underlying motivations from suicidal acts and should thus be categorized as different or whether they are indications of more serious suicidal risks in the future (Apter et al., 1995). Evans, Albert, and Macari (1996) describe a continuum with self-harming behaviors at one end, suicidal gestures and attempts in the middle, and suicide completion at the other. Research indicates that these behaviors are all related; Cox (2003) found 86 percent of prisoners who completed suicide in a five-year period had histories of physical self-destruction.

SCOPE OF THE PROBLEM

Research clearly indicates that suicide rates in prisons and jails far exceed suicide rates in the general public (Cox, Landsberg, & Paravati, 1989; Hall & Gabor, 2004; Hayes, 1997; Tartaro & Lester, 2005). The difference in suicide rates between inmates and the general public are inconsistent, however, ranging from three to nine times higher in correctional facilities (Hayes, 1997; Hall & Gaber, 2004; Tartaro & Lester, 2005).

The U.S. prison population was 258,165 in 1978, increased to 969,216 in 1996, and was over 2 million in 2005 (Tartaro & Lester, 2005; Travis, 2005). Logically, the number of inmate suicides increased along with the prison population. There were 60 prison inmate suicides in 1978, and this number increased to 155 in 1995. However, this seeming increase in prison suicides appears to be due, in part, to the large increase in the prison population, as suicide rates have actually decreased from 23 suicides per 100,000 inmates in 1978 to 16 suicides per 100,000 inmates in 1995 (Tartaro & Lester, 2005). Suicide rates in state prisons seem to have stabilized since 1995. In 2002, there was a minor decrease to 14 suicides for every 100,000 prison inmates, which equals approximately 280 suicides (Mumula, 2005).

Researchers have generally found that local jail suicide rates are consistently higher than state prison suicide rates (Bureau of Justice, 2005; Tartaro & Lester, 2005; Mumula, 2005). Jail suicide rates, however, have also declined steadily over the past two decades. In 1983, there were 129 suicides per 100,000 inmates reported (Hayes, 1995). In fact, the majority (56%) of jail deaths in 1983 were due to suicide. In 2002, the suicide rate in jails decreased to 47 suicides per 100,000 inmates (Bureau of Justice, 2005). In 1997, suicide was the leading cause in prisons (Hayes, 1997), however, natural causes (52%) recently surpassed suicide (32%) as the most frequently cited cause of death.

Certain types of facilities are at increased risk for suicide. Larger jails have fewer suicides than smaller jail facilities; with the nation's 50 largest jail systems (29 per 100,000 inmates) reporting half as many suicides as other jails (57 per 100,000 inmates). Offenders with a history of violence were most at risk; prisoners incarcerated for violent offenses in both local jails (92 per 100,000) and state prisons (19 per 100,000) had rates much higher than average. Consequently, facilities housing a high proportion of violent offenders may be especially at risk for prisoner suicide.

States differ considerably in reported rates of suicide. During a two-year period, three states reported no prison suicides (New Hampshire, Nebraska, and North Dakota), while South Dakota reported as many as 71 suicides per 100,000 inmates and Utah reported 49 suicides per 100,000 inmates (Mumola, 2005). The variation across states, while seemingly due to many factors, may underscore differing protocols that exist among states for identifying suicidal prisoners and implementing prevention and intervention plans. The implementation of suicide prevention programs in prisons is discussed in more detail later in this chapter.

RISK FACTORS

Over the past two decades, several important risk factors for suicide have been identified. The presence of several of these risk factors should alert mental health professionals to suicidal inmates and help professionals classify which inmates present a serious risk. The majority of risk factors are relevant for suicidal adults in the general population; however, some risk factors are specific to incarcerated individuals. For example, as previously mentioned, type of offense is related to suicide rates, with inmates convicted of violent crimes demonstrating higher suicide risk than nonviolent offenders (Way et al., 2005). Furthermore, White and Schimmel (1995) found that in their sample of prisoners who completed suicide, 28 percent of suicides were precipitated by new legal problems and 23 percent by inmate-related conflicts. Correia (2000) asserts that an inmate's sentence length and feelings regarding this sentence are important in determining potential suicide risk. Newly sentenced inmates and those with longer imposed sentences are at greater risk for suicide (Lester, 1987). Each inmate, however, may respond differently to his or her sentence. Professionals should assess individual responses to determine how the sentence may be affecting the inmate's self-esteem, family and interpersonal relationships, and employment (Rowan & Hayes, 1995).

Certain demographic characteristics have been associated with higher rates of suicide. Way et al. (2005) analyzed data from the mental health treatment charts of all completed suicides between 1993 and 2001 ($N = 76$) in New York state who had contact with mental health services. Suicidal inmates were compared to the patients on the mental health caseload and to all the New York state inmates in custody. Way et al. (2005) found that inmates who committed suicide were significantly younger than the total mental health group and the total prison population ($p < .001$). The mean age for inmates who committed suicide was 32.8, the mean age for the mental health caseload was 37.1, and the mean age for all New York prisoners was 34.6. Only 4 percent of the suicide victims were women, which is significantly different than the mental health caseload (14%), but not the total New York prison population. African American inmates were significantly less likely to commit suicide than inmates of other races. Approximately 24 percent of the inmates who committed suicide were African American, while 44.6 percent of the mental health caseload was African American, and 51 percent of the total New York prison population was African American. Furthermore, in an evaluation of several suicide prevention programs, White and Schimmel (1995) found that the majority of the inmates who committed suicide were White (65%) and male.

A prior history of suicide attempts is another important indicator of suicide risk (Moscicki, 1997). Thus, professionals should review inmates with several suicide attempts or patterns of increasing suicidal threats for severity of current risk. To examine the relationship between past self-harm and current depression, hopelessness, and suicidal ideation, Palmer and Connelly (2005) conducted a study to compare depressive symptoms among prisoners who had made a prior attempt at self-harm with prisoners who had never made prior attempts. The researchers matched the participants of the two groups, each consisting of 24 inmates, according to age, race, penal status, offense, whether they had previously been incarcerated, and the number of previous sentences. The following three scales were used to measure hopelessness, depression, and suicidal ideation: Beck's Hopelessness Scale (BHS), Beck's Depression Inventory-II (BDI), and Beck's Scale for Suicidal Ideation (BSSI).

Palmer and Connelly (2005) found significant differences between inmates who reported an experience of self-harm (the vulnerable prisoners) and the comparison group on all three measures. Inmates who had experienced self-harm in the past had significantly higher ratings of hopelessness, depression, and suicidal ideation. The vulnerable prisoners had a mean score of 10.13 on the BHS, 17.42 on the BDI, and 6.38 on the BSSI. In comparison, inmates who did not report an experience of self-harm in their past had a mean score of 6.29 on the BHS, 15.13 on the BDI, and 1.17 on the BSSI. These are differences of 3.84, 12.29, and 5.21, respectively, all statistically significant. The results of this study indicate the importance of previous self-harm as a risk factor for current suicidal ideation, with depressive symptoms acting as moderating variables.

In addition to the risk associated with personal experience with self-harm, inmates with a history of suicide in their families are also at increased risk, especially if the suicide involved an immediate relative, partner, or child (Brent et al., 1998). Similarly, inmates who have recently experienced loss of a significant person in their lives due to death or divorce are also particularly at risk (Hall, Platt, & Hall, 1999).

The way that inmates articulate their suicidal thoughts is also a useful indicator of risk. Inmates who describe suicidal impulses with anxiety and/or determination should be noted, as well as inmates who demonstrate problems with impulse control (Polvi, 1997). Charts are useful for noting histories of impulsive behaviors that have warranted disciplinary action in the past (Correia, 2000). While impulsivity is worrisome, so is careful planning. Inmates who articulate a plan for how they would commit suicide, especially with particularly lethal/realistic means, are considered an immediate risk compared to those who have not considered how they would commit suicide (Hall et al., 1999).

Inmates who are currently under the influence of substances and/or have severe addiction problems have an increased risk of suicide (Rowan & Hayes, 1995). In fact, because inmates sometimes smuggle drugs into correctional facilities, substances can affect inmates long after entrance into a facility. Subsequently, suicide prevention programs are wise to respond with immediate observation of those suspected to be under the influence (Correia, 2000).

Lack of social support has been shown to place inmates further at risk. Inmates with social networks in the facility may reduce their sense of hopelessness or fear, thereby reducing suicide risk, while inmates with familial social support outside the facility may be more open to prevention efforts (Correia, 2000).

PSYCHIATRIC DIAGNOSIS

Suicidal prisoners have been found to have elevated rates of psychiatric diagnosis (Cox, 2003). Fulwiler, Forbes, Santangelo, and Folstein (1997) found suicidal prisoners have more frequent diagnoses of depression and dysthymia, but fewer diagnoses of childhood hyperactivity, antisocial disorder, aggressive behavior, and impulsive personality traits than their self-harming counterparts. Thus, self-harmers may be using self-injurious behaviors as means of escape or coping, while a high percentage of suicidal prisoners have consistently been shown to be clinically depressed (69% Saarinen, Lehtonen, & Lonngrist, 1999; 62% Tatarelli et al., 1999).

Suicidal prisoners have also been found to have elevated rates of bipolar disorder (Fulwiler et al., 1997) and psychotic disorders (Tatarelli et al., 1999). In fact, Cox (2003) found 41 percent of prisoners who committed suicide were diagnosed with a psychotic disorder. Delusions of persecution are particularly dangerous; depressed inmates with delusions are five times more likely to commit suicide than depressed inmates who do not have delusions (Roose, Glassman, Walsh, Woodring, & Vital-Herne, 1983). Schizophrenia, in particular, is highly correlated with suicide. Research has shown that approximately 35 percent of inmates committing suicide in federal prisons carry a diagnosis of schizophrenia in their pasts (U.S. Department of Justice, 1999). White and Schimmel (1995) found that, of the 43 suicidal inmates studied, 11 inmates had severe psychotic disturbances, 6 had a mood or affective disorder, 4 had paranoid ideations, one had organic brain syndrome, and one had post-traumatic stress disorder. Personality disorders have also been linked to suicide in incarcerated individuals; Kullgren, Tengstrom, and Grann (1998) report that offenders with personality disorders are 12 times more likely to commit suicide than offenders without personality disorders.

A study by Way et al. (2005) extended the understanding of the psychiatric disorders specific to suicidal inmates when they compared the mental health disorders of New York inmates who committed suicide with inmates on the mental health caseload who were not suicidal. The primary or secondary diagnoses of major mood disorders were significantly underrepresented among the suicide victims compared to the mental health caseload (Way et al., 2005). Conversely, schizophrenia ($p < .001$), adjustment disorder ($p < .001$), and personality disorder ($p < .001$) were significantly overrepresented among the suicide victims.

With the elevated rates of psychiatric disorders reported in suicidal inmates, it is not surprising that a history of prior psychiatric treatment is the most consistent predictor of suicide in prisoners. Prisoners with a psychiatric history are eight times more likely to make a suicidal gesture during incarceration (Ivanoff, Jang, & Smyth, 1996). Cox (2003) reports that 85 percent of prisoners who committed suicide had histories of psychiatric care, with approximately 40 percent having been hospitalized in inpatient psychiatric hospitals prior to incarceration.

In addition to mental health histories, suicidal inmates have higher rates of chronic health conditions. Most prevalent are reports that 36–66 percent of inmates who committed suicide were HIV positive (Tatarelli et al., 1999). Research indicates that HIV-positive inmates are most at risk shortly after diagnosis rather than during later debilitating stages, indicating suicide may be a way of coping with this chronic illness (Conwell, 1994). Researchers have found other chronic and neurological health problems at elevated rates in suicidal inmates, including diabetes, prostate disorder, hyperthyroidism, closed seizure disorder, and history of head injury. Suicidal inmates are often in poor health and are likely to suffer from an array of serious psychiatric and medical conditions.

SUICIDE ASSESSMENT MEASURES

Most clinicians ask three simple questions to determine if a client is suicidal: (1) Are you currently thinking of committing suicide? (2) Do you have a plan to commit suicide? And if so, (3) What is your plan to commit suicide? If the client has a realistic plan to commit suicide, then the clinician generally considers the client to be acutely suicidal, and they follow suicide prevention protocol. Along with these three common questions, there are several suicide assessment measures that clinicians can administer to gauge the intensity of their client's suicidal behavior (www.endingsuicide.com).

In 2004, according to the American Correctional Association (ACA), mental health workers or trained officers at local jails and prisons must assess suicidal ideations and risk for all new inmates during the initial screening process. While there are several suicide assessment measures, this chapter will focus on two of the most popular: the Scale for Suicide Ideation (SSI) and the Suicide Behaviors Questionnaire (SBQ). For a more detailed discussion of other suicide assessment tools the reader is directed to a review by Range and Knott (1997).

The Scale for Suicide Ideation (SSI; Beck, Kovacs, & Weissman, 1979) is a 21-item, interviewer-administered rating scale that is one of the most widely used measures of suicidal ideation. The SSI measures the intensity of clients' attitudes, behaviors, and plans to commit suicide. Each item on the scale has three options, scored between 0 and 2, with a total rating of 28. There are five screening items: three items assess the respondents' wish to live or wish to die and two items measure the respondents' desire to commit suicide. Researchers have found the SSI to be associated with the suicide items from the Beck Depression Inventory and the Hamilton Scale for Depression. Additionally, internal consistency, interrater reliability, test-retest reliability, and concurrent validity have all been established (Beck, Brown, & Steer, 1997; Beck et al., 1979).

The Suicide Behaviors Questionnaire (SBQ; Linehan, 1981) is a self-report measure of suicidal thoughts and behaviors. The questionnaire uses a Likert scale to measure the frequency of suicide ideation, communication of suicidal thoughts, and attitudes and expectation of actually attempting suicide. The SBQ has been administered in psychiatric outpatient settings and with college students. Researchers found acceptable internal consistency and high test-retest reliability over a two-week period. Additionally, the SBQ has a relatively high correlation with the SSI. Finally, along with internal consistency and test-retest reliability, concurrent validity has been well established (Cotton, Peters, & Range, 1995).

The SBQ has been adapted into a four question, rater-administered, semi-structured clinical interview called the Prison Suicide Behaviors Interview (PSBI; Ivanoff & Jang, 1991). The developers have used the PSBI in several studies measuring suicidality in prisoners (i.e., Ivanoff & Jang, 1991), and it has been shown to have good test-retest reliability and to be a valid measure of prisoners' suicidal behavior (Smyth, Ivanoff, & Jang, 1994).

SUICIDE PREVENTION STANDARDS, PROTOCOLS, AND PROGRAMS

Although researchers have identified significant risk factors for suicide and developed standardized assessment tools, correctional facilities have been slow to respond to suicide risk among inmates. The threat of lawsuits provides motivation to large criminal justice systems to begin providing suicide prevention programs in their facilities. The following section begins with a case study of a recent prisoner suicide and subsequent lawsuit. The section then details efforts by national professional agencies to develop standards for suicide prevention, the resulting suicide prevention protocols suggested for all facilities, and the degree to which such correctional facilities adhere to national standards. Finally, this section concludes with descriptions of four comprehensive, effective, and innovative suicide prevention programs.

VERMONT DEPARTMENT OF CORRECTIONS

A 2006 lawsuit in Vermont, as reported by the *Bullington Free Press,* highlights the importance of departments of corrections (DOCs) adhering to suicide prevention protocol and standards. The parents of an inmate who committed suicide while in custody are suing Vermont's DOC, alleging that prison workers knew their son was contemplating suicide, but did not follow the suicide prevention protocol to prevent it from happening. In October of 2004, the parents' 24-year-old son was found hanging in his cell after being in jail for 15 months while awaiting trial. The inmate's parents stated that their son told correction officers four times in the previous year that he was thinking of killing himself, but he was never referred for mental health services. One of the correctional officers recommended to the parents that they seek legal representation because this was not the first occurrence of such a tragedy. The defendants in this case are the Vermont DOC, three specific employees, the correctional medical services, and the department's medical care contractor at the time (www.burlingtonfreepress.com).

This is the second lawsuit in three years brought against the Vermont DOC by parents of an inmate who committed suicide. The last family settled out of court for $750,000. In this most recent case, the particular jail correctly performed a suicide assessment upon the inmate's arrival. The mental health worker found the inmate to have the potential to become suicidal, which he documented it in the inmate's chart, but unfortunately there was no follow-up. Apparently, there was an existing suicide prevention protocol, but the lawsuit claims that the Vermont DOC did not adhere to the protocol for this suicide victim.

Developing Standards for Suicide Prevention

As previously mentioned, inmate suicide was the leading cause of death in jails and prisons throughout the United States in the late 1970s and early 1980s. Subsequently, in the mid-1980s, ACA and the National Commission on Correctional Healthcare (NCCHC) developed standards for prisons and jails to follow to reduce their suicide rates (Danto, 1997). Both organizations ultimately revised and modernized their standards in the early 1990s. The ACA developed the following five standards: (1) Correctional staff should observe all inmates every 30 minutes and more frequently for inmates who are suicidal; (2) health-trained staff should conduct medical screening on all inmates upon arrival to the facility; (3) professional staff should complete a health appraisal on all inmates within 14 days of arrival; (4) staff are required to have training in first aid and cardiopulmonary resuscitation (CPR), and should be able to respond to a medical emergency within four minutes; and (5) a written suicide prevention program has to exist and be approved by a medical or mental health professional (Danto, 1997).

The NCCHC standards state that there must be an intervention to handle a suicide attempt that involves notifying jail administrators and outside authorities such as family members (Danto, 1997). The NCCHC standards are more comprehensive than the ACA standards and specifically address suicidal inmates by developing the following four levels of suicide prevention:

1.   Inmates who recently tried to commit suicide should be housed in a safe room with visual checks every 5 to 10 minutes including when the inmate is asleep.
2.   Inmates considered at high risk to commit suicide should be in a safe room and observed every 5 minutes while awake and 10 minutes while asleep.
3.   Inmates considered at moderate risk for suicide should be observed every 10 minutes while awake and every 30 minutes while sleeping.
4.   Inmates who might be at risk for becoming severely depressed should be observed every 30 minutes while awake and sleeping.

Protocols for Suicide Prevention Programs

The ACA (2004) has continued to revise their suicide prevention standards over the years, with the intent of prison and local jail administrators using the standards as a guide for suicide prevention. The ACA standards state that all new employees who have regular contact with inmates must receive 40 hours of training during their first year of employment, which staff members must complete before working independently at an assigned position. This training includes recognizing signs of suicidal thinking and behavior, along with suicide prevention techniques. Furthermore, the ACA standards state that health care providers or specially trained officers conduct a suicide assessment during initial screening for new inmates. Finally, the jail or prison's mental health staff has the discretion to segregate suicidal inmates, if the inmates are considered an imminent threat, by placing them in an isolation room. Staff must observe inmates housed in an isolation unit at least every 15 minutes (ACA, 2004).

Protocols for assessing and preventing prisoner suicide are developed in institutions that attempt to incorporate decisions made in federal courts as well as national professional groups (Hayes, 1995). The degree to which individual prison systems follow these guidelines and recommendations varies greatly across states. The NCCHC created some of the first and most comprehensive national standards to move beyond implementation of adequate suicide assessment, prevention, and intervention, to identifying essential components of suicide prevention programs. The NCCHC's prevention program included 11 components:

1.   **Identification** (screening forms use observations and interviews to assess suicide risk)
2.   **Training** (all staff trained to recognize cues of suicide risk)

3. **Assessment** (mental health worker conducts thorough assessment and assigns risk level)

4. **Monitoring** (specify procedures for regular monitoring of prisoners at risk)

5. **Housing** (avoid isolation unless constant observation is possible; house with other inmates in safe environment with 10–15 minute checks)

6. **Referral** (refer potentially suicidal prisoners to mental health providers)

7. **Communication** (procedures for constant communication between mental health provider and corrections staff)

8. **Intervention** (Immediate intervention procedures for stopping a suicide in progress)

9. **Notification** (procedures for notifying authorities and family members of suicide attempts or completions)

10. **Reporting** (careful documentation of screening, monitoring efforts, and suicide attempts or completions)

11. **Review** (plan for review by prison administrators and medical professionals if suicide occurs)

The National Center on Institutions and Alternatives (NCIA) narrowed recommendations to include six critical components utilized to evaluate all 50 state Departments of Corrections' (DOC) suicide prevention protocols (Hayes, 1995). The six most critical components (staff training, intake screening/assessment, housing, levels of supervision, intervention, and administrative review) were found in only three DOCs across the country, and 14 DOCs (27%) had limited or no suicide prevention plans (Hayes, 1995). The degrees to which these six critical components are currently implemented in DOCs nationwide are described briefly below.

Staff Training.   Correctional staff have the most contact with prisoners, are usually present in a suicide attempt, and are responsible for most monitoring. It is therefore of concern that staff training was explicitly mentioned by only 27 DOCs (52%) in the suicide prevention plans.

Intake Screening/Assessment.   Assessments should consider a number of empirically supported factors shown to predict suicide attempts, including family history of suicide, recent significant loss, first incarceration, lack of social support, and psychiatric history. Brief screenings by intake personnel should identify prisoners with any level of risk, while more thorough assessment should be conducted by mental health professionals to clarify risk level and recommend preventative measures. A clear procedure for screening and assessment at intake was similarly present only in 29 DOCs' (56%) suicide prevention policies (Hayes, 1995).

Housing.   Housing potentially suicidal inmates in isolation, while convenient to correctional staff, increases risk of suicidality and is not recommended because it increases alienation and decreases monitoring. Suicidal prisoners should be housed with other inmates (or in mental health facilities) and in cells where dangerous objects have been removed, and should be located close to staff. Further, removal of prisoners' clothing (excluding belts and shoelaces) as well as physical restraints should be avoided and used as a last resort. The majority of DOCs' suicide prevention protocols considered housing concerns (39 DOCs or 75%; Hayes, 1995).

Level of Supervision.   The overwhelming majority of suicide attempts in custody are by hanging. Brain damage from strangulation can occur within 4 minutes, death often occurs within 5 to 6 minutes from oxygen loss (Yeager & Roberts, 2007). The ability of prison staff to respond promptly in suicide attempts is dependent on the level of supervision imposed by the suicide prevention protocol. Procedures should differentiate risk levels and assign levels of supervision according to risk level, with higher risk prisoners under continuous 1:1 observation. Standard observation includes roving staff persons making continuous or intermittent/unpredictable rounds and observations of suicidal prisoners. In addition, correctional officers should be examining the cell for slight changes in content (presence of sheets, blankets, shoelaces) and alterations to the safety features (altered room fixtures). Finally, staff are in a position to identify shifting inmate acuity levels or increased levels of anxiety and/or agitation (Yeager & Roberts, 2007). The use of cameras and television monitoring is recommended as a supplement to, but not a replacement for, to face-to-face observation. Among DOCs, 41 (or 79%) addressed supervision in their protocols, however policies varied with the frequency of observation (Hayes, 1995).

Intervention.   Correctional staff are likely to be the first to intervene in a suicide attempt or completion. Intervention procedures should include first aid and CPR training, assessment of genuine emergency, and alerting other staff to call for medical help. Staff should never assume the prisoner has died but instead follow lifesaving procedures until medical personnel can make a determination. Only 12 of the 50 DOCs (23%) included intervention procedures in their protocol (Hayes, 1995).

Administrative Review.   Should a suicide completion take place, administrators should conduct a thorough review to determine if the appropriate prevention and intervention procedures were taken and to identify any factors that could have indicated suicide risk. This review should result in recommendations for needed changes in policy/procedures. These assessments should include critical review of all personnel involved with the prisoner, including physicians, nurses, mental health professionals, and correctional staff and administrators. Only 14 DOCs (27%) addressed reviews in their suicide prevention protocols (Hayes, 1995).

Effective Suicide Prevention Programs in State Prisons

In 1995, Lindsay Hayes wrote an extensive and often-cited report on the prevention of prison suicide to the U.S. Department of Justice. While Hayes found that few state prisons had comprehensive suicide prevention policies, he did state that there are some effective suicide prevention programs that have reduced the rates of inmate suicide. Hayes (1995) conducted an evaluation of state prisons in search of a model suicide prevention program. The following two conditions had to be met in order to be considered a model program:

(1) The prison facility had to adhere to each of the six critical components of a written suicide prevention policy (staff training, intake screening/assessment, housing, levels of supervision, intervention, and administrative review), and (2) the facility had to have an extended suicide-free period. While Hayes did not consider any program to have model suicide prevention programs, he did find two highly effective programs: Elayn Hunt Correction Center (EHCC) in St. Gabriel, Louisiana, and the State Correctional Institution-Retreat (SCI-Retreat) in Hunlock Creek, Pennsylvania.

Elayn Hunt Correctional Center (EHCC).   The EHCC successfully implemented a suicide prevention program that incorporates a diagnostic center and all six critical components of a written suicide prevention policy. EHCC is fully staffed with four full-time physicians, two part-time psychiatrists, six psychological associates, nine clinical social workers, and one substance abuse counselor. All new inmates receive a complete medical examination, a thorough psychological assessment, and an in-depth classification review at the Adult Reception and Diagnostic Center. Along with providing medical and screening services, EHCC offers a variety of individual and group counseling sessions focusing on adjustment for newly incarcerated inmates, HIV/AIDS, substance abuse, problem-solving, and crisis intervention (Hayes, 1995). Below is a brief description of EHCC's implementation of the six critical components of a suicide prevention programs proscribed by the NCIA.

Staff Training.   Every staff member who works directly with inmates receives two hours of training in recognizing suicidal inmates *and* intervening when necessary. EHCC provides instructions on how to identify suicidal behavior and has a documented suicide prevention policy. Additionally, all staff is trained in CPR and first aid (Hayes, 1995).

Intake Screening/Assessment.   EHCC's mental health staff asks all new inmates questions about current and prior suicide risk and provides inmates with information about the risk of suicide. Additionally, all staff who work with and observe inmates must fill out a form indicating if a new inmate displays any of the following behaviors often associated with being suicidal: self-destructive acts, suicidal/homicidal ideations, depression, mood changes, agitation, hostility, insomnia, and overall bizarre behavior. Then, if the mental health professional considers an inmate to be suicidal, the inmate is placed on suicide watch for 24 hours at a time (Hayes, 1995).

Housing.   Suicidal inmates are housed away from the general prisoner population. If possible, each prison cell contains two suicidal inmates to avoid isolation. If an inmate is in a cell alone, however, the security officers have frequent conversations with the inmate, with the purpose of avoiding isolation. The cells that house suicidal inmates have high visibility to make it easy for the staff to observe inmates (Hayes, 1995).

Levels of Supervision.   EHCC has two levels of suicide watch: standard and extreme. While standard suicide watch is for inmates who have expressed a desire to commit suicide but are not considered actively suicidal, extreme suicide watch is for inmates whom mental health workers consider actively suicidal (Hayes, 1995).

Intervention.   Every housing unit at EHCC has two correctional officers who are the first responders if an inmate attempts suicide. Additionally, each housing unit has the following: paramedic shears, regular and large gauze bandages, ace bandages, elastic rolls, disposable pocket masks, latex gloves, bite block, and a tool designed to cut a variety of materials that could be used in attempted hangings (Hayes, 1995).

Administrative Review.   If an inmate successfully commits suicide at EHCC, an investigation must take place by a four-member team that includes a mental health worker, a correctional investigator, a security advisor, and a medical staff member.

Results of implementing the suicide and suicide prevention policies at EHCC have been promising. In the 11 years since implementation, only one inmate committed suicide, and that was during the first year (Hayes, 1995).

State Correctional Institution at Retreat (SCI-Retreat).   While SCI-Retreat does
not have the extensive reception and diagnostic services that EHCC has for newly admitted inmates, it does have a suicide prevention program that contains all six critical components of a suicide prevention policy. Staff at SCI-Retreat include a full-time psychologist, a social worker, a part-time psychologist, a part-time physician, and 15 nurses (Hayes, 1995). SCI-Retreat, like EHCC, is noted for addressing the six NCIA components.

Staff Training.   All staff who have contact with inmates are trained in symptoms of suicidal behavior and the facilities procedures to prevent suicide.

Intake Screening/Assessment.   All inmates are initially processed at the Department of Correctional and Classification Center before being transferred to SCI-Retreat. Upon arrival at SCI-Retreat, mental health professionals ask about current and past suicidal ideations. Additionally, security officers are instructed to inform the unit manager if they witness any of the following behaviors: threats, depression, or self-mutilation. Then, the psychologist uses the Suicide Potential Checklist to assess the inmate's suicide risk and will put the inmate on suicide watch if they deem necessary. Only mental health staff may remove an inmate from suicide watch (Hayes, 1995).

Housing.   All inmates on suicide watch are housed in the medical infirmary. Mental and medical staff must decide whether to give the inmate clothing and bedding, based on their level of supervision (Hayes, 1995).

Level of Supervision.   SCI-Retreat contains three different levels of supervision for suicidal inmates: close watch, constant watch, and regular watch. Close watch, which is the second highest level, is for inmates whom professionals do not consider actively suicidal but have the potential. Correctional staff members visually observe inmates on close watch every 15 minutes. Constant watch is reserved for inmates whom mental health professionals consider actively suicidal. Correctional staff observe inmates on constant watch continually. Lastly, regular watch is used as a step-down from the other two levels, and inmates are to be observed every 30 minutes (Hayes, 1995).

Intervention.   All of the housing units at SCI-Retreat contain first-aid kids, disposable pocket masks, and a tool for cutting materials in attempted hangings.

Administrative Review.   In the event of a suicide attempt, all staff who had contact with the inmate beforehand must submit a statement explaining the behaviors that may have led to the suicide attempt. A clinical review team interviews staff and inmates to determine the factors that may have led to the suicide attempt (Hayes, 1995).

Comprehensive Models and Innovative Suicide Prevention Programs

New York Model for Local Jails.   Based on the ACA and NCCHC standards, New York state developed a comprehensive crisis intervention program for local jails (Cox et al., 1989). Cox et al. (1989) explain that the New York Office of Mental Health and the New York Commission of Corrections collaborated with Ulster County Mental Health Services, the New York State Division of Criminal Justice, and a statewide advisory group to develop a suicide prevention crisis model. The model contains the following four components: (1) policy and procedural guidelines, (2) suicide prevention intake screening guidelines, (3) an eight-hour training program in suicide and suicide prevention, and (4) the development of a mental health practitioner's manual. Additionally, according to Cox et al. (1989), there are six essential requirements of the New York model, including an interagency conceptual agreement, essential direct services, delineation of responsibilities among agencies, interagency communication, staff education, and formal suicide investigations when suicides occur.

Interagency Conceptual Agreement.   The interagency conceptual agreement is between criminal justice and mental health agencies. The directors of these agencies have the responsibilities for implementing the crisis intervention program and to reach agreements regarding the target population, the specific goals to be achieved, and the anticipated consequences for the target population (Cox et al., 1989). Table 1 delineates the goals developed under the New York model.

TABLE 1   Client, Staff, and System Goals

Client Goals	Staff Goals	System Goals
1. Identify suicidal inmates	1. Provide all staff with training	1. Improve collaboration between mental health and criminal justice
2. Reduce incidence of suicide	2. Provide staff with orientation to jail rules	
3. Stabilize suicidal inmates		2. Develop operational guidelines
4. Prevent decompensation		
5. Provide services in timely manner		3. Provide cost-effective model
6. Provide care to all mentally ill inmates		

Essential Direct Services.   According to Cox et al. (1989), the essential direct services include identifying inmates at risk for suicide and referring them for necessary mental health and medical services. Mental health and medical interventions should include emergency mental heath services, psychiatric inpatient treatment, nonemergency mental health services, and emergency medical services. Additionally, for the suicidal inmates' protection, the New York model states that suicidal inmates should be housed in special units away from the general prison population.

Delineation of Responsibilities among Agencies/Interagency Communication.   Criminal justice and mental health agencies must know which aspects of suicide prevention they are responsible for. Through interagency communication, which is necessary to ensure continuity of care, directors should document their agencies' responsibilities.

Staff Education.   In the New York model, there are three components to staff education. First, the model includes activities to ensure that officer, medical, and mental health staff have the knowledge and skills necessary to conduct the suicide prevention services. Second, medical staff must be trained in psychotropic medications, program referral, and identifying suicide risk factors. Finally, mental health staff must be oriented to the criminal justice system (Cox et al., 1989).

Formal Suicide Prevention.   Formal suicide investigations are conducted for four reasons: (1) to determine the causes and circumstances of the suicide; (2) to make officers and staff accountable for providing security and treatment, making decisions, and being cognizant of structural failings; (3) to establish clear and curative actions, and (4) to provide services that deal with the emotional reaction by other inmates (Cox et al., 1989).

According to Cox et al. (1989), the preliminary results of the New York suicide prevention model were promising. The total number of suicides in local New York jails decreased from 21 the year before implementing the model, to 12 the following year, and just 5 the year after that.

Innovative Prison Suicide Prevention Program

Hall and Gabor (2004) published a paper discussing an innovative peer suicide prevention program in Alberta, Canada. Prison administrators in Alberta developed a peer suicide prevention program based on the idea that inmates are more likely to confide in one another than in staff members (Hall & Gabor, 2004). The name of the program is SAMS in the Pen. Volunteers meet with distressed inmates upon self-referral or request from staff or another inmate. Ninety percent of the inmates who sought services self-referred themselves.

The top three reasons that inmates self-referred themselves, or were referred by staff or another inmate, were emotional problems, incarceration-related problems, or family and relationship problems. In a documentation review, Hall and Gaber (2004) found that the percentage of inmates who sought services ranged from 21 to 28 percent. Between .6 percent and 2.1 percent were assessed as being acutely suicidal.

Results of the peer suicide prevention program were encouraging, but unfortunately administrators cancelled the program for unknown reasons. In the five years prior to implementation, there were four completed suicides, equaling a suicide rate of 131 suicides for every 100,000 prisoners. During the five-year period the program operated, there were two completed suicides, equaling a rate of 65.5 suicides for every 100,000 prisoners. In the two years following the cancellation of the program there were two successful suicides, equaling a rate of 165 suicides per 100,000 prisoners.

CONCLUSION AND RECOMMENDATIONS FOR THE FUTURE

Though national associations and federal courts began developing suicide prevention protocols for local jails and state prisons 20 years ago, there are still many departments of corrections that do not implement these standards. This is of concern, considering that prison and jail inmates are at elevated risk for suicide compared to adults in the general population. Empirical studies have greatly advanced our understanding of the particular factors that put inmates at risk for suicide. Demographic variables, attitudinal and emotional variables, psychological symptoms, and histories of suicide and loss have led to the development of standardized suicide risk assessment tools. These empirically tested tools help practitioners accurately identify prisoners at risk for suicide. Accurately assessing risk, however, is only helpful to the extent that employees at correctional facilities consistently use assessment tools and follow prevention protocol for at-risk inmates. Correctional treatment specialists and mental health practitioners working within the criminal justice system are challenged to advocate for more stringent adherence to suicide prevention program protocols. Such efforts are likely to prevent unnecessary deaths among vulnerable inmate populations and to protect facilities from the malpractice lawsuits that often follow completed suicides of adults confined in correctional facilities.

REFERENCES

AACAP. (2005). Practical parameter for the assessment and treatment of youth in juvenile detention and correctional facilities. *Journal of the American Academy of Child and Adolescent Psychiatry, 44*(10), 1085–1098.

American Correctional Association. (2004). *2004 standards supplement.* Lanham, MD: Author.

Apter, A., Gothele, D., Orbach, I., Weizman, R., Ratzoni, G., Hareven, D., & Tyano, S. (1995). Correlation of suicidal and violent behavior in different diagnostic categories of hospitalized adolescent patients. *Journal of the American Academy of Child and Adolescent Psychiatry, 34,* 912–918.

Beck, A. T., Brown, G., & Steer, R. (1997). Psychometric characteristics of the Scale for Suicide Ideation with psychiatric outpatients. *Behavior Research and Therapy, 11,* 1039–1046.

Beck, A. T., Kovacs, M., & Weissman, A. (1979). Assessment of suicidal intention: The Scale for Suicide Ideation. *Journal of Consulting and Clinical Psychology, 47*(2), 343–352.

Brent, D. A., Moritz, G., Liotus, L., Schweers, J., Balach, L., Roth, C., & Perper, J. A. (1998). Familial risk factors for adolescent suicide: A case-control study. In R. J. Kosky & H. S. Eshkevari (Eds.), *Suicide prevention: The global context* (pp. 41–50). New York: Plenum.

Burlington Free Press. (2006). Inmate suicide leads to lawsuit against corrections. Retrieved August 28, 2006 from www.burlingtonfreepress.com

Centers for Disease Control and Prevention. (2000). *Youth risk behavior surveillance—United States, 1999.* MMWR Publication No. 49 (No.SS-05), 1–96, Atlanta, GA: Author.

Coalition for Juvenile Justice. (2000). *Handle with care: Surviving the mental health needs of young offenders.* Washington, DC: Coalition for Juvenile Justice.

Conwell, Y. (1994). Suicide and terminal illness: Lessons from the HIV pandemic. *Crisis, 15,* 57–58.

Correia, K. M. (2000). Suicide assessment in a prison environment: A proposed protocol. *Criminal Justice and Behavior, 27*(5), 581–599.

Cotton, C. R., Peters, D. K., & Range, L. M. (1995). Psychometric properties of the Suicidal Behaviors Questionnaire. *Death Studies, 19*(4), 391–397.

Cox, G. (2003). Screening inmates for suicide using static risk factors. *The Behavior Therapist,* 212–214.

Cox, J. F., Landsberg, G., & Paravati, M. P. (1989). The essential components of a crisis intervention program for local jails: The New York local forensic suicide prevention crisis service model. *Psychiatric Quarterly, 60,* 103–117.

Danto, B. L. (1997). Suicide litigation as an agent of change in jail and prison: An initial report. *Behavioral Sciences and the Law, 15,* 415–425.

Evans, W., Albert, E., & Macari, D. (1996). Suicide ideation, attempts and abuse among incarcerated gang and nongang delinquents. *Child & Adolescent Social Work Journal, 13,* 115–126.

Fulwiler, C., Forbes, C., Santangelo, S. L., & Folstein, M. (1997). Self-mutilation and suicide attempt: Distinguishing features of prisoners. *Journal of the American Academy of Psychiatry Laws, 25,* 69–77.

Fremouw, W. J., de Perczel, M., & Ellis, T. E. (1990). *Suicide risk: Assessment and response guidelines.* New York: Pergamon.

Gallagher, C. A., & Dobrin, A. (2006). Deaths in juvenile justice residential facilities. *Journal of Adolescent Health, 38,* 662–668.

Gallagher, C. A., & Dobrin, A. (2005). The association between suicide screening practices and attempts requiring emergency care in juvenile justice facilities. *Journal of the American Academy of Child and Adolescent Psychiatry, 44*(5), 485–493.

Galloucis, M., & Francek, H. (2002). The Juvenile Suicide Assessment: An instrument for the assessment and management of suicide risk with incarcerated juveniles. *International Journal of Emergency Mental Health, 4*(3), 181–199.

Gray, D., Achilles, J., Keller, T., et al. (2002). Utah youth suicide study, phase I: Government agency contact before death. *Journal of the American Academy of Child and Adolescent Psychiatry, 412,* 427–434.

Hall, B., & Gabor, P. (2004). Peer suicide prevention in a prison. *The Journal of Crisis Intervention and Suicide Prevention, 25,* 19–26.

Hall, R. C. W., Platt, D. E., & Hall, R. C. (1999). Suicide risk assessment: A review of risk factors for suicide in 100 patients who made severe suicide attempts. *Psychosomatics, 40,* 18–27.

Hayes, L. M. (2004). *Juvenile suicide confinement: A national survey. Office of Juvenile Justice and Delinquency Prevention.* Alexandria, VA: National Center on Institutions and Alternatives.

Hayes, L. M. (2000). Suicide prevention in juvenile facilities. *Juvenile Justice, 7*(1), 40–53.

Hayes, L. M. (1997). From chaos to calm: One jail system's struggle with suicide prevention. *Behavioral Sciences and the Law, 15,* 399–413.

Hayes, L. M. (1995). *Prison suicide: An overview and guide to prevention.* Alexandria, VA: National Center on Institutions and Alternatives.

Ivanoff, A., Jang, S. J., & Smyth, N. J. (1996). Clinical risk factors associated with para suicide in prison. *International Journal of Offender Therapy and Comparative Criminology, 40,* 135–146.

Ivanoff, A., Smyth, N. J., Grochowski, S., Jang, S. J., & Klein, K. E. (1992). Problem solving and suicidality among prison inmates: Another look at state versus trait. *Journal of Consulting and Clinical Psychology, 60,* 970–973.

Ivanoff, A., & Jang, S. J. (1991). The role of hopelessness and social desirability in predicting suicidal behavior: A study of prison inmates. *Journal of Consulting and Clinical Psychology, 59,* 394–399.

Kullgren, G., Tengstrom, A., & Grann, M. (1998). Suicide among personality-disordered offenders: A follow-up study of 1,943 male criminal offenders. *Social Psychiatry and Psychiatric Epidemiology, 33*, 102–106.

Lester, D. (1987). *The death penalty.* Springfield, IL: Charles C. Thomas.

Linehan, M. M. (1981). *Suicidal behaviors questionnaire.* Unpublished inventory, University of Washington, Seattle, Washington.

Memory, J. (1989). Juvenile suicides in secure detention facilities: Correction of published rates. *Death Studies, 13*, 455–463.

Morris, R. E., Harrison, E. A., Knox, G. W., Tromanhauser, E., Marquis, D. K., & Watts, L. L. (1995). Health risk behavioral survey from 39 juvenile correctional facilities in the United States. *Journal of Adolescent Health, 17*, 334–344.

Moscicki, E. K. (1997). Identification of suicide risk factors using epidemiologic studies. *Psychiatric Clinics of North America, 20*, 499–517.

Mumula, C. (2005). Suicide and homicide in state prisons and local jails. Washington DC, U.S. Department of Justice. (NSJ No. 210036).

Online Education on Suicide Prevention for Professionals. Retrieved August 28, 2006, from www.endingsuicide.com

Palmer, E. J., & Connelly, R. (2005). Depression, hopelessness and suicide ideation among vulnerable prisoners. *Criminal Behaviour and Mental Health, 15*, 164–170.

Penn, J. V., Esposito, C. L., Schaeffer, L. E., Fritz, G. K., & Spirito, A. (2003). Suicide attempts and self-mutilative behavior in a juvenile correctional facility. *Journal of the American Academy of Child and Adolescent Psychiatry, 42*, 762–769.

Polvi, N. H. (1997). Assessing risk of suicide in correctional settings. In C. D. Webster & M. A. Jackson (Eds.), *Impulsivity: Theory, assessment, and treatment* (pp. 278–301). New York: Guilford.

Range, L. M., & Knott, E. C. (1997). Twenty suicide assessment instruments: Evaluation and recommendations. *Death Studies, 21*(1), 25–58.

Rohde, P., Seeley, J. R., & Mace, D. E. (1997). Correlates of suicidal behavior in a juvenile detention population. *Suicide and Life-Threatening Behavior, 27*, 164–175.

Roose, S. P., Glassman, A. H., Walsh, B. T., Woodring, S., & Vital-Herne, J. (1983). Depression, delusions, and suicide. *American Journal of Psychiatry, 140*, 1159–1162.

Rowan, J. R., & Hayes, L. M. (1995). *Training curriculum on suicide detention and prevention in jails and lock-ups.* Alexandria, VA: National Center for Institutions and Alternatives.

Saarinen, P. I., Lehtonen, J., & Lonnqvist, J. (1999). Suicide risk in schizophrenia: An analysis of 18 consecutive suicides. *Schizophrenia Bulletin, 25*, 533–542.

Sanislow, C. A., Grillo, C. M., Fehon, D. C., Axelrod, S. R., & McGlashan, T. H. (2003). Correlates of suicide risk in juvenile detainees and adolescent inpatients. *Journal of the American Academy of Child and Adolescent Psychiatry, 42*, 234–240.

Sickmund, M. (2006, June). *Juvenile Residential Facility Census, 2002: Selected findings.* Juvenile Offenders and Victims National Report Series Bulletin.

Smyth, N. J., Ivanoff, A., & Jang, S. J. (1994). Changes in psychological maladaptation among inmate parasuicides. *Criminal Justice and Behavior, 21*, 357–365.

Substance Abuse and Mental Health Services Administration. (2001). *Summary of findings from the 2000 National Household Survey on Drug Abuse* (NHSDA Series: H-13, DHHS Publication No. SMA 01-3549) Rockville, MD: Author.

Tatarelli, R., Mancinelli, I., Taggi, F., & Polidori, G. (1999). Suicide in Italian prisons in 1996 and 1997: A descriptive epidemiological study. *International Journal of Offender Therapy and Comparative Criminology, 43*, 438–447.

Tartaro, C., & Lester, D. (2005). An application of Durkheim's theory of suicide to prison suicide rates in the United States. *Death Studies, 29*, 413–422.

Travis, J. (2005). But they all come back: Facing the challenges of prisoner Reentry. Washington DC: The Urban Institute Press.

U.S. Department of Justice. (1999). *Annual refresher training—1998: Signgs of suicide risk*. Washington, DC: Author.

Wasserman, G. A., & McReynolds, L. S. (2006). Suicide risk at juvenile justice intake. *Suicide and Life-Threatening Behavior, 36*(2), 239–249.

Way, B. B., Miraglia, R., Sawyer, D. A., Beer, R., & Eddy, J. (2005). Factors related to suicide in New York state prisons. *International Journal of Law & Psychiatry, 28*, 207–221.

White, T. W., & Schimmel, D. J. (1995). Suicide prevention in federal prisons: A successful five-step program. In L. M. Hayer (Ed.), *Prison suicide: An overview and guide to prevention* (pp. 46–57). Mansfield, MA: National Center on Institutions are Alternatives.

Yeager, K. R., & Roberts, A. R. (2007). Prevention of prisoner sudden deaths by asphyxiation, hanging, and taser induced 50,000 volt shocks: Emerging safety guidelines and suicide screening protocols. In D. W. Springer & A. R. Roberts (Eds.), *Handbook of forensic mental health with victims and offenders*. New York: Springer.

14

Executive Functioning in the Brain

Assessment and Treatment of At-Risk Offenders

Mark H. Stone

The problem of criminal offending is complex and widespread. Criminal offending makes every occurrence a difficult problem for law enforcement, the judicial system, treatment providers, and the public. There is also much fear among people regarding criminal offending, which only complicates an already difficult matter.

The Department of Justice (http://www.usdoj.gov/dataonline) provides data on crime, and the published data for 2004 by the department gives these figures based on a U.S. population of 293,655,404:

Violent crime	1,367,009
Murder	16,137
Robbery	401,326
Rape	94,635

Further data is given, but these figures suffice to indicate that crime is a serious matter, and that steps must be taken to address the criminal actions that produce such consequences. Attacks upon children and adolescents are particularly heinous and provoke much anger. Naturally, we all are concerned with crime, and everybody seems to have an explanation of why criminal offending occurs. The most common explanations typically arise from a socioeconomic perspective. These explanations look to criminality as a consequence of social and economic forces.

The approach of this chapter is entirely different. It offers commentary on brain functioning together with data to explain why some criminal offending may occur. No excuses for criminal behavior are intended by these explanations and data. People are definitely responsible for their actions. Instead, the proffered information provides explanations for why some offending may occur, and what can be done to reduce its occurrence by means of assessment and treatment.

First, we discuss brain functioning, especially what has been designated as executive behavior, a condition that appears to be frequently encountered among criminals because it is deficiencies in this area of the brain that may give rise to criminal behavior. Second, the matter of assessing this condition, both informally and psychometrically, is presented together with data. Third, we offer strategies for dealing with deficiencies in executive behavior in treatment, and how treatment may assist at-risk individuals in achieving more appropriate behavior.

BRAIN ANATOMY

The human brain is a marvelous organ that provides for the stimulus-response and integration of all human thoughts, feelings, and behaviors. The brain is divided into left and right hemispheres, and each hemisphere is divided into four lobes for further delineating brain functioning. The brain is an integrated organ, although this discussion concentrates solely on the two frontal lobes. These frontal lobes lie in the most forward part of the brain just behind the forehead. Through evolution, this area has grown more than any other part of the human brain and now occupyies almost a quarter of the brain. The growth of the frontal area further distinguishes humans from other mammals. Not only are the frontal areas the last to develop in evolution, they are the last to mature in human development.

Anatomical/neurological studies and summaries (Eccles, 1970, 1989; Geschwind, 1965, 1972; Levin, Eisenberg & Benton, 1991; Pincus, 2003; Tobias, 1983) suggest that full development of the frontal lobes can be as late as early adulthood. Myelination of nerves occurs after birth, with dendrites and cell maturation developing through childhood and adolescence (Paus, 2005). Paus indicates, "In a shift from a caregiver-dependent child to a fully autonomous adult, the adolescent undergoes multiple changes in physical growth, physiology, and cognitive and emotional skills" (p. 60).

The frontal areas are described as "immensely rich connections to all sources of sensory information" (Walter, 1973). The association areas of the frontal lobes are profound, connecting them to many other areas of the brain. These areas are considered the master association areas of the brain. Consequently, the frontal areas of the brain are highly influential in the so-called executive functions of human behavior Goldberg, 2001). Lesions to the frontal lobes, sometimes designated as the frontal lobe syndrome, can occur from trauma and tumors, and are secondary to many other diseases. Accidents and the use of alcohol and drugs likewise contribute to their occurrence. Any dysfunction or damage to the frontal lobes has great consequences for impairing the executive functioning of the brain (Anderson, Bechara, Damasio, Tranel, & Damasio, 1999).

According to Luria (1973), the famous Russian physiologist and Nobel Prize winner, "They [the frontal lobes] are a superstructure above all the other parts of the cerebral cortex and perform a far more universal function of general regulation of behavior." Luria (1980) also stated that the prefrontal lobes play "a decisive role in the formulation of intentions and programs and in the regulation and verification of the most complex forms of human behavior." While much more sophisticated research has emanated from studies in this area since Luria's day, his generalizations are still valid.

The frontal lobes are also anatomically distinct in that they do not contain any pyramidal cells. Instead, this cell area is known as the "granular frontal cortex." While the brain is the seat of intellectual functioning, the frontal lobes, both left and right, show little effect on general measured intelligence, but they are very involved in the activities of paying attention, motivation, planning, and execution of thoughtful behavior. The frontal lobes are not without connection to the rest of the cortex. In fact, there are rich interconnections from the frontal lobes to the limbic system, which regulates behavior, to the voluminous interconnections forming the corpus callosum, which connects the two hemispheres, and many other areas of the brain (Goldberg, 2001).

EXECUTIVE FUNCTIONING

Executive area dysfunction is evaluated by impairment in motivation, attention, sequencing of actions, slowed thinking, poor judgment, social withdrawal, and irritability (Mesulam, 1986). Mood changes from apathy to sudden and impulsive acts frequently occur. The moody but violent murderer depicted in the popular movie *Fargo* is a good example. His sudden explosions from extreme reticence to extraordinary violence are excellent illustrations of this condition (Bechara, Damasio, Tranel, & Damasio, 1996).

Lezak (1995) defined executive functioning as inability for self-control, heightened irritability, excitability, impulsivity and difficulty in making shifts in attention. Bigler and Clement (1997) postulated executive functioning deficits to include loss of the ability to plan, to initiate behavior, and to accurately monitor the outcomes of behavior. Damasio (1994) indicated three deficiencies emanating from the frontal area of the brain. These include failure (1) to generate options, (2) to evaluate the consequences of actions, and (3) to conceptualize efficient means to achieve a goal. Disturbances in behavior resulting from lesions that damage the frontal lobes impair the ability to compare the result of one's actions with one's intent. Such damage makes a person incapable of recognizing mistakes. Simple memory tasks are frequently without impairment while more complex ones (two or more) are greatly affected when the frontal lobes are impaired.

When the frontal lobes are dysfunctional, the brain reacts to all stimuli in an uncontrolled manner. This may result in highly imitative, stereotyped, repetitive, and sensory-bound impulsive behavior with hyperactivity. These impaired persons are said to be "stimulus-bound" meaning they are always attracted to novel stimuli, and unable to ignore distracting stimuli. They have a profound disturbance in executing complex behavior, and a marked increase in making immediate responses to irrelevant stimuli. They often display a driven hyperactivity.

The right hemisphere is particularly involved in attention tasks. Mood is also moderated here. Mesulum and Geshwind (1978) wrote, "The fundamental role of 'attention' is to direct vigilance toward events which are of emotional or motivational significance to the organism." The frontal areas of the brain, as all areas of the brain, are readily damaged by a lack of oxygen, and from any impediments to the blood supply to the brain. Brain damage also results from injury and hemorrhages. Alcohol and illicit drugs directly affect brain functioning, and their use may damage cells forever. Alcohol and drug abuse are so frequently associated with criminal behavior that one expects these behaviors to accompany brain dysfunction. Persons at risk from any of these conditions or impaired by any of these causes may have serious malfunctioning of the frontal lobes as well as the entire brain (DeVries & Shippenberg, 2002; Kelley & Berridge, 2002). A life of constant exposure to the effects of violence further increases the likelihood of brain damage and dysfunction. Arrest and incarceration from criminal behavior may cause or further exacerbate these conditions.

Individuals must also develop and practice the behaviors associated with optimal executive functioning to become fully functional persons. While the frontal lobes provide the capacity for successful functioning they do not operate automatically in and of themselves. Like any other attribute, executive skills must be trained and practiced to be functional. Most persons learn these skills through practice by means of the modeling, training, and encouragement provided by their parents and teachers. Parental neglect and/or failure to learn at home or in school may impede development of the executive function of the frontal lobes.

With this short introduction to brain behavior, we proceed to explain how these matters may influence some criminal offenders. A useful illustration is provided by Gazzaniga (1998), who puts it this way:

> We all have had our interest sparked by an attractive stranger. Struggle ensues as we try to override the deeply wired circuitry provided by evolution to maintain our desire to reproduce. Allaying possible embarrassment, the mind gets around the brain's assertion this time and manages to maintain control. Society does have an effect through yet other brain representations, and thus we are not completely at the mercy or our brain's reproductive systems. (p. 22)

Why do some individuals exercise control in such instances, while others do not? There is no single answer applicable to all persons. We have to make careful assessments in order to determine the reasons for criminal offending behavior. To do so requires that we assess, diagnose and, treat the causes that occasioned the possible reasons why offenders have committed their criminal acts. In doing so we learn why they have not been able to modify their behavior and actions. Then we and they can proceed to remediate these deficiencies.

ASSESSMENT

Some of the conditions described here can be specifically assessed. We know some of the attributes and behaviors that need to be evaluated. While complete medical examinations are needed, and specialists such as neurologists and clinical neuropsychologists are exceedingly helpful, clinicians and treatment professionals can also do their part.

Clinicians can learn to accurately observe and record the special behaviors of criminal offenders especially associated with frontal lobe deficiencies. These criteria can enumerate by the degree to which the at-risk individual exhibits the following seven behaviors:

1. Impulsiveness and an inability to inhibit an inappropriate behavior.
2. Inability to change a task in midstream, so to speak.
3. Inability to withhold inappropriate responses.

4. Preservation on a task.

5. Stimulus-bound behavior, that is, always preferring novel stimuli and an inability to ignore distracting stimuli.

6. Inability to self-monitor thoughts, actions, and behavior.

7. Lack of forethought and the inability to anticipate the consequences of one's actions.

These attributes can be assessed and recorded with reasonable reliability and validity by making careful documentation of the behavior. It is especially important not to label the individual or the behavior, but instead to document exactly what behavior occurred, when it occurred, and under what conditions.

In order to assist in this informal assessment, a checklist has been developed and is given in Appendix A . This checklist will help identify the essential characteristics of executive functioning.

A skillful interview must be conducted and social history also obtained. Events such as accidents and illness may be factors that impair executive functioning, and such occurrences from past history need to be carefully documented so they can be evaluated. Any assessment must be comprehensive, and carefully completed in order to understand how the impact of dysfunction to the frontal lobes may impinge on observed actions and behavior. Since alcohol and drugs can greatly impair functioning, a comprehensive drug-alcohol history is also required.

Useful Instruments for Assessment

A formal assessment of executive function should include the following three areas:

1. A comprehensive social history should be conducted. It is best to follow a structured format to guarantee that all the relevant information has been gathered. Examples to use include the Human Behavior Questionnaire (Comings, 1990), which comes with both child and adult versions each of that cover all the major areas in 31 pages of questions. Achenbach (1997) has developed separate report forms for children, adolescents, and people in early and late adulthood. The later report forms are provided with scoring profiles and normative data. The SCID Screen Patient Questionnaire (First, Gibbon, Williams, & Spitzer, 1997) is a structured clinical interview available for use as an oral interview, and by computer using a CD, which comes also comes with a patient tutorial so the instrument can be self-administered via computer. Besides a comprehensive interview, the SCID also contains sections on alcohol and drug use. These are only a few of the many instruments that might be used.

2. As has been indicated, alcohol and drug abuse should be carefully assessed because of the role they play in criminal behavior. Inasmuch as denial is very common, the use of a structured assessment such as the Substance Use Disorders Diagnostic Schedule-IV (Harrison & Hoffman, 2001) is recommended in order to help determine the most accurate information from the client. It is wise to corroborate self-reports by conducting separate interviews with a spouse, family members, and employer(s).

3.   A specific assessment of *attention* as manifest in daily life is very important to determine. Levin, High, and Goethe (1987) have devised a Neurobehavioral Rating Scale (NRS) for assessing those behaviors associated with inattention resulting from head injury or other conditions. Twenty-seven items are rated using a 7-point scale to address inattention, distraction, and decreased alertness; cognitive thought processes such as disorganized tangential and preservative thinking; as well as other areas of inattention. Ponsford and Kinsella (1991) have developed a 14-item instrument using a 5-point scale for addressing lethargy, restlessness, distraction, and other aspects of inattention. Rater reliability for both of these instruments is reported as sufficiently high to make them useful for assessment.

SPECIFIC ASSESSMENT OF EXECUTIVE FUNCTIONING

The following eight tests are commonly used to evaluate the frontal lobes in contradistinction to tests used to measure intellectual functioning. These instruments, and others of a similar nature, require advanced skills and training for administration and interpretation. They may not be appropriate for use by clinicians who are not qualified to administer and interpret them, however, a referral to a clinical neuropsychologist can be made.

1.   *Vigil for Thought*—a test for measuring auditory and visual attention, and related concentration.

2.   *California Verbal Learning Test*—a test for the measurement of verbal learning and memory.

3.   *Rey Complex Figure Test*—a copying test of visual-spatial observation, and paper-pencil construction.

4.   *Controlled Oral Word Association Test*—a test of auditory association

5.   *Stroop Test*—a test for measuring visual attention requiring mixed modes of responding.

6.   *Wisconsin Card Sort*—a test for measuring flexibility, perseveration, and mixed modes of responding.

7.   *Trails A and B*—a test of visual-spatial sequencing with paper-pencil. Stone (2006) has produced *Trails L*, which continues beyond Trails A and B by providing even further identification of visual-spatial impairment.

8.   *Category Test*—a test of visual memory taken from an extensive neuropsychological test battery that has been shown to validly identify deficiencies in executive skill behaviors.

The complete references for these tests and the results in their study are given in Stone and Thompson (2001). A more complete description of the instruments and references can be found in Lezak (1995). Perusing test catalogs by the major test companies, and reading the reviews contained in the *Mental Measurement Yearbooks* (Impara and Plake, 1998) that are customarily found in libraries, will assist in identifying and evaluating additional instruments. The popular text *Psychological Testing*, by Anastasi and Urbina (1997), provides a list of test publishers and their addresses. One should be cognizant of the fact that purchasing and using instruments should follow ethical guidelines (APA, 1999).

A study by Stone and Thompson (2001) examined the executive functioning of 63 previously incarcerated males who were in treatment as a condition of parole. These criminal offenders produced test scores that were statistically different from the normative controls on 21 of 32 (66%) instruments used in a comprehensive assessment that included all the instruments mentioned above in addition to several others. The results indicated that criminal offenders showed marked discrepancies on those tests that are especially sensitive to frontal lobe impairment. These tests were those listed earlier. While these findings cannot fully explain all the issues of criminal offending, they support the contentions given above regarding the strong influence that frontal lobe impairment plays in the cycle of offending.

Stone and Thompson (2001) offered the following conclusions:

• Criminal offenders may have frontal lobe impairments that impede the acquisition of executive functioning skills needed to guide behavior, and especially in the acquisition of new behaviors. For example, a client may not be able to generalize from one setting to a different setting, or from one instance to a new situation. A client may not be able to abstract a behavioral concept from an incident, or draw conclusions about subsequent behavior, because this impairment precludes learning new skills.

• Therapist and mental health workers cannot assume that clients understand comments, suggestions, and recommendations simply because they acknowledge they do either by saying "yes" or nodding affirmatively. Instead, clients should be asked to repeat and especially to sequence correctly the steps to follow, or the new application to implement. Learning new skills requires simple but multimodal clues, much practice, constant review, and overt demonstrations of the acquisition of these new skills or behaviors.

• Reliance on moral imperatives is not a useful therapeutic device inasmuch as all abstract concepts are of limited application to at-risk criminal offenders. Individuals with brain impairments require numerous examples followed by much over-learning and reinforcement to ensure the acquisition of new skills.

• Treatment of at-risk criminal offenders requires a structured environment. Clients may be annoyed by this structure and feel their freedom is restricted. However, the results of this approach confirm what is already known about individuals with limited executive functioning—they lack the skills to direct themselves in their own environment.

• Clients should be taught ways to remember, to record, and to code the acquisition of skills. Learning good habits is required. At-risk criminal offenders usually resist any attempt to be structured, which is their own undoing inasmuch as they have already demonstrated that they do not possess the skills and habits to direct their actions appropriately.

• At-risk criminal offenders are usually not gainfully employed, interested in regular working conditions, or interested in achieving them without direction. They are used to having time on their hands to do as they please. Consequently, there must be a systematic approach to developing work skills, learning the appropriate behavior for a work environment, achieving regular employment, and especially receiving ongoing and constant monitoring with continual supportive supervision. These so-called adjunct skills for building work-related skills are sometimes dismissed as not treatment-oriented when, in fact, work skills constitute the essence of life for everyone. Adler stressed that there were three major tasks in a person's life— work, friendship, and the expression of intimate love.

- At-risk criminal offenders have a host of new skills to learn. These are best acquired and supported through structured group experiences. The value of group treatment cannot be underestimated.

ALFRED ADLER ON CRIME

Alfred Adler (1870–1937) addressed the matter of crime in 1930, but the original journal is no longer available. Stone and Drescher (2004) published a version of the paper based on the unpublished notes from Adler's writings found in the Library of Congress. This paper is printed as Chapter 21 in their book entitled *Adler Speaks*, which is a compilation of Adler's largely unpublished lectures. Adler begins by stressing that one sees "in the behavior of a person how he relates to the outside world." He continues by indicating that life's main goal is "to create, to go ahead, to develop, and to strive for success" (p. 94). This behavior shows that a person following criminal activities cannot relate to the outside world as other do, except to take and use in whatever way he can all that can be garnered from others. "Everybody is property," writes Adler in discussing a criminal's motives. Whatever variation occurs in such behavior (Adler says there are a million variations), the criminal always seeks to gain for self alone and not for others. Whatever goodness exists, and criminals have some manifestation of goodness, it is always secondary to their own gain, and never to truly benefit another except for receiving leftovers.

Adler argues that criminals operate from a "private intelligence" that must be recognized as selfish and self-centered. They must change their orientation so as to become active participants in society. For most individuals, it is parents and teachers who help young people to develop what Adler calls *social interest* or *community feeling*. This concept is a cardinal one for Adler's psychology, and its absence is clearly evident in criminal behavior. Criminal behavior must be changed from a private orientation to one of addressing concern for all. In fact, social interest or community feeling is Adler's index of normality. As such, the manifestation of social interest or community feeling indicates the absence of antisocial behavior (Carrich, Newbauer, & Stone, 2001).

The task is to show the criminal the loss that results from a lack of community feeling. At first, criminals will have no interest in hearing this idea in the same way that gamblers attend only to dreams about future winnings and not to past or present losses. These daydreams are self-delusions that are more prevalent in human behavior than is realized (Stone, 2002). The common denominator among all criminals is that their behavior is a response to not believing that they are prepared to meet the difficult problems of life. Consequently, they adopt an antisocial viewpoint because they dare not risk working at these problems like other people. Hiding their fear of possible failure, they choose to see themselves as special, an elite group that need not follow the road all others must travel.

Adler argues one cannot force anyone to adopt social interest or community feeling. Rather, we must by reason and artistry in psychotherapy help the person recognize that the path of crime cannot produce the superiority desired. This false superiority is temporary at best, if achieved at all. At-risk criminals must mobilize their creative powers to address the problems they fear facing, and not allow themselves to retreat from their striving for legitimate success.

Samenow's 1984 book on criminal behavior, *Inside the Criminal Mind*, describes a program for how to work with at-risk criminals. His ideas emanate from the work of Adler. In fact, Samenow calls attention to Adler's paper on crime in Chapter 2 of his book. Samenow rejects the myths for causing criminal behavior—parents, economics, peer pressure, and so on. Instead, he directly quotes Adler:

> . . . criminals have a private logic, a private intelligence. They are suffering from a wrong outlook upon the world, a wrong estimate of their own importance and the importance of other people. (p. 20)

Samenow argues that the task is to stop the search for causes and concentrate on how criminals think—the private thinking that has produced this condition. In a very reasonable, but strong and straightforward manner, one must help the at-risk criminals recognize their private logic and see that only by making a change in their thinking can they produce a change in behavior. The task is one of reeducation—reeducating the individual to recognize that the private thinking approach has to go. In its place must be a concern for others that replaces a concern for self. A careful examination of one's thinking and behavior must take place so that "common sense" replaces "private sense." Adler borrowed these two phrases from the German philosopher Immanuel Kant (1724–1804), who meant "common sense" to imply rational thinking as accomplished by any reasonable being with a goal of community. "Private sense" implied self-centered thoughts, largely self-delusions. Kant (1982) wrote that, "Enlightenment is man's emergence from his self-imposed immaturity." The goal for treatment is to overthrow private sense (logic) in favor or participation in the common sense (logic) involving others.

The task is not easy and a clinician must be a combination of psychologist who understands thinking and behavior, an educator who can refocus attention on meaningful issues, and a coach/support who encourages all the efforts taken to change. The shocker to the criminal is contained in the words of one client who said, "The more I do, the more there is to do." That is what life is all about, and now he is truly facing life. It also explains the underlying fear of failure that is the reason why at-risk criminals will not change—they fear failure from having to meet challenge following challenge.

One of the tools that is especially helpful at this point comes from the work of Prochaska and associates (1992, 1995, 2001, 2002) who have constructed a model for what is required in changing one's behavior. Their model views change as occurring over time and consists of six stages: precontemplation, contemplation, preparation, action, maintenance, and termination. They postulate that different processes produce change at these differing stages. Without reviewing the model specifically, our application to at-risk individuals on parole has produced beneficial results. Clients learn a strategy that deconstructs the process of change into steps that can be described and learned.

These steps have operational definitions that describe where the individual is throughout the process of changing behavior. When change is unpacked and operationalized, a client learns that making changes in one's life is not a dichotomous, either-or process, but a continuous one. Furthermore, changing behavior requires identifying the stage characteristics and processes required which help specify what needs to be done. We have found that this way of looking at change has been very beneficial to at-risk individuals on parole who meet regularly in groups for treatment. The content and process of treatment is much more focused and clear when the clients know the process, and then work together to help each other. Working together builds community feeling as Adler indicated. The stages of the model are explained to group members, and the model's steps are carefully delineated. Clients next determine what stage they are at, and they reevaluate themselves at every session. In some groups we have asked the participants to evaluate not only their own stage but also the stage for each member of the group. This is accomplished by each group member presenting his/her own problem/issues and describing the success and failure that has occurred. Other group members offer additional commentary and support the efforts made. They also monitor the process as peers and keep one another from making evaluations that are not based in fact according to self-reports. Peer monitoring has proved especially beneficial. The only disadvantage with applying this model has been that the six stages of this model require further subdivisions in order to help clients work on specific tasks with even more focused attention.

To further assist group members in making changes in their behavior, we have employed models taken from two industrial strategies for improving quality control: *Quality Is Personal* (Roberts & Sergesketter (1993) and *Kaizen* as described by Maurer (2004).

QUALITY IS PERSONAL

The content of Quality Is Personal presents simply strategies for making changes in individual behavior. These changes are supported by numerous illustrations for how personal change can be implemented using ideas drawn from business and industry. The advantage to clients is that these strategies are not the usual mental health approaches that can sometimes turn people off. We emphasize in our groups that these methods for making changes come from business and industry where making change is used to increase productivity, improve quality, and become profitable. It is only logical to apply these methods to a personal undertaking. As such we are not offering one more self-help method, but instead a proven approach from business and industry that can be applied as informally or as strictly as deemed appropriate. We have worked with these approaches in our own lives, and so we can address a client's needs and questions from the viewpoint of others who have used and profited by these methods.

The authors also reference Benjamin Franklin and his penchant for improvement. Franklin serves as an excellent example of someone desirous of making changes in his life. As described in his *Autobiography*, Franklin sought to improve his character by addressing these standards: temperance, silence, order, resolution, frugality, industry, sincerity, justice, moderation, cleanliness, tranquility, chastity, and humility. Overall, Franklin reported success, and this was probably due to his isolating specific traits and seeking to improve them. Franklin also acknowledged less success in improving some of these thirteen traits, and he identified order and humility as difficult ones to improve on in his behavior.

The Roberts and Sergesketter methods require developing *Personal Quality Checklists*. These are self-created checklists of what one wants to accomplish in change. (An example is given in Appendix B.) The authors address checklists applied to business applications: answering phone messages the same day, likewise for e-mail; not allowing papers to accumulate; checking one's appearance regularly; and so on. We have encouraged clients to create their own personal quality checklists, such as appearing clean and neat, smiling to those you meet, using "please" and "thank you," and other simple steps to introduce change. Later, we proceed to develop more complex ones around difficult issues that have frustrated them. However, the emphasis is always on having clear and simple tasks that can easily be accomplished—on selecting tasks that one can be largely successful in doing. This orientation is essential.

The next step is to keep records. We advocate using 3×5 index cards, writing only one topic on each card and leaving space to record every instance of success. Roberts and Sergesketter advocate recording one's failures and they give a rationale for why failures should be recorded. In essence, they argue the task selected should be one for which there is a high probability for success. Therefore, the number of failures should generally be few. We recommend using index cards because they are small, easy to keep in one's pocket, but strong enough to survive repeated handling. The emphasis is not just on keeping records, but on the process of recording behavior and being attentive to the recording process. We advocate focusing attention only on a few specific tasks, usually only three or four to begin the process. In group sessions we discuss progress, especially how to break down large tasks into smaller and smaller ones that can be specifically, identified, and accomplished. Progress and success on these tasks are things to be proud about. We celebrate in group about accomplishing them, and we give much attention to group members in their efforts to support one another in addressing their accomplishments. Group members frequently learn tasks and strategies from one another, and they revel in making progress. For the first time many group members now learn how to move from an internal sense of failure to an external mode of documented success.

THE KAIZEN APPROACH

Kaizen is a Japanese word signifying "change for the better" or "improvement." It is derived from an approach to industrial productivity pursed by post–World War II Japanese manufacturers that began from applications by statisticians such as W. Edwards Demming. Demming is noted internationally for his workshops on improving quality. Derived from a Buddhist term, *Kaizen* implies the phrase, "Renew the heart and make it good." Among the goals of *Kaizen* for industrial production is the elimination of "activities that add cost but do not add value." Another element is the ability to understand the "root causes" of a problem. These are the core issues that must be addressed to improve quality production.

Understanding a "root cause" is very similar to Adler's "fictive goal." Both represent the pursuit of useless issues in a quest for improvement. The key element applicable here is the emphasis to "take small actions." The *Kaizen* approach is to break down a problem into smaller and smaller segments. The task is to change by means of a small segment only, and not address the entire problem. This is in keeping with the philosophy of Lao-tzu, "A journey of a thousand miles begins with the first step."

This approach to industrial efficiency can be applied to personal matters by "taking one step at a time" (note the AA similarity for application), and striving for continuous improvement" instead of for an absolute change. The methodology includes making many, many changes, and always looking at the results, followed by readdressing the issue and positing another change. The model for making changes resembles a continuous spiral. It is not the end of the spiral that one focuses on, but the process. This is because the process of *Kaizen* never ends.

This approach is frustrating to those seeking a quick change, and to those who want change accomplished immediately. However, this approach builds upon a step-by-step model with slow steady growth as the goal that produces change. It has also been beneficial in our treatment groups because it focuses on making successful changes, and not on change itself. Importance is placed on making one small but useful change. This ensures that a change which has been selected can be forthcoming, enjoyed, and built upon. It has also been attractive for group members to apply a business approach to solving their problems rather than the usual mental health approach of only talking about making changes.

Robert Maurer (2004) has adapted *Kaizen* to solving personal problems in his book *One Small Step Can Change Your Life: The Kaizen Way*. Maurer illustrates that application of this approach by extolling the simple-step approach to weight reduction—one less mouthful; smoking—one less cigarette; exercise—one minute only to start. The emphasis is on continuing the small task that has been selected. The step identified and selected to work on should be so small that success is virtually guaranteed. This is the secret.

It is especially necessary to break the cycle of introducing change only to fail once more. That cycle of failure is what blocks any productive activity from beginning anew. At-risk criminals have a wealth of experience in failure. When we can anticipate the outcome—failure—we will avoid starting. But when we can virtually guarantee success it becomes a different matter. What keeps this process from being one more self-help approach is that there is a long history to this strategy, and it has been advocated in a number of different venues. For example, in behavioral psychology developing subjective units of disturbance (SUDs), one must select a small sequence of steps, and success depends upon the smallness of the steps in achieving change. In program learning, the sequence of skill acquisition is only as successful as the smallness of the learning steps. Self-instruction requires these steps be small and therefore achievable. Good instruction has always been conditional on the skill of the teacher in sequencing the steps and arranging the teaching units as reachable one from the other. In their book *Learning for Mastery*, Block, Airasian, Bloom, and Carroll (1971) have argued that mastery itself is possible for virtually everyone in any area of endeavor, and that learning is only a function of time and sequence, not of talent.

Making a change requires that step-by-step success be achieved. Gratification should be as immediate as possible. This sets the stage for continuity. We will typically do only what we know we can be successful at accomplishing. This is the key to making positive changes in behavior.

CONCLUSION

In order to address the issue of at-risk criminal offending it is necessary that these persons receive a comprehensive evaluation. While this evaluation should include the standard instruments of a psychological examination for assessing intelligence, achievement, and personality, it must further include the neuropsychological assessment described to address the executive functions, which are frontal lobe activities. A comprehensive psychological assessment is required in order to gain an understanding of the overall level of functioning of the person, and specific attention must be given to the assessment of executive functions. A social history, health assessment, and drug/alcohol history are also required.

Treatment must be arranged to address the area of executive function deficits. The need for introducing simple models for helping clients change their behavior is essential. This is particularly critical in the area of executive functioning because these frontal lobe deficits appear to be independent of general levels of intelligence.

Several approaches were introduced that have been successfully applied to our groups. We have found that an emphasis on making simple steps has been both attractive and successful with groups of at-risk offenders. These approaches work particularly well with individuals who show deficiencies in executive functioning.

REFERENCES

Achenbach, T. (1997). *Manual for the young adult self-report and young adult behavior checklist*. Burlington: University of Vermont Department of Psychiatry.

Adler, A. (1930). Individual psychology and crime. *The Police Journal 17*(6), 8–11. (See Stone & Drescher, 2004, Chapter 21.)

American Psychological Association. (1999). *Standards for educational and psychological testing*. Washington, DC: Author.

Anastasi, A., & Urbina, S. (1997). *Psychological testing* (7th ed.). Upper Saddle River, NJ: Prentice Hall.

Anderson, S., Bechara, A., & Damasio, H., Tranel, D., & Damasio, A. (1999). Impairment of social and moral behavior related to early damage in the human prefrontal cortex. *Nature Neuroscience, 2*, 1032–1037.

Bechara, A., Damasio, A., Tranel, D., & Damasio, H. (1996). Failure to respond automatically to anticipated future outcomes following damage to human frontal cortex. *Cerebral Cortex, 6*, 215–225.

Bigler, E., & Clement, P. (1997). *Diagnostic clinical neuropsychology* (3rd ed.). Austin: University of Texas Press.

Block, J., Airasian, P., Bloom, B., & Carroll, J. (1971). Mastery learning. New York: Holt, Rinehart and Winston.

Carrich, M., Newbauer, J., & Stone, M. (2001). Sexual offenders and contemporary treatments. *Journal of Individual Psychology, 57*(1), 3–17.

Comings, D. (1990). *Human behavior questionnaire*. Duarte, CA: City of Hope Medical Center.

Damasio, A. (1994). *Descartes' error: Emotion, reason, and the human brain*. New York: Avon Books.

DeVries, T., & Shippenberg, T. (2002). Neural systems underlying opiate addiction. *Journal of Neuroscience, 22*, 3321–3325.

Eccles, J. (1970). *The human psyche*. New York: Springer-Verlag.

Eccles, J. (1989). *Evolution of the brain*. London: Routledge.

First, M., Gibbon, M., Williams, J., & Spitzer, R. (1997). *SCID Screen Patient Questionnaire and SCID Scan Patient Questionnaire Extended*. North Tonawanda, NY: Multi-Health Systems, Inc.; American Psychiatric Association.

Gazzaniga, M. (1998). *The mind's past*. Berkeley: University of California Press.

Geschwind, N. (1965). Disconnection syndromes in animal and man. *Brain, 88*, 237–294.

Geschwind, N. (1972). Language and the brain. *Scientific American, 226*(4), 76–83.

Goldberg, E. (2001). *The executive brain: Frontal lobes and the civilized mind*. New York: Oxford University Press.

Harrison, P., & Hoffman, N. (2001). *Substance use disorders diagnostic schedule-IV*. Smithfield, RI: Evince Clinical Assessments.

Impara, J., & Plake, B. (1998). *The thirteenth mental measurements yearbook*. Lincoln, NB: Buros Institute.

Kant, I. (1982). *Perpetual peace and other essays on politics, history, and moral practice*. Indianapolis: Hackett.

Kelley, A., & Berridge, K. (2002). The neuroscience of natural rewards: scale. *Journal of Neurology, Neurosurgery, and Psychiatry, 50*, 183–193.

Levin, H., Eisenberg, H., & Benton, A. (1991). *Frontal lobe function and dysfunction*. New York: Oxford University Press.

Levin, H., High, W., & Goethe, K. (1987). The Neurobehavioral Rating Scale. *Journal of Neurology, Neurosurgery, and Psychiatry, 50*, 183–193.

Lezak, M. (1995). *Neuropsychological functioning* (3rd ed.). London: Oxford University Press.

Luria, A. (1973). *The working brain*. New York: Basic Books.

Luria, A. (1980). *Higher cortical functions in man* (2nd ed.). New York: Basic Books.

Maurer, R. (2004). *One small step can change your life: The Kaizen way*. New York: Workman.

Mesulam, M. (1986). Frontal cortex and behavior. *Annals of Neuropsychology, 19*, 320–325.

Mesulam, M., & Geschwind, N. (1978). On the possible role of neocortex and its limbic connections in the process of attention and schizophrenia. *Journal of Psychiatric Research, 14*, 249–259.

Paus, T. (2005). Mapping brain maturation and cognitive development during adolescence. *TRENDS in Cognitive Science, 9(2)*, 60–68.

Pincus, J., & Tucker, G. (2003). *Behavioral neurology*. Oxford: Oxford University Press.

Ponsford, J., & Kinsella, G. (1991). The use of a rating scale of attentional behavior. *Neuropsychological Rehabilitation, 1, 241–257.*

Prochaska, J., DiClemente, C., & Norcross, J. (1992). In search of how people change: Applications to addictive behaviors. *American Psychologist, 47*, 1102–1114.

Prochaska, J., Norcross, J., & DiClemente, C. (1995). *Changing for good*. New York: Avon.

Prochaska, J., & Norcross, J. (2001). Stages of change. *Psychotherapy, 38(4)*, 443–448.

Prochaska, J., & Norcross, J. (2002). Stages of change. In J. Norcross (Ed.), *Psychotherapy relationships that work*. New York: Oxford University Press.

Roberts, H., & Sergesketter, B. (1993). *Quality is personal*. New York: Free Press.

Samenow, S. (1984). *Inside the criminal mind*. New York: Random House.

Shapiro, D. (1965). *Neurotic styles*. New York: Harper Torchbooks.

Stone, M. (2002). *Life-lies and self-deception*. Chicago: Phaneron.

Stone, M. (2006). *Trails L: Manual for administration, scoring, and interpretation*. Wood Dale, IL: Stoelting.

Stone, M., & Drescher, K. (2004). *Adler speaks: The lectures of Alfred Adler*. New York: Universe.

Stone, M., & Thompson, E. (2001). Executive function impairment in sex offenders. *The Journal of Individual Psychology, 57(1)*, 51–59.

Tobias, P. (1971). *The brain in hominid evolution*. New York: Columbia University Press.

Walter, W. (1973). Human frontal lobe function in sensory-motor association. In K. Pribram & A. Luria (Eds.), *Psychophysiology of the Fontal Lobes*. New York: Academic Press.

APPENDIX A
Informal Assessment of Executive Functioning

		Almost Never	Rather Frequently	Almost Always
1.	Limited attention span	0	1	2
2.	Appears unmotivated	0	1	2
3.	Cannot plan ahead	0	1	2
4.	Difficulty executing tasks	0	1	2
5.	Unable to sequence tasks	0	1	2
6.	Slow thinking	0	1	2
7.	Poor judgment	0	1	2
8.	Poor insight	0	1	2
9.	Socially withdrawn	0	1	2
10.	Irritable	0	1	2
11.	Sudden mood changes	0	1	2
12.	No self-control	0	1	2
13.	Impulsive	0	1	2
14.	Cannot shift attention	0	1	2
15.	No ability to plan ahead	0	1	2
16.	Cannot monitor self	0	1	2
17.	Cannot foresee consequences	0	1	2
18.	Cannot see means to an end	0	1	2
19.	Cannot recognize own mistakes	0	1	2
20.	Cannot evaluate own actions	0	1	2

APPENDIX B

Personal Quality Checklists	Daily Record
On time for appointments	1 2 3 4 5 6 7
Clean and neat in appearance	1 2 3 4 5 6 7
Polite when speaking	1 2 3 4 5 6 7
Never makes fun of others	1 2 3 4 5 6 7
Sets one daily goal to achieve	1 2 3 4 5 6 7

15

Correctional Social Work

Harris Chaiklin

Some years ago I wrote a paper on developing correctional social services (Chaiklin, 1974). At that time I advanced some principles for developing such services based on my experiences directing a prerelease project (Chaiklin, 1972). I also believed that we were on the cusp of a change and that correctional systems would see a great increase in the numbers of social workers and the things they did would become. Time has cured me of those hopeful expectations, but I still believe that the principles I enunciated hold true and can be useful in understanding and implementing services in today's correctional world.

This chapter will expand on the principles and present a detailed view of what is involved in a service as contrasted to a treatment view of correctional social services. From this perspective, treatment is only one of several options available to the correctional social worker. First I will compare a treatment and a casework approach. Then I will present the need for social services and finally look at what the profession is doing to meet the identified needs.

TREATMENT ORIENTATION

One of the few textbooks directed toward criminal justice practice is Roberts's (1997) *Social Work in Juvenile and Criminal Justice Settings*. Ten of the 25 chapters focus on institutional and community-based treatment with adult offenders. Correctional social work provides a number of opportunities for a career that is clinically and personally challenging. The major dilemma is that social workers are both agents of social control and social change in correctional settings. Correctional administrators usually believe that all staff need to be authoritative, regimented and militaristic, and coercive in managing large groups of inmates. This can be problematic and frustrating for a clinical social worker who is not comfortable working with involuntary clients. On the other hand, a growing number of correctional administrators have started their careers as correctional social workers, case-workers, or correctional treatment specialists. These types of prison administrators are much more receptive in promoting rehabilitation and treatment programs (Ivanoff, Smyth, & Dulmus, 2007). Most critical for all correctional treatment specialists, regardless of whether they have graduate training in social work, counseling, or psychology is to understand the environmental and daily crisis-inducing events that often occur in prisons. For example, it has been documented that the risk of inmate suicide is highest for first-time offenders during the first 24 to 72 hours of incarceration (Ivanoff et al., 2007).

Another book, Ellis and Sowers's (2001) *Juvenile Justice Practice*, focuses on recommended treatments for juvenile offenders, but the underlying similarity in all correctional treatment practice makes it useful here. The core depends on using a DSM diagnosis as the basis for treatment (APA, 1994).

Intervention Priorities

Following Bazemore and Day (1996), Ellis and Sowers identify three priorities in intervention. These are:

1.   Rehabilitation
2.   Protection of the community
3.   Restitution to the victim

Continuing to follow Bazemore and his associates, Ellis and Sowers say that the priorities should be used in a "balanced and restorative approach" that emphasizes accountability, competency, and public safety.

Principles of Effective Intervention

*   Individual counseling and related services
*   Behavioral contracting
*   Institutional settings
*   Service delivery systems

Sanctions Monitoring and Supervision

*   Schedules of sanctions
*   Administering sanctions

CASEWORK ORIENTATION

A Definition of Social Casework

The social caseworker (Chaiklin, 1978):

1.   Utilizes the physical, emotional, social, and cultural factors that influence behavior.

2. Pays attention to *all* the problems the person has.

3. Examines the social situations in which problems manifest themselves.

4. Where appropriate works with an individual's problems in a family or group context.

5. Knows the community and its resources.

6. Coordinates services.

7. Meets need without requiring attitude change.

Intervention Principles

1. Realism

2. Primacy of custody

3. Social services help meet essential human needs

4. Including family and significant others in service planning

One way of explicating the idea of *realism* is to say that it means "don't promise too much." It is often the case that in order to get money and support to provide needed services the providers must promise to do what they can't do (Lee, 1937). The causes of deviant behavior and the number of different people and institutions that influence this behavior are so plentiful that it is too much to expect that social services alone will have a significant impact on the crime rate. For some individuals they may be the source of major change but these cases do not add up to impacting the crime rate.

Some service providers do not recognize the gap between promise and reality and others know they cannot bridge the gap. Regardless of the reason, the situation helps to put services providers perpetually on the defensive, trying to justify the worth of their service. There is only one justification for providing social services to prisoners: They are entitled to them because they are human beings.

Conflicts between "treatment and punishment" personnel in institutions have clouded understanding the *primacy of custody*. There is no inherent conflict between custody and either treatment or providing services. Staff on both sides of the issue may point to the conflict as a way of justifying their ideological position, while overlooking the fact that they are not doing the job. Unless an institution is secure, neither correctional nor service staff is safe and it is not possible for any personnel to do an effective job. What is worse is that when prison staff engage in a power struggle over whose views dominate the inmates attain great power by playing one side off against the other. This further reduces institutional security.

In providing *social services [to] help meet essential human needs* the aim is neither to explain crime nor "cure" the individual. There are numerous theories of crime. They all play some role in explaining crime. When the aim is to "treat" criminals so that they are cured, then it is necessary to fit components from numerous theories to the individual. This only provides a theory of explanation. While sometimes the explanation may indicate what the treatment is, it is usually the case that a separate theory of intervention is required. For example, it is known that the AIDS virus is transmitted through unprotected sex or by sharing needles. Stopping these practices will not cure AIDS. As yet there is no known cure, only a set of palliatives that do not cure the disease. The AIDS virus may mutate into harmlessness before a cure is found. Where social deviance is concerned there are not even good palliatives available.

Providing social services to prisoners means that needs are met without reference to whether the person is good or bad. Social workers must be aware that they are not used as part of a "game" a prisoner is running. Needs occur throughout a person's prison career. Meeting them may or may not help deter the offender from future criminal activity. If the person is emotionally disturbed, psychotherapy or other forms of psychological intervention are required. Where appropriate, a social worker who is qualified can provide these services but it is only one element of the casework job.

What this means can be seen from a matter which comes up frequently, receiving "bad news" from home. Social workers may facilitate anything from getting quicker or more frequent access to phones to having a community agency get involved so that the offender's family receives necessary service. Another continuing problem concerns inmates who have a domestic relations offense related to paying court-ordered family support. This offense can be the one for which a person is in prison or concurrent with another charge. In a prerelease project that I directed some years ago 15 percent of the 273 men served had such an offense and 37 percent of the 86 men who had children had an offense (Chaiklin, 1972). These men had complex relationships both with their "families" and the agencies that dealt with their being in arrears. There were difficulties in communication and coordination that made this a challenging group to work with (Chaiklin & Kelly, 1975). Many of those charged with this offense did everything they could to avoid paying the charges against them and others were paying and had trouble because the systems that were supposed to help them did not function well. Providing casework service to help offenders resolve real problems and meet needs benefits both them and society. This is especially so with this group because society and corrections officials tend to look down on them.

Finally, there is the question of *including family and significant others in service planning.* In the Community Reintegration Project of the 273 men served, only one could be considered a true isolate. Family issues were almost always present in any service that was provided. Since this was a prerelease center where men were scheduled for release in six months and many were on work release, it would seem strange that men would want to escape. When they did, the Camp Center staff referred to them as "walkaways." Most of those men were soon "caught." We did a special study of 20 of these men and found that in 18 situations the reason given for walking was that they had received bad news from home and could not communicate with the family or influence what was happening.

The project made a special effort to work with older offenders about release issues. Many of these men were lifers who may have already made parole but whose release was held up because the conditions of the parole had to be met. In one instance project staff located the 67-year-old ex-girlfriend of an 84-year-old man. She said that she didn't "want that drunken bum back," but she found a room for him, came in and cleaned it, and cooked meals for him. In another instance, the project located in a Midwestern state the relative of a 76-year-old offender who had not seen him in 30 years. When asked why they had not been in contact, the relative said, "No one asked, we just drifted out of contact." He went on to say that if he had known that help was needed, he would have responded. He welcomed this man into his home.

The family looms larger in the offender's life than correctional personnel usually think. "More than half of incarcerated men have children under age 18 and more than half of these men were living with their children at the time of their incarceration" (Drucker, 2006, p. 168). These men are more involved with their families than is usually perceived and imprisonment has disastrous effects on the families.

A SERVICE PLAN

The principles of practice are of little use unless they can be reflected in an organized service plan that is understandable and visible. The vehicle for this is the case record. Important information should be created and stored in a concise and easily available form. Today, there is no reason not to have all records online.

A Structure of Practice

A generic "structure of practice" is used to develop initial information. In addition to the usual face sheet data, the structure consists of items that are not fixed. They can be modified as needed.

1. Ask the client what he or she want? Write down exact words and make a part of the record.

2. What is the problem?
    a. How viewed by client.
    b. How viewed by worker.

3. What has client done up till now?
    a. Include nature of relationship with former workers, if applicable.

4. How does client expect change to occur—How does client expect it will turn out?
    a. What will they do—what will worker do.
        1. Explain how what will be done works.
    b. Keep goal in mind—identify what needs to be accomplished so that both know the end is reached.

5. A social work review of systems
    a. Physical
        1. Compliance
    b. Emotional—do a brief mental status
    c. Social
    d. Financial
    e. Legal
    f. Other agencies—not already identified—in contact with
    g. Anything else that interferes in ability to live life the way you want to

In developing the information for the structure, the focus is on current reality and meeting needs. A detailed life history is only used if it is deemed that the person is either greatly at risk for mental illness or already ill. Personality changes slowly so that even if psychotherapy is needed reality needs should be met first.

A full analysis of the structure will not be given here. Most of the questions that flow from the outline are obvious. I will stress a few that are either slighted or not well developed in other assessment tools. The outline reflects the client's view. It is important to know this. At the same time, all problems identified either by the worker or the client need to be confirmed.

It is important to write down what the client wants because these statements are frequently discounted, especially in prison. Experience shows that most of the time people mean exactly what they say. Workers in their education often learn that initial problem statements may be masking something, or that they change after the client comes to trust the worker. In prison this can be part of "running a game." All of these things are possibilities and it only takes a few sessions to find this out.

The worker who initially discounts statements the client makes proceeds at great risk. In one delinquency project I was associated with, there was a youth who was a chronic liar (Chaiklin, Chesley et al., 1977). He began complaining that his stomach ached. His probation officer discounted it as another effort to get out of probation requirements. Fortunately this project has a mandatory physical examination for all participants. This young man turned out to have a bleeding ulcer.

Explaining what will be done is something that workers need to work on. It is not enough to say, "I will refer you for treatment" or "I am here to help you." If clients don't understand what they are committing to, it is hard if not impossible to work with them.

In getting a history it is important to know all medications a client is taking. Often times this is the only indication that there is an emotional disturbance. In other instances drugs are prescribed by different clinics and no one checks for interaction effects. Other times people complain about their medications. To reinforce the point about not discounting, I have found that even in psychotic patients when they complain about the effects of drugs on them they are right about one-third of the time.

The above remarks illustrate the factual information that needs to be developed. It is reality based. The slogan I use is "manifest before latent, overt before covert, reality before fantasy." This is to reinforce the idea that the worker only turns to the personality base when the facts are established and further exploration is indicated.

This initial assessment should be printed and a copy given to the client. Worker and client can then together agree on a service plan. An important element in this plan is deciding on the level of service needed. All clients do not need the same intensity of time and attention. The levels are:

1. Information
2. Negotiation
3. Support
4. Treatment

The meaning of these levels can be illustrated by a simple example. Many offenders have questions or problems with their Social Security accounts. Even though the Social Security program is projected as an insurance program for people have paid, in 1950 the Supreme Court ruled it to be a welfare program. While offenders are in prison they are denied benefits but their family can get them. Some offenders are illegal aliens and unaware that their families can qualify for benefits, some have no social security number, and some have multiple numbers.

When any of these issues comes up, there will be some people who will handle it themselves when they are given the correct information about the resources to consult. Others will find this difficult and a call will be made, in the offender's presence, to the appropriate office and then the phone turned over to the person. Sometimes a person is so anxious that the worker must accompany him or her to a necessary appointment, even if the person representing Social Security is in the prison. Finally, while some prisoners have a real Social Security issue, their emotional state is such that what they need is psychological treatment and it may be that the worker will have to take care of the matter.

Determining needs and providing services according to the plan outlined above is neither time-consuming nor does it demand huge resources. Most of the work consists of clarifying issues and connecting offenders to appropriate agencies. The one exception to this is when treatment for mental illness is required. This is often an unmet need. It does not prevent meeting other service needs.

Given that so much can be accomplished by facilitating the meeting of reality needs, it is a mistake for prison social workers to get involved in psychiatric treatment. A few people can tie up all their time. There is a real problem with emotionally disturbed people in prison. In 2006 there were almost 2.2 million people in jail, 350,000 of whom were estimated to have a mental illness. (Gibbons & de B. Katzenbach, 2006). This presents a peculiar problem to prisons. Mental hospitals, but not prisons, can refuse admissions when they are full. This results in a practice of putting prisoners in "chemical straightjackets," as they are over-medicated to control them. Deinstitutionalization has meant that there are more mentally ill people in prison than in the past (Fazel & Lubbe, 2005). At present about 80 percent of those who enter U.S. prisons have a problem with drug abuse or alcohol dependency. This country seems stuck with a put-them-in-jail-and-forget-about-them mentality. About one-third of all prisoners are in jail for a nonviolent drug offense (Drucker, 2006). There are much cheaper and humane alternatives that do not threaten community safety or security.

Comparison

The Ellis and Sower treatment configuration approach is comprehensive, stresses the importance of the family and community, and takes a mental health stance. The casework model I use focuses more on direct services to individuals, groups, and families. Psychotherapy is one option under this rubric. We share an emphasis on the importance of community and families. When community agencies and institutions are dealt with, it is in relation to the client's need. The aim is not to change the agencies or get involved in broader efforts at change. I have consistently found that as short as services are, much more can be available to prisoners if caseworkers know what the resources and intake requirements of service providers are. The field is still too disorganized to have any agreed-on service protocols. What is offered here is only one way of going about the job. Moving in this direction is going to be slow because American social work has become so dominated by the need for insurance reimbursement that "social casework" has almost been replaced by "clinical social work." *Clinical* is a word that has medical connotations, so its use helps to create a false impression in situations in which therapeutic treatment is not the issue.

THE NEED

How great is the need for services by those caught up in the criminal justice system? While a definitive answer can't be given, it is possible to show that there are many matters requiring casework help. The sheer number of people involved helps outline the dimensions of the problem. The total number of people inside during 2005 was 13.5 million. The

United States has 5 percent of the world's population but 25 percent of its prisoners. Where race is concerned, African Americans are about 12 percent of the population but they account for 50 percent of the prisoners. In 2001 those who served time in a state or federal prison constituted almost 17 percent of African Americans, almost 8 percent of Hispanics, and almost 3 percent of Whites. If incarceration rates remain the same, 32 percent of African American boys born in 2001 will go to prison. Large numbers of black man think they have been unfairly stopped by police and even more are afraid of this. This represents no improvement in conditions documented by Miller (1996) a decade earlier. In Washington D.C., more than 75 percent of African American males will be in jail at some time during their life (Drucker, 2006).

The return to a punishment philosophy in prison has exacerbated the needs for services. Despite what politicians like to project and the public likes to believe, this way of handling offenders creates more problems than it controls. Burnett and Maruna (2004), who followed the careers of 130 men released from an English prison which has a punishment orientation said, "And, here lies the failing of the 'prison works' doctrine. The notion that Britain's 'decent but austere' prisons can both scare inhabitants straight through sheer deterrence, and also somehow become hotbeds for hope and developing self-efficacy seems a far-fetched fantasy to say the least" (p. 401). That such an obvious contradiction in aims cannot get a fair hearing offers proof that people believe what they want to believe and the evidence makes no difference.

One of the trite expressions about prison life is that "Everyone who enters eventually leaves even if it is only feet first." It is too bad that this phrase has become so hackneyed because it contains an essential truth that must be kept in focus. That is, planning for a person's release must start the day they enter the system and continue throughout their tenure. Today, overcrowding and shortage of personnel have placed prisons under great stress. The general rule is that to do proper classification a prison should not be more than 85 percent full. Jammed prisons not only make it difficult to provide services they make prisons unsafe for both offenders and staff.

The Commission on Safety and Abuse in prisons begins its report this way:

> For all of the hard work and achievements of corrections professionals—most of which the public does not hear about—there is still too much violence in America's prisons and jails, too many facilities that are crowded to the breaking point, too little medical and mental health care, unnecessary uses of solitary confinement and other forms of segregation, a desperate need for the kinds of productive activities that discourage violence and make rehabilitation possible, and a culture in many prisons and jails that pits staff against prisoners and management against staff. There is too little help and hope for the individuals we incarcerate and too little respect and support for the men and women who work in our prisons and jails. And notwithstanding these conclusions, we know less about safety and abuse in America's prisons and jails than we should. It is simply not enough to be better than we were. We must confront and solve today's problems. (Gibbons & de B. Katzenbach, 2006, p. 6)

This is a strong statement. The content of the report backs it up. The commission's focus on safety and abuse was developed because of a concern about violence in the prison and its causes and cures. Conditions that lead to violence are overcrowding, poor medical care, overuse of high-security segregation, and poor training and morale among correctional workers.

Among the things preventing reform is the ability of prisons to wall themselves off from both internal and external scrutiny. Improvement requires changing these conditions. They particularly stressed that poor data hampers efforts to change things and advocate uniform nationwide data standards, objective classification, and direct supervision. It is all presented in a reasonable and rational tone, a surefire formula for early obscurity. An example of a stronger statement comes from England where Levy (1997) states that prison health services should be the equal of those in the community.

Social services and social work are not mentioned in the report but they do say, "Support community and family bonds. Reexamine where prisons are located and where prisoners are assigned, encourage visitation, and implement phone call reform" (Gibbons & de B. Katzenbach, 2006, p. 35).

While safety in prisons is a major issue the problems with prisons go beyond that. For example, California's once vaunted correctional system has been described as being in crisis (Pomfret, 2006). The California Rehabilitation Center is supposed to hold 1,800 inmates, but it has 4,700. The building is in such bad shape that they have to shut the electricity off in rainstorms because it is feared that prisoners will be electrocuted. In April 2006, U.S. District Judge Thelton E. Henderson took over the prison medical system because of inadequate services.

Newspapers provide an ample source of case illustrations that show the depths of malfunctioning in the criminal justice system (Jones, 2006). Mr. Elias Fishburne IV, a gay Washington D.C. hairdresser, had a minor auto accident. The officer on the scene said he was wanted under another name. Mr. Fishburne protested his innocence. He was given bad advice by a correctional officer and did not protest extradition. This kept him in the system without bail and forced a trip to Georgia. In addition to the police the following entities handled his case, the Maryland State Police, the state Department of Corrections, the Prince Georges County Sheriff's Office, the state's attorney, the District Court administrator, and the Georgia sheriff who issued the warrant.

Part of his problem was that the arresting officer did not make the mandatory check at the National Criminal Justice Information Center because the computer was down. Fishburne's protests went unheeded because each office with jurisdiction assumed that it had been done and disclaimed responsibility. They did not even listen to his mother, who had worked as a technician in a police office. Another part of his problem is that some years previously he had been the victim of identity theft. This came back to haunt him because it was this person who had an outstanding warrant. The physical description of this person in the warrant bore no resemblance to him. No official paid attention to it.

His experience in jail was painful. His dreadlocks were cut. He said that Black correctional officers treated him worse than the white. He earned respect from the inmates by doing their hair. The costs to him were enormous. He lost his business, home, and car. He does not have the energy or resources to pursue a suit. While there is much to discuss in this story, the relevant point is that if a social worker had been present at the police station and lockup it is probable that this would have never happened. With the exception of Treger's (1980, 1981) pioneering work, relatively little has been done to promote the use of social workers in conjunction with the police. It would also have helped if anyone at any point had both looked at Mr. Fishburne listened and matched his description to the wanted person.

THE SOCIAL WORK RESPONSE

Historically, the fields of social work and correctional services had a joint beginning. The era when the Conference of Charities was created in 1875 was one of great reform. For example, in 1883 the Pendleton Act was passed. This laid the basis for a modern civil service free of political interference. From 1882 until 1916, the conference was known as the Conference of Charities and Correction (Chaiklin, 2005). Even after the split, social work continued to be influential in prisons. A unified Federal Bureau of Prisons was created in 1930, with Sanford Bates as the first director. He was a strong supporter of social work and taught at the Columbia University School of Social Work after retirement. At its initiation the bureau had a social work supervisor. In 1932 this supervisor, Ruth E. Collins, laid out practice principles that contain elements of what I have proposed. She said that the social worker should coordinate services inside and outside of the prison and that for the prisoner, "His social study, analysis and treatment should commence the moment of his admission to the institution and continue throughout his entire career rather than be postponed to the date of his parole consideration" (Collins, 1932, p. 867). It is doubtful if social work in corrections, except for a few states such as Wisconsin and New York, has had the widespread acceptance it had during these early years.

The 1930s also saw a rise in the criticism of the roles that social workers were playing in corrections. In 1936 Papurt (1936), a prison psychologist, noted the extensive use of caseworkers in prisons but said they were making trouble for themselves because they oversold what they could do, they were so eager to demonstrate their usefulness they intruded in areas not their responsibility, and they overvalued what they were doing. He said that the vast majority of crimes were committed by normal people and that these were the ones who most needed casework help. There was just not enough time to do therapy. He concluded that, "The caseworker must realize, for his own good, sooner or later, that he is but one unit in a necessary machine that has as its purpose the smooth functioning of a correctional machine" (Papurt, 1936, p. 69). This underscores the importance of the practice principles that I specified in the beginning of this paper.

By the 1960s, sociology and criminal justice were offering competing programs (Roebuck & Zelhart, 1965). There was still a strong belief that social work provided the best option for correctional work but this was challenged. Johnson (1961) wondered whether correctional workers, including social workers, could achieve professional status because the different occupations involved had no sense of togetherness, lacked professional qualification standards, and failed to adapt professional practice to institutional requirements. During this time, the Council on Social Work Education had a corrections educational consultant. No such position is now listed. The critique of social work correctional practice was also sharpening. These criticisms included that education did not prepare social workers for working with nonvoluntary clients and too much emphasis was placed on emotional as opposed to environmental factors. Social work education was seen as tending to portray offenders as sick, and consequently as neglecting institutional and community safety. While there was a belief that generic training was best for working in corrections there was also the complaint that not enough specialized knowledge was provided. Finally, it was felt social workers identified with the profession and not with corrections (Roebuck & Zelhart, 1965). The response within the profession to these criticisms was to gradually withdraw interest in the field.

Given social work's vaunted interest in social justice and racial equality, one would think that the conditions described in this paper would lead to a major effort by the organized profession to mount a campaign to bring about improvement at the policy level. It is far from doing that. The profession is at a stage where it recognizes the problems and the need, but so far it has taken little action (Stoesen, 2004). In an *NASW News* story Jeffrey Draine says:

> What I am concerned about in this field right now is the extent we're allowing the criminal justice system to drive the process. All the initiative and innovation is not coming from the treatment community as much as it is from the criminal justice side. Social work as a profession checked out of this field in the 1970s and left it to criminal justice. The professionalization of criminal justice took off. People who might have been interested in going into social work went into criminal justice which has a different set of professional standards. Social workers need to reclaim this. (Stoesen, 2006, p. 4)

And Diane Young said, "Social work used to be quite involved in correction issues and criminal justice in the early 1900s. . . . Almost none of the schools of social work have a concentration on criminal justice, and a minority of them even have a course. There is not a lot of emphasis in our curriculum" (Stoesen, 2006, p. 4).

Recent efforts to get the profession and social work education involved in criminal justice education have been duds (Chaiklin, 2000). The profession is very good at convening experts to talk about the problem (Pace, 2006), what it doesn't do is take action. For example, Barry C. Scheck and Peter J. Neufeld, who in 1992 founded the nonprofit Innocence Project at the Benjamin N. Cardozo School of Law at Yeshiva University, have shaken the credibility of the American justice system with DNA testing. NASW is not systematically collecting this information and it is not urging social workers to identify clients who might benefit from such a service. College and law students are very involved in doing this. If the profession could even emulate Charles Dickens and have all state chapters arrange periodic prison visits, great things might happen.

In England social workers are more involved in criminal justice work than American social workers. One concern they have is that the American Justice Model is replacing their traditional emphasis on welfare and rehabilitation. Barry (2000) discusses these issues in a study of the views of offenders in aftercare. She describes how in the 1980s there was a buildup of literature that said nothing worked and there was a shift to a justice model, which emphasized science, prevention, and control. The aim was to demonstrate effectiveness. This movement came to England and practice has shifted to being political and managerial. Practice objectives became more punitive by emphasizing responsibility and choice and relegating social needs to a secondary role. She conducted studies of what clients want and found that they wanted someone who was understanding and gave practical advice. What is interesting about this report is that I have not found a comparable study by an American social worker. Apparently English social workers still believe in the importance of casework.

CONCLUSION

In this paper I have laid out a reality-based approach to doing social casework with presumed offenders at any stage of their involvement in the criminal justice system. The point is that most of the needs of people involved in the criminal justice system are practical everyday things. If psychotherapy is needed this should be obtained. Unless this is the specific job of a social worker in the justice system treatment, should not be the goal because it takes up too much of a worker's time. Classification officers are not well positioned to help prisoners maintain family contact. Even if they are interested, which many are not, they would not have time for this. One can duplicate many times the situation of Mr. Fishburne where the lack of someone willing to listen and check had a severe impact on his life. If the kind of social work I have described here can become established in the correctional system, it is possible that social caseworker can once again become an honored title.

REFERENCES

American Psychiatric Association. (1994). *Diagnostic and statistical manual of mental disorders.* Washington, DC: APA.

Barry, M. (2000). The mentor/monitor debate in criminal justice: "What works" for offenders. *British Journal of Social Work, 30*(5), 575–595.

Bazemore, G., & Day, S. E. (1996). Restoring the balance: juvenile and community justice. *Juvenile Justice, 3*(1), 3–14.

Burnett, R., & Maruna, S. (2004). So "prison works," does it? *The Howard Journal, 43*(4), 390–404.

Chaiklin, H. (1972). *Final report: The community reintegration project.* Baltimore: University of Maryland School of Social Work and Community Planning.

Chaiklin, H. (1972). Integrating correctional and family systems. *American Journal of Orthopsychiatry, 42*, 784–789.

Chaiklin, H. (1974). Developing correctional social services. In A. R. Roberts (Ed.), *Correctional treatment of the offender* (pp. 294–308). Springfield, IL.: Charles C. Thomas.

Chaiklin, H. (1978). Role and utilization of the social worker in clinical practice. In G. U. Balis, L. Wurmser, E. McDaniel, & R. G. Grenell (Eds.), *The psychiatric foundations of medicine: Psychiatric clinical skills in medical practice* (Vol. 5, pp. 475–481). Boston: Butterworth.

Chaiklin, H. (2000). Needed: more education for social work practice in criminal justice. *Journal of Law and Social Work, 10*(1/2), 165–174.

Chaiklin, H. (2005). Franklin Benjamin Sanborn: Human services innovator. *Research on Social Work Practice, 15*(2), 127–134.

Chaiklin, H., Chesley, F. D., et al. (1977). Delinquency and health status. *Health and Social Work, 2*(3), 25–37.

Chaiklin, H., & Kelly, G. B. (1975). The domestic relations offender. *The Social Service Review, 49*, 115–121.

Collins, R. E. (1932). Contributions of social work to parole preparation. *Journal of Criminal Law and Criminology, 22*(6), 864–872.

Drucker, E. M. (2006). Incarcerated people. In B. S. Levy & V. W. Sidel (Eds.), *Social injustice and public health* (pp. 161–175). New York: Oxford University Press.

Ellis, R. A., & Sowers, K. M. (2001). *Juvenile justice practice: a cross-disciplinary approach to intervention.* Belmont, CA: Brooks/Cole. Thomson Learning.

Fazel, S., & Lubbe, S. (2005). Title Prevalence and characteristics of mental disorders in jails and prisons. *Current Opinion in Psychiatry, 18*(5), 550–554.

Gibbons, J. J., & de B. Katzenbach, N. (2006). *Confronting confinement: A report of the commission on safety and abuse in America's prisons.* Washington, DC: Vera Institute of Justice.

Ivanoff, A., Smyth, N., & Dulmus, C. (2007). Preparing social workers for practice in correctional institutions. In A. Roberts & D. Springer (Eds.), *Social Work in Juvenile and Criminal Justice Settings* (3rd ed.). Springfield, IL.: Charles C. Thomas.

Johnson, E. H. (1961). The professional in correction: status and prospects. *Social Forces, 40*(2), 168–176.

Jones, T. (2006). The wrong man: Mistaken for a fugitive an innocent hairdresser landed in jail. *The Washington Post*, A1, A12–A13.

Lee, P. R. (1937). The future of social work. In *Social work as cause and function* (pp. 133–149). New York: Columbia University Press.

Levy, M. (1997). Prison health services. *British Medical Journal, 315*, 1394–1395.

Miller, J. G. (1996). *Search and destroy: African-American males in the criminal justice system*. New York: Cambridge University Press.

Pace, P. R. (2006). Experts examine rise in female offenders. *NASW News, 51*, 6.

Papurt, M. J. (1936). A psychologist looks at prison casework. *Journal of Criminal Law and Criminology, 27*(1), 68–74.

Pomfret, J. (2006). California's crisis in prison systems a threat to public. *The Washingon Post*, A3, A8.

Roberts, A. R. (Ed.) (1997). *Social work in juvenile and criminal justice settings* (2nd ed.). Springfield, IL: Charles C. Thomas.

Roebuck, J., & Zelhart, P. (1965). The problem of educating the correctional practitioner. *The Journal of Criminal Law, Criminology, and Police Science, 56*(1), 45–53.

Stoesen, L. (2004). Corrections: public safety, public health. *NASW News*, 49.

Stoesen, L. (2006). Prisoner reentry: reclaiming the challenge. *NASW News, 51*, 4.

Treger, H. (1980). Guideposts for community work in police-social work diversion. *Federal Probation, 44*(3), 3–8.

Treger, H. (1981). Police-social work cooperation: problems and issues. *Social Casework, 62*(7), 426–433.

Index

❖